The Architecture
of Pipelined
Computers

McGRAW-HILL COMPUTER SCIENCE SERIES

Allen: Anatomy of LISP
Bell and Newell: Computer Structures: Readings and Examples
Donovan: Systems Programming
Feigenbaum and Feldman: Computers and Thought
Gear: Computer Organization and Programming
Givone: Introduction to Switching Circuit Theory
Goodman and Hedetniemi: Introduction to the Design and Analysis of Algorithms
Hamacher, Vranesic and Zaky: Computer Organization
Hamming: Introduction to Applied Numerical Analysis
Hayes: Computer Architecture and Organization
Hellerman: Digital Computer System Principles
Hellerman and Conroy: Computer System Performance
Kain: Automata Theory: Machines and Languages
Katzan: Microprogramming Primer
Kohavi: Switching and Finite Automate Theory
Liu: Elements of Discrete Mathematics
Liu: Introduction to Combinatorial Mathematics
MacEwen: Introduction to Computer Systems: Using the PDP-11 and Pascal
Madnick and Donovan: Operating Systems
Manna: Mathematical Theory of Computation
Newman and Sproull: Principles of Interactive Computer Graphics
Nilsson: Problem-Solving Methods in Artificial Intelligence
Rice: Matrix Computations and Mathematical Software
Rosen: Programming Systems and Languages
Salton: Automatic Information Organization and Retrieval
Siewiorek, Bell, and Newell: Principles of Computer Structures
Stone: Introduction to Computer Organization and Data Structures
Stone and Siewiorek: Introduction to Computer Organization and Data Structures: PDP-11 Edition
Tonge and Feldman: Computing: An Introduction to Procedures and Procedure-Followers
Tremblay and Bunt: An Introduction to Computer Science: An Algorithmic Approach
Tremblay and Bunt: An Introduction to Computer Science: An Algorithmic Approach, Short Edition
Tremblay and Manohar: Discrete Mathematical Structures with Applications to Computer Science
Tremblay and Sorenson: An Introduction to Data Structures with Applications
Tucker: Programming Languages
Watson: Timesharing System Design Concepts
Wiederhold: Database Design
Winston: The Psychology of Computer Vision

McGRAW-HILL ADVANCED COMPUTER SCIENCE SERIES

Davis and Lenat: Knowledged-Based Systems in Artificial Intelligence
Feigenbaum and Feldman: Computers and Thought
Kogge: The Architecture of Pipelined Computers
Lindsay, Buchanan, Feigenbaum, and Lederberg: Applications of Artificial Intelligence
    for Organic Chemistry: The Dendral Project
Nilsson: Problem-Solving Methods in Artificial Intelligence
Watson: Timesharing System Design Concepts
Winston: The Psychology of Computer Vision
Wulf, Levin, and Harbison: HYDRA/C.mmp: An Experimental Computer System

The Architecture of Pipelined Computers

Peter M. Kogge

IBM Federal Systems Division

⬤ Hemisphere Publishing Corporation

Washington   New York   London

McGraw-Hill Book Company

New York   St. Louis   San Francisco   Auckland   Bogotá
Hamburg   Johannesburg   London   Madrid   Mexico
Montreal   New Delhi   Panama   Paris   São Paulo
Singapore   Sydney   Tokyo   Toronto

This book was set in Press Roman by Hemisphere Publishing Corporation. The editors
were Diane Heiberg, Valerie M. Ziobro, and Elizabeth Dugger; the production supervisor
was Miriam Gonzalez; and the typesetter was Linda Holder.
BookCrafters, Inc. was printer and binder.

THE ARCHITECTURE OF PIPELINED COMPUTERS

1 2 3 4 5 6 7 8 9 0 BCBC 8 9 8 7 6 5 4 3 2 1

Library of Congress Cataloging in Publication Data

Kogge, Peter M   date
    The architecture of pipelined computers.

    (McGraw-Hill advanced computer science series)
    Bibliography: p.
    Includes index.
    1. Computers, Pipeline. 2. Computer architecture.
I. Title. II. Series.
QA76.5.K587   001.64'25   80-26122
ISBN 0-07-035237-2

To my mother, father, wife, and children
In appreciation of their love and support

Contents

Preface

In the world of very high-speed computers, there are two complementary design philosophies—parallelism and pipelining. Parallelism achieves high speed by replicating some basic function many times and providing each replication with one piece of the input data. Pipelining takes the same function and partitions it into many autonomous but interconnected subfunctions. Operation is analogous to fluid in a physical pipeline, with throughput dependent only on the rate at which new inputs are provided to the pipeline and not on its length. Of the two approaches, parallelism is the most frequently discussed, with literally hundreds of scientific papers and several major conferences devoted to its study. Yet despite all this attention, relatively few truly parallel machines have been built.

Just the opposite is true of pipelining. The technique is virtually as old as electronic computers, with each generation of machines using ever more sophisticated variations, but the subject has received nowhere near the attention in the literature that parallelism has. This text is an attempt to fill this void. Its purpose is twofold: first, to document and unify in one place much of the theory, techniques, and understanding we currently have about pipelining, and second, to present the material so that the reader can recognize and use the techniques in future designs. As such, it is more an engineering than a theoretical text; discussions range from logic design considerations, through the construction, cascading, and control of pipelined structures, to the architecture of complete systems and the development of programming techniques to efficiently use such machines. Whenever possible, examples from real machines are used to amplify the development and presentation of the various concepts. Questions at the end of each chapter are largely practical in nature, with emphasis on using the various techniques and concepts to solve real design problems. Because one of this text's goals is documentation, references are given whenever possible. The format for each reference is an author's surname followed by the year of publication. In addition to identifying the source of the material, this format also gives the reader a sense of the time frames involved and consequently the historical sequence of development.

The text itself addresses a graduate-level audience with a presumed background in logic design, programming, and computer architecture. It would easily fill roughly one-half of a first-year graduate course on high-speed computing, with the other half spent on equivalent discussions on parallelism.

The information contained here is a combination of the author's design experiences on several pipelined machines, including the IBM 3838 Array Processor, and an extensive literature survey. The actual text itself has grown from a series of courses taught by the author at the University of Massachusetts at Amherst, the State University of New York at Binghamton, and in-house engineering courses at IBM, Owego, N.Y.

Finally I would like to express my appreciation to all those who helped in the preparation of this book, particularly my wife, Mary Ellen, for her continual patience and support, Harold S. Stone for the initial suggestion to prepare such a text and for his typically excellent reviews and comments, Jordan B. Pollack for both his suggestions and programming of many of the state diagram search algorithms, and finally the IBM Corporation, particularly the talented co-workers at the Electronic Systems Center, for help in producing the original drafts and in performing detailed reviews.

Peter M. Kogge

The Architecture
of Pipelined
Computers

Chapter 1

Introduction

At any time the technology available to a computer architect limits the maximum rate at which data may be processed by a single circuit. In the last 30 years this basic technology has gone from relays, tubes, and acoustic delay lines, through transistors, integrated circuits, and large-scale integration, with charge-coupled devices, magnetic bubbles, Josephson junctions, and surface acoustic waves looming on the near horizon. However, regardless of the technology's intrinsic speed, there has always been the need for much more computer performance than is feasible with a simple straightforward design. For example, there currently exist several projects with requirements of 10^9 instructions per second (1 ns per instruction) balanced against technologies that are approaching the speed of light transmission limitation (30 cm/ns). A textbook design of such a machine packaged in a physical sphere of less than 30 cm in diameter is impossible to imagine in any current technology.

To overcome these limitations, computer architects have long resorted to a series of design techniques that are classified under the general term of *concurrent operation,* where at any instant the computer's hardware is simultaneously processing more than one basic operation. Within this general category are two well-recognized techniques, *parallelism* and *pipelining.* Although rooted in the same origins, and often hard to distinguish in practice, the two terms are discernibly different in their general approach. Parallelism emphasizes concurrency by replicating (often exactly) a hardware structure several, perhaps many, times. High performance is attained by having all structures execute simultaneously on different parts of the problem to be solved.

Pipelining, the subject of this book, generally takes the approach of splitting the function to be performed into smaller pieces and allocating separate hardware to each piece, termed a *stage*. Much as water flows through a physical pipeline, instructions, or data, flow through the stages of a digital computer pipeline at a rate that is independent of the length of the pipeline (number of stages) and dependent only on the rate at which new entries may be fed to the input of the pipeline.

This rate in turn depends primarily on the time for one piece of data to traverse a single stage. As does a physical pipeline, a computer pipeline may do more than simply move its contents unchanged from one location to the next. A physical pipeline in a chemical plant, for example, may have separate stages dedicated to filtering its contents, adding chemicals, and boiling it (Fig. 1-1), whereas a computer pipeline may have stages devoted to instruction fetch, decode, and execution (Fig. 1-2).

The operation of both physical and digital pipelines is similar. As a particular item flows through either pipeline, it occupies only one stage at a time. Simultaneously, an item that enters the pipeline before this item occupies a stage farther down the pipeline, and an item that enters after the referenced item occupies a previous stage. As time goes on, the stage vacated by one item is occupied by the one immediately following it. This concurrent use of many different stages by different items is often called *overlap*. The net result is that the maximum rate at which new items may enter the pipeline depends strictly on the longest time required to traverse any single stage and not on the number of stages.

The goal of designing a computer using pipelining is clearly performance. If some function can be executed with a straightforward design in C ns, and the design is partitionable into N stages, then a pipeline designed to execute the same function repeatedly can perform the function at rates up to C/N ns—an N-fold increase in performance. Of course, in practice there are conditions due to both hardware technology and the function being pipelined that will tend to limit actual achievable rates. However, even with these limitations dramatic performance gains are possible and have been achieved regularly in real systems.

The key to how much performance gain is possible depends on what basic operation in a system is pipelined and on the quality of the partitioning of that function into individual subfunctions to which stages can be assigned. In real systems this basic

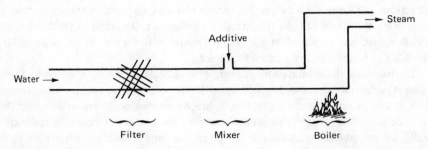

Figure 1-1 Physical pipeline.

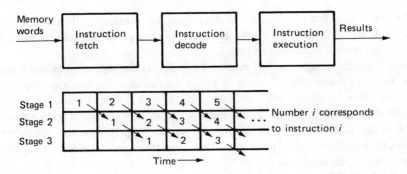

Figure 1-2 Digital computer pipeline.

operation ranges from floating-point arithmetic, through machine-level instruction execution, to the overlapped execution of significant amounts of function such as an entire central processor and an I/O (input-output) processor. In fact, such systems are often hierarchically designed with each stage for one level of pipelining itself actually designed as a pipeline.

This text attempts to look at all aspects of the design and use of pipelining in modern systems. Areas included are definitions and historical perspectives, hardware and control design technology, computers where the pipelining is "visible" in some sense to the programmer, those where it is not, and finally, an overview of possible future trends. Constant consideration is given throughout to perhaps the most difficult problem facing the designers of a digital pipeline, that is the detection and avoidance of *hazards*. Although defined in detail later, a hazard in a pipeline is basically an aspect of its design or use that prevents new data from continually entering at the maximum possible rate.

The remainder of this first chapter more formally defines a pipeline and possible variations and gives a historical overview of how the concept of pipelining has developed. A final section compares pipelining with the companion concept of parallelism.

Chapter 2 is devoted exclusively to the hardware of pipelines. It begins with the properties of logic for pipelines, moves through different kinds of memory structures found in pipelines, and ends with some constructive examples of the buildup of pipelines from individual stages.

Chapter 3 examines the control aspects of designing pipelines, namely scheduling when to permit new data to enter a pipeline to maximize total throughput. The theory developed here is used throughout the book to illustrate the effects of various hazard-avoidance techniques.

One class of highly concurrent processors frequently encountered is a *vector processor*. In such machines the programmer organizes data into sets, or *vectors*, that are processed en masse by single instructions. When implemented on a pipelined machine, these instructions can set up the hardware to pipeline the processing of the data vectors and thus achieve truly remarkable levels of performance. Pipelining in such machines is often very visible to the user. Chapters 4 and 5 discuss these organizations in detail, Chap. 4 defining the typical hardware designs and architectural features and Chap. 5 describing techniques for developing algorithms for efficiently using them. The applications range from implementations of the vector instructions themselves to procedures typical of large programs.

In the other major class of pipelined computers the pipelining is much less rigid than in vector processors and is usually much less visible to the end user. This is typical of cases where "conventional" computer architectures are implemented with pipelined organizations. Here the hazards are much more complex than in vector processors, because the pipelining must recognize and handle properly the dependencies among individual instructions in a program as they flow through the pipeline. Chapter 6 concentrates on such machines.

The final chapter looks at possible relationships between pipelining and new technologies, some novel approaches to hazard processing in pipelines that are under investigation, and other areas of system design where the theory of pipelining may be applicable; it ends with some thoughts on pipelining and its relation to programming.

1.1 FUNCTIONAL PARTITIONING AND STAGING

The term pipelining as used in this text refers to design techniques that introduce concurrency into a computer system by taking some basic function to be invoked repeatedly in the system and partitioning it into several subfunctions with the following properties:

   1   Evaluation of the basic function is equivalent to some sequential evaluation of the subfunctions.
   2   The inputs for one subfunction come totally from outputs of previous subfunctions in the evaluation sequence.
   3   Other than the exchange of inputs and outputs, there are no interrelationships between subfunctions.
   4   Hardware may be developed to execute each subfunction.
   5   The times required for these hardware units to perform their individual evaluations are usually approximately equal.

The hardware required to evaluate any of these subfunctions is termed a *stage*. Unlike a physical pipeline handling liquid, the typical digital pipeline does not accept data in a continuous flow. Instead it accepts discrete inputs that traverse from stage to stage according to the commands of a fairly regular clock. A good physical analogy is the handling of bottles in a bottling plant.

Since the logic that actually does the processing at each stage is itself normally without memory, this discreteness in the presentation of data to each stage usually demands that some kind of memory element be included at either the beginning or end of each stage. This element prevents data being processed in one stage from overrunning its stage and falsely influencing the next stage before a single time period has ended. Such overruns might occur because of differing amounts of logic per stage or variations in the time delays per logic element. These interstage memory elements prevent overruns by causing all stages to resynchronize at least once per processing step. The occurrence of a clock pulse at the end of each processing-step time unit forces each memory element to sample the outputs of the previous stage and to hold that sample in its own output until the next clock pulse. During the next time period this sampled output is the input to the logic of the next stage, and in turn it will be sampled by the next memory device at the succeeding clock. In the literature these memory devices have gone by various names, including *staging latch, staging platform,* or *reservation station.* This text will use the term staging latch or latch.

1.2 PIPELINING VS. OVERLAP

In current usage the terms *pipelining* and *overlap* have similar, but not identical, meanings. They both employ the idea of subfunction partitioning, but in slightly different contexts. Pipelining occurs when all of the following are true:

1 Each evaluation of the basic function is relatively independent of the previous one.

2 Each evaluation requires approximately the same sequence of subfunctions.

3 The subfunctions are closely related.

4 The times to compute different subfunctions are approximately equal.

Overlap, on the other hand, is typically used when one of the following occurs:

1 There may be some dependencies between evaluations.

2 Each evaluation may require a different sequence of subfunctions.

3 The subfunctions are relatively distinct in their purpose.

4 The time per stage is not necessarily constant but is a function of both the stage and the data passing through it.

The distinctions between pipelined processing, overlapped processing, and parallel processing often become quite fuzzy in practice.

From time to time in this text we will refer to pipelining of the first kind as *synchronous* or *static.* Similarly, overlapped processing may be referred to as *asynchronous* or *dynamic pipelining.*

A classic example of static pipelining is the design of a pipelined unit built to do repeated independent floating-point additions on data provided by some other unit. Here the basic function, floating-point addition, is relatively simple. As far as the adder is concerned, the result of one add in no way depends on the previous, next, or any other add. Further, there are a variety of ways of partitioning the add function into stages, ranging from two (cf. IBM System/360 Model 91—Anderson et al., 1967a) to six (cf. TI ASC—Watson, 1972a,b) or more. However, once a partition is made, all adds follow the same path. For example, Fig. 1-3 diagrams the result of partitioning the function floating-point addition into five subfunctions as follows:

1 Subtraction of the exponents;

2 Shifting right the fraction from the number with the smaller exponent by an amount corresponding to the difference in exponents;

3 Addition of the other fraction to the shifted one;

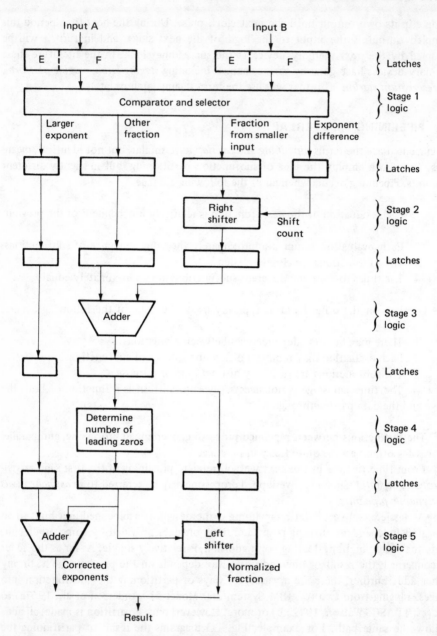

Figure 1-3 Example of a five-stage floating-point adder.

4 Counting the number of leading zeros in the sum; and

5 Shifting left the sum by the number of leading zeros and adjusting the exponent accordingly.

Although this partitioning is typical, there are variations in real units to account for such things as different number bases, over- and underflow detection, and representation of zero.

The pipeline in Fig. 1-3 has separate logic for each of these subfunctions with staging latches positioned between each set of logic to hold the output of the stage for processing by the next stage. Every addition follows the same path through these stages. Further, the time required by each stage to do its subfunction is about equal, and the transitions from stage to stage are rigidly controlled by an external timing source common to all stages. The analogy to a physical pipeline is direct.

The simplest example of overlap or dynamic pipelining is a computer system where all I/O is handled by one processor, all computation by another, and most communication is through a common memory module (Fig. 1-4). A typical task in this system would alternate between the computational and I/O processors while the execution of some other task is overlapped by using the other processor. In our terminology there are two stages, each of which is an entire processor, coupled by a staging latch, which is actually an entire memory system. Here operation is a great deal less synchronized than in a floating-point adder; the partitioning of the basic function (task) is dynamically changing and even the time per stage is not predictable in advance.

Another common example of overlapped operation is in the design of high-speed CPUs such as the IBM System/360 Model 91 (Anderson et al., 1967a). Here the basic function to be evaluated is repeated machine-level instruction execution, and the partitioning itself is both data and sequence dependent. As with the floating-point adder, the hardware is typically divided into a fixed number of well-defined stages. However, because of, among other things, format differences, each instruction may take a different path through the pipeline. A branch instruction, for example, would not follow the same sequence of stages as a floating-point multiply. In addition, dependencies between successive instructions may perturb both the path taken and the time spent in each stage. Again as an example, a floating-point multiply instruction may be held up waiting for the result of some previous instruction, whereas a branch instruction started several cycles later may not depend on the multiply's output and may race ahead. The result is a very dynamic process where the order of intermediate handling and completion of instructions may be totally different from the sequence in which they were started. For example, Fig. 1-5 (from Anderson, 1967b) shows the partitioning of RS format floating-point operations in the IBM System/360 Model 91. Totally different partitioning occurs for different types of instructions.

For simplicity throughout this text, any design employing either pipelining or overlap as defined above will be called a pipeline. When it is necessary to make the distinction, the appropriate term will be used to qualify it.

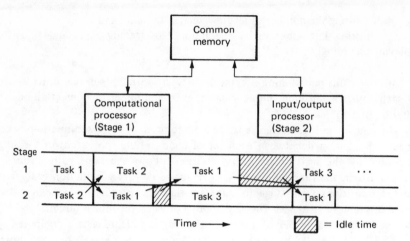

Figure 1-4 Simple overlapped system.

1.3 CLASSIFICATION OF PIPELINES

Pipelines can be classified both according to their capabilities and according to how they are actually used. A *unifunction pipeline* is one that is capable of only one basic kind of function evaluation. The pipeline performs the same operations on every set of inputs given it with no variations. The floating-point adder described earlier is unifunction in nature. On the other hand, a *multifunction pipeline* is one that is capable of several different kinds of function evaluations. Thus, in addition to the data inputs, there is some kind of control input directing the pipeline's activity. Examples include the IBM System/360 Model 91 where the path selection is in fact derived from the input instructions themselves, the TI ASC (Watson, 1972a) where an eight-stage arithmetic unit can be configured for a variety of operations, and the IBM 3838 Array Processor (IBM, 1976) where the connections between various pipelined multipliers and adders are under microprogrammed control.

For multifunction pipelines the frequency at which changes to the function being performed are made leads to another classification. If the pipeline system is capable of only relatively infrequent changes to the function type being run, then the pipeline is said to be *statically configured*. Between changes the pipeline acts as if it were unifunction and simply repeats the same set of operations over and over again on the incoming data. Very often this configuration change is under direct programmer control, resulting in a class of computer architecture termed a *vector processor*. Here a single instruction specifies both the function to be performed and the location of a long string of data elements (a vector) to which this function is to be applied. The pipeline is then configured to perform the operation, and the data is "streamed" through it. After one of these vector instructions completes, a different one may be started. Examples of machines with such capabilities include the IBM 2938 Array Processor (Ruggiero and Coryell, 1969), CDC STAR-100 (Hintz, 1972), the TI ASC (Watson, 1972a), the IBM 3838 Array Processor (IBM, 1976), and the CRAY-1 (Cray, 1976).

Other multifunction pipelines allow more frequent changes to the functions they

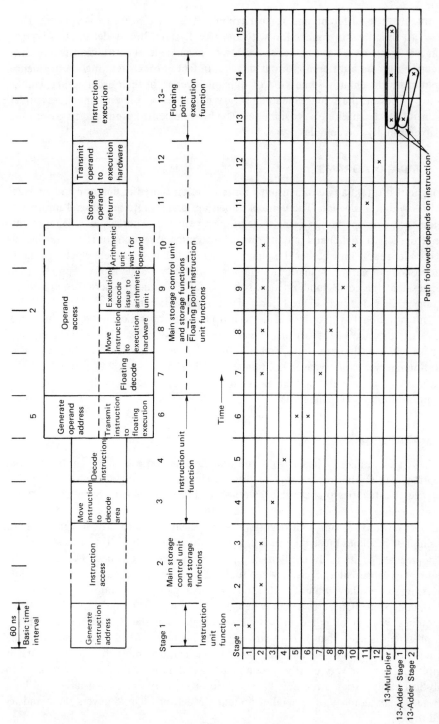

Figure 1-5 IBM System/360 Model 91.

9

perform, up to a different one for each input. These are termed *dynamically con-figured*. As described in connection with the IBM System/360 Model 91, this type of pipeline is most often used in the execution of machine-level instruction where each instruction may be a different format or type. In fact, most current high-performance computer designs employ some kind of dynamic overlap in their architecture. Unlike a vector processor, the actual pipelining is very seldom even visible to, much less under the control of, the machine's programmer. The internal controls required to govern the overlap are simply too complex.

1.4 TIMING DIAGRAMS

Throughout this text a two-dimensional representation is used to describe and analyze activities within a pipeline. The vertical dimension divides into an integral number of entries, each corresponding to one stage in the pipeline. The horizontal axis represents time (from left to right) and may be divided into integral sections or left a continuous variable, depending on whether the pipeline is controlled by a discrete clock or is more asynchronous in nature. A mark at some place in this two-dimensional representation indicates that the corresponding stage is in use for the indicated period of time. The diagrams in Figs. 1-2 and 1-5 are typical of this representation.

This notation has its origin in the Gantt charts of operation research, the space-time charts of Chen (1971a,b), and the reservation tables of Davidson (1971). In most cases we will use the latter term, *reservation table,* since such diagrams define how an operation reserves various stages as a function of time.

Chapter 3 uses reservation tables extensively in derivations of a theory that guides the optimization of a pipeline's use.

1.5 HAZARDS

A hazard is something in the design or use of a pipeline that prevents the pipeline from accepting data at the maximum rate that its staging clock might support. There are two general categories of hazards: *structural* and *data dependent.* Structural hazards are cases where two different pieces of data attempt to use the same stage at the same time. For obvious reasons such occurrences are called *collisions.* The design of all but the simplest pipelines must take such hazards into account from the earliest point in development. For statically configured pipelines, the theory of Chap. 3 describes how the designer can predict precisely when such hazards might occur and how to schedule processing so that they will not occur, thus optimizing processing rates.

Data-dependent hazards occur when what is going on in one stage of a pipeline determines whether or not data may pass through other stages. A simple example is two different stages that must share a single memory. When one stage uses the memory, the other stage, if its data also requires memory, must idle until the first is complete. These are very clearly system- and usage-dependent, and not as amenable to analytical study as are structural hazards. However, they are encountered and have spawned a fair number of general techniques. Much of Chap. 6 covers these and related topics.

1.6 HISTORICAL PERSPECTIVES

The recognition of the usefulness of pipelining dates back to the earliest days of computer design, with each succeeding generation employing more pervasive and sophisticated techniques. This section briefly charts the growth of these techniques, in terms of both actual computer systems and their underlying basic design concepts. At each stage of development we will list only a representative sampling of machines because a complete list of all machines employing pipelining would be overwhelming.

One of the earliest machines to employ a form of overlap was the UNIVAC I. This machine overlapped program execution with certain limited I/O activities. Succeeding machines amplified this technique until today it is not unusual for a single computer system to have several processors dedicated to strictly I/O functions.

Use of pipelining and overlap within the computing facility itself started with techniques for speeding up instruction fetch times. The IBM 7094 had a 72-bit-wide memory and 36-bit instruction. Each time a memory access was made to fetch an instruction, the unused 36 bits were saved. This eliminated half of the instruction fetches when the CPU was executing sequential code.

Machines like the IBM 7094 II went one step farther with the use of interleaved memory to speed up memory access time. In an *interleaved memory* several different memory modules are activated in a cyclic fashion as memory locations are specified sequentially. For example, in a four-way interleaved memory, all location addresses of the form $4i$ are in one module, all those of the form $4i + 1$ in another, $4i + 2$ in a third, and $4i + 3$ in the remaining module. This arrangement might be considered a four-stage pipeline, where in the time required to do one memory access up to four separate accesses can be in different stages of completion.

Partitioning of the instruction execution process itself began with the STRETCH (Block, 1959; Bucholz, 1962) and the LARC (Eckert et al., 1959; Chen, 1975). The goals for the STRETCH design were a 100-fold improvement over the older 704, where memory technology gave only a factor of 6 and logic technology a factor of 10. The rest of the performance increase was to come from a combination of heavy interleaving of memory with partitioning of the instruction execution process into two stages: an instruction fetch/decode and a data execution phase. The LARC took this partitioning farther and broke the process into four stages: instruction fetch, address index operations, data fetch, and execution.

Although the theoretical speedup due to pipelining alone for such systems over a conventional design is equal to the number of stages, this was not fully achievable. Actual performance increase was limited by dependencies between instructions. An instruction at one stage of the pipeline may depend on the result of a previous instruction that has not yet completed and consequently must be held up from advancing to the next stage. Furthermore, in these early systems a holdup of one stage holds up all stages in back of it, even though some of the instructions in back of it may not depend on it and could advance through the unused stages.

The CDC 6000 series of computers (Thornton, 1964, 1970) were among the first to attempt to overcome this dependency holdup problem. Although not pipelined in the strict sense defined above, many of the techniques used were forerunners of more modern approaches that have been used in pipelined machines. First, for example, the architecture of the instruction set was specifically designed to remove as many potential dependencies as possible. This included simple formats, simple memory addressing, and separate hardware register sets for separate functions. For example, all computation is done in a three-register format where the registers are 60-bit central registers. Likewise, all addressing is done via separate address and index registers. This separation and dedication of function increases the independence of many of the steps of instruction execution, permitting more partitioning and consequently more overlaps. In addition, the 6000 series included a central scoreboard with status on each resource in the machine that might be used by some instruction currently at some stage of processing within the system. When an instruction reaches a stage where continuance is dependent on some resource that might be in use for some other instruction, the scoreboard is checked. If the instruction is not permitted to continue, it is temporarily put aside. In the case of the 6600, this deferring of an instruction also halted the flow of instructions in back of it. When the dependency is satisfied (e.g., the other instruction completes), the scoreboard recognizes that the deferred instruction may now be allowed to continue and returns it to an active state. Since there are many possible dependencies (register usage, store followed by a load from the same address, conditional branches, etc.), individual instructions might be delayed more than once during their execution.

One other notable feature of the 6000 series machines was the inclusion of many independent function units (multipliers, adders, etc.) for the data execution stage. As each instruction reached this stage the operands were delivered to a free function unit of the proper type for processing. That function unit is marked busy until the operation is complete and the result removed. This again results in the overlap of many different instructions.

Although not strictly pipelined, many of the 6000 series features paved the way for future pipelined machines. It is a good example of where the differences between pure pipelining, overlap, and pure parallelism become quite indistinct, but where the basic notions of functional partitioning and hazard detection and removal were clearly considered in the design phase. Later machines such as the 7600 amplified these techniques by more heavy pipelining, particularly in the function units.

The IBM System/360 Model 91 took a somewhat different approach.[1] Here the goal was to use pipelining to speed up the execution of a more conventional instruction set (the System 360 architecture) as much as possible. Since this instruction-set architecture was not specifically tailored to a pipelined implementation, there are more possibilities for interinstruction dependencies. Consequently, a great deal of attention was paid to interlocks and partitioning the system to allow as much overlap as possible. This resulted, for example, in partial fetching of both possible sets of code following a conditional branch instruction when the results of the conditional test depend on instructions not yet complete. When the result is known, the unwanted sequence is purged.

As shown in Fig. 1-5, the whole process of instruction execution was heavily pipelined with a myriad of paths and special functions designed to increase throughput. In

---

[1] The January 1967 issue of the *IBM Journal of Research and Development* describes this machine in great detail.

fact, the System/360 Model 91 was one of the first machines to employ a hierarchy of pipelines, with the outermost level consisting of two stages: an *I-Unit* for instruction fetch and preprocessing and an *E-Unit* for execution. Both of these units were themselves pipelined.

As an example, the data-execution phase of the floating-point instruction execution process is itself heavily pipelined with individual pipelined multipliers and adders doing the actual computation. Further, these units are interconnected by a decentralized common data bus, which initiates operations as soon as data operands are available, largely independent of the original order of instructions listed by the programmer. The resulting "chaotic," out-of-order execution sequence could at times be quite different from what the programmer might expect, but because of the design, the computed results were as expected.

The next development in pipelined machines grew out of the need in certain applications for execution rates much higher than could be achieved with conventional architectures. Further, these applications were often characterized as series of steps, where at each step a single function was used successively in many individual elements of data. Such sets of data were called *vectors*. A new class of instructions, termed *vector instructions*, were then developed to allow a programmer to specify in a single instruction one of these basic vector steps. Besides eliminating the overhead due to loop control instructions, this type of instruction allowed the computer designer to set up the internal pipelines to run at maximum rates without fear of encountering unforeseen dependencies and hazards. Such machines are termed *vector processors*.

Three such machines were the IBM 2938 Array Processor, the CDC STAR-100, and the Texas Instruments Advanced Scientific Computer. The IBM 2938 Array Processor (Ruggiero and Coryell, 1969) was a pure vector processor optimized to do multiply-adds that attached to the memory bus of more conventional machines and received strings of vector instructions from those machines.

The CDC STAR[2] included both conventional scalar instructions and vector instructions. As in the 6000 series machines, there were multiple independent functional units for the execution stage, but in the STAR these units were themselves pipelined. In addition, special addressing modes called *bit vectors* were developed to allow the programmer to treat in compact form vectors that contained many zero elements. The TI ASC machine (Watson, 1972a) went in another direction with the inclusion of vector instructions capable of handling up to three-dimensional vectors. This design was also different in that internally a single arithmetic pipeline could be configured dynamically to perform any of the basic operations (multiply, add, etc.) on either fixed- or floating-point data. The machine would support anywhere from one to four of these pipelines.

The most recent developments in pipelined design have emphasized increased overlap of higher level functions. The IBM 3838 (IBM, 1976), for example, is an attached vector processor like the previous 2938 but with a richer and higher level of vector instructions. Within this unit there are several independent processing components, all of which perform different parts of the vector instruction execution

---

[2] The *Proceedings of COMPCON 1972* include many articles on this machine.

process, and some of which are themselves pipelined at several levels. This again permits several levels of pipelining and overlap to be active at any one time, with the simultaneous interleaving of several different programs for several different and independent users.

Another example is the CRAY-1 (Cray, 1976). The architecture of this machine includes both scalar and vector instructions, but with a twist. Instead of applying to vectors in memory, the CRAY-1's vector instruction set applies to sets of elements in *vector registers*. At any one time a programmer can specify the simultaneous loading and unloading of some of these registers with vector processing (multiplies, adds, etc.) of the contents of other vector registers. Additionally, the programmer may specify the *chaining* of vector operations, where the outputs of one vector operation are directly fed to the next as they are generated without having to wait for completion of the first instruction. To a large degree the pipelining in this machine is very visible to the user. By careful programming, large amounts of overlap are achievable.

In more recent work, the concept of chaotic instruction execution has driven the study of *data flow* machines where there is no order of execution implied by the order of instructions in storage. The only hazards left are data-dependent ones where, for example, instruction j explicitly requires data to be produced from instruction i.

1.7 COMPARISON WITH PARALLELISM

During the mid-1960s, the price of hardware dropped sufficiently to allow computer architects to consider wholesale "replication" of computers or computer subsystems as a viable technique for developing high-performance systems. This replication of hardware may be to allow similar processing of different data to occur simultaneously or to allow different hardware to handle distinctly different parts of the problem. In today's terminology these machines are termed *parallel*. Although, as said before, both parallelism and pipelining have the same origins and are hard to separate in practice, the mental image many current practitioners have of each is sufficiently distinct to justify a high-level comparison of the two. Both techniques attempt to increase the performance of some function by increasing the number of simultaneously operating hardware modules. For a conventionally designed module to do some generic function, either technique can be used to derive a new design running up to N times faster. However, whereas in the pure pipelined design the basic module is split into N pieces, in the pure parallel design the basic module may be replicated N times with all replications running simultaneously on different data. A mixture of the two results in an overlapped design. Although in terms of performance a parallel and a pipelined machine may be equivalent, the resulting organizations will be dramatically different. For example, both the ILLIAC IV (Barnes et al., 1968) and the CDC STAR-100 were built with very large scientific problems in mind. However, the ILLIAC IV, which is heavily parallel, employs 64 copies of what is similar to the arithmetic unit of a more conventional machine. Each copy has its own registers, adder, and memory, and all can run simultaneously. In contrast, the STAR emphasizes modules that are heavily pipelined. The organizations of the two machines bear little resemblance to each other.

Figure 1-6 and Table 1-1 summarize major differences between the two approaches. Of course in real machines the contrast is not so sharp, since often techniques are mixed. For example, the highly parallel ILLIAC IV employs a pipelined/ overlapped control-unit design, whereas the highly pipelined STAR has replicated function units.

The distinctions between the two approaches are most easily seen if we consider the variations in the basic *architecture* a computer might have. One definition of computer architecture is the characteristics of a machine as seen by a programmer or high-level logic designer, such as its instruction set, memory size, and organization. A scheme proposed by Flynn (1966) breaks computer architecture into four distinct categories: SISD, SIMD, MISD, and MIMD. SISD stands for Single-Instruction-Stream/ Single-Data-Stream and corresponds to conventional computers where instructions are executed one by one, and a single instruction deals with at most a single data operation (such as an add). A SIMD machine, Single-Instruction-Stream/Multiple-Data-Stream, contains instructions that can directly trigger a large number of data operations on different data. The vector processors discussed earlier fall into this category. MIMD machines are Multi-Instruction-Stream/Multi-Data-Stream, and are characterized by the simultaneous execution of many different instruction streams (programs) where

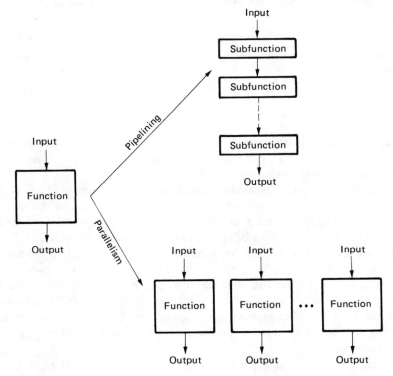

Figure 1-6 Parallelism and pipelining.

Table 1-1   Comparison of Parallelism and Pipelining

Parameter	Parallel organization	Pipelined organization
Basic design	Independent execution of subproblems on separate hardware	Partitioning of function into N subfunctions
Performance	N results every T seconds	One result every T/N seconds
Basic clock	Time for one function evaluation	Time for one stage
Typical supported architecture	SIMD, MIMD	SISD, SIMD
Preferred problem structure	Array problems with lengths multiples of number of processors; partitionable, independent processes	Speedup of conventional instruction sets, favors one-dimensional vectors of arbitrary long length
Timing diagram	Two-dimensional processor no. vs. time	Two-dimensional stage no. vs. time
Typical memory organization	Multiple, independent memory modules	Single, multiway-interleaved memory
Typical memory bandwidth	High instantaneous	Constant average
Detailed control	Handled by user	Handled largely by hardware
Performance limitations	Cost, problem structures	Technology, memory bandwidth
Reliability considerations	Easy to "hot" spare	Expensive, not modular

the instructions in each stream deal with different data sets. Multiprocessor systems are perfect examples of this category. Finally, MISD machines pass a single data item simultaneously by many instructions.

Within these categories, pipelining is used most often to support SISD or SIMD machines. As described in the previous section, most conventionally architected computers employ pipelining/overlap to some extent, ranging from simply interleaved memories up to heavy pipelining of all phases of an instruction's execution. Further, machines previously defined as vector processors fall into a strongly SIMD category. Some attempt has been made to design MIMD machines from primarily pipelined designs, although usually for cost-effective rather than performance reasons. Examples of this latter class include the peripheral processors on the CDC 6000 series machines and on the TI ASC. Other proposals, for example by Shar (1974), have examined supporting multiple minicomputers (at least as seen by the programmer) by a single pipelined device.

In contrast, parallelism is most extensively used in both SIMD and MIMD class designs where entire processing elements are replicated. For SIMD parallel machines, replication factors range from 64 for ILLIAC IV, through 288 for PEPE (Enslow,

1974), up to the thousands in more recent proposals. True MIMD machines replicate entire conventional computers and range from the very common dual multiprocessor up to the 16 PDP-11's in C.mmp (Wulf and Bell, 1972), and the hundreds in CM* (Swan et al., 1977).

This difference in preferred architecture also manifests itself in the kinds of problems that fit best on machines using either technique. Parallel SIMD machines are good matches for problems where the dimensions of the basic data structures are multiples of the replication count. Parallel MIMD machines are most useful when a task can be split into many semi-independent subtasks, each of which can be run on a distinct processor. Pipelined SISD machines appear little different to the programmer from classical nonpipelined processors; the major difference is an increase in speed. In contrast to parallel SIMD machines, pipelined SIMD machines are most suited for handling very long vectors to minimize the effect of pipeline startup/shutdown times.

Another characteristic affected by these techniques is the way in which activity within a computer is drawn as a function of time and algorithm being executed. For example, activity within a parallel machine is often diagrammed as a two-dimensional graph with time on one axis and processor identification on the other. A mark or line then indicates time periods when each processor is busy, with arrows connecting points in the graph if the result produced by one processor is used by another. As an example, Fig. 1-7 diagrams a four-processor SIMD machine that is computing the sum of eight numbers. In comparison, timing for pipelined machines is a two-dimensional graph with time on one axis and stage number on the other. Again markers or lines are used to indicated activity, but now the total activity for a task appears slanted in relation to the diagram for a parallel machine. Figure 1-8 diagrams the timing for a four-stage adder that solves the same problem as Fig. 1-7.

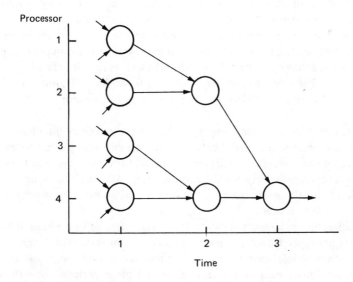

Figure 1-7 Parallel computer timing diagram.

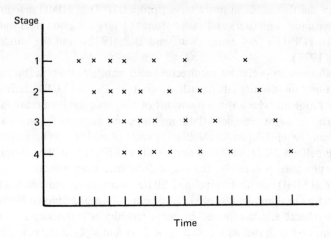

Figure 1-8   Pipelined computer timing diagram.

On a more detailed level, the differences between parallelism and pipelining also show up in memory organization and bandwidth, internal interconnection of modules, and control. Today, parallel machines with N processors nearly always have at least N distinct memory modules so that each processor can access data simultaneously. Because there are often requirements for each processor to access data from different memories at different times, there is usually a switch or interconnection network between the memories and processors with controls to dynamically interconnect the two. Similarly, there are often interconnections between processors to allow direct exchange of data. In either case the optimal, and by far most costly, interconnection scheme is a *cross-bar switch* allowing any processor combination to talk to any memory combination at one time. Depending on the nature of the problems being solved, real systems employ less complex switches, which results in reduced generality. In many systems, however, even these reduced switches account for a large percentage of system cost. The interested reader is referred to works by Thornton (1977), Siegal (1977), and Thompson (1978) for introductions to modern switch design technologies.

In contrast, pipelined machines typically employ multiway-interleaved memories with only one or very few paths between the memory and the processor. Further, since the nature of a pipeline implies some natural flow, there are usually only a small number of internal paths between the various stages. As a result, although the memory organization is usually more complex than for a parallel machine, no expensive interconnection network is needed.

This difference in memory organization is also reflected in the kind of bandwidths (read/writes per second) that the memory must sustain in current design. In a parallel machine with multiple memory modules there are periods when all the memory modules must deliver data at the same time and other periods where there is more quiescence. The result is a memory bandwidth that varies, reaching very high values for short periods of time when all processors demand simultaneous service. Again in contrast, a memory system for a pipelined machine typically accesses data at a much smoother, more constant rate, since the pipelines themselves accept data at constant intervals. Of course, because most data in the system travels to and from this single memory, the actual bandwidth for a pipelined machine at the same performance level as a parallel machine can be extremely high. In both cases a great deal of modern research is going into how to design memory subsystems capable of meeting such demands.

There are also substantial differences in the control of such processors. In parallel processors, speedups are possible only when the user has allocated individual tasks to individual processors. This typically requires that the user be given a very high degree of visibility and control over what happens in the system such as the interconnection networks and processor-processor communication. In pipelined machines, however, the designer has already specified to a large extent the partitioning of the basic functions, so that a user needs and typically has little access to the controls of the pipeline. Instead the user's problem is to write a program to avoid sequences that might slow the execution of the task by not permitting the pipeline to be kept full. For example, instruction sequences that force interlocks to be invoked during their execution should be avoided, as should processing very short vectors where the time to fill the pipeline initially is large in comparison with the number of operations to be started and with the depth of the pipeline.

The final point of contrast between pipelining and parallelism is in *scalability,* that is, how big the degree of partitioning can be made. For parallel architectures the primary constraints to arbitrarily high replication counts are cost, particularly in the interconnection network, and the speed of light, because as the number of processors increases, the physical distances between them increase, in turn limiting the speed of data exchange. In contrast, a function cannot be subpartitioned into an arbitrarily large number of pipeline stages, even if cost is not an issue. In any given technology there is some limit on the minimum time to pass through each stage; that is, there must be at least one level of processing logic per stage in order to do anything other than transfer data. This in turn is also limited by the speed of light, but not to the extent that parallel machines are, since most pipelines are highly linear and one stage can be packaged near its predecessor.

Another big problem in the scalability of pipelined machines is, as mentioned above, the high bandwidth typically required of memory systems to support pipelines. Parallel designs can usually replicate memory modules with perhaps an increase in switch costs to get more bandwidth, but pipelines typically funnel all memory operations through small numbers of interconnections.

The final point of comparison is in the capacity of the design to support some redundancy to improve reliability. In many parallel machines it is possible to add at little cost additional copies that can be "switched in" as needed. This is not true of many pipelined designs where each stage is different. Separate redundancy techniques may have to be used at each stage and designed in at the beginning.

PROBLEMS

1-1   Consider a digital bus connecting several sources of data that compete for the bus to talk to one of several destinations. What functions have to be performed to get data from one source to a destination? How might you partition these functions into a pipelined bus? How much extra bandwidth does your partitioning provide over a nonpipelined version?

1-2   A standard method of computing the square root of X is with the recurrence $X(i) = \frac{1}{2} [X(i-1) + X/X(i-1)]$ where $X(0)$ is some estimate of $\sqrt{X}$.

   a   Assuming that you have available an arbitrary number of multipliers, adders, and dividers, how might you partition the computation of $X(3)$ where $X(0) = X$? What kind of performance results when you have a lot of square roots to do? How long does it take to do each square root?

   b   Repeat, assuming you have only one adder, one multiplier, and one divider. What hazards slow you down?

1-3   The text gave one possible partitioning of floating-point addition. Develop two others. Show a rough logic diagram for each.

1-4   Try partitioning the process of instruction execution for some computer instruction set with which you are familiar. What problems do you encounter?

Chapter 2

Hardware Design and Stage Cascading

The use of pipelined design techniques requires a somewhat different approach to the actual logic design of a system than that for more conventional design techniques. For example, as in any design, the type of logic available influences directly the minimum time for a basic logic cycle of a processing unit. However, perhaps much more critical for pipelines are the characteristics of the staging latches, since they determine to a large extent the characteristics of the clock used to govern the pipeline. In turn this affects the finest possible level of partitioning and consequently the maximum speed of the system. Further, even when all these individual stage characteristics are determined, a partitioning of the desired function must be found that allows all stages to run concurrently but without an excessively high cost (e.g., total number of bits in staging latches kept at an affordable level).

This chapter attempts to give some insight into the above problems by first reviewing the basic mathematics relating the characteristics of the staging latches to the logic involved. This has ramifications on the latch design, logic partitioning, and hardware packaging. Next is a review of some additional characteristics of staging latches, and then by example some ways in which functions can be built up out of cascaded arrangements of individual stages. Included are problems that on the first glance are nonpipelineable but by proper recasting can be solved efficiently with pipelined techniques. Finally, a development of some cost criteria and cost equations yields insight into determining what partitions of a function result in the most cost-effective pipelined design.

Although couched primarily in terms of synchronous pipelines, the results given here are equally applicable to asynchronous (overlapped) designs.

2.1 LOGIC DESIGN TECHNOLOGY

There are two components to any stage in a pipeline: the logic to do the required subfunction and the mechanism to save the output of one stage as input to the next. Although they are typically separate hardware elements (we will discuss some alternatives later), the characteristics of each have a strong influence on the design of the other. This interaction was not formalized on the early pipelined machines (of the 7094 or STRETCH vintage) because there were relatively few, rather specialized stages. When one stage wanted to communicate with another, special resyncing hardware delayed one until the other was ready. Neither great generality nor extremely high speeds were needed.

These requirements changed in the mid-1960s with the emergence of machines with more concurrency such as the IBM System/360 Model 91 (Flynn, 1966; Anderson et al., 1967b). These machines had on the order of a dozen stages, all being clocked at a relatively high rate. The technology available was either discrete transistor components or low-level integrated circuits (two to five gates per chip for the Model 91). In such systems, performance was not so much a function of the number of stages as it was the basic stage clocking rate. The designers' goal was to minimize this basic clock, perhaps at the cost of relatively few logic levels per stage and the corresponding increase in the number of stages required. When this was attempted, two design constraints became evident, both concerning the nature of the clock pulse used to trigger the staging latches into accepting new information. In Fig. 2-1 this clock pulse has two basic components, T and W. T is the time available for signals to propagate from the output of one latch, through the logic for that subfunction, to the input of the next latch. W is the width of the clock pulse and represents the time spent in accepting the computed result into the latch and stabilizing the output.

The first, and most obvious, design constraint was that the time T_{max} for a signal to traverse the longest path through the logic must be no greater than T. The second constraint is not so obvious; it deals with the possibility that a data path through the logic might be so short that if a latch changes its output a little early during W then the change might reach the next staging latch and change it during the same clock. This situation was termed a *critical race* by Cotten (1965). To avoid it, the shortest paths of logic in each stage might have to be augmented by do-nothing circuits that simply introduce a time delay.

Together these two constraints place limits on the minimum and maximum amount of logic that can be placed in any path from the output of one latch to the inputs of the next. These limits are further tightened when another phenomenon called *clock skew* is considered. Ideally all stages in a pipeline receive the same pulse at the same time. However, in reality differences in cabling, loading, and driver circuits make it practically impossible to guarantee identical arrival times. The term S for clock

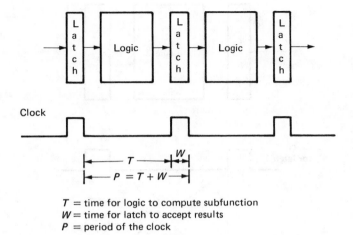

T = time for logic to compute subfunction
W = time for latch to accept results
P = period of the clock

Figure 2-1 Basic pipeline clock.

skew represents this difference in actual arrival times of the same pulse at different stages and must be taken into account in both constraints. First, if the skew is such that one stage receives its clock a little before its predecessor, then the total time available for logic propagation is reduced. In terms of T_{max}, T, and S, it is required that

$$T_{max} \leqslant T - S \tag{2-1}$$

Figure 2-2 diagrams this case. Similarly, the critical race conditions are worsened if the clock for one stage is delayed relative to the same clock for the previous stage (Fig. 2-3). This delay simply allows more time for changes in the output of the earlier stage to propagate through the minimum logic path and affect its successor during the "same" clock. To avoid this problem requires that

$$T_{min} \geqslant W + S \tag{2-2}$$

Cotton (1965) first documented bounds equivalent to these.

2.1.1. Latch Design—The Earle Latch

From these investigations it is obvious that the key to very high performance is in the design of the latch. Those characteristics of a latch that make it particularly well-suited are high speed and consistency of timing. By high speed is meant that a minimum time is required to accept an input and save it. This directly translates into smaller pulse widths, more usable logic time, and consequently higher performance. Consistency of timing means that when the output of a latch must change to follow a new input value, it always takes about the same amount of time to make the change independent of which output is observed or whether the change is from 1 to 0 or 0 to 1. Inconsistency of timing in a latch is equivalent to introducing additional skew into the circuit with the concurrent loss of processing time.

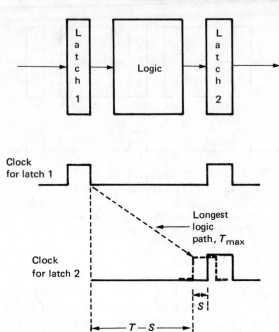

Figure 2-2 Effects of clock skew on longest logic path.

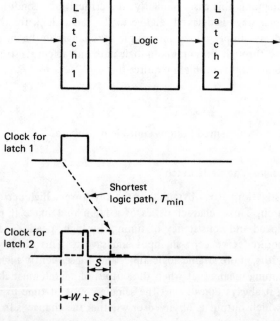

Figure 2-3 Effects of clock skew on critical race.

As an example of a latch having neither of the above characteristics, Fig. 2-4 diagrams a classical latch circuit constructed from four NAND gates.[1] In current terminology this circuit is called a *flip-flop*. We assume that each gate has an inherent delay of d time units. There are three inputs to this latch: DATA, $\overline{\text{DATA}}$ (the complement of DATA), and CLOCK. The two outputs OUT and $\overline{\text{OUT}}$ are complements of each other. When the clock is high (logic 1), the output follows the input. When the clock is low, the output freezes its values at whatever it was just before the clock dropped. The actual clocking of the latch is thus the time from the rise of CLOCK from 0 to 1 to its fall back to 0. This time corresponds to the minimum possible W in the previous equations. Detailed timing for a particular case, namely where OUT is initially 0 and DATA is 1, is shown in Fig. 2-5. Here one gate delay after the clock rises, the output of gate 1 drops to 0. One gate delay later OUT rises to 1; and after yet another gate delay $\overline{\text{OUT}}$ drops to its final value 0. Any time after this the clock may fall and the outputs will remain stable.

The disadvantages of this latch are several. First, $\overline{\text{DATA}}$ must always be available as an input, which requires either double rail logic, where both the true and complement signals are generated at each level of gating, or an inverter between DATA and $\overline{\text{DATA}}$. The first approach costs hardware; the second reduces the amount of time available for logic propagation in the stage by the delay of the inverter. The second disadvantage is that the latch takes up to three equivalent gate delays to have stable outputs. Finally, even within these three gate delays the timing of the individual gates is not consistent. In Fig. 2-5 the line OUT changes at time $2d$, but $\overline{\text{OUT}}$ waits until time $3d$. During this third d period both OUT and $\overline{\text{OUT}}$ have the same value— a violation of the desired logical characteristics. For other combinations of input and output values this relationship will switch, $\overline{\text{OUT}}$ becoming stable before OUT.

A series of latch designs for pipelines has been proposed to overcome these problems (cf. Cotten, 1965). One of the more successful ones was the *Earle latch* (Earle,

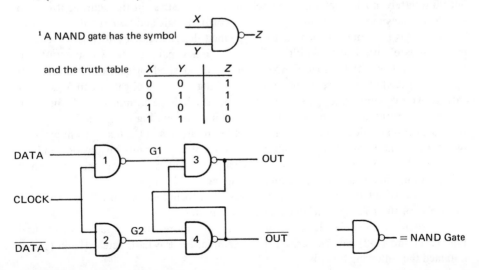

[1] A NAND gate has the symbol ... —Z

and the truth table

X	Y	Z
0	0	1
0	1	1
1	0	1
1	1	0

= NAND Gate

Figure 2-4 Classical NAND gate latch.

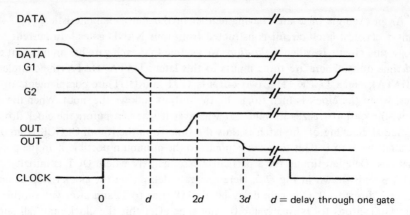

Figure 2-5 Typical timing for NAND gate latch.

1965; Hallin and Flynn, 1972), a simplified version of which appears in Fig. 2-6. This latch has several differences from the more classical design of Fig. 2-4. First, it requires only a single data input, thus avoiding the complement input problem. Second, it has only two levels of logic, and for any combination of input or initial state, the output is always stable after exactly two gate displays. This is both faster and more consistent than the latch of Fig. 2-4. Finally, there are two clock inputs, CLOCK and $\overline{\text{CLOCK}}$, that are normally complements of each other. However, because of the design of the latch, the operation is remarkably insensitive to any skewing differences between the two clocks. In fact, by varying the timing between clock inputs several useful functions other than a simple latch can be obtained.

In addition to all these advantages the Earle latch has one other excellent characteristic, namely that one level of AND–OR logic can be built into the basic latch with absolutely no impact on its switching characteristics. In the equivalent of two total gate delays we can get two gate delays' worth of logic and two gate delays' worth of latch. This is of obvious benefit to a pipelined design. The key to this is the replication of gate pairs 1 and 2 in Fig. 2-6 where each new pair of gates will substitute for the data input one of the logical AND terms of the desired logical expression. Thus if there are N AND terms, there will be N gates taking the place of gate 1 and N gates for gate 2. At the same time, gate 4 in Fig. 2-6, which is performing an OR-function, grows from three inputs to $2N + 1$ inputs. For example, Figs. 2-7 and 2-8 together form a carry-save adder and latch with three inputs A, B, and C_{in} (carry from previous bit positions) and two outputs S and C_{out} representing the same bit position and the carry into the next bit position. These particular designs were first proposed by Earle (1965) for use in a high-speed pipelined multiplier.

Because of all these characteristics, this latch technique was used extensively in the design of the IBM System/360 Model 91 computer.

As soon as a detailed latch design is available, more accurate versions of bound Eqs. (2-1) and (2-2) can be derived. For example, for the Earle latch, Hallin (1970) obtained the following bounds:

$$T_{\min} \geq (2d + S_{C-\overline{C}}) + S_{C_{i-1} - C_i} + U \tag{2-3}$$

$$2d + S_{C-\overline{C}} \leqslant T_{min} + M \tag{2-4}$$

where T_{min} = the time for the shortest path through the logic
d = the maximum gate delay
U = the maximum variation in the pulse width
$S_{C-\overline{C}}$ = the maximum skew between signals CLOCK and $\overline{\text{CLOCK}}$ at the same latch
$S_{C_{i-1}-C_i}$ = maximum skew between CLOCK signals of neighboring latches
M = the minimum width of any pulse that would propagate through a gate and cause a pulse in the output

After analyzing these equations with numbers characteristic of the logic technology available at the time, Hallin concluded that the longest logic path had to include at least the equivalent of four gate delays.

2.1.2 Packaging

As described above, pipelines are particularly sensitive to clock skew and variations in logic delays. In practice there are three sources for these problems: the wiring in physical interconnections of components, variations in the electrical characteristics of the

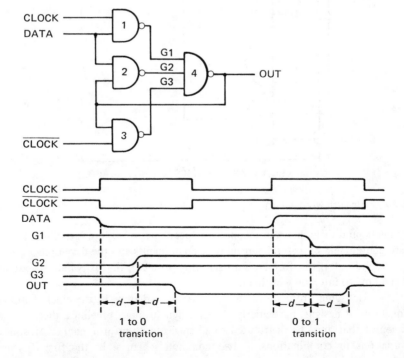

Figure 2-6 Earle latch and timing.

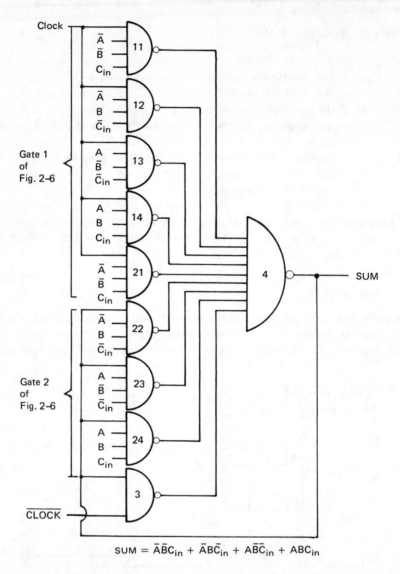

$$SUM = \bar{A}\bar{B}C_{in} + \bar{A}B\bar{C}_{in} + A\bar{B}\bar{C}_{in} + ABC_{in}$$

Figure 2-7 Earle latch with sum logic.

components, and differences in component speed due to loading variations. The latter two are containable by careful screening of components and the development of good design ground rules; the former is a packaging problem, that is, where to put which parts and how to interconnect them.

These packaging problems show up most immediately in the clock distribution system. In most designs, particularly for large synchronous pipelines, there is a single clock source that must be distributed to all stages in a uniform manner. Most designs use variations or combinations of two common schemes. In the first (Flynn and

Amdahl, 1965), related logic is grouped into "islands," with a single clock entry point per island. Uniform length cables connect each island to the central clock regardless of the actual physical distance between clock and island (Fig. 2-9). Once on an island, a similar approach can be used in a recursive fashion to distribute the clock to individual boards and from there to individual components. As the number of islands increases, the resulting topology of such a configuration can begin to resemble a two- or even three-dimensional star with the islands on the periphery and the clock at the center. This formation can be observed in current high-speed computing systems where the main processing cabinets are arranged roughly along the radius of a circle with the clock generator at the center.

The other approach to clock distribution is to use a "timing chain" (Cotten, 1965). With such an arrangement (Fig. 2-10), the clock pulse enters only the first stage, and each succeeding stage delays and reshapes the clock pulse from the previous stage. Extreme care must be taken to produce clock regenerator circuits with highly repeatable and consistent delays. The clock frequency must be chosen so that the period between any two pulses is no shorter than the longest possible delay from any timing stage.

Several variations of these approaches are possible. For example, within an individual island a relatively short timing chain approach can distribute the clock from the entry point to individual stages. In cases where an island represents one or more complete stages, a timing chain can interconnect the stages roughly as they are used, the main clock feeding only the first island stage.

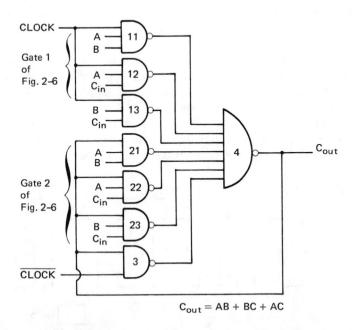

$$C_{out} = AB + BC + AC$$

Figure 2-8 Earle latch with carry logic.

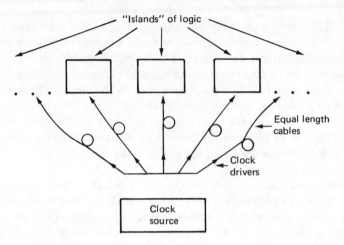

Figure 2-9 Central clock source.

Another possibility is to distribute the clock in a starlike fashion to each stage and use a timing chain to select which clock to pass to the staging latch (Fig. 2-11). The delays in the chain are deliberately set to less than the clock period with the output pulse somewhat wider than the actual clock pulse width. Because it is a central clock pulse that activates the stage, the previously mentioned problems with variations in delay characteristics and thus clock skew are greatly reduced. An additional advantage of this configuration is that now the initial source of the timing chain can be independent of the clock; in particular, it can be generated only when a datum is entering the pipeline, thus serving a control rather than timing function. This idea is discussed more fully in Chap. 3.

The actual logic circuit used in this chain has been discussed by Cotten (1965) and others. In many cases variations of the circuit used for the staging latch, such as the Earle circuit with its two clock inputs, represent good designs for the combined gate-delay function.

Another major concern in the packaging of pipelined systems is the delay introduced by wiring including to various degrees the wiring between individual components in a board, between boards (particularly through connectors), and between

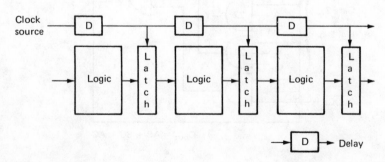

Figure 2-10 Timing chain.

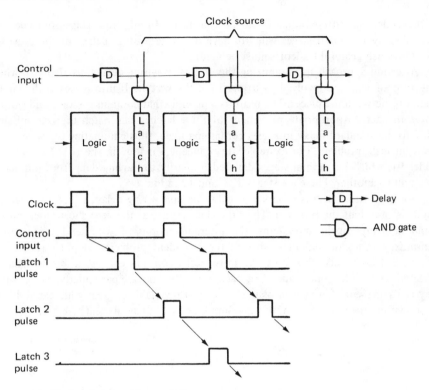

Figure 2-11 Timing chain used for control.

cabinets containing sets of boards. These delays are due to the limited propagation speed of electrical signals in the wiring and cannot be avoided. In some real systems these delays are so significant that even if a perfect zero-delay logic were available and substituted for all parts in the machine, the machine's performance would only increase by a factor of 2. Intercomponent wiring delays approximately match the logic delays.

As in the clock distribution system, there are several ways of alleviating this problem. First, special care can be taken as to what logic is placed on what printed circuit boards. For example, Fig. 2-12 diagrams two ways of partitioning logic components onto boards or modules. In the first approach, Fig. 2-12a, there is one board for each stage. Consequently, the time for each stage must include an interboard delay. Although proper placement of boards can minimize this delay, and proper selection of wire lengths equalizes the effects, in general the clock pulse rate must be slower than the intrinsic logic would otherwise allow. An alternative approach, Fig. 2-12b, partitions a slice of several stages onto a single board. In this approach the intermediate stages have no extra delays between them and can be made logic-intensive. However, there may be new delays introduced in the interconnection of logic from board to board for a single stage. An example of this is a stage that must include a 32-bit adder partitioned over four separate boards. There is no board-to-board delay introduced in data feeding the adder or sampling the results, but all carry signals between those parts of the adder on different boards do have a delay. In addition, stages preceded or succeeded by off-board stages will still have the stage-to-stage delays of the previous case. Obviously, careful tradeoffs must be made.

A second approach to minimizing the effects of wiring delays, particularly when long runs of wire are involved, is to partition the wire itself into pieces with staging latches in between the pieces. The result is a pipeline that contains no logic and simply moves the data. Appropriate placement of these latches can match the transmission delay to the standard delay in stages containing logic, thus eliminating the wire delay as an intrinsic problem. For example, this concept was used in the IBM System/360 Model 91, which has several stages devoted primarily to moving data from one hardware unit to another. These are stages 3, 8, and 12 in Fig. 1-5.

For both the concerns of clock distribution and wiring delay, selection of wiring length is only half the problem. The other half is that at the very short clock pulses found in many pipelined systems, the interconnections of wire tend to resemble transmission lines or antennas with all the attendent problems of pulse reflection, echoes, and cross talk. Problems like pulse reflection and echoes, where a signal is reflected back to its source and then back down the line, are particularly severe, since they can represent alternate paths in the logic with variable or greatly increased delay. As shown in an earlier section, this maximum delay can have a great effect on the per-

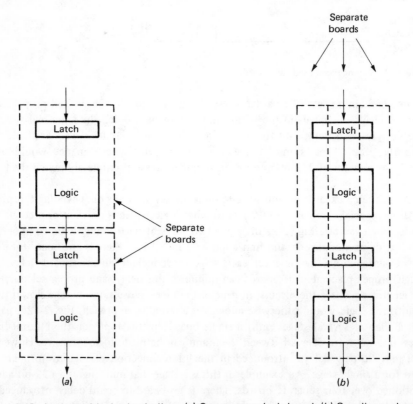

Figure 2-12 Logic partitioning in pipelines. (a) One stage per logic board. (b) One slice per board.

formance of a pipeline. The problem can get particularly severe at connectors (plugs and jacks) because an improperly selected connector may have a different impedance than the wiring itself, causing large reflections. The solution in many systems is to treat all interconnections and wiring as transmission lines and properly match their impedance to the intrinsic impedance of the circuit drivers and the loading of the circuit receiver. Impedance-matching circuits may also have to be added where the component characteristics themselves are not satisfactory. In cases where even this is not sufficient, such as in very large systems, the final step of manufacture often involves technicians tuning the machine by measuring delays and impedances and physically adjusting individual wire lengths and electrical terminators. Additional retuning may be necessary during the life of the machine to counterbalance aging components.

2.1.3 Maximum-Rate Pipelined Design—An Alternative

All of the design techniques mentioned so far use explicit storage elements to separate different data items as they move through a pipeline. There is an alternative technique based on observations of real fluid flows that eliminates these latches and allows much higher throughput rates. The mathematics behind its development was first presented in the context of electronic pipeline designs by Cotten in 1969. Although the technique has not been widely used for a variety of reasons discussed later, the potential performance advantages are sufficient to merit its exposition here.

A physical pipeline often consists of hundreds of miles of pipe with valves and pumps at appropriate places to allow the fluid being transported to enter or exit the system. In this configuration there is no need for staging latches. Instead the common velocity of all molecules in a local group in the fluid tends to keep that group together as it goes through the pipeline. Knowing the time at which a group of molecules enters the pipeline and the transit rates through the pipeline allows one to predict when the group will pass by any point in the pipeline and to draw out that group by opening a value as pictured in Fig. 2-13. This technique is used in pipelines for petroleum products where at any one time several different grades of gasoline or oil may be inside a single pipeline with no barrier separating them. Time at the receiving end determines when each fluid is available.

A major problem preventing this from being a perfect system where all of each fluid type can be withdrawn at the end is friction and other losses causing molecules near the walls of the pipeline to slow down in relation to those at the center. The result is a dispersion of the interface between fluid types as shown in Fig. 2-14. As the pipeline gets longer, the time during which a pure fluid type is present with no mixture decreases and the region of mixture increases. Consequently, if so many gallons of a pure fluid type are desired at some point in the pipeline, then a greater amount of that fluid must be fed in, the difference depending on how much mixture occurs by the time the fluid reaches the destination. After a certain point it becomes impossible to remove any pure fluid since the dispersal for the front of the fluid group begins to overlap that for the rear of the group. Where this point occurs depends solely on the difference in transport velocities, not on the absolute velocities themselves.

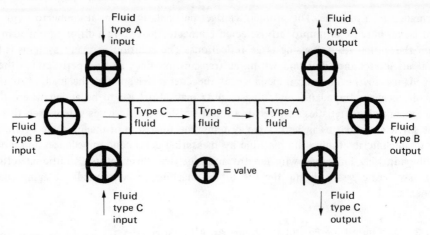

Figure 2-13   Perfect frictionless pipeline.

An identical situation occurs in the design of electronic pipelines. If all logic had exactly the same delay, and if the logic was designed in levels, with the inputs for one level connected to outputs of gates in the previous level and all paths through a level traversing exactly one gate, then no latches would be needed and the situation of Fig. 2-15 results. In this figure, P is the period during which a new set of data is presented to the first level and d is the gate delay. The output of the kth level can be sampled for answers every P seconds, where this output sample clock is the same as the input one, except phased by an amount kd mod P. The only limit to how small P can be made is the minimum pulse width to which a gate will respond with a valid output (delayed d seconds). This pulse width is typically less than the delay, meaning that a potential order-of-magnitude increase in performance is possible over the designs using the Earle latch. For obvious reasons these designs are called *maximum-rate pipelines.*

As in physical pipelines, however, variations in speed through the circuits affect the time during which the output of any level is valid. Some gates may have a shorter delay than the average; others may have a longer delay. This variation may be due to differences in part types, variations from component to component, intercomponent wire lengths, or loading on the gate. Regardless of the cause, some of the outputs of one level will come valid earlier than the average; others will come valid later. This variation in output timing means that the next level of logic will get inputs that change over a period of time without an abrupt transition. Variations in delays in this next

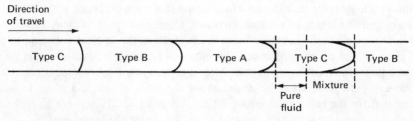

Figure 2-14   Effects of friction.

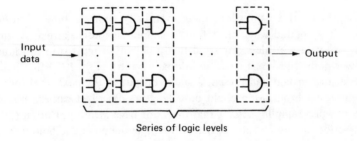

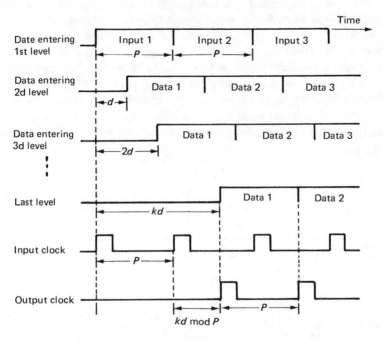

Figure 2-15 Uniform delay logic pipeline.

level add to the confusion by further spreading the time over which its outputs change. Figure 2-16 diagrams this situation in detail. As in physical pipelines, the increasing uncertainty cuts into the time when the output of a level is known to be "pure," that is, when it gives a stable and correct answer. Mathematically, after the kth level there is exactly $P(k)$ time per P-second interval when the output is known to be good, and this $P(k)$ is

$$P(k) = P - \sum_{i=1}^{k} (d_{\max\ i} - d_{\min\ i}) \tag{2-5}$$

where $d_{\max\ i}$ is the longest delay through any path in the ith logic level, and $d_{\min\ i}$ the shortest.

As indicated by this expression, there eventually comes a time when $P(k) \leqslant 0$; that is, there is no period when all outputs are simultaneously correct. At this point the pipeline becomes worthless. To avoid this problem we must stop cascading levels at some lower point and insert some additional circuitry (Fig. 2-17) that will sample the outputs at one instant and present a stable output to the next level for at least P seconds. This resynchronization could be a latch as described earlier, although it is possible to design a sampling circuit that does not have memory. Cotten (1969), for example, describes a very fast circuit that will sample the input and hold it stable for a short period of time. Succeeding logic levels could then be added and a new resampling circuit included only when the delay differences again become excessive.

As with the latch-per-stage approach, the properties of this sampling circuit directly affect the minimum value of P. Such a circuit is typically clocked, with a clock pulse used to indicate when the input should be sampled. Inherent delays in the circuit will then hold the output stable for a period of time. Regardless of the clock characteristics, however, there is some minimum time W during which the input to this sampling circuit must be stable. If the clock occurs at exactly the right time, then the sampling circuit should be installed after the kth level where k is the last level at which

$$W \leqslant P - \sum_{i=1}^{k} (d_{\max\ i} - d_{\min\ i}) \tag{2-6}$$

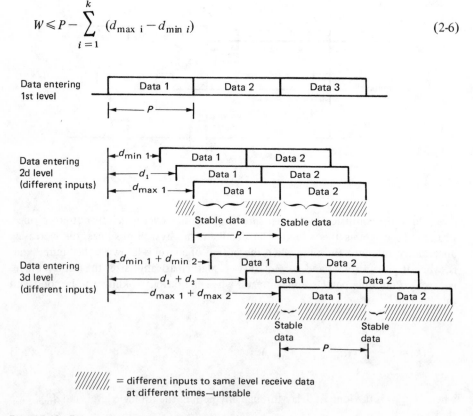

$\frac{/////////}{}$ = different inputs to same level receive data at different times—unstable

Figure 2-16 Effects of variations in delay in same level.

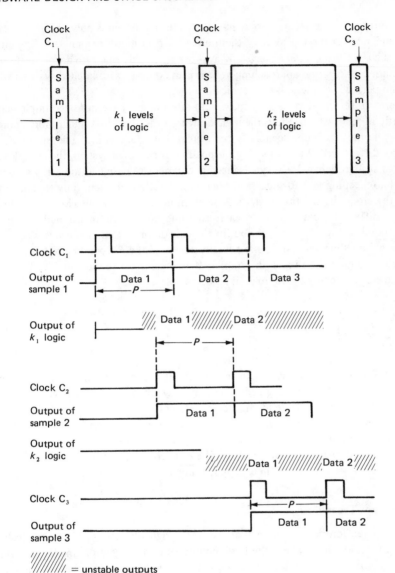

Figure 2-17 Use of resampling circuits.

Skew in the arrival of the clock pulse is handled much as it was for the latched designs; its application is left as an exercise for the reader.

Assuming a skewless clock distribution, this relation leaves us with a fundamental clock period of

$$P \geqslant W + \sum_{i=1}^{k} (d_{\max i} - d_{\min i}) \tag{2-7}$$

In contrast to the latched approach, this equation depends only on *differences* in delays and not on the logic delays themselves. Furthermore, certain sampling circuit designs such as Cotten's can achieve a W as short as roughly one gate delay, resulting in a minimum clock period approaching d. This is in contrast with latched systems where minimum periods of at least $4d$ are typical.

There are several reasons why maximum-rate designs have not been implemented frequently in real systems. First, the logic designer's task becomes much more complex as he or she must account accurately for a great many factors in the determination of the delay differences. While this may be possible for a small system, the complexities of a large system demand a very advanced and expensive design automation system to do the bookkeeping and to suggest alternatives. Another problem only touched upon here is the clock distribution system. Besides minimizing skew, the clock system must deliver a different *phase* clock to each sampling circuit. As mentioned earlier and demonstrated in Fig. 2-17, the period for the clocks for all sampling levels is the same, but the relative time when the pulse actually occurs in the P-second period depends on the levels of logic separating each sampler. If two samples are separated by k levels of logic, the clocks feeding the samples must be out of phase by

$$\left(\sum_{i=1}^{k} d_{\max\ i} \right) \bmod P \text{ seconds} \tag{2-8}$$

A final and severe problem with maximum-rate designs is that they are extremely hard to debug. Conventional pipeline designs may be single-stepped with the entire state of the machine available at the staging latch outputs. Maximum-rate designs cannot be single-stepped, since stopping the machine even momentarily causes the loss of all data not saved in a sampling circuit. If the pause is too long, even the data in these sampling circuits may fade and be lost. These machines must be debugged from the start while they are running at their designed rate.

2.1.4 Recent Technologies

The clock equation bounds defined above were originally developed for the technologies of the mid-1960s where the basic component was a gate or smaller (individual transistor). All latches and logic were built from combinations of these components. Although technology has advanced considerably since then, to varying extents these bounds are still valid for the mainstream technologies of today. Machines where very high performance via short clock periods is the primary goal still use individual, very high-speed gates as their basic components. The CRAY-1 (Cray Research, 1976), for example, achieves up to 160 million operations per second through a design employing a 12.5-ns clock for staging and repeated use of only three part types from a high-speed ECL (emitter-coupled logic) technology. These types are a dual NAND gate circuit, a register file, and a memory chip. To a large extent all the design equations and packaging concerns mentioned previously are directly applicable.

Other machines such as the IBM 3838 (IBM, 1976) use more dense integrated circuit technology to achieve cost effectiveness where slower clock rates are acceptable.

In such machines the individual logic components that must be considered are not individual gates but more complex functions such as adders, shifters, and decoders. Even the latch designs are different; a wide variety of flip-flops, latches, and hold circuits are available. The primary difference between this and earlier technologies is density: each function is still built out of gates but is packaged and described as a module. Consequently, although the staging latch analysis may change, the basic form and intent of the clock bound equations is still valid. Similarly, the packaging discussion is still valid, although because the logic is more dense physically, much of the primary delay concerns shift from board-to-board wiring to part-to-part wiring.

The advent of LSI (large-scale integrated circuits) will not have a noticeable impact on these equations. The design of individual LSI chips employing pipelining internally will use the equations almost directly, particularly if a component like the Earle latch is present. At the next level, where sets of LSI chips are combined, the basic form of the equations is still valid, although, again, the source of the delays moves up one functional level.

2.2 MEMORY HIERARCHY

At this point the importance of the basic staging latch design is obvious. However, in the typical pipelined computer system there are several other memory structures whose designs are equally important to total system performance. These include the main memory, a local or cache memory, and the replacement of certain staging latches by register files. As in any memory hierarchy, these structures are ordered in decreasing size, main memory having the most capacity and register files the least, and they are ordered in increasing speed, register files being the fastest and individual memory modules the slowest. In addition to this ordering, however, in the context of a pipeline these structures all provide different functions. The main memory not only must hold all data files but also must have sufficient speed to match the overall demands of the pipelines. The local memories are primarily rate-matching and temporary storage devices between the main memory and pipeline. The register files are embedded in the pipelines and are involved in the intimate timing and flow of data through the individual stages. The following sections examine each of these structures in more detail.

2.2.1 Main Memory

The main memory in any computer holds the majority of data and instructions and is the memory structure most visible to a programmer. Its two major attributes are *size* (number of words) and *bandwidth* (words accessed per second). Its basic building block is a *module* that contains a fixed number of words only one of which can be accessed at a time. By combining modules in different ways, increases in overall memory size and bandwidth are possible. Size is a function of problem requirements and will not be discussed further. Required bandwidth, however, depends strongly on the speed of the pipelines, since there is little sense in building a system where the pipeline cannot be fed at full rate with data or instructions from memory.

The *demand ratio,* or ratio of memory bandwidth to pipeline clock rate, can run from 2 to 1 to well over 10 to 1 depending on the nature of the pipeline. As one example, the IBM System/360 Model 91 CPU can initiate the execution of instructions at rates up to one every 60 ns. At the time of the design, analysis of typical benchmark programs indicated that each instruction required 1.25 memory accesses (Boland et al., 1967). In addition, simultaneous I/O transfers must be added to this. The net result was a requirement of two or more memory word accesses per pipeline clock.

Other machines such as the TI ASC and the CDC STAR-100 make much greater demands on their main memories primarily because of the presence of vector instructions in the instruction set and vector-oriented arithmetic pipelines in their hardware. In one case, the ASC machine, there can be up to four pipelined arithmetic units operating simultaneously. Since each unit can make up to three memory requests per clock (two inputs and a result), the main memory can see up to 12 requests for word access during each clock interval. The inclusion of instruction fetches and I/O can push this ratio even higher.

In most real systems, the intrinsic bandwidth of the basic memory module is seldom sufficient to match this required demand ratio. Consequently, multiple modules must be accessed simultaneously to yield higher effective access rates. The general technique employed, called *interleaving*, typically arranges the modules so that N sequential memory addresses, i, $i + 1$, $i + 2, \ldots, i + N - 1$, fall in N distinct modules. The ith memory module holds only words whose addresses are of the form $kN + i$ (for $0 \leqslant k \leqslant M - 1$, and M the number of words in one module). By keeping all N modules busy accessing data, effective bandwidths up to N times that of a single module are possible.[1]

There are a variety of ways of implementing such interleaved structures. Most of them begin to resemble pipelines where the "logic" function is the accessing of a word in a module. Figure 2-18 diagrams a single module, and Figs. 2-19 and 2-20 diagram two extremes of interleaving of this simple module. The elementary structure of Fig. 2-19 accesses N words in parallel for each request. If $N = 2^k$ and $M = 2^m$, then out of $m + k$ address bits, m of them are sent to all memory modules, with the bottom k bits used to pick which of the N words to read first. Thus for each request to the

---

[1] An alternate form of interleaving places all words with addresses of the form $iN + k$ ($0 \leqslant k \leqslant M - 1$) in one module. Multiple accesses can be made simultaneously but only if the accesses are to addresses separated by more than M words.

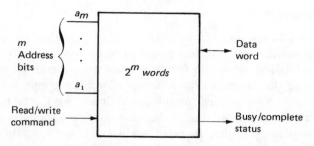

Figure 2-18 Typical memory module.

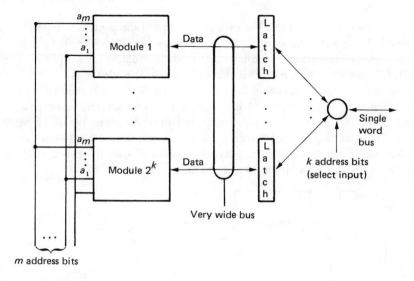

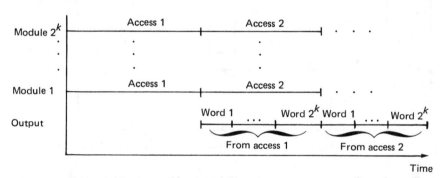

Figure 2-19 Simple interleaved memory and timing.

memory system, N sequential words (with the addresses $iN + j$ for fixed i and $0 \leqslant j \leqslant N - 1$) are read out. These words may be latched up and during the next access read out over a single-word-wide bus at a rate N times faster than the access time of a single module. Although Fig. 2-19 shows only the timing for a multiple-word read, the timing for a multiple-word write is similar.

This simple structure is ideal for cases where memory is typically accessed sequentially, as in the fetching of a vector in a vector processor, or the execution of sequential instructions. However, the performance degrades dramatically whenever non-sequential accesses are needed (for example, in a program with a high percentage of jump instructions). To partially overcome this, memory systems such as that in Fig. 2-2-20 have been designed. Here the latches have been moved from the outputs of each module to its address inputs. This allows each module to be using a different relative address than the others. To handle this increased flexibility a *memory controller* is introduced. This unit accepts a stream of one-word access requests from the pipelines and processes them one at a time. For each access request the controller determines if the module holding that word is currently busy with a previous request, and if not, the appropriate relative address is loaded into that module's address latch and the operation started. If the module is busy that request is delayed. While the memory module is accessing the appropriate location, the controller handles other requests in a similar fashion. When a module's command is complete the controller either starts a new command, if the old one was a memory write, or (for reads) routes the data from the module to the requesting pipeline before starting a new command. The timing diagram of Fig. 2-20 shows the sequence of activity for a stream of reads from sequential locations. As in Fig. 2-19, the extension to writes is direct.

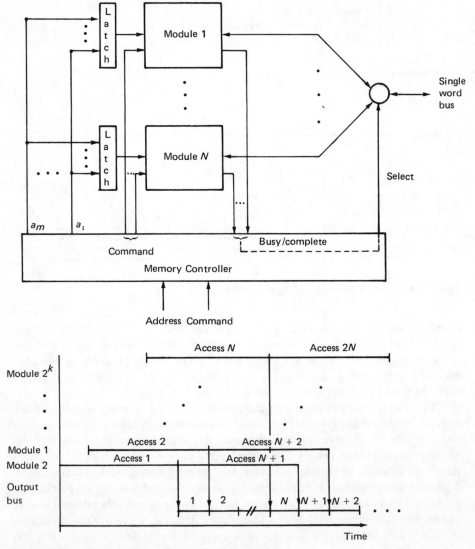

Figure 2-20 Complex interleaved memory and timing.

As will the simpler version, this system will handle requests for sequential words N times faster than that for a single module. In addition, however, it will handle at the same high speed any series of accesses where in N consecutive requests no module is needed more than once. For example, an eight-way interleaved memory designed along the lines of Fig. 2-20 will run eight times faster than a single module whenever the sequence of addresses is uniformly spaced by not only 1 but any of either 3, 5, 7, 9, 11, . . . , locations. For the spacing of 3, the address sequence is of the form 0, 3, 6, 9, 12, 15, 18, 21, 24, 27, . . . , and the sequence of modules usage is 1, 4, 7, 2, 5, 0, 3, 6, 1, 4, 7, ... Other spacing values will not run at this maximum rate but will still run faster than a single module would provide. The timing for a uniform spacing of 2 is shown in Fig. 2-21; it still achieves a factor of 4 over a single memory module. In general any accessing sequence other than one with a uniform spacing of N will run at least twice as fast on an N-way interleaved memory over a memory having only a single module. This can be stated as a specific rule as follows:

Theorem 2-1 Assuming that a memory design consists of N individual modules interleaved in the complex fashion and the access time for any module is T, then for an address sequence with a uniform spacing of S the average time per element access is the product of all prime factors of S that are also prime factors of N, times T/N.

Lemma 2-1 If N and S are relatively prime (i.e., have no common factors other than 1), then data may be accessed at the maximum rate of T/N seconds per word.

The proofs of these are left to the reader.

The performance degradation is even worse when a nonunity spacing is used on the addresses fed to a memory with simple interleaving. In this case the rule is as follows:

Theorem 2-2 Assuming that a memory design consists of N individual modules interleaved in a simple fashion as pictured in Fig. 2-19, and the access time for any module is T, then for an address sequence with a uniform spacing of S the average time per element access is

$$\frac{ST}{N} \quad \text{for } S \leqslant N$$
$$T \quad \text{for } S > N$$

The proof of this is also left to the reader.

Because of the complexity of the controller most real memory systems requiring very large interleave factors of 8 or more use a combination of these two techniques. For example, in the IBM System/360 Model 91 (Boland et al., 1967) basic memory modules were paired together as in Fig. 2-19 so that each access retrieved two words. These paired modules were then interleaved 4 to 16 times as in Fig. 2-20. The

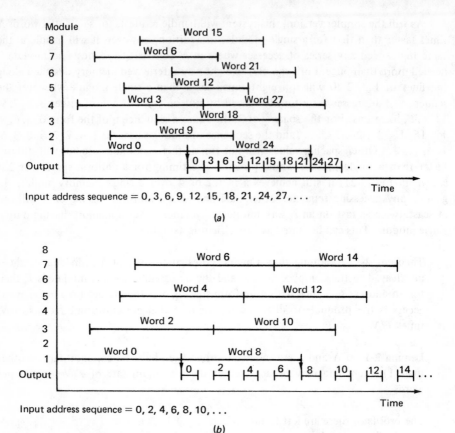

Figure 2-21 Uniformly spaced accesses in eight-way interleaved memory. (a) Spacing of 3. (b) Spacing of 2.

TI ASC main memory design (Watson 1972a) is similar, with an eight-way interleave as in Fig. 2-20 and each module returning 8 consecutive words per access. In such cases predicting the performance for a nonunity spacing becomes quite complex.

2.2.2 Local Memory

In nearly all pipelined computers, the main memory delivers its maximum bandwidth when accessing relatively long sets of sequentially located words. Although this rate may match the aggregate rate at which the pipeline requires accesses, the order in which the data is accessed is not usually what the pipeline really needs. A good example of this is a vector processor executing vector add. At each clock the pipeline performing the add needs one element from each of the two input vectors and delivers one element of the result vector. The memory, on the other hand, provides a string of elements from one operand, followed by a string from the other, followed by a write of part of the output vector. As another example, a pipeline that is interpreting instructions may get N of them at a time from memory, but must handle each individually with special consideration for jumps or loop instructions. Further, the data operands requested by the instructions very seldom follow any particular pattern.

In both cases the typical solution is the insertion of a small, very high-speed memory between the main memory and the pipeline. Such memories are often called *caches* or *local memories.* These memories may or may not be visible to the programmer. In structure they may be small, random-access memories, first-in-first-out queues, or associative memories. Since many people connect the term cache with an associative structure, and this is not always the case, this text will call all such structures by the more general term, local memory.

Regardless of how they are constructed, all local memories operate in roughly the same way. They are organized to permit block transfers between themselves and main memory simultaneously with more random transfers to the pipeline. Consequently, they perform a joint rate-matching and address translation function. Because of the simultaneity of transfer to memory and the pipeline, the total bandwidth capacity of the local store system must very often exceed twice the demand ratio for the pipeline.

Figure 2-22 diagrams four typical methods of implementing a local memory. First is the *associative cache,* where each entry contains both a main memory address and the corresponding data word. It is typically bulk loaded from the main memory and randomly read by the pipeline. On a load, both the contents of a location and its address are placed in a free entry. On a read, the pipeline provides the particular main memory address it desires, and a simultaneous comparison occurs between that address and the address portion of all entries. The entry with a matching address will respond with the appropriate data. To the pipeline the local memory is invisible and simply makes the main memory appear very fast and free from interleave problems. For these reasons it is used in many, if not most, high-performance computers. Chapter 6 includes detailed discussions of some of the design tradeoffs possible for such local memories.

The second most complex structure used in local memories is the *swinging* or *dual* buffer. Here two or more very fast random-access memories are connected together so that while one of them is being loaded or unloaded by the main memory, the other is connected to the pipeline. When both the main memory and the pipeline have finished using their respective buffers, the buffer connections switch and the pipeline gets the buffer just loaded by main memory, and vice versa. This structure appears quite often in vector processors. The *vector registers* of the CRAY-1 (Cray, 1976) and the dual 2048-word working stores of the IBM 3838 (IBM, 1976) are real examples, which will be discussed in Chap. 4.

The next most complex local memory is a true dual-ported random-access memory. Here a small memory has two sets of address decode and select logic allowing the main memory and the pipeline simultaneous access to different words in the array. The cost of such devices confines their use to applications where only a small amount of buffering is required.

The simplest local memory structure is a true first-in-first-out (FIFO) queue (cf. Knuth, 1969). Here data enters the queue at one rate and leaves at another. The order in which it leaves is the same as it entered. A typical application is around an arith-

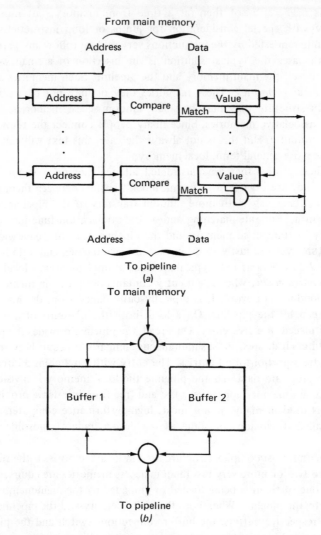

Figure 2-22 Typical local memory structures. (a) Associative local memory. (b) Swinging buffers.

metic pipeline for a vector processor. Two FIFOs feed the two pipeline inputs while a third receives the results. The main memory loads the input queues and unloads the output. As long as there is something in each input queue and the output queue has not overflowed, the main memory is free to load or unload an arbitrary amount of any queue in whatever order is optimal.

For all these structures we have assumed that it is the main memory that actually performs the transfers from itself to the local memory. In real systems the responsibility for governing the transfers is actually up to a memory controller situated between the main memory and the local memory. This controller receives transfer commands from some part of the pipeline and provides synchronizing information in return to the pipeline indicating completion of transfer. More detail on such controllers will be included in later discussion of specific pipeline types.

2.2.3 Register Files

In many modern pipelines it is not uncommon to find selected staging latches replaced by more complex memory structures. Though scaled down in size, any of the structures defined in the context of local memories (Sec. 2.2.2) may replace a staging latch. Of course, because of timing considerations the amount of logic following the latch may have to be drastically reduced. This may force the addition of an extra stage to the pipeline, but it has little effect on pipeline throughput.

Perhaps the most useful of these structures in the context of a pipeline latch is the

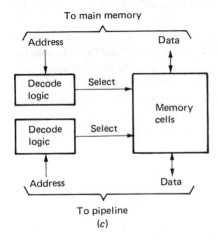

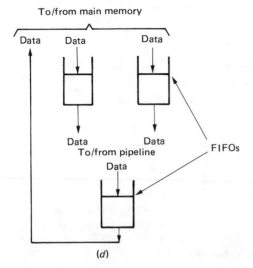

Figure 2-22 Typical local memory structures (*continued*). (*c*) Dual-port memory. (*d*) FIFO queues.

dual-ported random-access memory. Integrated circuits performing this function for a small number of words have been commercially available for some time. They are called *register files*. In a pipelined circuit one data port is connected to the output of the previous stage's logic, and the other data port is connected to the input of the next set of logic. As pictured in Fig. 2-23, the first port is configured to write into the file and the second port to read. The two sets of addresses are provided to the pipeline by a control unit.

A register file provides at least three capabilities not possible with a simple staging latch. First, it allows one set of data to be used several times without having to regenerate it. This is useful, for example, when a common multiplier term has been computed and will be used as one input to a multiplier pipeline for the next several clock periods. The next use is as a local reshuffler of data. Part of the pipeline may generate intermediate results in one order, but the rest of the pipeline may need them in some other order. Separate control of the address busses permits this reordering to occur.

The third and most common application of register files is as a variable *delay*. A one-unit *noncompute delay* is equivalent to replacing one latch with two latches having no intervening logic besides the noncompute logic needed to prevent timing races, as in Fig. 2-24. The usefulness of such delays will become apparent in later sections.

A single register file can automatically generate any number of delay units K up to the capacity of the file by simply using a cyclically increasing address sequence for the write port and exactly the same address for the read port but delayed K cycles. Figure 2-25 diagrams the timing for a delay of 2.

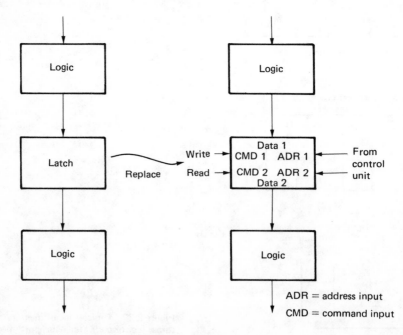

Figure 2-23 Replacement of latch by dual-ported memory.

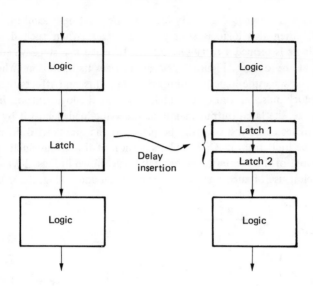

Figure 2-24 One-unit delay insertion.

2.3 CASCADING OF PIPELINED STAGES

Although most pipelines are designed by careful partitioning of a function into stages, a great deal can be learned about the interactions of such partitions by considering the reverse problem, the construction of complex pipelines from an elementary stage. In this section a variety of pipelines for performing primarily arithmetic operations will be developed from cascaded combinations of simpler stages. Though feasible, not all of these designs are optimal. In Sec. 2.5 measures of cost effectiveness and tradeoffs between these and alternative partitions will be examined.

Perhaps the most elementary but still nontrivial stage is a unit with three equally weighted binary inputs and two binary outputs. The outputs represent the binary sum of the three inputs. Because each input can take on the value 0 or 1, the output must be capable of representing any value from 0 to 3, which is handled by the conventional two-bit representation $00, 01, 10,$ and 11.

File location loaded	$Data_i$	$Data_{i+1}$	$Data_{i+2}$	$Data_{i+3}$	$Data_{i+4}$
	M_0	M_1	M_2	M_3	M_0
File location read	$M_1 = Data_{i-3}$	$M_2 = Data_{i-2}$	$M_3 = Data_{i-1}$	$M_0 = Data_i$	$M_1 = Data_{i+1}$

|←————— Delay of 2 ————→|

$M_i = i$th location of register file

Figure 2-25 Addressing of register file to induce variable delay.

If one input is designated a "carry-in," and the most significant bit of the output a "carry-out," then this logic is simply a *full adder.* When such designations are ignored, the logic is termed a *carry-save adder.* To make it a stage we add two bits of staging logic at the output. Figure 2-26*a* summarizes its operation. When inputs are presented to the stage the logic computes the sum. This sum affects the latch output only after a clock pulse has caused the latch to sample the logic output. In the absence of a clock pulse, the latch output maintains the value loaded into it by the previous clock. The latches could just as easily be placed at the inputs with no change to the structures to be built from it. One implementation of this circuit including latches is the combinations of the two Earle latches with logic shown in Figs. 2-7 and 2-8.

The simplest use of such a stage is as a bit serial adder (Fig. 2-26*b*). The two in-

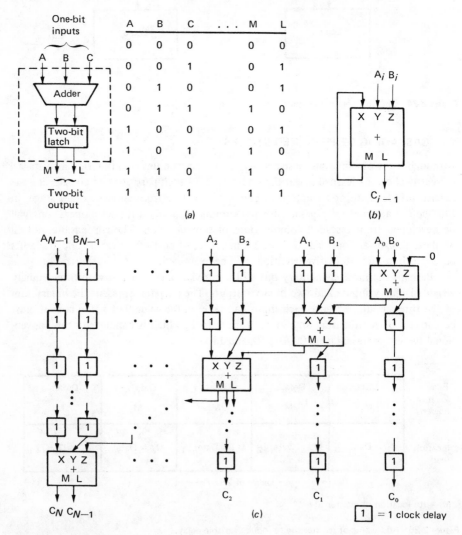

Figure 2-26 A simple stage and some applications.

puts represent the bit serial representation of two binary numbers, least significant bit first. The feedback path between output and input serves to propagate the carry from one bit position to the next. This structure adds two N-bit numbers in N clocks.

2.3.1 Pipelined Adders

In building conventional multibit parallel adders out of full-adder logic, the simplest and slowest approach is the *ripple adder,* which takes the most significant bit of each output (the M output) and feeds it into one of the inputs to the next full adder. The time to add two N-bit numbers is roughly N times the time to go through one full adder, since a carry generated by the lowest adder may propagate up through the array one adder at a time. Faster techniques involve adding logic to look ahead and predict the carries early, but the best such adders are capable of are times proportional to $\log_2 N$. In contrast, Fig. 2-26c diagrams a pipelined ripple adder that can add numbers at a rate of one per clock independent of N. Each add, of course, still requires N clocks, but as soon as each bit position is computed, the hardware associated with it is freed for use by another set of numbers. Likewise, no full adder is used until all of its inputs are available. The extra staging latches at the input with no intervening logic are there simply to guarantee this arrival condition. Similarly, the extra latches on the outputs delay those bits until the entire sum is complete. For a generalized N-bit pipelined ripple adder, on the order of N^2 unit delays are needed. This can be expensive for even moderate N if each delay is implemented with latches and noncompute logic. The use of register files, as discussed in a previous section, can simplify this count but cannot eliminate it.

2.3.2 Pipelined Multiplier

The basic adder stage may also be used in the construction of a variety of pipelined integer multipliers. Figure 2-27 diagrams a 4×4 bit multiplier based on the classical one-bit-at-a-time partial product generation, followed by a series of pipelined ripple adders to sum these terms. Extensions of this method can compute arbitrary $N \times N$ bit products at a rate of one per clock (independent of N), but again at a potentially explosive cost in the number of delays needed to align and save intermediate results. In comparison, the best rate at which a nonpipelined multiplier can compute results is time proportional to $(\log N)^2$.

Because of its cost in implementing the delays, the above method is seldom used in real machines. Instead, variations of the Wallace tree (Wallace, 1964) can substantially reduce the total number of stages and thus the number of delays needed. In this approach the adder logic is used as a three-input, two-output adder, and at each stage for each term as many three-input adds as possible are performed. Thus in the 4×4 example, the first stage includes an adder to sum up three of the members from the set $(A_3 B_0, A_2 B_1, A_1 B_2, A_0 B_3)$. The second stage then includes an adder to sum the remaining term with the least significant bit of the output of the first adder, plus the most significant output from the first stage adder that computed the sum of $A_2 B_0$, $A_1 B_1, A_0 B_2$. For an arbitrary-sized multiplier this three-to-two reduction continues until for each bit position of the result there are only two bits left to add. These two numbers may then be added together in a conventional fashion. Figure 2-28 diagrams a Wallace tree multiplier for the 4 × 4 case. A pipelined ripple adder sums the final two partial sums. We note that the total number of stages and latches has been greatly reduced over the simplistic approach of Fig. 2-27. Anderson et al. (1967a) give a good description of a variation of this approach in the multiplier of the IBM System/360 Model 91.

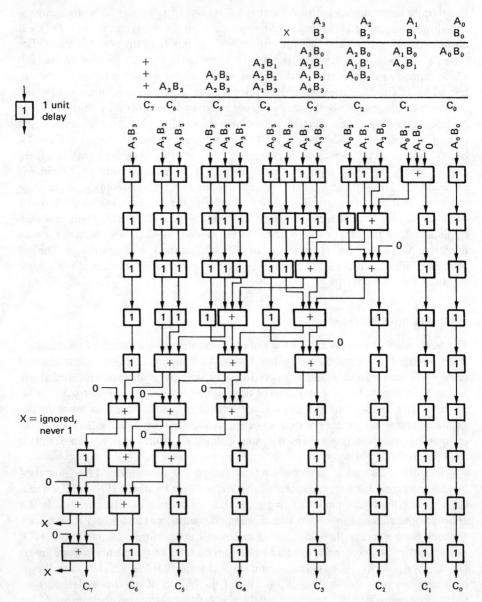

Figure 2-27 Pipeline multiplier using ripple adder.

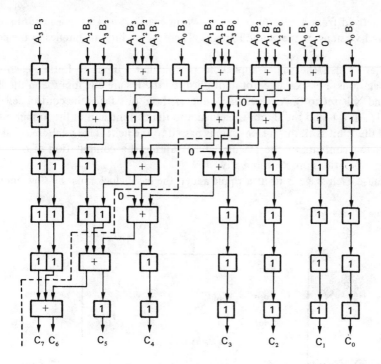

Figure 2-28 Wallace tree pipelined multiplier. Logic above dashed line is Wallace tree; logic below is ripple adder.

2.3.3 A Multifunction Pipeline

All the structures described in the preceding section are capable of only one basic type of operation, addition or multiplication. In terms of our previous definitions they are unifunction pipelines. It is possible to use the same kind of iterative cascading of stages to construct multifunction pipelined units. A good example proposed by Kamal, Singh, and Agrawal (1974) is capable of multiplication, division, squaring, and square roots, all within a single pipelined structure. In this case the basic computational cell is a combined adder/subtractor with two control inputs, four data inputs, and four data outputs. Figure 2-29a diagrams this cell and its logic equations. The data outputs S, D, and E are latched. For simplicity the carry-out is not latched. The effects of this on performance will be discussed later. The control input X indicates whether or not the data input B is to be left alone or complemented. A 0 on control input F passes the input A to the output S; a 1 adds A to B as modified by X. The data outputs D and E pass various logical functions of B and C as selected by F.

Figure 2-30 diagrams how these cells may be combined to produce the desired pipeline. Each stage of the pipeline consists of a horizontal line of computation cells connected as a ripple adder/subtractor. There are four sets of data inputs A, B, C, and P, and one set of outputs S. Depending on which operation is being performed, a different set of these outputs is used. The X and F controls for each stage are unique and are derived from a control cell as shown in Fig. 2-29b. This cell in turn is driven by delayed versions of the X and P inputs. There are no internal latches to the control cell.

Table 2-1 lists the values applied to the pipeline's input to initiate each of the basic operations. For example, for multiplication the B's are one input, and the P's the other, and X is set to 0. At each stage, one of the P bits feeds the control cell. If the bit is a 1, F is a 1, and the B input is added into the current sum in the proper bit positions. If the P bit is 0, the current sum is passed to the next stage unaltered. Table 2-2 diagrams the contents of the staging latches during the computation of $4 + 3 \times 6$. The other operations proceed similarly.

Because each stage is itself a ripple adder, the basic clock must be slow enough to

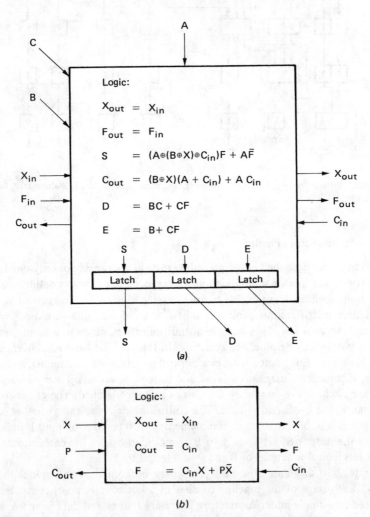

Figure 2-29   (a) Multifunction computation cell. (b) Associated control cell.

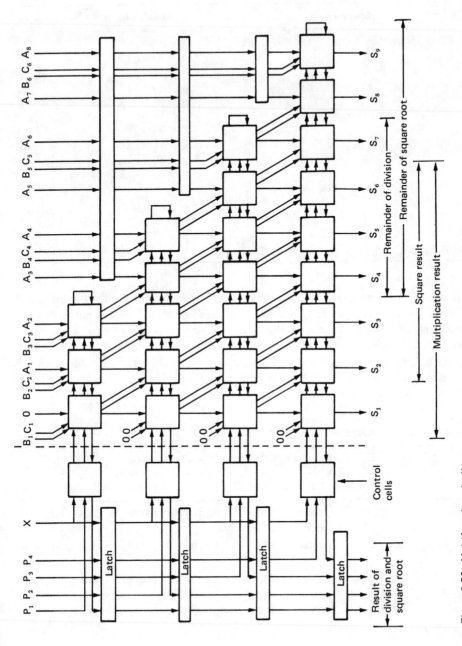

Figure 2-30 Multifunction pipeline.

55

Table 2-1 Operations for Generalized Array

Operation	Required Input
$(A_1 \ldots A_6) + (B_1 \ldots B_4) \times (P_2 \ldots P_4)$	$X = 0 = P_1$ $B_i = 0$ for $i > 4$ $C_i = B_i$
$(A_1 \ldots A_6) \div (B_1 \ldots B_4)$	$X = 1$ $B_i = 0$ for $i > 4$ $C_i = B_i$ $P_i = 0$
$(P_2 \ldots P_4)^2$	$X = 0 = P_1$ $B_i = 0$ for $i > 4$ $C_i = B_i = P_i$ for $i \leqslant 4$
$\sqrt{(A_1 \ldots A_8)}$	$X = 1$ $P_i = 0$ $B_1 C_1 = 00$ $B_2 C_2 = 01$ $B_i C_i = 10$ for $i \geqslant 3$

allow a carry to propagate from a rightmost cell to the leftmost cell in that stage and back to the control logic. In general the last stage has $2N + 1$ cells, meaning that the clock speed depends primarily on this stage. If a longer pipeline is tolerable, the carry-out from each computation cell may also be latched as was done in the previous simple adder cell. By adding more unit delays, as in Figs. 2-26, 2-27, and 2-28, the clock can be sped up to match the time to transit only a single cell. The cost is again of course an increased number of unit delays.

Table 2-2 Sample Multiplication on Multifunction Pipeline

	Input to Logic			Output from Logic		
	A	B,C	P	S	D,E	Comment
Stage 1	00010000 $= 4$	110000 $= 6$	0011 $= 3$	000100	011000	Since $P_1 = 0$, leave A alone
Stage 2	000100	011000	0011	000100	001100	Since $P_2 = 0$, leave A alone
Stage 3	000100	001100	0011	010000	000110	Since $P_3 = 1$, add 2×6 to A
Stage 4	010000	000110	0001	010110	0000110	Since $P_4 = 1$, add 1×6 to A

Output $= S_1 \, S_2 \ldots S_6 = 010110 = 22 = 6 \times 3 + 4$

All $X = 0$

In the terminology of Chap. 1, this pipeline is a good example of a multifunction, dynamically configurable design, since not only can it perform a variety of operations, but at each clock the operation started may have no relationship whatsoever to any operation initiated previously and still in progress within the pipeline.

2.3.4 A Multifunction Pipeline with Multiple Paths

The previous section diagrammed a pipeline that was multifunction in operation capabilities but still linear in terms of the path taken by the data. The flow for each initiation was from one stage to the next, independent of the operation. As an example of a pipeline where the path may change, in this section we consider a multifunction pipeline for fixed- and floating-point additions, subtractions, and multiplications. In general outline it is similar to the arithmetic pipeline of the TI ASC machine (Stephenson, 1973) described in Chap. 4.

At a first level, floating-point multiplication can be partitioned into three subfunctions: fraction multiplication, exponent addition, and result normalization. For the first two subfunctions individual subpipelines could be constructed from arrays of adder cells as described earlier. The normalization is an equally simple thing to pipeline since it consists primarily of leading-zero detectors and shifters. Floating-point addition also partitions into three subfunctions: initial alignment including exponent compare, fraction addition, and result normalization. The normalization function conceptually is similar to that for the multiplication. The addition can again be implemented as an array of adder cells if so desired, and the initial alignment again requires exponent arithmetic and shifting. The fixed-point operations require only one subfunction each from the above collection.

A single pipeline can be constructed to perform all of these functions by the appropriate combination of five subpipelines each of which performs one of the five unique subfunctions. Figure 2-31 diagrams such a pipeline. What makes this unique from previous examples is that no single operation uses all stages in the pipeline. Instead each of the desired operations uses a different pattern of subpipelines as diagrammed in Fig. 2-32. A control mechanism (such as that described in Chap. 3) is responsible for providing the routing information for each initiation.

This multiple-path pipeline also introduces a problem not previously encountered, that is, the possibility of *structural hazards* or *collisions* between different initiations each of which uses a different path. For example, we consider a floating-point addition operation followed some time later by a fixed-point add. If the add operation is started at the wrong time, it will attempt to use the adder subpipeline at exactly the same time that the aligned number from the floating-point add attempts to use the unit. The control mechanism clearly must prevent such collisions from occurring. One theory for handling such problems is developed in Chap. 3.

2.4 PIPELINES WITH FEEDBACK

None of the pipelines constructed so far have any *feedback*, that is, a pipeline input fed by a later pipeline output. The existence of feedback implies a certain "sequential-

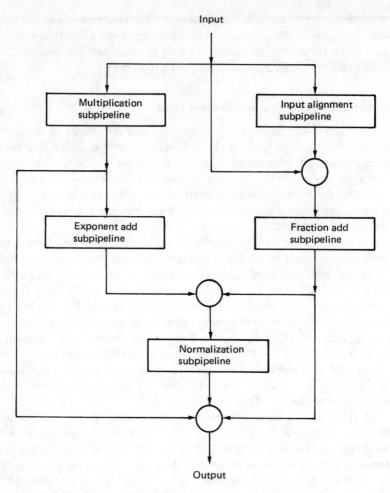

Figure 2-31 A multifunction multipath pipeline.

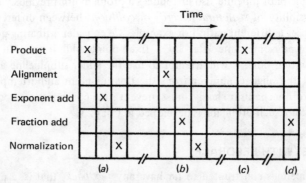

Figure 2-32 Subpipeline usage. (*a*) Floating-point multiply. (*b*) Floating-point add. (*c*) Fixed-point multiply. (*d*) Fixed-point add.

ism" to the function being computed—that is, each output of the pipeline depends on previous outputs. The improper use of such feedback around a pipeline can destroy its efficiency, since if a new computation cycle cannot be started until the previous one is complete, then only a few stages of the pipeline will be in use at any one time, and the throughput will drop much below that for problems with no feedback. This section studies the construction of pipelines that for certain classes of problems have substantial feedback but still run at a very high rate.

The most common problems involving feedback are *recurrences*, which accept as their input a string of values $a(1), a(2), \ldots, a(n)$, and produce as output another string $x(1), x(2), \ldots, x(n)$ where for some $m > 0$ each $x(i)$ is a function of $a(i)$ and $x(i-1)$ through $x(i-m)$. That is,

$$x(i) = f(a(i), x(i-1), \ldots, x(i-m)) \qquad (2\text{-}9)$$

The function f is termed the *recurrence function*. In addition, each input $a(i)$ may actually be a small set of values such as a real and imaginary part or a set of filter coefficients. This set of values is called a *parameter vector*. A pipeline to solve this system would ideally accept one new $a(i)$ as input at each clock and produce a new $x(j)$ at the same rate. A good example is a real-time digital signal processor where part of each $a(i)$ is a measurement of an incoming signal and each $x(i)$ is the corresponding filtered output.

A direct implementation of such a problem is to design a pipelined module to perform the function f and simply wrap the output back into the inputs as pictured in Fig. 2-33. This implementation, however, has a disastrous impact on performance. If the number of stages in the module to compute f is df, then the time the calculation of $x(i)$ is started to the time it is complete is df clock periods. Since $x(i+1)$ depends on $x(i)$, however, we cannot start the calculation of $x(i+1)$ until $x(i)$ is totally finished. During the intervening time there is nothing the pipeline can do so it is idle. The result is that a new calculation is initiated only once every df clocks. This is in contrast to normal problems where the initiation rate is totally independent of the number of stages in the design.

One way to overcome this poor performance was described in a series of papers by Kogge (1973b, 1974, 1977a). In this approach the basic recurrence equation for computing $x(i)$ from $x(i-1), \ldots, x(i-m)$ is backed up on itself by substituting appropriate copies of the original Eq. 2-9 for one or more of the $x(i-1), \ldots, x(i-m)$ terms:

$$\begin{aligned}
x(i) &= f(a(i), x(i-1), \ldots x(i-m)) \\
&= f(a(i), f(a(i-1), x(i-2), \ldots, x(i-m-1)), x(i-2), \ldots x(i-m)) \\
&= f(a(i), f(a(i-1), x(i-2), \ldots, x(i-m-1)), f(a(i-2), x(i-3), \ldots, \\
&\quad x(i-m-2)), \ldots f(a(i-m), x(i-m-1), \ldots, x(i-2m))) \qquad (2\text{-}10)
\end{aligned}$$

This procedure removes the dependence of $x(i)$ on $x(i-1)$ completely, thus easing the feedback problem. Further backups can remove the dependence on $x(i-2)$, $x(i-3), \ldots$. The problem with this substitution in general is that the pipeline to implement the backed-up recurrence mushrooms in complexity. Figure 2-34 diagrams how even a simple single backup can double the hardware. Furthermore, this doubling of hardware doubles the pipeline delay; and even with the freedom brought by the loosened dependency, the net performance is no better than the original pipeline (cf. the timing diagram of Fig. 2-34).

Fortunately, for many common problems the explosion in hardware caused by the backup can be avoided. In these cases the backed-up recurrence can be mathematically rewritten in the form

$$x(i) = f(b(i), x(i-df), \ldots, x(i-df-m+1)) \tag{2-11}$$

where the new values or sets of values $b(i)$ are computable strictly from $a(i), \ldots,$ $a(i-df+1)$. If this backing up is possible, as it is for a great many common recurrence functions, then the pipeline of Fig. 2-33 with $b(i)$ substituted for $a(i)$ will in fact start a new $x(j)$ through the pipeline at each clock as pictured in Fig. 2-35. Here the computation of $x(i+1)$ does not depend directly on $x(i)$. Instead, once df of the answers are known (such as $x(0), x(1), \ldots, x(df-1)$) further answers can be grouped into sets of df results, $[x(kdf), x(kdf+1), \ldots, x((k+1)df-1)]$, each set depending only on the previous set. At the ith clock $x(i)$ is available as an output and is the last element needed to start the computation of $x(i+df)$. Since this occurs at each clock pulse, there is always a computation to start, and unlike Fig. 2-33, the pipeline is always busy and running at 100% capacity.

To expand the pipeline computing f into a complete system requires adding an additional pipeline that can take the $a(i)$ parameter vectors at a rate of one per clock and compute the corresponding $b(i)$ values. The output of this new pipeline will then feed the f module directly. If it is possible to construct such a module, then the cascaded system will run at one $x(i)$ per clock regardless of how many stages are involved.

One example of this procedure is the design of a pipeline to compute $x(i) = a(i) + x(i-1)$ assuming that a four-stage pipelined adder is available. This adder might be similar in design to those of Sec. 2.3.1. Backing up this recurrence yields

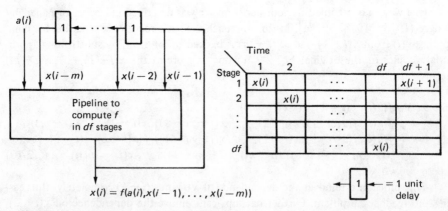

Figure 2-33 Direct implementation of recurrence.

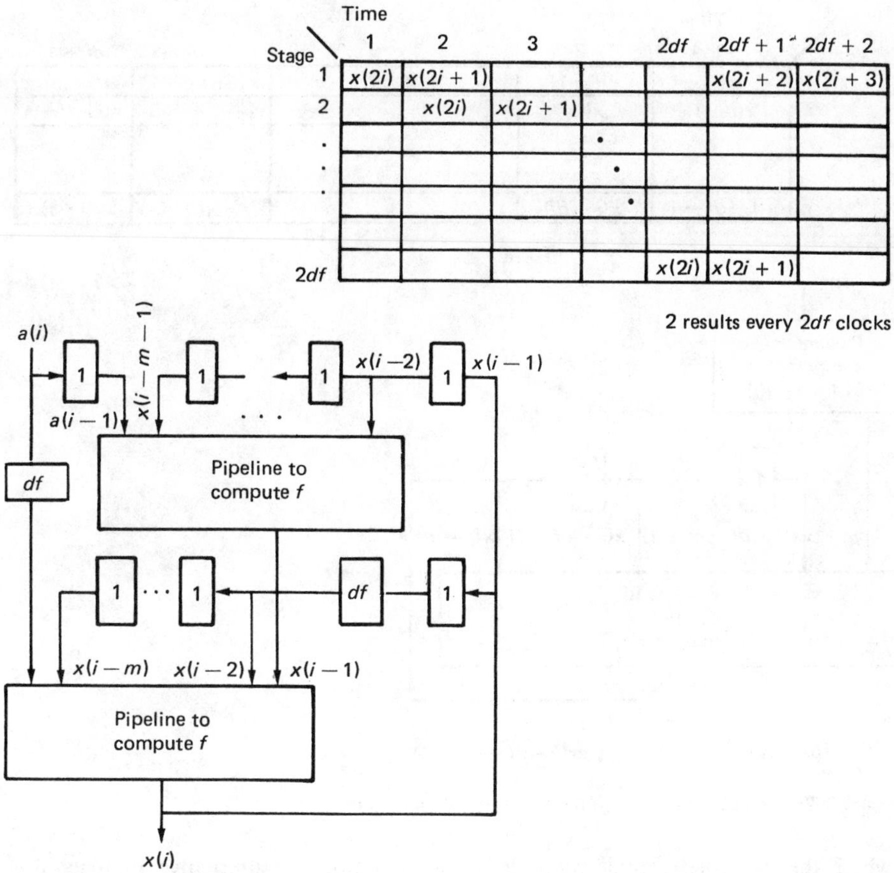

Time Stage	1	2	3		2df	2df + 1	2df + 2
1	x(2i)	x(2i + 1)				x(2i + 2)	x(2i + 3)
2		x(2i)	x(2i + 1)				
.				.			
.				.			
.				.			
2df					x(2i)	x(2i + 1)	

2 results every 2df clocks

Figure 2-34 Backing up the recurrence.

$$x(i) = a(i) + x(i-1)$$
$$= a(i) + (a(i-1) + x(i-2))$$
$$= a(i) + a(i-1) + (a(i-2) + x(i-3)) \qquad (2\text{-}12)$$
$$= a(i) + a(i-1) + a(i-2) + (a(i-3) + x(i-4))$$
$$= b(i) + x(i-4)$$

where $b(i) = a(i) + a(i-1) + a(i-2) + a(i-3)$. The additional pipeline to compute $b(i)$ is functionally a four-input adder. Starting from scratch the most cost-effective design would be a Wallace tree approach using the carry-save adder module of a previous section. If instead we wished to use more replicas of the available four-stage adder, several other designs are possible. The most direct, a serial implementation (Fig. 2-36), uses three adders with a total delay of 12. It assumes that $b(i)$ is computed as

$$b(i) = (a(i) + (a(i-1) + (a(i-2) + a(i-3))))$$

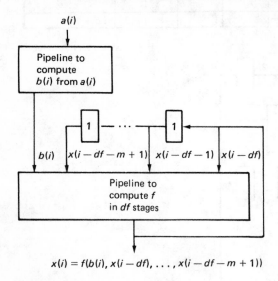

Time Stage	1	2		df	df + 1
1	$x(i)$	$x(i + 1)$		$x(i + df - 1)$	$x(i + df)$
2	$x(i - 1)$	$x(i)$			$x(i + df - 1)$
⋮	⋮	⋮		⋮	⋮
df	$x(i - df - 1)$	$x(i - df)$		$x(i)$	$x(i + 1)$

$a(i)$

Pipeline to compute $b(i)$ from $a(i)$

$b(i)$ $x(i - df - m + 1)$ $x(i - df - 1)$ $x(i - df)$

Pipeline to compute f in df stages

$$x(i) = f(b(i), x(i - df), \ldots, x(i - df - m + 1))$$

Figure 2-35 Cascaded high rate implementation of recurrence.

where the parentheses guide the order of computation. An alternative approach uses the associativity[1] of the + operator to perform the additions in a different order:

$$b(i) = ((a(i) + a(i - 1)) + (a(i - 2) + a(i - 3)))$$

Figure 2-37 diagrams this arrangement. We note that the adders are arranged in a "treelike" fashion. Although there is no change in the number of adders, both the number of noncompute delays and total pipeline delay have been reduced. This arrangement is equivalent to the *log-sum* reduction algorithm used for many years on parallel computers (cf. Kuck, 1968). Upon careful observation of the timing of this organization we note that in all cases the upper right adder duplicates the result computed by the upper left adder two clock units ago, and consequently can be replaced by a simple delay. The resulting pipeline (Fig. 2-38) uses only two adders and has a total delay of only 8.

This log-sum technique is in fact so general that as pictured in Fig. 2-38 it may be used to reduce to one quantity an input set of 2^k quantities where the reduction

[1] The function f is associative if for all a, b, c, $f(a, f(b,c)) = f(f(a,b),c)$. It is commutative if for all a, b, $f(a,b) = f(b,a)$.

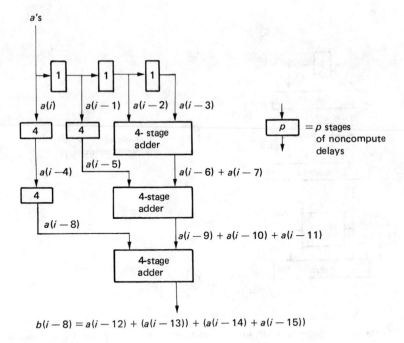

$$b(i-8) = a(i-12) + (a(i-13)) + (a(i-14) + a(i-15))$$

Figure 2-36 Serial cascade for four-input adder.

operation is any associative function. The pipeline requires only k levels of the basic module and is totally independent of the intrinsic number of stages in that module.

Figure 2-39 diagrams the complete solution to the sample additive recurrence. It uses three adder modules and has three extra latches used strictly as delays; it can accept one new input at each clock.

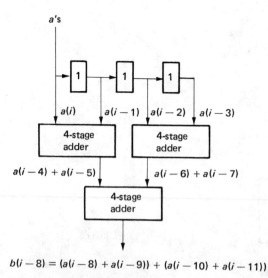

$$b(i-8) = (a(i-8) + a(i-9)) + (a(i-10) + a(i-11))$$

Figure 2-37 Log-sum cascaded four-input adder.

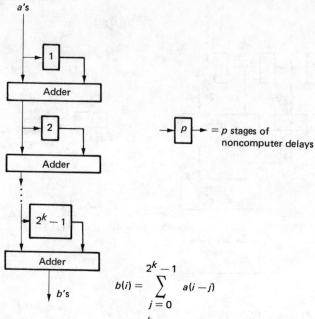

$$b(i) = \sum_{j=0}^{2^k - 1} a(i-j)$$

Figure 2-38 Reduced log-sum cascade for 2^k adder. Add may be replaced by any associative operator.

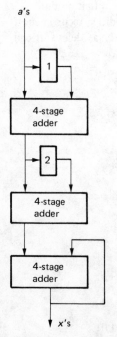

Figure 2-39 Complete pipeline for $x(i) = a(i) + x(i-1)$.

This technique generalizes directly to the solution of any first-order recurrence ($m = 1$) where the function f has only the property that there exists some other function g such that for all a, b, and x of the proper domains,

$$f(a,f(b,x)) = f(g(a,b), x) \tag{2-13}$$

The function g is termed a *companion function.*

Any recurrence with this property allows itself to be backed up as follows:

$$
\begin{aligned}
x(i) &= f(a(i), x(i-1)) \\
&= f(a(i), f(a(i-1), x(i-2))) \\
&= f(g(a(i), a(i-1)), x(i-2)) \\
&= f(g(g(a(i), a(i-1)), a(i-2)), x(i-3)) \\
&= f(g(g(\ldots, g(a(i), a(i-1)), \ldots, a(i-df+1))), x(i-df)) \\
&= f(b(i), x(i-df))
\end{aligned}
\tag{2-14}
$$

where $b(i)$ is computed from the a's using only the g function. Further, it is easy to show that insofar as its effects on f are concerned the function g is associative (Kogge, 1973a). Therefore, if we design pipelined modules to compute f and g, and the delay through the f module is df, then a cascaded pipeline consisting of $\log_2 df$ levels of g arranged as in Fig. 2-38 and feeding a single f module will compute the recurrence at maximum rate.

One demonstration of the efficiency of this approach was made by Loomis (1966), who reported a pipelined adder design where the basic bit-by-bit sum and carry equations were manipulated into a companion-function-like form. Specialized staging similar in topology to Fig. 2-38 (with different logic functions in each stage) then resulted in an adder capable of several times the performance of more conventionally designed pipelined adders.

This companion function concept is not limited simply to first-order recurrences. Kogge (1973b) shows that equivalent pipelines can be constructed for mth order recurrences, $m > 1$, whenever a pair of companion functions g and h exist with the following properties for any $a(i)$, $x(i)$:

$$
\begin{aligned}
&f(a(0), f(a(1),x(1), \ldots ,x(m)), x(1), \ldots ,x(m-1)) = f(g(a(0), a(1)), \\
&\quad x(1), \ldots ,x(m))
\end{aligned}
\tag{2-15}
$$
$$
\begin{aligned}
&f(a(0),f(a(1),x(1), \ldots ,x(m)),f(a(2),x(1), \ldots ,x(m)), \ldots ,f(a(m),x(1), \ldots , \\
&\quad x(m))) = f(h(a(0),a(1), \ldots ,a(m)),x(1), \ldots ,x(m))
\end{aligned}
$$

If g and h can be implemented as pipelines of delay dg and dh, respectively, then k levels of Fig. 2-40, configured as in Fig. 2-41, will output results at a rate of one per clock. Here k is the smallest integer such that

$$k((m-1)dg + dh) + df \leqslant m2^k - m + 1 \tag{2-16}$$

As in many of the previous pipeline constructions, the major disadvantage of these

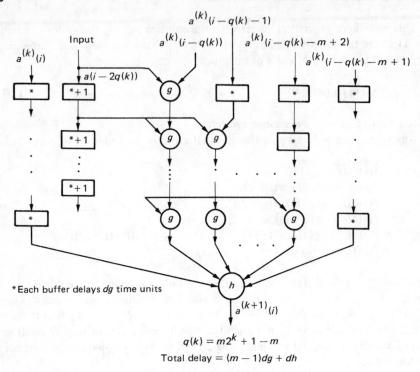

$$q(k) = m2^k + 1 - m$$
Total delay $= (m-1)dg + dh$

Figure 2-40 Basic pipeline for mth order recurrence.

techniques is the potentially explosive increase in hardware. Unlike the previous non-feedback pipelines, however, these constructions must also be initialized very carefully; either degraded speed or special values must be forced into the feedback inputs until enough outputs are available to fill all feedback inputs with proper values.

2.5 COST-PERFORMANCE TRADEOFFS

Very few real systems have performance as the sole criterion for design effectiveness; somewhere in the process *cost* becomes a concern. Depending on the situation this cost may be expressed in terms of gate counts, space utilization, or design time, but it nearly always increases with increasing performance. A tradeoff is usually necessary to balance maximum achievable performance with minimum acceptable cost. This section investigates briefly some basic methods that have been used to perform such tradeoffs. Although not always applicable, these methods give general indications of the range of possibilities. Of course, it is critical to remember the design objectives might not be strict cost-performance optimization, but instead may be a certain level of performance at minimum cost. Such different objectives would require different optimization criteria.

One of the easiest cost relationships to derive is between speed, cost, and the number of stages into which a piece of combinational logic is to be partitioned. If the time for this total logic (without latches) to compute one answer is T, then after the partitioning of the logic into k stages of equal delay, the time per stage, and thus the time per computation, decreases to roughly

$$\frac{T}{k} + S \tag{2-17}$$

where S is the time required to traverse the staging latch. Similarly, if the cost of the logic (in whatever measure is meaningful) is C, and the cost of a single level of staging latches is L, then the cost of a k-stage pipelined version is roughly

$$Lk + C \tag{2-18}$$

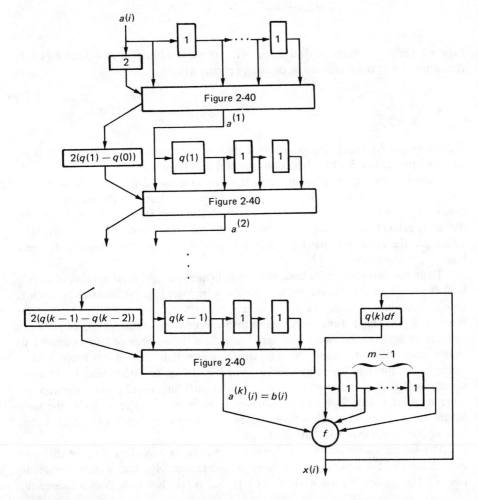

Figure 2-41 Pipelined computation of mth order recurrence.

The shape of these two curves as a function of k is shown overlapped in Fig. 2-42. As the number of stages increases, the cost increases while the performance in calculations per second (the reciprocal of stage time) also increases, but not as fast as cost. One method of comparing these two terms is by computing *cost-performance* or cost per calculation rate as a function of k. Since the performance is the reciprocal of stage time, the cost-performance ratio is:

$$\frac{\text{Cost}}{\text{Calculation rate}} = \text{cost} \times \text{time per calculation}$$

$$= (Lk + C)\left(\frac{T}{k} + S\right) \tag{2-19}$$

$$= LT + CS + \frac{LSk^2 + CT}{k}$$

Figure 2-42c diagrams the general shape of this curve as a function of k. Larson (1973) first showed that the minimum of this curve occurs when

$$k = \sqrt{\frac{CT}{LS}} \tag{2-20}$$

This minimum represents the point where the cost per calculation is lowest, or equivalently where the number of calculations per cost unit is highest.

Though good for initial sizing estimates, this cost model neglects two important considerations. First, how the logic is actually distributed among the different stages affects how many bits of staging latch are needed at each stage of the pipeline. This obviously affects the cost per stage. Second, the cost model assumes a particular logic design for the combinational logic and thus overlooks potential savings by different logic implementations.

There are two good guidelines that can help minimize the total number of staging latches needed in the design. First, a partition of logic that produces more outputs than it needs inputs should be placed as late as possible in the pipeline. The converse is also true, that logic using more inputs than it produces outputs should be placed as early as possible in the flow. This tends to reduce the number of latches needed to simply pass data unchanged through several stages that do not reference it. For example, all the pipelines constructed from Fig. 2-26a, an adder cell, would work equally well if the latches were moved to the inputs but would require significantly more total latch bits. The second guideline is to group all logic requiring the same inputs in the same stage. This again reduces the number of times a string of latches does nothing more than pass data unchanged.

The second objection to the simple cost model, namely the effects of different formulations of the basic logic, has been studied extensively. The Wallace tree multiplier of Fig. 2-28 is a good example of a typical result. Not only does it reduce the

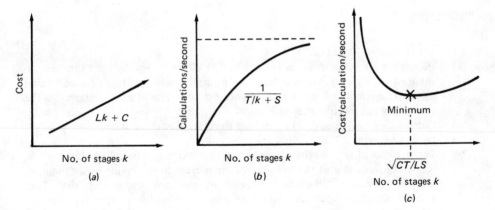

Figure 2-42 Cost and performance. (a) Cost. (b) Performance. (c) Cost-performance ratio.

number of stages required to perform the function (thus reducing the number of latches) but also it actually decreases the amount of adder logic needed.

To fairly compare different circuits that perform the same function, several researchers have extended the concept of cost-performance ratio to represent a measure of how many basic calculations are produced by a circuit with a given gate count. This measure, termed efficiency, is given by

$$\text{Efficiency} = \frac{\text{number of bits processed}}{(\text{number of gates})(\text{time per stage})} \tag{2-21}$$

where the number of gates includes those used in the latch, specifically the Earle latch described earlier. The number of bits processed allows comparison of a design optimized around one size of input operands (such as a 32-bit adder) with another design optimized for a different size. By making the various factors a function of the number of stages, as was done earlier, not only different circuits but also different numbers of stages can be compared. Hallin and Flynn (1972), for example, studied a variety of pipelined adders, including carry look-ahead and conditional sum designs, and found that a maximally pipelined condition sum adder was the most efficient approach. Equivalent studies of multipliers by Hallin and Flynn and by Deverell (1975) have found multipliers even more efficient than the basic Wallace approach, particularly when there is a strong desire to produce them from LSI parts.

This whole approach to cost tradeoffs can be extended to encompass entire systems. In one study by Larson and Davidson (1973), the cost-effectiveness of various degrees of pipelining and parallelism was studied in relationship to a processor built to compute fast Fourier transforms (FFT). The cost equations described above were amplified to more accurately represent 10 structured variations, each with cost and varying degrees of pipelining.

PROBLEMS

2-1   Verify Eqs. (2-3) and (2-4).

2-2   Design a logic stage from Earle latches that either passes its input through unchanged or logically shifts it left one position under control of a command signal. Diagram the logic for the rightmost four bits of such a stage. Do the same using circuits like that of Fig. 2-4. Compare.

2-3   Correct Eqs. (2-6) and (2-7) to include the effects of clock skew.

2-4   Prove Theorems 2-1 and 2-2.

2-5   The method of interleaving described in the text might be called "low-bit" interleaving since it uses the low bits of an address to determine which memory module to access. "High-bit" interleaving uses the uppermost bits of an address. Describe when this might be a useful alternative, either for speed or other reasons.

2-6   Assume a memory system consisting of a complex interleaving of four subsystems, each of which consists of four simply interleaved modules. Describe how addresses are broken down to select modules. Assuming a single module takes T seconds per access, at what rate can accesses uniformly spaced by 1, 2, 3, 6, or 9 words be made?

2-7   Simulate executing the pipelined adder (Fig. 2-26) and both pipelined multipliers (Figs. 2-27 and 2-28) where during the first three clock periods the pairs (0110, 0111), (1001, 0101), and (1111, 0001) are presented to the A and B inputs. Run the pipes until all answers have been provided. Show all intermediate latched results.

2-8   Work out for the pipeline of Fig. 2-30 the sequence of calculations for 37/9, 5^2, and $\sqrt{26}$.

2-9   Express the carries in a binary addition as a recurrence and find a companion function. Use the result to guide the logic design of a pipelined binary adder. How does it compare to the ripple adder of Sec. 2.3.1?

Chapter 3

Timing, Control, and Performance

Efficient use of a pipeline demands that there be a timely source of inputs to drive it. Without such a stream, successive stages in the pipeline become idle, and system throughput decreases accordingly. However, providing this input stream is only half the problem; care must be taken in *scheduling* when each input starts through the pipeline to guarantee both high performance and avoidance of internal conflicts. If all pipelines were purely *linear,* that is, each stage connecting to only a single succeeding stage, such scheduling would be trivial. Inputs would be given to the pipeline as they arrive at a rate of one per clock pulse. Real pipelines are usually more complex. Some stages may require different time periods. There may be feedback from a stage to a previous one or multiple paths out of a stage to later stages. More than one stage may be used by an input at one time. There may be dependencies between inputs that force certain orderings to the computations involving these inputs. Furthermore, for multifunction dynamically configured pipelines the path to be taken through the pipeline may vary dramatically with each input. All these factors place constraints on new starts and make the overall performance of a machine critically sensitive to the procedures used to schedule and control its activities. Unfortunately, they also make the task of defining optimal schedules very difficult.

The development of procedures for determining schedules for pipelines has been studied by several groups. Ramamoorthy and Li (1975) have shown that the general problem is "intrinsically difficult" and is a member of the "NP Complete" class of problems (Karp, 1972). It is conjectured that any such problem of this class has no "fast" solution, that is, a scheduling algorithm whose execution time is a polynomial function of the number of items to be scheduled. Other groups, such as Ramamoorthy and Li (1974), Ramamoorthy and Kim (1974), and Sze and Tou (1972), have studied suboptimal scheduling algorithms and their characteristics with mixed results.

Despite the intrinsic difficulty of the general case, there are subclasses of pipelines for which optimal or at least heuristically good scheduling algorithms exist and are useful in an engineering sense. The most important of these algorithms handle the scheduling of pipelines where the only restrictions are that

1   The execution time for all stages is a multiple of some basic clock.
2   Once a computation starts through a pipeline, its time-pattern of stage usage is fixed.

There may be any pattern of stage usage, but that pattern is known precisely as soon as the data enters the system. This is an excellent model for many real pipelines, particularly those used in vector processors (see Sec. 1.3 and Chap. 4). Scheduling algorithms for this class compute sequences of new calculation start times that optimize the total number of calculations performed per second. In addition, outgrowths of these algorithms can also go back to the original stage-time usage patterns and indicate how modifications to those patterns can increase total throughput. The original work on these techniques was developed in a series of papers by Davidson (1971, 1974, 1975), Shar (1972), Patel and Davidson (1976), and Thomas and Davidson (1974). Sections 3.2 and 3.3 draw heavily on this work as a foundation.

Another class of problems for which a good solution exists deals with the pipelining of instruction execution for an SISD architecture. The major difference between this and the above class is that there may be dependencies between inputs (instructions to be executed) that may not become apparent until after an input has started through a pipeline. The techniques developed here are useful for partial control of the pipeline, but they are not a complete answer. Chapter 6 addresses the design of such systems in more detail.

The control of pipelines does not end with the development of a good scheduling algorithm. Hardware must be implemented to dynamically generate the schedules and to control the individual stages so that each computation flows through the pipeline according to plan. Later sections of this chapter discuss both concerns.

It should be stressed that the results of this chapter, particularly in the manipulation of reservation tables, will be used throughout the rest of the book. Therefore, it is worth the reader's time to fully understand at least the high points of this chapter. These include determination of optimal schedules for static pipelines and the use of delay insertion for increased performance.

3.1   COMMON NOMENCLATURE

The scheduling procedures described in this chapter assume that the exact pattern of stage usage is known for each input before it is started through a pipeline. These patterns may be described in a two-dimensional tabular description known as a *reservation table*. One reservation table represents exactly one pattern taken by one data input. An *initiation* of a reservation table occurs when a computation is started that will follow this designated path. An initiation thus corresponds to the start of a single function evaluation. When an initiation is made, the pipeline's controller must reserve for that initiation at the appropriate times the stages called out by the reservation table. Any attempt by two or more initiations to use the same stage at the same time is a *collision* and clearly must be avoided by both the scheduling algorithm and the controller executing it. Not avoiding a collision is equivalent to asking a single piece of logic to compute two different results simultaneously.

Each row in the reservation table corresponds to the time usage of a unique stage in the pipeline. Time, the other dimension, is partitioned into segments, usually fixed and equaling the basic clock rate of the pipeline. Each column thus is a diagram of the internal usage of the pipeline at a particular instant of time. To simplify analysis the time segments are assigned integer values; the first time segment where there is some pipeline activity is denoted time unit or clock cycle 0. A mark in entry (i,j) indicates that for this pipeline to execute the given function, stage i is needed j time units after the initiation of the function evaluation. If there are several possible reservation tables for a single pipeline (labeled A, B, C,...), the mark used as an entry in the table is the same as the table's name. Where there is no possible ambiguity, the mark "X" will be used. The total number of clock units from time 0 to the last segment where there is activity is called the *compute time* for that reservation table.

Figure 3-1 illustrates two reservation tables for a pipeline having three stages. Figure 3-1a (table A) has a compute time of 7 time units and that for Fig. 3-1b (table B) is 8 units. It is important to keep in mind that each reservation table represents exactly one evaluation of a given function.

In terms of the nomenclature of Chap. 1, a *static pipeline* is one where all initiations are of the same reservation table, and a *dynamic pipeline* is one where the initiation sequence includes copies of different reservation tables.

As shown in Fig. 3-1, it is possible to have within one reservation table multiple marks in a row or column. Multiple marks in a row may represent either repeated usage of the same stage several times in the same function evaluation or, if the marks are contiguous, simply a stage that is slower than others.

Likewise, multiple marks in a given column are also permissible and represent multiple stage usage in a single time unit. This corresponds to the introduction of parallelism into the function evaluation.

A reservation table does not uniquely specify or correspond to a hardware pipeline. Instead a large number of pipelines can have data flows represented by the same reservation table. For example, Fig. 3-2 diagrams four separate pipelines that would support one or both of the reservation tables of Fig. 3-1. All are different. The pipeline of Fig. 3-2a, for example, implements the pattern of reservation table B by feeding back from one stage to a previous stage over different paths. Each stage takes exactly one clock cycle for its operation. In contrast the first stage for the pipeline of Fig. 3-2b is assumed to take two clocks to process data; and the repetitive use of stages 2 and 3 in reservation table B is implemented by a register file (see Sec. 2.2.3) in front of stage 2's logic, which repeats the value from stage 1 after a delay of 2 cycles.

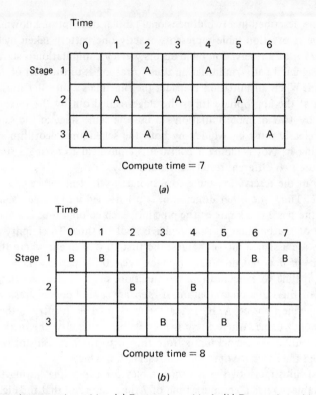

Figure 3-1 Sample reservation tables. (*a*) Reservation table A. (*b*) Reservation table B.

As a further example, Fig. 3-3 diagrams how the pipeline of Fig. 3-2*c* implements one initiation of reservation table A. This example illustrates many of the points mentioned above such as nonlinear flow of data, multiple paths, and multiple simultaneous stage utilizations. It also demonstrates how collisions might occur. At times 2 or 6, for example, any attempt to enter new data into the pipeline, i.e., start a new initiation, will conflict with the initiation started at time 0. Both will need to use the same stage (logic set 3) at the same time.

A key parameter in determining the performance of a pipeline is the *latency*, or number of time units, separating two initiations of the same or different reservation tables. A latency may have any positive integer value including 0. Figure 3-4 illustrates the effects of different latency values between various combinations of the reservation tables of Fig. 3-1. The notation is again a tabular one, although now it represents the total dynamic usage of the pipeline when several initiations are active simultaneously. As shown in Fig. 3-4, although more than one latency between two initiations may be possible, not all latencies are permitted. For example, on a static pipeline a latency of 0 is impossible because both evaluations would attempt to use the same hardware stages at exactly the same moments. As another example, a latency of 2 for reservation table A causes dual use of stage 2 during times 3 and 5 and thus is never allowed. In general a latency value that results in a conflict is said to cause a collision.

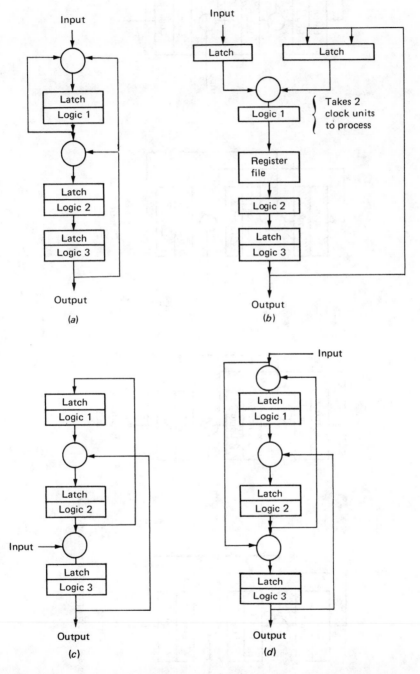

Figure 3-2 Some sample pipelines. (*a*) For reservation table B. (*b*) For reservation table B. (*c*) For reservation table A. (*d*) For either A or B.

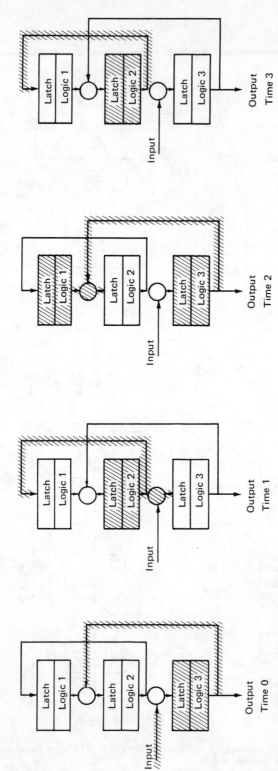

Figure 3-3 Flow of data for reservation table A.

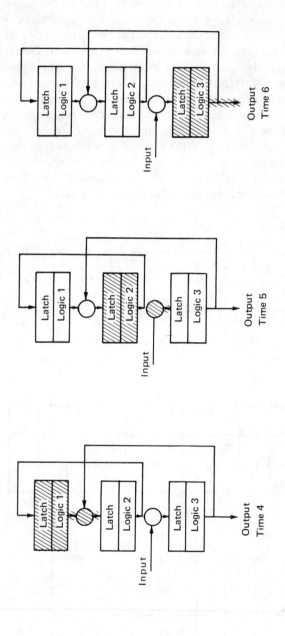

Figure 3-3 Flow of data for reservation table A. (*Continued*)

///// = Flow of data at that time

Since the goal of a pipeline is to compute as many evaluations as possible in as short a time as possible, the prime measure of actual system performance is the *initiation rate,* or average number of initiations per clock unit. The larger the initiation rate, the faster the machine operates. However, mathematical techniques to be described later make it more convenient to discuss the reciprocal of the initiation rate, or *average latency,* the average number of time units between two initiations. Obviously, the smaller the average latency, the faster the pipeline performs. For static pipelines the lower limit to any average latency is clearly 1, since a latency of 0 always causes collisions. This corresponds to an upper limit on the initiation rate of 1. For dynamic pipelines latencies of 0 are possible because two different reservation tables might not overlap. The reservation tables of Fig. 3-1 have this property. In such cases an upper limit to the initiation rate is the minimum of the number of reservation tables and the number of stages in the pipeline. We can overlap reservation tables directly on one another until either we run out of tables or all stages are utilized at time 0. The average latency is then bounded below by the reciprocal of the initiation rate.

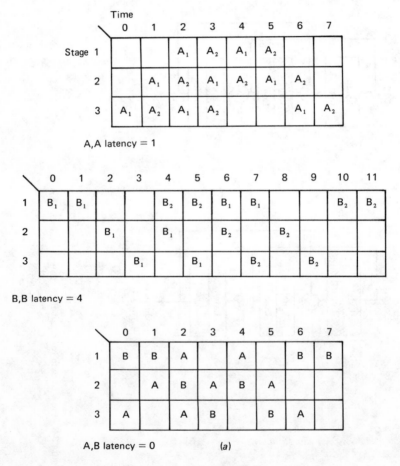

Figure 3-4 Sample latencies. (*a*) Latencies with no collisions.

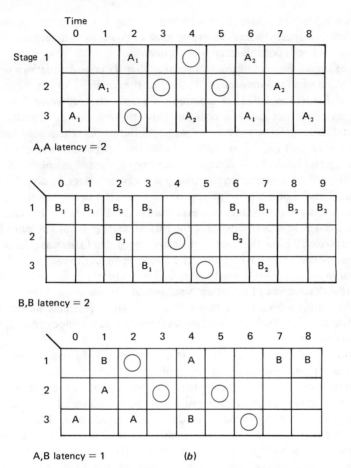

Figure 3-4 Sample latencies. (*Continued*) (*b*) Latencies with collisions (circled).

Another measure of pipeline performance is *stage utilization.* There is one such number for each stage in the pipeline; it indicates on the average how often that stage processes data over a long set of initiations. For each initiation of a reservation table the number of marks in the *i*th row indicates the number of times stage *i* is used in one evaluation. The average utilization of a stage by a function is thus the initiation rate times the number of marks. If several different reservation tables are active at the same time, the total utilization of a stage is the sum of the utilizations by each function type. The maximum utilization of any stage is 1.

Given a set of one or more reservation tables, the purpose of a *control* or *scheduling strategy* is to develop the sequence of times when initiations should be made, or equivalently the sequence of latencies between initiations, that will minimize the average latency (maximize the initiation rate). As described previously, not all latencies are possible; furthermore, the choice of which latency to use between one pair of initiations directly affects which set of latencies is permitted between future pairs. Consequently, a strategy that always chooses the minimum currently permitted latency between two initiations, called a *greedy strategy,* may not always attain the maximum possible performance. Optimal strategies must look ahead to determine the effects on performance of each possible latency sequence.

For example, Fig. 3-5 diagrams a strategy that starts new initiations of reservation table B at alternating latencies of 3, then 8, time units. This results in an average latency of 5.5 $[(3 + 8)/2]$. It represents a greedy strategy since 3 is the smallest latency that does not cause a collision between two separate initiations. A more patient and more effective strategy would be to wait to start the second initiation until the fourth time unit (Fig. 3-6); then new initiations can be made regularly at intervals of 4. The average latency of 4 is clearly superior to the previous one.

In terms of stage utilization the greedy strategy uses stage 1 only 73% of the time, and stages 2 and 3 only 36%. The rest of the time some of the hardware remains idle. In contrast, the patient strategy achieves nearly 100% utilization of stage 1, and 50% of stages 2 and 3. In at least one sense the patient strategy is optimal since it uses some of the hardware 100% of the time. It is clearly impossible to increase the initiation rate above this because there are no free cycles from stage 1 left to use.

When initiations must come from several reservation tables, the strategy must also consider the desired mix of initiation types and any dependencies between them.

Other factors relevant to either static or dynamic pipelines are discussed in the appropriate sections. Table 3-1 summarizes important terminology used in this chapter related to reservation tables.

Before examining the theoretical results, we should emphasize that a reservation table represents an abstraction of the problem by divorcing the way in which data flows through the pipeline from the hardware implementation of the pipeline. As the rest of this chapter will show, this abstraction leads to many theoretically important results that are largely independent of the underlying hardware. However, it is critical to remember that the end goal is the scheduling of initiations on the hardware and this goal influences the mechanisms used to control the pipeline and in some cases the structure of the pipeline itself. One example of the latter effect occurs in the deliberate insertion of delays into a reservation table to increase overall initiation rate. A delay, however, is often modeled by addresses leading to a register file (see Sec. 2.2.3). Therefore, knowing where in a pipeline register files are used as latches and how many are available affects the number of delays that may be inserted. The reverse is also true.

3.2 STATIC PIPELINES

A static pipeline is one where for some period of time only repeated evaluations of the same function with different data are performed. In this case pipeline performance is simply the initiation rate (or average latency) of the corresponding reservation table and control strategy. This section analyzes the properties of a reservation table that determine its theoretical maximum initiation rate, the set of all possible initiation strategies, the strategies that yield the maximum realizable performance, and methods for modifying a reservation table so that its maximum realizable rate achieves the theoretical maximum rate.

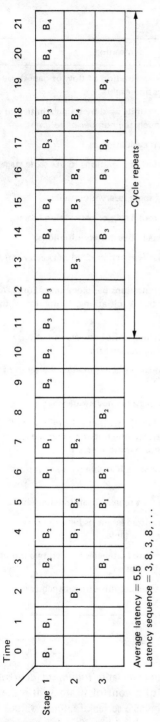

Average latency = 5.5
Latency sequence = 3, 8, 3, 8, . . .

Figure 3-5 Greedy initiation sequence for reservation table B.

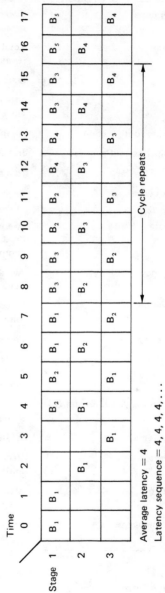

Average latency = 4
Latency sequence = 4, 4, 4, 4, . . .

Figure 3-6 Optimal initiation sequence for reservation table B.

Table 3-1 Summary of Important Terms

Terminology	Meaning
Reservation table	Two-dimensional representation of flow of data through pipeline for one function evaluation.
Compute time	Total number of time units used by a single initiation of a reservation table. Equals the number of columns.
Initiation	Start of one function evaluation.
Collision	Attempt by two different initiations to use same stage at same time.
Static pipeline configuration	All initiations are of same reservation table.
Dynamic pipeline configuration	Initiations may be from a mix of reservation tables.
Latency	Number of time units between two initiations.
Latency sequence	Sequence of latencies (written in < >) between successive initiations.
Initiation rate	Average number of initiations per clock unit. Equals N divided by time to start N initiations. A function of the control strategy.
Average latency	Average number of clock units between initiations. Equals reciprocal of initiation rate.
Stage utilization	Percent of time that each stage is used over a series of initiations.
Control strategy	Procedure that chooses a latency sequence.
Greedy strategy	A control strategy that always picks the minimum possible latency between one initiation and the last without regard to any future initiations.
Minimum achievable latency (MAL)	Smallest average latency achievable by any control strategy.
Latency cycle	A latency sequence that repeats itself indefinitely.
Collision vector	Vector showing permitted latencies between two initiations from the same table.
Collision matrix	Matrix showing permitted latencies betwen two initiations from any of a set of tables.
Forbidden latency set	Those latencies that cause collisions between two initiations.

3.2.1 Key Terms

Two key terms in this discussion are *latency sequence* and *minimum achievable latency* (MAL). The latency sequence is the output of a control strategy; it is the list of latencies between successive initiations. It is written as a series of latency values surrounded by < >. For Fig. 3-5 this sequence is < 3,8,3,8,3,8,...>. A *latency cycle* occurs when a latency sequence consists of the same subsequence repeated indefinitely. The cycle is written as a series of latencies surrounded by ( ). For Fig. 3-5 this cycle is (3,8). The *period* of a cycle is the sum of its latencies. The *average latency* of a cycle is the period divided by the number of latencies. It represents the average time between initiations during that cycle. Likewise the average latency of a latency sequence is the time from the start of the first initiation to the end of the last, divided by the number of initiations. Again for Fig. 3-5 the period is 11 and the average latency is 5.5.

A latency sequence is *permissible* if during the course of all the initiations there are no collisions. A valid control strategy must generate only permissible sequences.

The *MAL* is the smallest average latency that can be achieved by any permissible latency sequence. A lower bound on MAL can be determined from the reservation table alone according to the following lemma:

Lemma 3-1 (Shar, 1972) For any statically configured pipeline executing some reservation table, the MAL is always greater than or equal to the maximum number of marks in any single row of the reservation table.

Proof Let the initiation rate over a long period of time be r initiations per time unit, and the number of marks in the ith row of the reservation table be $N(i)$. Then the utilization of the ith stage is $rN(i)$. Since no utilization may pass 100%, $rN(i)$ must be less than 1 for all i, and thus r must be no greater than $1/\text{MAX}(N(i))$. Since the average latency is the reciprocal of r, it can be no less than $\text{MAX}(N(i))$. Q.E.D.

In Fig. 3-1 reservation table A has 3 marks in rows 2 and 3, and consequently its MAL is at least 3. Likewise the MAL of reservation table B is bounded by 4.

This lower bound gives the design engineer a quick estimate of the maximum performance possible for the given pipeline and reservation table. However, there is no guarantee that the actual MAL equals this bound—that is, that there is some latency sequence whose average latency achieves it. The reason is, of course, that the desirable small latencies may not always be permissible; they may cause collisions and therefore cannot appear in a sequence. For example, while there is an optimal sequence for reservation table B as illustrated in Fig. 3-6, the lowest average latency of any schedule for reservation table A is 4—one-third greater than the bound. This is due, to a large extent, to the fact that a latency of 2 causes a collision (Fig. 3-4b).

3.2.2 A State Diagram

The purpose of the control or scheduling strategy is to determine when to make new initiations. This cannot be done without knowledge of the pipeline's activity at each step in time. However, what is of value to the strategy is not really the actual pattern of stage usage. Instead what counts is a description of whether or not a new initiation at a certain time can cause a collision with any previous initiation. One method of developing and presenting such information is through a *state diagram* where at each time unit the current pipeline configuration corresponds to one of the states. The arcs from one state to the next indicate what new state the pipeline might be in at the next time unit. All possible latency sequences correspond to paths in such diagrams. By analyzing all such paths, particularly those that form closed loops, those with minimum average latency can be identified. The latency sequences that they correspond to are thus optimal strategies.

The particular information encoded into each state is termed a *collision vector*. This vector is a d-bit binary sequence, where d is the compute time of the reservation table. The d bits are labeled 0 to $d - 1$ from left to right, with a 0 in position i indicating that a new initiation i time units from now will not conflict with any currently uncompleted initiations. A 1 indicates that a collision will occur, and therefore an initiation at that time must be avoided. The collision vector for each time period takes into account whether or not a new initiation was made in that period.

The collision vector for the initial state has the special name *initial collision vector*. Since it corresponds to the time unit when the pipeline is first started, it is a representation of what latencies are permissible between just two initiations, one at time 0 and one at time i. As such it is also a representation of permissible latencies between any two initiations without regard to earlier pipeline activity.

Computing this initial collision vector is straightforward. For each value of i between 0 and $d - 1$, one copy of the reservation table is shifted i time units to the right and overlayed on an unshifted copy of the same table. If there are two marks in the same stage-time entry anywhere in the overlay, bit i of the initial collision vector is 1; otherwise it is 0. In all cases bit 0 of this collision vector is 1 because overlaying a reservation table on itself causes a collision everywhere there is a mark. Likewise bit positions beyond the dth are always 0 because the shifted and nonshifted tables never overlap. Because this is always true, these bit positions need not be shown in the collision vector representation.

Figure 3-7 illustrates the development of the initial collision vector for reservation table B.

An alternative approach is to construct the *forbidden latency set*. The number i is a member of this set if, and only if, in at least one row of the reservation table there are two marks separated by i columns. Analysis of the marks in each row quickly identify all members of this set. We note that 0 is always in the set. Finally, for all i in the set the corresponding bit of the initial collision vector is 1. All other bits are 0. For an example, for reservation table B, row 3 indicates that the forbidden latency set must contain a 2. Row 2 also indicates that 2 is a member. From row 1 we set that 1, 5, 6, and 7 are members. The resulting forbidden latency set is thus $\{0,1,2,5,6,7\}$ and the corresponding collision vector is 11100111.

Once the initial state of the pipeline at time 0 is available, the equivalent states for all future time may be computed. The rules for this generation assume that if the collision vector for time t is known, then the states corresponding to time $t + 1$ have collision vectors computed as follows:

Procedure: GENERATE STATE DIAGRAM (Davidson, 1971)

1   The collision vector for time t is left-shifted one bit position, with the leftmost bit discarded and a 0 appended to the right.

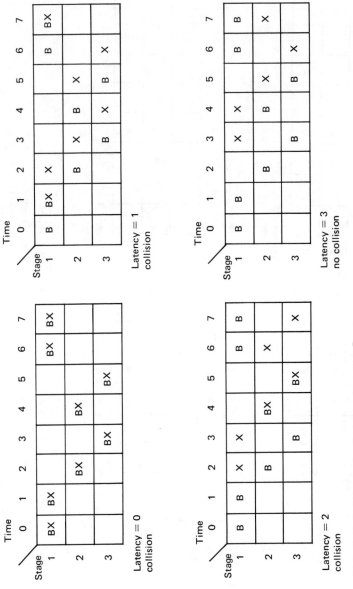

Figure 3-7 Collision vector for reservation table B.

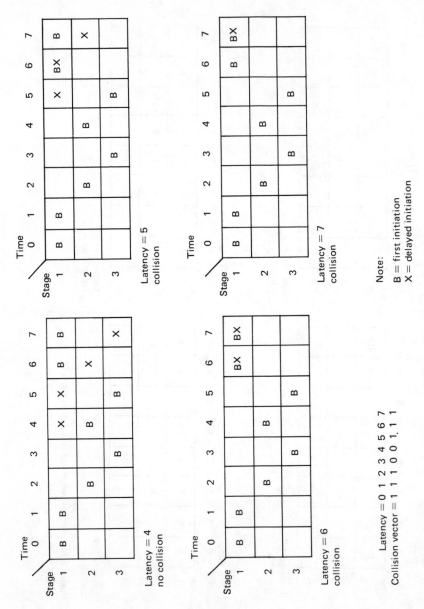

Figure 3-7 Collision vector for reservation table B. (*Continued*)

2 If bit 0 of this vector is 1, then this is the new collision vector.

3 If bit 0 is 0, then two different states at time $t + 1$ are possible depending on whether or not an initiation is made at time $t + 1$. If an initiation is not made, then the shifted collision represents the successor state. If an initiation is made at time $t + 1$, then the new collision vector is the bit-by-bit logical OR of the shifted vector and a copy of the initial collision vector.

4 In any event if the new collision vector is identical to that for a previous state, the arc from the current state returns to that previous state. If the collision vector is new, a new state is defined with an arc from the old to new state. An asterisk (*) is placed on arcs corresponding to time units when a new initiation is made.

The correctness of this procedure follows directly from the definition of a collision vector. If at time t a collision vector has a 1 in bit i, then an initiation at time $t + i$ must be avoided. Consequently the collision vector at time $t + 1$ must also indicate this, but that requires a 1 in bit $i - 1$. If no new initiations are made at time $t + 1$, then the converse is also true, namely that there is a 1 in bit $i - 1$ only if at time t bit i was 1. This justifies steps 1 and 2.

Step 3 handles the possibility of an initiation at time $t + 1$. This is the case only if at time t bit 1 of the collision vector was 0 (or conversely at $t + 1$ after step 1 bit 0 is 0). If all possible latency sequences are to be covered by this diagram, both the possibilities of making and not making a new initiation must be considered. This results in two arcs from the state corresponding to time t. Of course any real latency sequence will take only one of them. The first arc handles the case where no initiation is made. Here the state for time $t + 1$ has the collision vector from step 1. The second arc handles a new initiation at time $t + 1$. In this case any further initiation made after time $t + 1$ must avoid collisions with *both* the initiations made before $t + 1$ *and* the one made at $t + 1$. However, these latter collisions are identified completely by a copy of the initial collision vector. Logically ORing this with the shifted vector of step 1 yields a vector listing all and only those future times when either kind of collision might occur.

Step 4 keeps the diagram a closed finite graph. Because many different time units may have the same collision vector and thus the same state, and new states depend only on previous ones, there is no loss of information in this simplification.

Figure 3-8 is the state diagram constructed from the above rules for reservation table B. At time 0, the very first initiation, the pipeline is in the initial state. The first new initiation is not possible until time 3 (the third arc). If an initiation is made, the new state 11111111 prohibits any new initiations until all previous initiations have run their course 8 or more time units later. If an initiation is not made at time 3 (state 00111000), another decision arises at time 4 (fourth arc). Here again there are two successive states. If a new initiation is made, a loop of four states (11110111, 11101110, 11011100, 10111000) is entered where at every fourth clock a new initiation can be made. This loop is left only when an initiation is not made.

These loops indicate directly the equivalent latency sequences. For example, the loop just discussed corresponds to the cycle (4), while an initiation at time 3 leads to cycles (3,8), (3,9). (3,10),. . . . Other cycles such as (8) and (4,8,3,8) are also present.

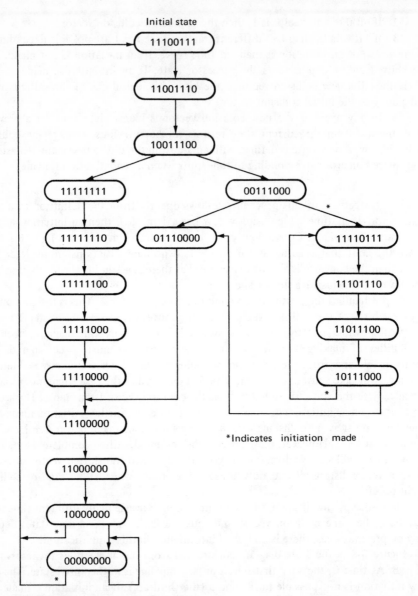

Figure 3-8 State diagram for reservation table B.

3.2.3 A Modified State Diagram

Although the collision vector for reservation table B is relatively simple, the resulting diagram is rather large. For more complex vectors the number of states grow at an alarming rate. Because of their complexity they rapidly lose their usefulness in designing real systems. To overcome this bottleneck a *modified state diagram* (Davidson, 1971) may be constructed. Such a diagram is similar to the original diagram but includes only those states resulting from new initiations. In the original diagram these are the states with * on some incoming arc. Two states in this new diagram are connected by an arc if and only if they were connected by some series of arcs in the original diagram, of which only the last was marked *. Further, this new arc has on it a number corresponding to the number of arcs between the two states in the original diagram. This number is the latency between two initiations. For example, a modified version of Fig. 3-8 would include the states 11100111 and 11110111 with an arc of value 4 connecting them. Figure 3-9 lists this modified diagram in its entirety.

Such modified diagrams clearly contain all relevant information found in the unmodified ones. There is a one-to-one correspondence of loops in the two graphs. Valid latency sequences are simply listings of the arc values. The period and average latency of loops comes immediately from summing the latencies around a loop and counting the number of states. The only information not included are the collision vectors for states where initiations are not made. These, however, are simple shifts of the last state when an initiation was made.

Although a modified diagram can be constructed by first constructing an unmodified one, it is easier to modify the rules for generation to create the new diagram directly. These modified rules are:

Procedure: GENERATE MODIFIED STATE DIAGRAM

   1 Start with the initial collision vector as the initial state.
   2 For each unprocessed state and for each k such that the kth bit of the corresponding collision vector is zero,
      a Shift the collision vector k bits left.
      b Delete the first k bits.
      c Append k zeros to the right.
      d Logically OR with a copy of the initial collision vector.
      e This is a new state. Connect to the current state by an arc of value k.
   3 Include an arc with value $\geq d$ from each state back to the initial state where d is the compute time of the reservation table.

For simplicity the arcs of step 3 are not always shown but simply are taken for granted.

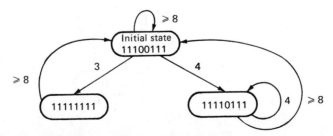

Figure 3-9 Modified state diagram for reservation table B.

The validity of this procedure follows directly from the previous one. Step 2 takes each state and generates from it a list of all states where another initiation is possible. One of these states exists for each 0 in the collision vector. Step 3 covers the degenerate case where all activity in the pipeline ceases before a new initiation is made. This corresponds to all paths that go through state 00. . .0 in an unmodified diagram.

Figure 3-10 is the modified state diagram for reservation table A developed from the above procedure. The number of states is greatly reduced from an equivalent unmodified diagram, but in contrast the cycles are much more apparent. Some of these cycles include (3,5), (1,7), (3,5,7), (5), and (5,7). The MAL is clearly 4 with a greedy cycle of (1,7) among those that achieve it.

3.2.4 Analyzing the Modified State Diagram

The modified state diagram represents in compact form all possible initiation sequences. The main goal of an optimal scheduler is to pick from these the sequence or sequences that provide the highest possible performance, or lowest MAL. When the number of initiations to be made is relatively small (less than the number of states), an exhaustive search of all possible paths is feasible. However, when the pipeline configuration is truly static, that is, if it makes the same kind of initiation an arbitrarily large number of times, an exhaustive search becomes impractical. A more constructive approach is needed.

The key to an efficient scheduling algorithm lies in an analysis of the *cycles* in a modified state diagram. A cycle consists of a set of states and their interconnecting arcs such that the sequence of arcs out of any one state eventually leads back to that state. With an indefinitely long series of initiations but only a finite number of states, all initiation sequences will eventually form cycles. Since the average latency of a cycle repeated many times is simply the average latency of the cycle (period divided by number of arcs traversed), an optimal scheduling algorithm need only enumerate all possible cycles in a state diagram and pick the ones with the lowest average latency.

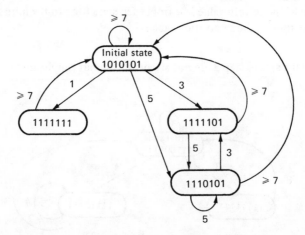

Figure 3-10 Modified state diagram for reservation table A.

An optimal schedule will then consist of a minimum time sequence of initiations leading from the initial state to any state in one of these minimum cycles, followed by
repeated executions of the cycle.

As defined in Sec. 3.1 paths are characterized by their *latency sequence,* or series
of latencies between successive initiations in the path. For a path that forms a cycle
the equivalent latency sequence is termed a *latency cycle* with the latencies for one
iteration of the cycle written as a list of numbers enclosed by ( ). Thus in Fig. 3-10
the cycle of states 1010101, 1111101, 1010101, 1110101, and back to 1010101 has
the equivalent latency cycle (3,7,5,7).

Simple cycles are an important class of cycles in which each state appears no more
than once per iteration of the cycle. The latency cycle (3,7,5,7) of Fig. 3-10 is not
simple because the state 1010101 is traversed twice. However, the sequence (3,5,7) in
Fig. 3-10 is simple. The utility of simple cycles comes from the following lemma:

Lemma 3-2 (Shar, 1972) In any modified state diagram if there is a cycle with
an average latency L, there is at least one simple cycle with average latency no
greater than L.

Proof If the cycle is itself simple, then the lemma is trivial. If the cycle is not
simple, then it is some combination of simple cycles as illustrated in Fig. 3-11.
We assume the cycle is constructed of m simple cycles, the ith of which is traversed $K(i)$ times and has a period $P(i)$ with $S(i)$ states.

The average latency of the entire cycle is thus

$$\frac{\sum_{i=1}^{m} K(i)\ P(i)}{\sum_{i=1}^{m} K(i)\ S(i)}$$

If the lemma is false, then the latencies of all m simple cycles must exceed
this average, i.e.,

$$\frac{\sum_{i=1}^{m} K(i) P(i)}{\sum_{i=1}^{m} K(i) S(i)} < \frac{P(j)}{S(j)} \quad \text{for all } j$$

We choose r such that $P(r)/S(r)$ is the smallest over all j. Then by rearranging
the above equation we find

$$\sum_{i \neq j} K(i)\ (P(i)\ S(r) - P(r)\ S(i)) < 0$$

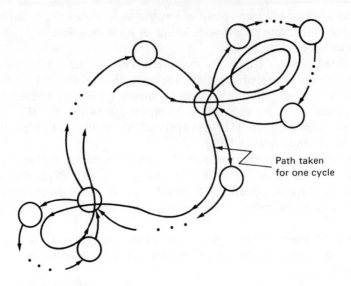

Figure 3-11 Compound cycles.

Since $K(i) \geqslant 0$ for all i, at least one of the terms $P(i) S(r) - P(r) S(i)$ must be negative. If this is the case, then for that value of i, $P(i)/S(i) < P(r)/S(r)$, which contradicts the assumption on r. Q.E.D.

This lemma allows the scheduling algorithm to limit its search for optimal cycles to simple cycles because it guarantees that no nonsimple cycle can have a lower average latency than one of the simple ones. This is a considerably easier task than enumerating all possible cycles since there are a variety of rather obvious algorithms available to help automate the process. As an example, the following is a list of all simple cycles and their average latencies for Fig. 3-10:

Simple Cycle		Average Latency
(7)		7
(5)		5
(1,7)	(greedy)	4
(3,7)		5
(5,7)		6
(5,3)	(greedy)	4
(3,5,7)		5
(5,3,7)		5

As this list shows, the optimal cycles are (1,7) and (5,3), both of which have an average latency of 4. The value of MAL for this diagram is 4. An optimal scheduling algorithm for this pipeline and reservation table should pick either of these cycles as a guide to when to make new initiations. Using any other cycle or path is non-optimal.

So far we have reduced the selection range for the optimal strategy algorithm from all possible paths to all simple cycles, a substantial reduction in work. But there is still a potentially large amount of work, particularly for a complex state diagram. Sometimes other reductions are possible, and our next step is to determine when they occur. Under certain conditions to be defined later, we may need to enumerate only greedy cycles where, from each state in the cycle, the next outbound arc chosen is always the one with minimal latency. In Fig. 3-10 a greedy cycle (1,7) encompasses states 1010101 and 1111111; (5,3) is also greedy and covers 1111101 and 1110101. While both of these cycles are optimal, this is not always the case. In Fig. 3-9 (3,8) is greedy but not optimal.

The enumeration of all greedy cycles is a particularly simple procedure.

Procedure: FIND ALL GREEDY CYCLES

   1 From the modified state diagram pick any state.

   2 Follow the sequence of minimum latency arcs until either the state from step 1 is encountered or there are no more arcs.

   3 In the former case the traced sequence is a greedy cycle. Record it and remove all states in it from the diagram.

   4 Pick another state and go back to step 2.

The validity of this procedure is obvious. The procedure takes at most N iterations of steps 2–4, where N is the number of states in the diagram. The average number is considerably less.

The conditions under which the restriction of the search to just greedy simple cycles is a direct consequence of the following lemma:

Lemma 3-3 (Shar, 1972) The average latency of any greedy simple cycle is less than or equal to the number of 1s in the initial collision vector.

Proof We assume the states making up a greedy cycle are labelled $S(1), S(2), \ldots,$ $S(n)$ with arcs of latency $L(1), \ldots, L(n)$ as in Fig. 3-12. Let $X(i)$ be the total number of 1s in the collision vector for state $S(i)$, and let X be the number of 1s in the initial collision vector. Now for these states and arcs to form a greedy cycle, the collision vector for $S(i)$ must have $L(i)$ left-most leading 1s, followed by a 0; otherwise $L(i)$ could not be a greedy arc.

Thus in the collision vector for $S(i + 1)$ there are at most $X(i) - L(i)$ 1s from the shifted $S(i)$, and X 1s from the copy of the initial collision vector. Stated as an inequality:

$$X(i + 1) \leqslant X(i) - L(i) + X$$

Starting at $S(2)$ and generating the chain of inequalities to $S(m)$, we get:

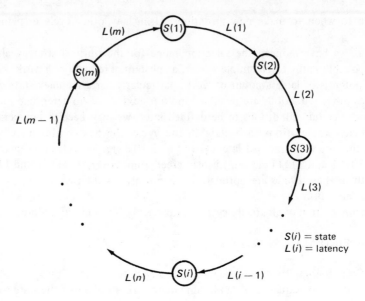

Figure 3-12   Diagram for Lemma 3-3.

$$X(2) \leqslant X(1) - L(1) + X$$
$$X(3) \leqslant X(2) - L(2) + X \leqslant X(1) - L(1) - L(2) + 2X$$
$$X(m) \leqslant X(m-1) - L(m-1) + X \leqslant X(1) - L(1) - \cdots - L(m-1) + (m-1)X$$

Using the relation $X(1) \leqslant X(m) - L(m) + X$ for the closing arc gives:

$$X(1) \leqslant X(1) - \sum_{i=1}^{m} L(i) + mX$$

Simplifying and rearranging the terms yields:

$$\frac{\sum\limits_{i=1}^{m} L(i)}{m} \leqslant X$$

But the left-hand side is the average latency of the cycle, and X is the number of 1s in the collision vector. Q.E.D.

This lemma places an upper bound on the average latency of any greedy cycle. Lemma 3-1 placed a lower bound on the average latency of any cycle. Together they bound the optimal simple cycles as follows:

Lemma 3-4 For any reservation table or state diagram:

$$\left.\begin{array}{r}\text{Maximum number of marks in any row}\\ \text{MAL}\\ \text{Average latency of any greedy cycle}\end{array}\right\}\begin{array}{l}\leqslant \text{MAL}\\ \leqslant \text{average latency of any greedy cycle}\\ \leqslant \text{number of 1s in initial collision}\\ \quad\text{vector}\end{array}$$

Proof From previous lemma.

This gives an immediate test for whether or not a greedy cycle is optimal. If the maximum number of marks in any row of the reservation table equals the number of 1s in the initial collision vector, then all greedy cycles are optimal and any of the ones enumerated by the previous procedure may be chosen. Further, even if the bounds are not equal, if any greedy cycle has an average latency equalling the lower bound, then it too is an optimal cycle. For example, reservation table B has a lower bound of 4 and an upper bound of 6. Enumerating the greedy cycles finds one cycle, (4), with an average latency equaling the lower bound. Once this case is found no further search need be done.

These bounds and the greedy cycles do not always directly determine the optimal cycle. For example, for reservation table A the lower bound is 3 and the upper bound is 4. Both greedy cycles (1,7) and (5,3) have average latencies equal to the upper bound. It is not until all simple cycles have been searched is it apparent that 3 is in fact unattainable and that 4 is the MAL.

To aid the designer the appendix lists the achievable MAL for all collision vectors of 9 bits or less, all greedy latency cycles, and all optimal cycles. By combining this information with the characteristics of the actual reservation table the designer can quickly develop optimal schedules for small problems.

3.2.5 Generation of Reservation Tables from Cycles

The previous sections have assumed as input a specification of a reservation table and developed from it the optimal cycles. The purpose of this section is to illustrate the possibility of a reverse analysis, that is, to start with a cycle and determine the properties of a reservation table that supports it. Such an analysis is useful in at least two applications. The first is during initial pipeline definition where the stages have not yet been partitioned, but the functions they are to compute and the overall solution rates are known. The second application occurs when dealing with a given reservation table whose MAL does not reach the lower bound and where explorations of slightly different or modified reservation tables may yield improved performance. This latter application is discussed in a later section. Much of the theory described in the following paragraphs originated with the work of Patel and Davidson (1976).

The key to determining which reservation tables can support a particular cycle lies in studying the structure of objects similar to the forbidden latency set. As defined earlier, an integer i is a member of this set only if two marks in any row of the reservation table are separated by i clocks. Position i in the equivalent collision vector has a value 1. Further, no latency or sum of successive latencies can equal this value i.

When starting with a cycle, the key is not in where 1s occur in the collision vector but where there *must* be 0s. This indicates how not to place marks. We define the *initiation interval* set G_C for a particular cycle C as the set of all integers i such that the time between some pair of initiations, but not necessarily successive ones, equals i. In more detail, if a latency cycle C is $(L(1), L(2), \ldots, L(K))$ then the equivalent latency sequence is

$$<L(1), \ldots, L(K), L(1), \ldots, L(K), L(1), \ldots>$$

and the initiation time sequence is

$$T(0), T(1), T(2), \ldots$$

where $T(j)$ is the starting time of the $(j + 1)$st initiation and equals the sum of the latencies between the previous initiations; i.e.,

$$T(j) = \sum_{i=1}^{j} L(i \bmod K)$$

Now G_C is:

$$G_C = \{ T(i) - T(j) \mid i > j \}$$

where $T(i)$ and $T(j)$ are in the initiation time sequence. Thus G_C is the set of all intervals between initiation when the initiations are made according to the cycle C.

For the cycle $(3,5,7)$ the latency sequence is $< 3,5,7,3,5,7,3,5,7, \ldots >$, the initiation time sequence is $[0,3,8,15,18,23,30,33, \ldots]$, and G_C is $\{ 3,5,7,8,10,12,15,18, 20,22,23,25, \ldots \}$. For example, the entry 22 is in G_C because initiations occur at 30 and 8. Other entries are in for equivalent reasons.

If an integer i is in G_C, then any reservation table supporting cycle C cannot have two marks in any row separated by i clocks. Otherwise i would be a forbidden latency and could not appear in G_C. Thus the ith bit in the initial collision vector must be 0. While this is key information, it is more constructive to consider the complement set H_C where $H_C = Z - G_C$ and Z is simply the set of all nonnegative integers. If i is a member of H_C, then it is permissible (but not mandatory) to separate two marks in a row by i clocks. Equivalently, it is permissible to have either a 0 or a 1 in position i of the initial collision vector. In fact such positions are the only places where 1s may be placed. Defining a row of a reservation table as equivalent to a set $\{z(1), z(2), \ldots \}$ where there is a mark only in time slot $z(i)$ yields the following lemma.

Lemma 3-5 Given a cycle C, all rows of any reservation table that support it must be representable as sets $\{z(1), z(2), \ldots\}$ where for all i, j, $|z(i) - z(j)| \in H_C$.

Proof Immediate.

When stated somewhat differently, this lemma gives a direct and easily applied test as to whether or not a particular reservation table can support a particular cycle as an initiation sequence. Such a test allows the designer to use experience and insight to guess an optimal solution and verify it without having to develop the entire modified state diagram.

Theorem 3-1 If a reservation table has a forbidden latency set F, then the cycle C is a valid initiation sequence only if F is a subset of H_C, or alternatively only if the intersection of F and G_C is null.

Proof From previous lemmas.

Although useful, these lemmas and theorems are difficult to deal with in practice because the sets G_C and H_C are infinite. More useful results are possible if instead of G_C and H_C we use the finite sets

$$G_C \bmod p = \{i \bmod p \mid i \in G_C\} - \{0\}$$
$$H_C \bmod p = Z_p - G_C$$

where p is the *period of the cycle* (i.e., *the sum of the latencies*), and Z is the set of integers $\{0, 1, 2, \ldots, p-1\}$[1].

$G_C \bmod p$ is simply the set of latencies between initiations separated by at most p clocks, and since the sequence repeats with period p, it is an accurate categorization of all latencies. For the cycle $(3, 5, 7)$ mentioned earlier, the period is 15; $G_C \bmod p$ is simply $\{3, 5, 7, 8, 10, 12\}$; and $H_C \bmod p$ is $\{0, 1, 2, 4, 6, 9, 11, 13, 14\}$.

The following lemmas define properties of $G_C \bmod p$ and $H_C \bmod p$ that are often useful in their construction:

Lemma 3-6 If g is in $G_C \bmod p$, then for all $i \geqslant 0$, $g + ip$ is a member of G_C.

Lemma 3-7 If $g \neq 0$, then g is a member of $G_C \bmod p$ only if $(p - g)$ is in $G_C \bmod p$ also.

Lemma 3-8 If $h \neq 0$, h is a member of $H_C \bmod p$ only if $(p - h)$ is in $H_C \bmod p$ also.

Proof Direct.

Direct modifications of Lemma 3-5 and Theorem 3-1 to the use of these finite sets in place of the infinite ones simplifies the testing of reservation tables for particular cycles. However, the construction of such reservation tables is still somewhat

---

[1]$x \bmod p = y$ if for some j, $x + jp = y$ and $0 \leqslant y \leqslant p - 1$. Example: 13 mod 7 = 6.

nebulous. What is needed is a simple set of relatively finite rules governing their construction. Such rules may be developed from the following definitions:

  1 If Z_p is the set of integers $\{0,1,\ldots,p-1\}$, two integers i, j from Z_p are *compatible with respect to* H_C mod p if $|i-j|$ mod p is in H_C mod p.
  2 A *compatibility class* with respect to H_C mod p is a subset of Z_p in which all pairs of elements are compatible.
  3 A *maximum compatibility class* with respect to H_C mod p is a compatibility class that is not a subset of any other compatibility class.

As an example, for the cycle $(3,5,7)$, the integers 9 and 13 are compatible because $|9-13|$ mod $15 = 4$ is a member of H_C mod p. Likewise, the set $\{0,9,13\}$ is a compatibility class, while $\{0,9,11,13\}$, $\{5,6,7\}$, and $\{0,1,2\}$ are each maximally compatible.

If some set of integers $\{z(1),z(2),\ldots\}$ is compatible, then it automatically satisfies Lemma 3-5 and is a valid representation of a row of a reservation table that supports the cycle. The converse is also true: the index set of any row of a reservation table supporting the cycle must be compatible. Summarizing and extending this gives the following key theorem

> **Theorem 3-2** For any cycle C with period p, any reservation table that supports this cycle as an initiation sequence must have rows of the form
>
> $$\{z(1) + i(1)p, z(2) + i(2)p, \ldots\}$$
>
> where $\{z(1), z(2), \ldots\}$ is a compatibility class of H_C mod p, and $i(1),i(2),\ldots$ are arbitrary integers.

Proof From previous lemmas.

This theorem allows us to construct the entire set of reservation tables that support some cycles. We simply compute all the maximal compatibility classes, and for each subset of some class use the above theorem to construct all possible rows.

While not difficult, the computation of the maximally compatible classes is more tedious than one might expect. The compatibility relation is not transitive; that is, x is compatible to y, and y is compatible to z, does not imply x is compatible to z. Thus it is not an *equivalence relation,* and therefore none of the algorithms for computing equivalence classes are applicable. Instead a more enumerative algorithm must be used. One example is the following, where compatibilities are checked one element at a time. Once an incompatibility is found, the set is split into two new ones, neither of which includes the incompatibility. The process is then repeated on each of the new sets. While all sets found by this algorithm are compatible, some are subsets of others and must be discarded after the algorithm is complete. Further, the algorithm computes only those maximally compatible subsets containing $z(1)$ (typically 0). A direct extension of the previous lemmas indicates that if some subset S is maximally compatible, then so is S' given by

$$S' = \{(s + a) \bmod p \mid 1 \leqslant a \leqslant p - 1, s \in S\}$$

Consequently, after completion of the basic algorithm the rest of the maximally compatible sets are computed by simple addition.

Procedure: FIND MAXIMALLY COMPATIBLE SUBSETS

1 Call FIND SETS ($H_C \bmod p$, 0). (Comment: This finds all compatible subsets that include 0.)
2 Remove from set of compatible sets all those that are subsets of others.
3 For each set and each value a in the range 1 to $p - 1$, create a new set where each element is the sum of a and an element of the original set, mod p.

Procedure: FIND SETS (S, j) (Comment: This computes all compatible subsets of set S.)

1 If $j \geqslant p$, then add S to the set of compatible sets and return.
2 If j is not in S, then call FIND SETS ($S, j + 1$) and then return.
3 If j is compatible with all other elements of S, then call FIND SETS ($S, j + 1$) and return.
4 Let U be set of all elements of S that are incompatible with j.
5 FIND SETS ($S - \{j\}, j + 1$).
6 FIND SETS ($S - U, j + 1$).

As an example, Fig. 3-13 illustrates the compatibility relation for the cycle (3,5,7) and Fig. 3-14 diagrams the application of the procedure FIND SETS to the appropriate $H_C \bmod p$. Note that not all the results are maximally compatible. The additive process (not shown) then forms the other maximally compatible sets. For example, from {0,2,4,13 } would come the sets {1,3,5,14 }, {2,4,6,0 }, {3,5,7,1 }, ... Note that some of these sets themselves are redundant and need not be listed.

The number of reservation tables that may be generated from these maximal sets is very large. Nothing in Theorem 3-2 constrains either the number of stages or the classes used to form any particular stage. Figure 3-15 illustrates several such variations for the cycle (3,5,7). To the right of each row is a listing of the set used in its generation. There are examples of all variations here. Some rows are simply maximally compatible sets; others are subsets of such a set. Some have a constant offset added to each element of some subset. Others have different multiples of 15 added to each. The example in Fig. 3-15e is of particular interest; it is reservation table A of Fig. 3-1 from which previous sections derived the (3,5,7) cycle. Given just the cycle, we have re-created a reservation table that accepts it as a valid initiation sequence.

3.2.6 Perfect Cycles

The previous section permits generation of reservation tables to support arbitrary latency cycles. With this capability in mind, one obvious question is whether a particular cycle is intrinsically better than another cycle. The primary parameter of comparison is, of course, average latency, and this can be computed directly from the

	j														
i	0	1	2	3	4	5	6	7	8	9	10	11	12	13	14
0	C	C	C	X	C	X	C	X	X	C	X	C	X	C	C
1	C	C	C	C	X	C	X	C	X	X	C	X	C	X	C
2	C	C	C	C	C	X	C	X	C	X	X	C	X	C	X
3	X	C	C	C	C	C	X	C	X	C	X	X	C	X	C
4	C	X	C	C	C	C	C	X	C	X	C	X	X	C	X
5	X	C	X	C	C	C	C	C	X	C	X	C	X	X	C
6	C	X	C	X	C	C	C	C	C	X	C	X	C	X	X
7	X	C	X	C	X	C	C	C	C	C	X	C	X	C	X
8	X	X	C	X	C	X	C	C	C	C	C	X	C	X	C
9	C	X	X	C	X	C	X	C	C	C	C	C	X	C	X
10	X	C	X	X	C	X	C	X	C	C	C	C	C	X	C
11	C	X	C	X	X	C	X	C	X	C	C	C	C	C	X
12	X	C	X	C	X	X	C	X	C	X	C	C	C	C	C
13	C	X	C	X	C	X	X	C	X	C	X	C	C	C	C
14	C	C	X	C	X	C	X	X	C	X	C	X	C	C	C

C = i and j are compatible
X = i and j are incompatible

Figure 3-13 Compatibility table for cycle (3,5,7).

cycle. However, comparing average latencies is valid only if the cycles themselves are supported on the same reservation tables or on reservation tables supportable on the same pipeline.

Perhaps a more intrinsic property of a cycle is how well it can utilize the underlying hardware of the pipeline. To repeat a previous definition, the *utilization* of a stage is the percentage of clock cycles during which data is flowing through it. Obviously, during any initiation cycle it is desirable to have at least one stage of the pipeline 100% utilized, for if no stage is so utilized, then some percentage of the pipeline's capability is wasted. Further, in such cases the cycle may not be optimal; there may be some other cycle with lower average latency (and thus higher performance) that does force utilization of at least one stage to 100%.

Using some of the results of the previous section it is possible to place an upper bound on the utilization of any stage of a pipeline/reservation table supporting a particular cycle. Cycles where this upper bound is 100% are called *perfect* and clearly hold at least the promise of more economic implementation than nonperfect cycles.

As mentioned earlier, the utilization of a stage can be computed from the ratio of the number of marks in that row of the reservation table to the average latency of the cycle. However, Theorem 3-2 states that any row in a reservation table supporting a particular cycle must originate with a compatibility class of H_C mod p. Combining these two statements yields the following theorem:

Theorem 3-3 For any particular cycle C the maximum possible utilization of any stage of any pipeline/reservation table supporting that cycle is no greater than

m/L, where m is the number of elements in the largest compatibility class of H_C mod p and L is the average latency of the cycle.

Further, for any cycle there exist pipelines/reservation tables that achieve this bound for one or more stages.

Proof The bound m/L follows directly from Theorem 3-2, because the number of marks in any row equals the number of elements in the compatibility class used

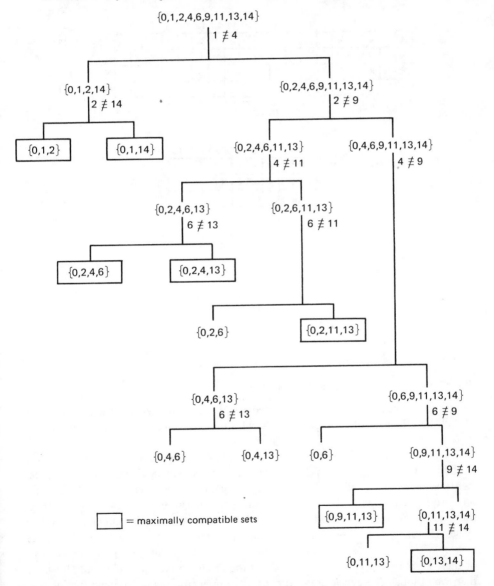

Figure 3-14 Application of procedure FIND SETS.

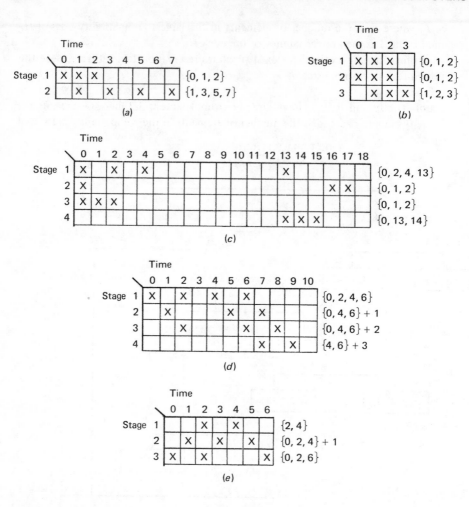

Figure 3-15 Sample reservation tables to support (3,5,7).

to construct it. The bound can be achieved by using in the construction of any or all rows the maximal compatible class with the largest number of elements. Q.E.D.

According to this theorem a cycle is perfect only if m equals L. For the example of the previous section, the cycle (3,5,7) with average latency 5 has at most four elements in any compatibility class (see Fig. 3-14) and consequently has a maximum stage utilization of only 80%. Thus, it is not perfect. This is particularly evident from the analysis of reservation table A—one of the reservation tables supported by this cycle. The analysis of Sec. 3.2.4 indicates that there are several cycles with average latency of 4 that are also valid for this reservation table including (5,3) and (1,7). Both of these cycles are perfect and optimal for the given reservation table. Note however that even though the cycles are optimal for the reservation table, the fact that no row represents an entire maximal compatible class means that no stage is used 100% of the time even with the optimal cycle. We could add other marks to the table in certain spots and not change the MAL. For example, a mark at (3,4) has no effect on the modified state diagram, but when the table is scheduled by (5,3), 100% utilization of stage 3 occurs. This may help the designer in managing and partitioning logic.

One important class of cycles is always perfect, as given by the following lemma.

Lemma 3-9 If a cycle is *constant,* i.e., of the form (L), then it is perfect.

Proof For such a cycle, $H_C \bmod p$ is $\{0,1,2,\ldots,L-1\}$ and the set $\{0,1,\ldots,L-1)$ is compatible. This set has L elements and thus the bound on utilization is $L/L = 1$. Q.E.D.

When starting from scratch to develop a reservation table, it is clear that a designer should consider primarily perfect cycles of the desired latency. In addition, if some row in the final reservation table is constructed from the largest maximally compatible class, then the original cycle is automatically optimal and no further state analysis is required. Further, even if the constructed reservation table does not achieve 100% utilization in any one stage, the original cycle may still be optimal. This is true of reservation table A where all rows have 3 marks, but the optimal latency is 4. Verification, however, does require a state analysis.

3.2.7 Delay Insertion for Increased Performance

Perhaps the most common problem in pipeline control occurs when an existing set of pipelined hardware is asked to perform a new type of computation. In such cases the designer has little if any control over the new reservation table to implement that computation, and a state analysis shows that the best possible initiation sequence does not reach the lower bound predicted by Lemma 3-1.

Therefore, a direct implementation will leave the hardware under-utilized.[2] It would clearly be of benefit if the reservation table could somehow be modified so that the overall structure is unchanged but overall performance increased.

Such a technique does exist, and paradoxically it decreases the average latency down to the lower bound from Lemma 3-1 by increasing the time per computation. This increase in individual computation time occurs as a byproduct of selectively delaying some of the marks in each row of the reservation table. The number of marks per row is unchanged. Each unit of delay moves a mark one clock unit to the right. Briefly, the location of the delays is chosen to force each row of the reservation table to match some compatibility class of a cycle that the designer wishes the reservation table to follow. For example, Fig. 3-16a illustrates a reservation table (due to Patel and Davidson, 1976) where the lower bound on achievable latency is 3 but for which the optimal cycle (4) has an average latency of 4. Judicious insertion of delays results in Fig. 3-16b—a reservation table with the same number of marks in each row and nearly doubled compute time, but for which the cycle (1,5) is a valid initiation sequence.

---

[2] This has happened many times to the author during the implementation of new algorithms for the IBM 3838 Array Processor.

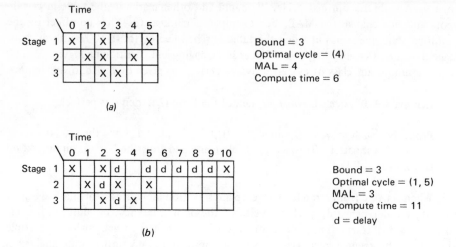

Figure 3-16 Sample use of delays. (a) Unmodified reservation station. (b) Delayed version.

This cycle has an average latency of 3, equaling the theoretical lower bound, and is 25% faster than the nondelayed version. The rest of this section describes the procedures involved in developing such modifications.

There are two kinds of delays, an input delay and an output delay. A one-unit *input delay* is equivalent to inserting an extra stage of noncompute logic just in front of the logic for a stage (cf. Fig. 2-24). Thus, although a value to be input to the delayed stage is computed by the previous stage at the same time as in the nondelayed version, it does not reach the actual logic of the delayed stage until an extra clock has passed. Similarly a one-unit *output delay* is equivalent to inserting an extra stage of noncompute logic just after the logic for a stage. Thus, although a value is computed at the same time as it would be in the nondelay case, it is not delivered to the next stage until an extra clock has passed. An output delay on one stage is clearly equivalent to an input delay on the rest.

Such delays may be implemented through the physical addition of more logic, or as is more commonly the case, by selectively replacing staging latches within the pipeline by dual-ported register files as described in Sec. 2.2.3 and then controlling the addresses going to each port. The latter approach is by far the most common since it allows flexible microprogrammed control over the amount of delay inserted on an as-needed basis.

The basic technique for delay insertion guides the placement of input delays in each row of the original reservation table. Such delays may force either input or output delays on marks in other rows. Whether they are required depends on factors not expressible directly within the reservation table, such as which stages' inputs depend on which other stages' outputs. This in turn depends on how the functions performed by the stages interrelate at the original problem level. For example, Fig. 3-17a illustrates a piece of a reservation table where the mark at stage 2, time i is to be delayed two units. If none of the other marks shown in the segment depends on this mark, then the reservation table after the delay would look like Fig. 3-17b. Only two units of input delay are needed at stage 2 starting at time i. The input to the first of these extra delays must be the same quantity input to $(2, i)$ in Fig. 3-17a.

As another example, if the mark at $(4, i + 1)$ represents a computation that requires the output of both the $(2, i)$ mark and other information present in the pipe at time i, then additional input delays would be needed for $(4, i + 1)$ with its mark moved two places to the right. This is shown in Fig. 3-17c. If $(4, i + 2)$ depended on $(4, i + 1)$, then moving $(4, i + 1)$ to the right also requires moving $(4, i + 2)$ to the right (plus moving all other marks representing dependent calculations). Yet another possibility is shown in computations dependent on both marks $(1, i)$ and $(2, i)$. Here the output of $(1, i)$ must be delayed two clocks. It is clear that in addition to the reservation table, the designer must know the precise dependency constraints for the problem being solved.

Under certain conditions any reservation table, even considering interrow dependencies, can be modified in a similar fashion to accept any cycle as an initiation sequence. The key to this lies in the following theorem:

Theorem 3-4 Given (1) any compatibility class from any cycle, and (2) any row of any reservation table, such that the number of marks in the row equals the

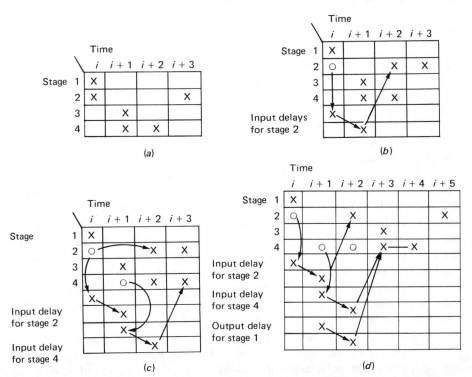

Figure 3-17 Sample delay and effects of processing constraints. (a) Mark at $(2, i)$ to be delayed two units. (b) After delay—no dependencies. (c) After delay: $(4, i + 1)$ depends on $(2, i)$. (d) Dependencies on $(1, i)$ and $(2, i)$.

number of elements in the compatibility class, then assuming no inter-row dependencies, sufficient delays can always be added to that row to force it to match the compatibility class or a modification to that class as described in Theorem 3-2.

Proof By construction as follows: We assume the marks in the rows fall at indices $a(1)$, $a(2)$, ..., and the values in the compatibility class are $c(1)$, $c(2)$, ... (not necessarily in increasing order). Starting with the first element of each, if $a(1)$ is less than $c(1)$, then $c(1) - a(1)$ input delays are inserted in front of the first mark of that row, and all marks to the right also move right $c(1) - a(1)$ positions. If $a(1)$ is greater than $c(1)$, then the value $a(1) - c(1)$ is added modulo the cycle's period p to each element of the compatibility class to create a new but equivalent class to be used for the rest of the processing. The rest of the marks are then processed in order from left to right. If $a(i)$ is less than $c(i)$, the ith mark is delayed $c(i) - a(i)$ clocks, and all marks to the right of i in that row move right. If $a(i)$ is greater than $c(i)$, then sufficient multiples of the cycles period p are added to $c(i)$ to reverse the inequality. Mark $a(i)$ is then delayed by the difference. Q.E.D.

As an example of this procedure, the maximal compatibility classes of the cycle (1,5) include $\{0,2,4\}$ and $\{0,3\}$. The first row of Fig. 3-16a has three marks at $\{0,2,5\}$. When matched against $\{0,2,4\}$ the first two elements already match $[a(1) = 0 = c(1)$, and $a(2) = 2 = c(2)]$. However, $c(3) = 4$ is less than $a(3) = 5$. Adding the period 6 to $c(3)$ yields 10, a number greater than $a(3)$. Delaying $a(3)$ by the difference of 5 clocks yields the first row of Fig. 3-16b.

In row 2, $a(1) = 1$ is greater than $c(1)$ in $\{0,2,4\}$. Therefore we construct the equivalent compatibility class $\{1,3,5\}$ and delay the second mark by one clock. The third mark falls in immediately.

The third row of Fig. 3-16a is matched against the class $\{2,4\}$ by applying a one-unit delay to the second mark. Note that $\{2,4\}$ is a subset of $\{0,2,4\}$ but is still a compatibility class.

Although other delay patterns are possible, this one, Fig. 3-16b, has the distinct advantage of being a valid computational sequence regardless of what inter-row dependencies exist. In fact the placement of the delays was made assuming that the computation represented by any mark at times $i + 1$ and beyond requires all outputs of stages active at time i. Thus when the mark at (2,2) is delayed, the mark at (3,3) is delayed equivalently so that it does not start until the first is complete. Likewise the mark at (2,4) moves to (2,5) to accommodate the delay in (3,3), but no new delays are needed because it remains in the same position relation to (2,2) after the delay. The delay to (3,4) has another effect, that is the introduction of an output delay after (1,2) to save its result one additional clock. Although input delays are shown applied to the original mark (1,5), an equivalent implementation would delay the output of (2,5).

Theoretically the procedure described by Theorem 3-4 allows the designer to pick *any* cycle whose average latency is not less than the maximum number of marks in any row and to adjust the reservation table to accept it as a latency sequence. This includes constant cycles, and in particular constant cycles (L), where L equals the maximum number of marks in any row of the reservation table. Such cycles are perfect (Lemma 3-9), resulting in reservation tables whose MALs achieve the bound of Lemma 3-1 and for which at least one stage of the pipeline is 100% utilized. Further, as shown by the previous examples, even dependencies between the computations implied by each mark can be factored in, although perhaps at the expense of additional delays.

Although all this is theoretically possible, there are constraints in real systems that sometimes prevent optimal performance from being achieved. First, not all staging latches are designed in as files or other complex structures. Thus we are not free to insert delays arbitrarily. This is not usually a severe restriction since typically the latches that are not replaced are those that are within some piece of linear pipeline where there is only one way for data to flow under any conditions. A good example of this is within a pipelined multiplier. The latches at the entry and exit are converted into files, but within the multiplier simple staging latches are used.

Perhaps a more severe constraint on implementing an arbitrary cycle is that the register files used for implementing the delays are finite. Since each unit of delay applied to a particular mark requires roughly one register in the file, there is a maximum delay that can be inserted in any one spot. In some cases this may prevent some cycles from being implemented. A good example of such a potential situation is in the first row of Fig. 3-16 where the third mark must be delayed by an amount approaching the period of the cycle. As the number of stages of a pipeline increases, the period of a typical cycle also has a tendency to increase with a concurrent increase in potential delay requirements. The designer of a pipeline should take these delays into account when planning the initial architecture.

3.3   DYNAMICALLY CONFIGURED PIPELINES

In dynamically configured pipelines each initiation may be from a different reservation table. This has a profound effect on scheduling. First, there may be times when more than one initiation may be made simultaneously during the same clock. This occurs when two or more different reservation tables have no overlap of stages and have no collisions with any previous initiation of any type. Second, there is no single definition of an optimal schedule. In a static pipeline all initiations are of the same type; therefore a strategy that maximizes the processing rate of this type is clearly optimal. When multiple reservation tables are handled there may be several equally valid optimal strategies including:

1   Maximizing the total number of initiations of any kind.

2   Maximizing the total number of initiations given that out of this total a percentage must be from each type of reservation table.

3   Minimizing the total time required to handle a specific sequence of initiation table types.

Depending on the circumstances, a designer may wish to optimize in any of these ways.

This section extends the state diagram approach of Sec. 3-1 to handle the dynamic case. Although the procedures are more complex and the available analysis techniques less thorough, they still give more insight into the problem than any other current approach.

3.3.1 Modified State Diagrams

The notion of characterizing the state of a static pipeline as a collision vector directly generalizes to the dynamic case. At each clock a *collision matrix* indicates the set of possible initiations. A collision matrix C is an $r \times d$ binary matrix, where r is the number of reservation tables and d the maximum compute time of any of the tables. In comparison with a collision vector, the (j,k)th element of a collision matrix is 0 only if making a new initiation k time units from now from reservation table type j will cause no collisions with any current initiation. At this point we could develop the rules for constructing state diagrams much as we did for the static case. However, such diagrams increase in complexity even faster than before, making use of a modified state diagram almost mandatory.

The first difference in such diagrams from those for the static case is that there is no single initial state. Instead for r reservation tables there are r initial states, the ith of which assumes that the first initiation at time 0 is of type i. The collision matrices for these states have the special name *initial collision matrices*. As in the static case these matrices represent collisions resulting from one initiation following exactly one other. The jth row of the ith such matrix, $\mathbf{CM}_i$, is the collision vector between an initiation of type i and a later initiation of type j. Thus $\mathbf{CM}_i$ (j,k) is 0 only if shifting reservation table j k places right, and overlaying it on to a copy of reservation table i results in no collisions. In all cases the ith row of $\mathbf{CM}_i$ is the same as the initial collision vector if reservation table i were used in a static configuration. The other rows of $\mathbf{CM}_i$ are thus *cross collision vectors*. For example, the collision matrices for a pipeline employing only reservation tables A and B of Fig. 3-1 are:

$$\mathbf{CM}_A = \begin{bmatrix} 10101010 \\ 01111000 \end{bmatrix} \qquad \mathbf{CM}_B = \begin{bmatrix} 01111100 \\ 11100111 \end{bmatrix}$$

Actual construction of the rest of the diagram is similar to that for the static case. For each state and each column within that state's collision matrix containing at least one 0, there is a set of arcs leading to new states. Generation of the new state consists of shifting the old collision matrix left and ORing in copies of the appropriate collision matrices. The complication in this process occurs when a column contains more than one 0. Here several different initiation types are possible, and there must be a separate arc for each possible combination of initiations. Each combination is termed an *initiation set*. For example, if in some collision matrix column k has 0s in rows 1, 3, and 4, then there are seven possible arcs with latency k, namely those associated with initiation sets $\{1\}$, $\{3\}$, $\{4\}$, $\{1,3\}$, $\{1,4\}$, $\{3,4\}$, and $\{1,3,4\}$. Further, a 0 in a column means only that there is no danger of collisions with any of the previously started initiations; it says nothing about collisions with any other initiation in the same initiation set. Consequently, not all initiations sets are valid. For any initiation set to have its own arc, there must be no possible collisions among the set when all are started simultaneously. This is equivalent to saying that the composite overlay of all reservation tables in a set has no matches. Such a set is called a *compatible initiation set*. Thus out of a state where the kth column has multiple zeros, there will be an arc with latency k for every, and only those, compatible initiation set that is a subset of the rows containing zeros. Each such arc typically leads to a different state. To keep track of which initiation causes which transition, each arc includes as its label not only the latency but also the equivalent compatible initiation set.

Any easy way to generate all compatible initiation sets from the location of zeros in a column is to consider at first only maximally compatible initiation sets. For any initiation set S a subset C is maximally compatible with respect to S if C is compatible and the addition to C of any reservation table in S but not in C causes the resulting set to be noncompatible. For any set S there may be more than one, possibly overlapping, maximally compatible subsets. Once all such maximally compatible sets are known, then the set of all compatible sets from S consists of all subsets of the maximally compatible set. The following lemma yields an efficient procedure for determining these maximally compatible sets.

Lemma 3-10 An initiation set S is compatible only if for all i and j in S, $CM_i (j,0)$ $= 0$, where CM_i is the initial collision matrix for reservation table i.

Proof Left to reader.

A procedure for creating these maximally compatible sets may then be constructed from the procedure described in Sec. 3.2.5 with the above lemma used as the test for compatibility. Once these maximally compatible sets are computed, construction of all subsets of these sets gives the complete collection of compatible initiation sets.

Bringing all the above discussion together yields the following procedure for creating the modified state diagram for a dynamically configured pipeline:

Procedure: DYNAMIC MODIFIED STATE DIAGRAM

1 Include as states one for each of the initial collision matrices.

2 For each unprocessed state and for the kth column in the state's collision matrix such that there is at least one zero in it, generate all compatible initiation sets.

3 For each initiation set take all specified initial collision matrices and OR together.

4 Delete the first k columns of the current states collision matrix, pad zeros on the back, and OR with the result of step 3. Call this a new state and couple it with the original state by an arc having both the value k and the initiation set on it.

5 Construct all initiation sets assuming a column of all zeros. Then for each state in the diagram and each initiation set construct an arc and appropriate destination state with value $\geqslant d$ and the listing of the set, where d is the compute time.

Figure 3-18 illustrates the modified state diagram when either reservation table A or B of Fig. 3-1 may be chosen. As can be seen, it is considerably more complex than either diagram for reservation table A or B alone (Figs. 3-9 and 3-10).

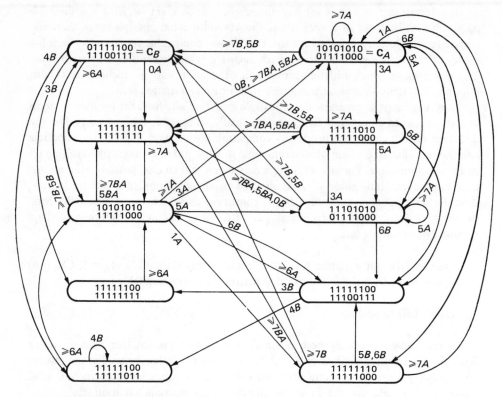

Figure 3-18 Modified state diagram for dynamic pipeline.

3.3.2 Analysis for Dynamic Pipelines

As in the static case, the modified state diagram for dynamic pipelines represents all possible valid initiation sequences. As mentioned earlier, however, there is no single globally applicable measure of performance. Depending on the system one of several different performance criteria is possible. Of course, each criterion requires a totally separate method of analysis.

There are at least three different performance criteria that make sense in the real world. These are:

1 Determination of the maximum number of initiations of any kind in any order per time unit.

2 Determination of the maximum number of initiations per time unit given that a certain percentage must come from each reservation table, but there is no order imposed on the sequence.

3 Determination of the maximum number of initiations per time unit given some specific sequence of initiation types to be performed.

From 1 to 3 these criteria become more and more restrictive. The first is a measure of the maximum possible throughput of the pipeline under any circumstances and represents an upper bound for the other two. The second criterion is useful when it is known that there is some statistical mix to the initiation types (e.g., 50% type A, 20% type B, and 30% type C), but there is little knowledge of the interrelationship of one initiation to the next. The third criterion, the most restrictive, is a measure of performance when a specific sequence of events is to occur.

If the pipeline under consideration is one that executes SISD instructions (i.e., a conventional computer), then the first measure is simply the maximum possible number of instructions per second that may be executed under any circumstances. Measure 2 attempts to bring in some real characteristics of programs (such as approximately 40% of all instructions are typically LOAD). Measure 3 asks for maximum performance for some benchmark program. Depending on what the designer is trying to do and the amount of information available, any of the above criteria may be used.

Performance measurements of the first kind are most easily performed since they are similar to the analyses applied to static diagrams. The major difference is that when computing the average latency of a cycle, the period is not divided by the number of elements in the cycle. Instead it is divided by the total number of entries in all initiation sets in the arcs making up the cycle. This accounts for all initiations made even when two or more are started at the same time. For example, in Fig. 3-18 the cycle $(5AB, 7A)$ has an average latency of 4, not 6. Since more than one initiation may be made per clock, this average latency may drop below 1, a situation not possible in the static case.

Because more than one reservation table may be initiated at any one time, there is no way of determining simply from the reservation tables an accurate lower bound on the average latency. This is again in contrast to the static case where Lemma 3-1 bounds latency by the number of marks in a row. About the only bound that can be computed a priori is given by the following lemma:

Lemma 3-11 The average latency of any cycle for a dynamically configured pipeline is bounded below by $1/n$, where n is the maximum number of elements in any initiation set.

Proof From the definition of initiation sets.

The second measure of performance asks for the minimum average latency given that some percentage of all initiations came from each reservation table. The collection of percentages is termed a *mix*. The goal of an optimal scheduling algorithm in this case is to find a cycle with minimum average latency whose initiations achieve the mix. Several variations of this are possible, only one of which has been studied in detail. This variation makes the additional assumption that at any time the scheduling algorithm is free to pick any of the reservation tables to make an initiation. There are no constraints either on the times when each reservation table may be initiated or on the order of initiation. Adding such constraints complicates the problem tremendously.

The work of Thomas and Davidson (1974) attempts to solve this problem by extending some of the results for the static case. As before, a simple cycle is defined as one that does not traverse any node in the state diagram more than once. Each such simple cycle has its own mix of initiation types that it achieves. For example, in Fig. 3-18 the simple cycle $(3A,5A,5AB,7A,7A)$ has the mix $\frac{1}{6}$ B's and $\frac{5}{6}$ A's. Not all such simple cycles need be considered. Instead we find only those simple cycles that achieve the lowest average latency for their particular mix. These cycles are termed *good simple cycles*. For example, for the mix $\frac{1}{6}$ B's and $\frac{5}{6}$ A's, the cycle $(1A,7A,3A,5A,0B, 7A)$ is good.

Given any set of good simple cycles, any mix within certain ranges may be implemented by some combination of the component cycles. These combinations may include multiple copies of some cycles. For example, the cycles $(1A,7A,3A,5A,0B,7A)$ and $(3B, 8B)$ will implement any mix where the percentage of B's is between 16.66 and 100%. Repeating the first cycle twice and the second cycle three times results in a mix with 44.44% B's.

Extending this idea results in a rather complex branch-and-bound and linear programming algorithm that for any mix computes a collection of good simple cycles to achieve that mix with minimum average latency (see Thomas and Davidson, 1974). The only drawback to this algorithm is that the collection of cycles is not guaranteed to be *connected;* that is, it may not be possible to form a single closed path in the state diagram that traverses all and only those desired cycles. Implementing such a schedule may then require coupling of the cycles by paths that are less than optimal with a resulting loss in performance. Consequently, the algorithm is not an optimal scheduler as much as it is a determination of a potentially reachable lower bound in minimum average latency.

The third measure of performance specifies some definite sequence of initiation types to be followed. This corresponds to the specification of a benchmark, a much better indication of real machine performance. Unfortunately, not much is known about determining optimal performance in such circumstances except for the obvious exhaustive search approaches. Further, a schedule that is optimal for one benchmark is probably not optimal for another one. About the best that can be done in such circumstances is to study simple variations of a greedy strategy that at each state always choses from those arcs with appropriate initiation sets the one with minimum latency.

3.4 IMPLEMENTATION OF CONTROL FUNCTIONS

Up to now the discussion has been largely theoretical, that is, what are the properties of and how does one determine an optimal schedule for controlling a pipeline. Real pipelines, of course, must somehow develop and be guided by such schedules while they are operational. This guidance consists of two points: the first is determining when a new initiation is to be started; the second is the actual shepherding of each initiation through the pipeline on a stage-by-stage basis. Depending on the pipeline these functions may be done by hardware, microprogramming, or a combination of the two. This section addresses these variations.

3.4.1 Hardware Initiation Control

The first major control responsibility is determining when a new initiation can be made. This is a function of both the properties of the reservation tables involved and the timing of when data is actually available for input to the pipeline. There are several

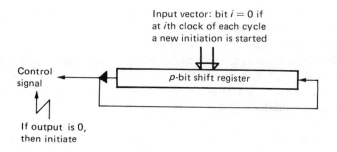

Figure 3-19 Initiation for a static pipeline.

typical combinations ranging from statically configured pipelines with rigid timing to dynamically configured pipelines with the arrival times of data indeterminant in advance.

The simplest case is a statically configured pipeline where the function to be performed rarely if ever changes and input data is always available when called for. In this situation all the theory of the previous sections can be used to determine what is an optimal or at least acceptable schedule. From this cycle of period p a p-bit vector may be created. The ith bit of this vector is 0 if at the ith time unit of each cycle a new initiation is started. For the cycle (2,3,2) this would correspond to 1010010. Then a simple shift register controller such as in Fig. 3-19 can take this vector and cyclically rotate it once per clock. If at the start of any clock the left-most bit is 0, then during this clock a new initiation is started.

Other variations of this simple timing scheme are possible. This particular one is presented because of versatility and commonality with the more complex case discussed below. The versatility in the controller lies in its ability to adapt to new schedules to accommodate periodic changes in either the function to be performed or the timing of input data arrival. However for each variation the desired schedule must be computed in advance. The system has no self-scheduling capabilities.

The next most complex and relatively common case is that of a statically configured pipeline where the arrival of data cannot be predicted in advance. This might be the case when the data comes from a shared memory, and periodically the memory may be busy with other requests when the pipeline wants data. In such cases it is not possible to determine the exact optimal schedule to be followed either in advance or even in real-time; we cannot look into near future and determine data arrival time. However, an ingenious controller due to Davidson (1971) can follow in real-time a greedy strategy. With this in mind the pipeline designer can configure the reservation table so that all greedy cycles are either optimal or near optimal. The techniques of Sec. 3.2 are used to do this. The result is a simple controller that delivers very nearly the full potential of the pipeline even under dynamically changing circumstances.

Figure 3-20 illustrates this controller. The organization is basically an implementation of the rules for generating the original state diagram representation of the pipelines activities (Sec. 3.2.2). As before, the central element is a shift register. Here, however, the shift register contains during each clock the collision vector representation of the pipeline's current state. Operation is as follows:

1 At the beginning of each clock the shift register is shifted left one bit position, with the rightmost bit filled with a 0.

2 If the leftmost bit is a 1, no initiation may be made during this clock period.

3 If the leftmost bit is a 0 and data is available, an initiation is started, and the initial collision vector is ORed into the shift register.

4 If the leftmost bit is a 0 but no data is available, no initiation is made, and the shift register is not modified.

If data is always available, the contents of the shift register clearly follow greedy cycles. If data is not available when a greedy latency comes up, the opportunity is skipped, causing the controller to leave the greedy strategy. However, as soon as data is available, the next available latency is chosen, and after that the controller follows the greedy cycle out of the resulting new state.

As before, this is a very versatile controller; only a change to the initial collision vector is needed to change the behavior of the system.

If the initial collision vector never changes, then a modification of this controller (Fig. 3-21) can follow other than greedy strategies. Here the output of the shift register feeds a read-only memory (ROM) or programmable logic array (PLA) in a table look-up mode. For each possible state of the pipeline that has a leading 0 there is an entry in the table that indicates whether or not an initiation may be made at this time. This output is combined as before with a "data available" signal to determine whether or not an initiation is actually made. The entries in the table are selected to guide the pipeline back to an optimum cycle whenever possible. Of course, as before, this system has no way of determining future data arrival times; therefore it still may not produce optimal initiation sequences.

Perhaps the most complex case arises when the pipeline is dynamically configured and data for each kind of function arrives independently of the others and with no time predictability. A good example is a stream of instructions arriving at an instruction decode unit. Again it is not feasible to dynamically compute and follow optimal schedules. However, as in the previous case it is possible to implement a controller that

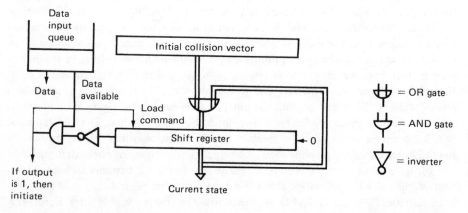

Figure 3-20 Greedy cycle initiation.

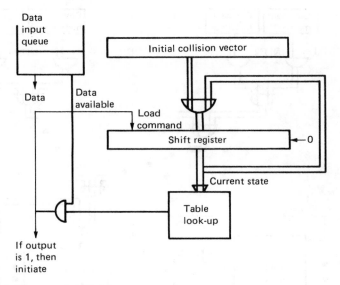

Figure 3-21 Arbitrary cycle initiator.

will consistently follow a greedy strategy where as many initiations as possible are made at the first opportunity. Figure 3-22 represents such a unit and is a generalization of Davidson et al. (1975). There are m initial collision matrices with m shift registers representing the current collision matrix state. All shift registers shift and load together. The output of the ith shift register indicates whether or not an initiation of type i may be made at the current time. These outputs are ANDed with the appropriate data available signals from the input data buffers, and they are presented to a table look-up function (again perhaps a ROM or PLA). From these inputs the table selects the largest possible compatible initiation set (Sec. 3.3), and all chosen data types are initiated into the pipeline simultaneously. The collision matrix is then updated by ORing it with copies of the appropriate initial collision matrices. As in Fig. 3-20 this controller could be expanded to handle somewhat more arbitrary initiation sequences, but because of the increased size of the collision matrix the expansion is probably too costly for all but the most trivial pipeline.

3.4.2 Intrapipeline Control

Once an initiation has been started the data associated with the initiation is to flow through the pipeline along the path depicted by the associated reservation table. The mechanism that scheduled and triggered the initiation is no longer concerned with the data and its handling. However, in all but the most trivial pipelines a great deal of control activity is still needed to complete the initiation and guide it to conclusion. These activities are all related to direct control of the pipeline's operations and include:

1 Generation of an "initiation complete" signal
2 Activation of logic within a stage

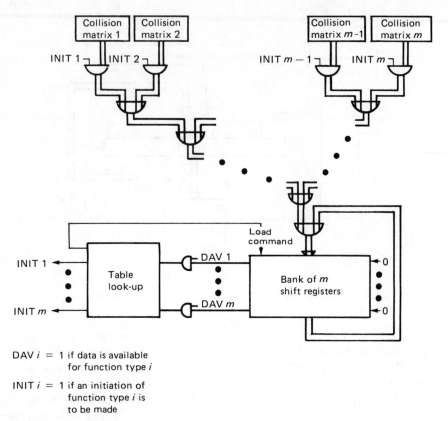

DAV i = 1 if data is available
            for function type i

INIT i = 1 if an initiation of
            function type i is
            to be made

Figure 3-22 Greedy initiator for dynamic pipelines.

3 Route control
4 Function selection within a stage

Generation of an initiation complete signal may not be related to the pipeline's control as much as to external devices that may need notification of a function's completion. A common example is a memory controller that must know when a function completes so that the result can be captured and stored in memory.

Although not always necessary, there are cases where the logic within a stage must know whether or not it is processing data during any particular cycle. For example, the stage of a floating-point adder pipeline that includes overflow and underflow error checks does not want to flag the occurrence of an error unless it is sure that the bit pattern being processed is truly data and not simply a null cycle.

Route control involves setting up the paths between stages needed to implement the reservation tables. For some simple statically configured pipelines no such control is necessary. For very complex dynamic pipelines the route control may depend on the initiation type being executed and the current execution step. This may require individual control of the inputs to each stage at each clock unit.

Even assuming that all paths are set up and that each stage knows when it has valid data, it may still be necessary to deliver unique control messages to each stage at each clock. These messages may alter in some way the function performed by the stage. A good example is a stage containing a general logic unit capable of ANDing or ORing its two inputs. Different reservation table types and different steps within the reservation table may require different logical operations.

There are many ways of implementing all these control modes. A simple implementation of the first two, "initiation complete" and "data valid," involves adding an extra bit per staging latch that is clocked just as the others in its groups are, but is connected to the extra bit in the next staging latch by "noncompute" logic that simply replicates the value (cf. Cotten, 1965). Figure 3-23 illustrates such an implementation. Whenever a new initiation is begun, a 1 enters the first of these extra bits. This signals the first stage that it now has valid data. At each clock this 1 propagates to the next stage and activates it. Finally, at the last stage this extra bit represents completion of the operation. We note that whenever two or more stages are activated at the same time (multiple marks in one column of the reservation table) both stages will receive a 1 in their extra bit positions. Likewise when two stages feed a single stage with two operands, its extra bit is set only once. Finally this implementation provides some error detection capabilities such as detecting when two different stages attempt

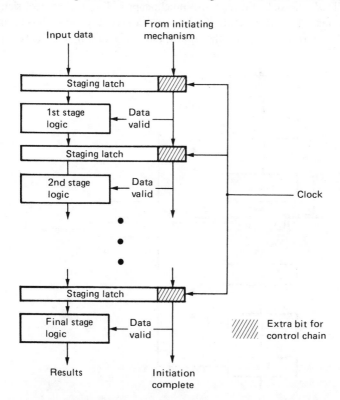

Figure 3-23   Timing chain for stage activation.

to load the same staging latch at the same time (a collision). Of course if the initiation mechanism is working correctly, this should never occur.

The route control and function selection modes are also closely related, and they are often provided by similar hardware mechanisms. Depending on the initiating mechanism, the complexity of the reservation table, and degree of reconfiguration, these mechanisms may fall between two extremes of *time-stationary* controls and *data-stationary* controls (Kogge, 1977a).

A time-stationary control mechanism provides the route control and function select signals for the entire pipeline from a single source external to the pipeline. In Fig. 3-24 the time-stationary control signals provide simultaneous control of the logic of one stage, the route into another stage's latch, and addresses for a register file in a third.

For statically configured pipelines these controls may be hardwired or changed only occasionally when the cycle or reservation table changes. For more dynamic pipelines there may be a change in these global signals at every clock. The source of the controls may be anything from a register to the output of a microprogrammed control unit (Sec. 3.4.3). The main characteristic, however, is that at each unit of time these controls govern the entire state of the machine.

The opposite extreme is represented by data-stationary controls. Here the control signals "follow" the data through the pipeline providing the control signals at each stage as needed. There is no centralized control source. Instead each time an initiation is made the control signals for the appropriate reservation table enter the pipeline

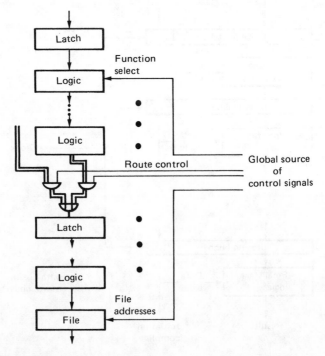

Figure 3-24 Time-stationary hardware controls.

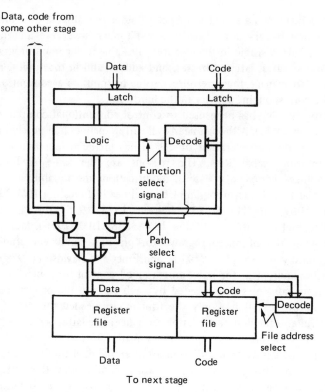

Figure 3-25 Data-stationary hardware controls.

along with the data. As long as the initiation unit has guaranteed that no collisions will occur, there is no danger of two controls attempting to use the same stage simultaneously. Figure 3-25 diagrams one possible data-stationary controller patterned after the timing chain of Fig. 3-23. Here the extra stage activation bit has been replaced by a set of bits containing some kind of code (perhaps initially the number of the reservation table).

As this code enters each stage it may be decoded to determine what the logic should do, what path to take next, and perhaps what file entry to save the results in. In addition, some logic may modify this code on the basis of the stages result or other information. Although this arrangement is certainly more flexible than the time-stationary approach, it is also more expensive in terms of hardware. It is up to the designer to determine whether the cost is warranted.

3.4.3 Microprogrammed Controls

A computer program as it is conventionally defined is a stored sequence of steps that directs a computer to perform a calculation. The resources the programmer must control to perform these calculations include registers, memory, and I/O devices. *Micro-programming* is an extension of this concept down to the control level of the com-

puter. Here too there is a stored sequence of steps that directs the computer to perform some action, but the desired results are at a much lower level and more related to
the hardware. This is visible in the resources available to the microprogrammer, which
include registers, gates, latches, busses, and adders, and in the typical microprogram
whose goal is to manage these resources so as to translate a conventional program's
code into the corresponding activity in the hardware.

Microprogramming has been used to control conventional computers for over 20
years (cf. Husson, 1970). Although nearly all early pipelines had purely hardwired controls, the more recent generation of design has included increasingly sophisticated
microprogrammable capabilities. The reasons are the same as for conventional
machines: reduced complexity, ease of modification, and flexibility for new applications. A partial list of microprogrammed pipelines includes the IBM 2938 (Ruggiero
and Coryell, 1969), the TI ASC (Stephenson, 1973, 1975), the Proteus Arithmetic
Element (Kratz et al., 1974), and the IBM 3838 (IBM, 1976). More recently, the
unique characteristics of microprograms for pipelines have been studied by Kogge
(1977a), Kaminsky and Davidson (1978), and Emer and Davidson (1978).

The basic requirement for microprogrammed control for a pipeline is that it provide the various control signals needed by each stage in the proper sequence. These
signals include by default not only the four modes needed for intrapipeline control
(Sec. 3.4.2) but also the desired initiation sequence. The latter is achieved by explicitly
coding into the structure of the microprogram the steps where new initiations are to
be started. The details of each initiation are then handled by the succeeding steps in
the microprogram. This has the drawback of demanding that the initiation sequence
be computed in advance with little or no variation possible at execution time. However for a large class of machines such as many of the vector processors this is not a
restriction.

The conceptually simplest microprogrammed control unit is one that provides to
the pipeline a new *microinstruction* at each clock, with the microinstruction interpreted as a series of *bit fields*. Each field is associated with exactly one particular
operation within the pipeline such as a function select for a particular stage's logic.
When a field is executed its value is interpreted to provide the controls for this function during that clock period. This particular method of partitioning microinstructions
is termed a *horizontal format*. Other variations are possible but this is by far the most
common.

To demonstrate the principles involved in microprogramming a pipeline, Fig. 3-26
illustrates a sample two-stage pipeline and the heart of a microprogrammed controller
for it. The pipeline is built for floating-point number additions where the first stage's
logic (the F module) performs exponent comparison and fraction alignment. The
second stage logic (the G module) performs fraction addition and postnormalization.
Data originates in the memory, passes through the pipeline, and back to memory. The
latch on the output of the G module is a two-entry register file where at any time any
entry may be loaded from G, written to memory, or passed back to the inputs of the
F module. Each microinstruction contains five fields:

1 The *read field* indicates which two words to read from memory into the X
and Y latches.

2 The *F field* indicates which inputs to use (from X, Y, F0 (file entry 0), or F1 (file entry 1)) and what the F logic should do (such as start the alignment of the inputs, start a subtract, or pass the left input unchanged).

3 The *G field* selects what to do in the G module (do an add, subtract, or pass X' unchanged), and where to put the result (F0 or F1).

4 The *write field* selects which file entry to write back to memory, and where to write it.

5 The *sequence control field* specifies how to select upcoming microinstructions from the microstore. It may include both conditional and unconditional branches with the former based on either results from the pipeline (the output of G is zero) or a settable loop control counter.

At each clock period there is exactly one field of each type active.

As in pure hardware controls, there are two extremes in the way the control signals from a microinstruction are distributed to the pipeline. With a *time-stationary* scheme each microinstruction specifies all controls of the pipeline for a single clock period. In terms of Fig. 3-26 the output fields of the control unit go directly to the pipeline control inputs. The entire state of the pipeline is thus defined by the current microinstruction. With a *data-stationary* scheme each microinstruction specifies the path to be taken through the pipeline by a single datum entering the pipeline at the beginning of the current clock period. Thus at any instant of time, portions of several microinstructions may be concurrently active. Figure 3-27 illustrates one way of

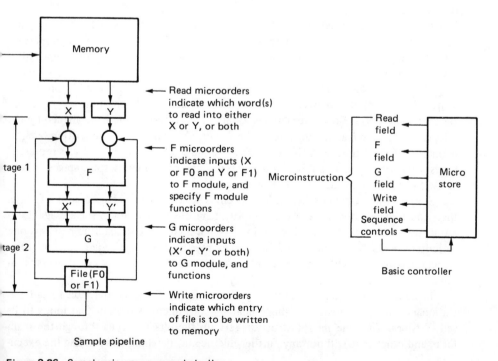

Figure 3-26 Sample microprogrammed pipeline.

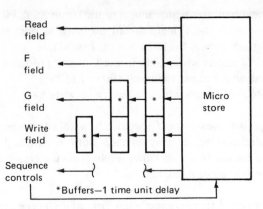

Figure 3-27 Modified data-stationary microprogrammed controller.

implementing this for the sample pipeline. As in Fig. 3-25 extra levels of staging latches are added to those in the pipeline. At each level, one field is stripped off and executed and the remaining fields passed on to the next level.

As examples of the differences between time- and data-stationary controls, Figs. 3-28 and 3-29 illustrate the equivalent microprograms for two different problems. In each figure the diagram on the top lists the contents of the pipeline's staging latches as a function of time. On the bottom are two different microprograms, one assuming a time-stationary controller and the other a data-stationary controller. The microinstructions are listed in a simple symbolic form with the fields for Read, F, G, Write, and Sequence written from left to right. A — indicates that the field should specify a "no-operation." To the left of each microinstruction is an indication of the clock periods during which it is executed. Also included is the reservation table for one iteration of the inner loop.

The first problem, Fig. 3-28, represents the element-by-element addition of two vectors (**A** and **B**) in memory. The result is a new vector **C**. At any time $i - 1$, two inputs $A(i)$ and $B(i)$ are read into latches X and Y, respectively. These are aligned by the F logic during time i, added together and normalized at time $i + 1$, and written back to memory as $C(i)$ at time $i + 2$. Note particularly the first and last three clocks represent times when the pipeline is filling and emptying, and consequently some stages are not in use. At clocks 4 through $N - 1$ all stages are in use.

Since a time-stationary controller specifies what happens at each unit of time, there must be a unique microinstruction for each different pattern of stage usage. Consequently, at least seven microinstructions are required, three to load the pipeline, one to loop on itself $N - 3$ times, and three to empty the pipeline. Further, each microinstruction is written with four different initiations at different stages of processing in mind.

In contrast the microprogram to perform exactly the same function for a data-stationary control consists of a single unambiguous microinstruction that loops to itself N times. This one microinstruction sets up the pipeline, runs through the main loop, and empties it without any further microcode. Fetching and starting the execu-

(a) Timing

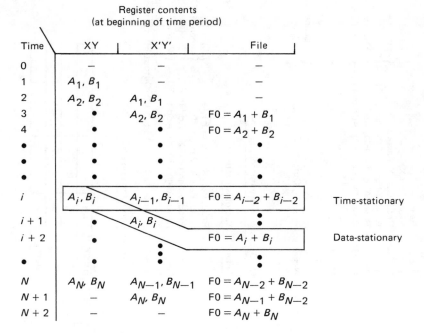

Time	XY	X'Y'	File	
	Register contents (at beginning of time period)			
0	—	—	—	
1	A_1, B_1	—	—	
2	A_2, B_2	A_1, B_1	—	
3	•	A_2, B_2	$F0 = A_1 + B_1$	
4	•	•	$F0 = A_2 + B_2$	
•	•	•	•	
•	•	•	•	
•	•	•	•	
i	A_i, B_i	A_{i-1}, B_{i-1}	$F0 = A_{i-2} + B_{i-2}$	Time-stationary
$i+1$	•	A_i, B_i	•	
$i+2$	•	•	$F0 = A_i + B_i$	Data-stationary
•	•	•	•	
N	A_N, B_N	A_{N-1}, B_{N-1}	$F0 = A_{N-2} + B_{N-2}$	
$N+1$	—	A_N, B_N	$F0 = A_{N-1} + B_{N-2}$	
$N+2$	—	—	$F0 = A_N + B_N$	

(b) Time-stationary microprogram

Time	Microinstruction
0	Read, —, —, —
1	Read, Align (X, Y) —, —
2	Read, Align (X, Y), Add (F0), —
3 to (N — 1)	Read, Align (X, Y), Add (F0), Write F0, Repeat N — 3 times
N	—, Align (X, Y), Add (F0), Write F0
N + 1	—, —, Add (F0), Write F0
N + 2	—, —, —, Write F0

(c) Data-stationary microprogram

Time	Microinstruction
0 to (N — 1)	Read, Align (X, Y), Add (F0), Write F0, Repeat N times

(d) Reservation table

	0	1	2	3
READ	A(i), B(i)			
F		X + Y		
G			X' + Y'	
WRITE				C(i)

Figure 3-28 Sample microprogram 1. Problem: Compute $C(i) = A(i) + B(i)$, for $1 \leqslant i \leqslant N$.

(a) Timing

Register contents (at beginning of time period)

Time	XY	X'Y'	File
0	—	—	—
1	A_1	—	—
2	A_2	A_1	
3	A_3	A_2	$F1 = A_1$
4	A_4	$F1, A_3$	$F0 = A_2$
5	.	$F0, A_4$	$F1 = A_1 + A_3$
6	.	.	$F0 = A_2 + A_4$
.	.	.	$\cdots$
$2i$	A_{2i}	$F1, A_{2i-1}$	$F0$
$2i+1$	A_{2i+1}	$F0, A_{2i}$	$F1 = \sum_{j=0}^{i-1} A_{2j+1}$
$2i+2$	$A_{2(i+1)}$	$F1, A_{2i+1}$	$F0 = \sum_{j=1}^{i} A_{2j}$
$\cdots$	$\cdots$	$\cdots$	$\cdots$
N	A_N	$F1, A_{N-1}$	$F1 = \sum_{j=1}^{N/2-1} A_{2j+1}$
$N+1$	—	$F0, A_N$	$F0 = \sum_{j=1}^{N/2} A_{2j}$
$N+2$	—	—	
$N+3$	—	$F1, F0$	$F0 = \sum_{i=1}^{N} A_i = C$
$N+4$	—	—	$F0 = \sum_{i=1}^{N} A_i$

Main loop (brace around $2i$ … rows)

(b) Time-stationary microprogram

Time	Microinstruction	
0	Read, −, −, −, −	} Initial pipeline
1	Read, Pass X, −, −, −	
2	Read, Pass X, Pass to F0, −, −	
3	Read, Align (X, F0), Pass to F0, −, −	
4 to	Read, Align (X, F1), Add to F1, −	} Main loop DO $(N-4)/2$ times
$N-1$	Read, Align (X, F0), Add to F0, −	
N	−, Align (X, F0), Add to F1, −	
$N+1$	−, −, Add to F0, −	} Empty pipeline
$N+2$	−, Align (F0, F1), −, −	
$N+3$	−, −, Add to F0, −	
$N+4$	−, −, −, Output F0	

(c) Data-stationary microprogram

Time	Microinstruction	
0	Read, Pass X, Pass to F1, −	} Initiate pipeline
1	Read, Pass X, Pass to F0, −	
2 to	Read, Align (F1, X), Add to F1, −	} DO $(N-2)/$ 2 times
$N-1$	Read, Align (F0, X), Add to F0, −	
N	No-Op	} Empty pipeline
$N+1$	−, Align (F0, F1, Add to F0, Output F0	

(d) Inner loop reservation table

	0	1	2
READ	$A(i)$		
F		$F0' + X$	
G			$X' + Y'$
WRITE			

Figure 3-29 Sample microprogram 2. Problem: Compute $C = \sum_{j=1}^{N} A_j$.

124

tion of a microinstruction is equivalent to starting a new initiation of the reservation table.

In addition to the greatly simplified microprogram, this approach has one other advantage: it is possible to precede or follow this microprogram by any other microprogram without needing special microcode to simultaneously empty the pipeline of one kind of operation while filling with the next. This is not true of the time-stationary version, which must explicitly define each time by itself.

Figure 3-29 illustrates a problem involving a more complex configuration. In this problem a single number C must be computed as the sum of $A(1)$ through $A(N)$. For reasons to be discussed more fully in Chap. 5, the most efficient solution involves alternating initiations between two similar reservation tables. One takes $A(2i)$ and adds it into file register F0. The other adds $A(2i + 1)$ to F1. The result is the sum of all even subscripted $A(i)$'s in F0 and all odd subscripted $A(i)$'s in F1. There must be two initial initiations of reservation tables to initialize F1 and F0 to $A(1)$ and $A(2)$, respectively, and a final initialization of a reservation table to add F0 to F1 and output the result.

As before, the time-stationary program is rather complex: the same microinstruction includes fields that are part of different initiations, even from different reservation tables. Special code is needed to start the pipeline, run through the main loop, empty the main loop, and perform the final add. In contrast the data-stationary microprogram has exactly one microinstruction for each type of reservation table initiated plus one no-operation microinstruction that is placed purely to give the proper latency between the next-to-last and last initiations. Also as before, the time-stationary approach requires special microcode to join the main loops of two separate microprograms if maximal use of each stage is a goal. This does not occur with data-stationary controls.

The results of these examples are generally true of all microprogrammed pipelines. A time-stationary approach to the execution of the various fields often results in clumsy and difficult to write microprograms. A data-stationary approach costs more hardware but allows more direct generation of microprograms from the desired sequence of reservation table initiations, requires less microcode, and has some slight performance advantages. However, care must be taken in the design of the data-stationary path that it be one that closely fits a wide range of possible reservation tables. Otherwise the microprogrammer must again force-fit several parts of several initiations into the same microinstruction. For a real pipeline there may be quite a few dramatically different reservation tables, so the best design may often be a combination of time-stationary and data-stationary approaches.

There are several other aspects of time-stationary and data-stationary microprograms for pipelines that are beyond the scope of this section. The articles by Kogge (1977a) and Emer and Davidson (1978) should be seen for more detail.

3.5 A SAMPLE DESIGN

To demonstrate the use of all the above techniques, this section outlines each step of the design of a fictitious yet reasonable pipeline. Although most of the results will be obvious by inspection, we will go through the formal demonstrations to solidify for the reader the concepts of the previous sections.

The problem to solve is to design a pipeline that samples at periodic intervals an analog signal X, at each interval taking the last four samples $X(i), X(i-1), X(i-2)$, and $X(i-3)$ and applying a symmetric filter to produce an output $Z(i)$ where

$$Z(i) = a(X(i) + X(i-3)) + b(X(i-1) + X(i-2))$$

The components assumed available include a one-stage pipelined analog-to-digital (A/D) converter, a two-stage pipelined adder, and a one-stage digital-to-analog (D/A) converter, all with a minimum stage time T. We also have a four-entry memory capable of one read or write operation every T seconds, and a two-stage multiplier capable of accepting a new input every $2T$ seconds. Finally, we assume whatever random logic is needed to glue the system together.

Partitioning the desired function into subfunctions results in an initiation that does something like:

1 Use the A/D converter to get $X(i)$.
2 Circularly write this value into the four-entry memory so that $X(i), X(i-1)$, $X(i-2)$, and $X(i-3)$ are stored.
3 Read out $X(i)$ and $X(i-3)$ and add.
4 Multiply the result of (3) by a.
5 Read out $X(i-1)$ and $X(i-2)$ and add.
6 Multiply the result of (5) by b.
7 Add the results of (4) and (6).
8 Output the result of (7) through the D/A.

From this partitioning we can sketch out a possible reservation table (Fig. 3-30). From this the forbidden latency set is $\{0,1,2,3,4,5,7\}$, and the initial collision vector is 11111101. The output $Z(i)$ appears 13 cycles after $X(i)$. From the reservation table the lower bound on MAL is 5 (five marks in the second row), and from the collision vector there is at least one greedy cycle of average latency 7 or better (7 ones in the vector). This indicates that we can start a new initiation on the average at least once every 7 cycles, but no better than once every five cycles. To find out what is possible we can generate and analyze the state diagram (or in this case look up 11111101 in the appendix). The result is that (6) is an optimal greedy cycle. This does not achieve the MAL bound of 5 and leaves every stage underutilized.

We now assume that the designer of this system wants to improve the performance to an average latency of 5, and in fact wants to implement a constant latency cycle (5). The delay insertion theorem indicates that this is possible if all rows of the reservation table can be expressed in terms of the maximally compatible classes of H_C mod 5 for the cycle (5). From Lemma 3-9 these classes include $\{0,1,2,3,4\}$ and all sets generatable from it by adding a constant to all elements and/or any multiple of 5 to individual elements.

There is no problem with row 1. Row 2 has the form $1 + \{0,1,2,3,4\}$, so it meets

	0	1	2	3	4	5	6	7	8	9	10	11	12	13
1. A/D converter	1													
2. Four-entry memory		2	3	3	5	5								
3. Adder stage 1					3		5					7		
4. Adder stage 2						3		5					7	
5. Multiplier stage 1							4	4	6	6				
6. Multiplier stage 2								4	4	6	6			
7. D/A converter														8

Figure 3-30 First possible reservation table. The number in each square corresponds to that step in the partitioning.

the constraints. Likewise rows 5 and 6 have the form $X + \{0,2\}$, and row 7 has the form $13 + \{0\}$. The problem is in rows 3 and 4, which have the form $X + \{0,2,7\}$; 7 is $2 + 1 \times 5$, and thus the element 2 is used twice. This is not allowed. We must then insert delays to change the form of these rows. The easiest and most obvious way is to delay starting operation (7) by one cycle. This also requires delaying the output operation (8), which is no problem. Delaying (7) by one unit results in row 3 of the form $4 + \{0,2,3 + 1 \times 5\}$, which is permissible by Thoerem 3-2. Figure 3-31 diagrams the resulting reservation table. As a check we find that the initial collision vector is 111110101. A look-up in the appendix verifies that a greedy cycle of (5) is possible and is optimal.

Figure 3-32 diagrams one possible hardware implementation of this reservation table. Notice that certain of the staging latches have been replaced by two-entry register files. Some of these, for example the A and B files, are there because the problem calls for two separate adds. Thus the pair A0, B0 supports the add $X(i) + X(i - 3)$; and A1,B1 supports $X(i - 1) + X(i - 2)$. Likewise the E and F files support the two multipliers. We assume part of initialization is to load F0 and F1 with the two filter constants a and b. Finally, the C and D files support the final add with its input delay.

The next step after finding a latency sequence (the scheduling strategy) and a pipeline (the hardware data flow) is to lay out the actual timing that the control mechanism, whatever it is, must follow. Since the period is 5 and the compute time is 15, in any set of 5 cycles there are different parts of $15/5 = 3$ initiations. One of the initiations is just starting, another is in the middle of its calculations, and the third is finishing up. As was shown in the section on microprogramming, it is important that the control mechanism keep track of where all three initiations are in their calculations. To formalize this Fig. 3-33 divides all time into sets of 5 cycles. At time $5i$ the ith initiation is assumed just starting at relative time 0 in the reservation table, the $(i-1)$st initiation is at time 5 of its computation, and the $(i - 2)$nd is starting its 10th step. At time $5i + 1$ all three have advanced one step. At time $5i + 5$ the $(i + 1)$st initiation starts, and what was the ith initiation now starts executing the second column of Fig. 3-33. At time $5i + 10$ the ith initiation starts the third column.

The box in Fig. 3-33 at time $5i + 1$, column 3, represents the one-unit delay inserted into the reservation table to increase its throughput. Note that register D0 is written into at time $5i$, and read out at time $5i + 2$, just as required for a one-unit delay. However, in this problem no other initiation is attempting to write into the D file during this time. Therefore, it is not strictly necessary to use a register file here. A simple latch would have sufficed. In general however it is necessary to do an analysis like this one to determine whether or not a file is needed. It would have been needed if another initiation was writing into the D file at time $5i + 1$.

Once a timing analysis like Fig. 3-33 has been performed, it is possible to use any of the control techniques described in Sec. 3.3. Because of the relatively straightforward nature of this application, we leave it to the reader to consider the exact implementation details.

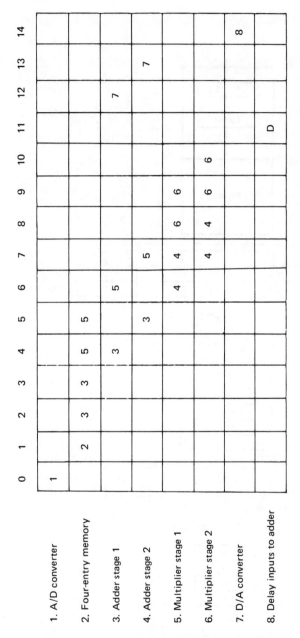

	0	1	2	3	4	5	6	7	8	9	10	11	12	13	14
1. A/D converter	1														
2. Four-entry memory		2	3	3	5	5									
3. Adder stage 1				3	3		5						7		
4. Adder stage 2						3		5						7	
5. Multiplier stage 1							4	4	6	6					
6. Multiplier stage 2								4	4	6	6				
7. D/A converter															8
8. Delay inputs to adder												D			

D = new delay

Figure 3-31 Delayed reservation table.

129

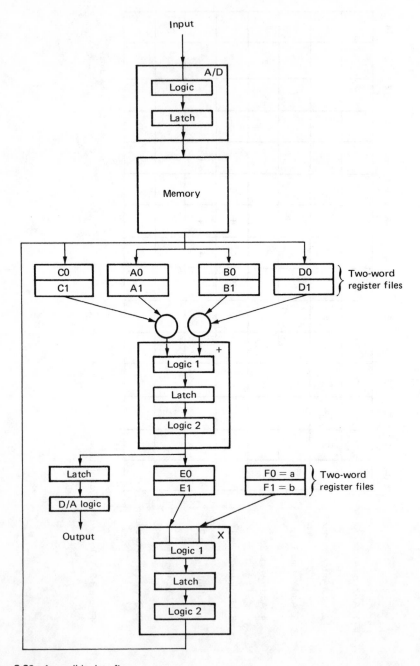

Figure 3-32 A possible data flow.

Cycle	i	$i-1$	$i-2$
$5i$	Sample A/D	Read $X(i-1-2)$ into B1 Route output of adder to E0	Route output of multiplier to D0
$5i+1$	Save A/D in memory	Start add of A1, B1 Start multiply of E0, F0	
$5i+2$	Read $X(i)$ into A0	Route output of adder to E1 Continue E0 $\times$ F0	Start add of C0 to D0
$5i+3$	Read $X(i-3)$ into B0	Start multiply of E1, F1	Route output of adder to D/A
$5i+4$	Read $X(i-1)$ into A1 Start add of A0, B0	Route output of multiplier to C0 Continue E1 $\times$ F1	Perform D/A

Figure 3-33 Timing information.

PROBLEMS

3-1 Given that c is the number of 0s in the initial collision vector, show that for any static pipeline and any modified state diagram:
   a The number of 0s in any noninitial state is always less than c.
   b The total number of states is no greater than 2^c.

3-2 Can you make similar statements for a dynamic pipeline?

3-3 For the collision vector 1101000011011 do a complete state analysis.

3-4 Show that Fig. 3-16a has an optimal cycle of (4).

3-5 Show that if a latency cycle includes $L_1, L_2, \ldots, L_n$, when the sum of $L_1, \ldots, L_n$ is L, then it is a valid cycle for some reservation table only if bit L of the corresponding initial collision vector is 0.

3-6 For the following reservation table find the initial collision vector, modified state diagram, optimal cycles and latencies, and all greedy cycles. Compute the initial collision vector using forbidden latency sets.

	0	1	2	3	4	5	6	7	8
1	X								X
2		X						X	
3			X				X		
4				X		X			
5					X				

3-7 How much increased performance can you get by inserting one unit of delay in the previous reservation table? Reanalyze your modified table.

3-8 Recast Theorem 3-1 into one referencing H_C mod p and G_C mod p. Prove. Take particular care with deciding what to do about a latency of 0.

3-9 Formally prove Theorem 3-2.

3-10 Find all maximally compatible classes for the cycle (1,9) that contains 2. Is the cycle perfect?

3-11 Show that the cycle (5,3) is perfect.

3-12 What is the maximum possible utilization of any stage of a pipeline that is computing initiations from some reservation table with the latency cycle (2,3,7)?

3-13 Without drawing the state diagram, determine whether or not the following reservation table supports the cycles (3,4) and (2,3,7).

	0	1	2	3	4	5	6	7	8
1	X								X
2		X	X					X	
3				X					X
4					X	X			
5		X					X	X	

3-14 Given that X is a positive nonzero fraction (i.e., $0 < X < 1$), an expansion for $1/X$ is (where $1 - X = Z$):

$$\frac{1}{X} = \frac{1}{1 - Z} = \frac{1 + Z}{1 - Z^2}$$

$$= \frac{(1 + Z)(1 + Z^2)}{1 - Z^4}$$

$$= \dots$$

$$= (1 + Z)(1 + Z^2)(1 + Z^4)(1 + Z^8) \dots$$

Assume you have available a one-stage pipelined adder and a two-stage pipelined multiplier. Work out a reservation table for the approximation $(1 + Z)(1 + Z^2)$. (You may wish to try alternate but equivalent algebraic forms.) Do a state analysis and find the optimal latency sequence. If it does not achieve the MAL bound, pick a perfect cycle and insert appropriate delays. Design a pipeline that will support this reservation table, showing feedback paths, which if any latches are replaced by files, and how many registers are needed in each file.

3-15 Prove Lemma 3-10.

3-16 Pick out six different cycles from Fig. 3-18 and compute the average latency. Of these which one(s) is (are) the best for each of the performance criteria addressed in Sec. 3.3.2?

3-17 Develop the state diagram for a dynamic pipeline having the following two reservation tables:

A			A	
	A		A	
		A		A

B				B
			B	
B		B		

    a What is the maximum number of initiations per cycle of any kind in any order? At what percentage of A initiations out of the total does this occur?

    b What is the best average latency when the sequence of initiations is AABB? ABB?

3-18 Develop a state diagram for the reservation tables of Fig. 3-31.

3-19 For the problem $X(i) = X(i-1) + X(i-2) + b(i)$, $X(0) = 0$, $X(-1) = 0$, write a time-stationary and data-stationary microprogram for the sample pipeline of Sec. 3.4.3. Try using the techniques of Sec. 2.4 to speed up the solution.

3-20 Describe a possible microprogrammed controller for the sample design of Sec. 3-4. Sketch the outline of a time-stationary microprogram to solve the filter problem.

Chapter 4

Static Pipelined Systems—Vector Processors

Since the beginning of the electronic computer, a major force in the development of very high performance computers has been the scientific community. Problems such as those found in weather forecasting, nuclear physics, thermodynamics, and seismology always seem to exceed the capabilities of conventionally architected machines. Despite these demands, however, the kernels of such problems are typically more structured than those of other applications, making it feasible to consider adding special architectural features to a computer to increase its effectiveness on these problems. Mathematically these problems can usually be expressed in linear algebra with all elements of rows or columns of large matrices manipulated in some identical fashion. When translated into a programming language such as FORTRAN the problems take forms such as

```
        DO 10 I = 1,N
    10  C(I) = A(I) * B(I)
```

or

```
        DO 20 I = 1,N
        DO 20 J = 1,M
    20  C(I) = C(I) + A(I + J) * B(J)
```

Translated into conventional machine code, such sequences include not only the instructions to do the desired operations, but also instructions to compute indices, access data, do loop counter tests, and branch back to the beginning of a loop. This extra overhead considerably slows down the computation rate.

It was recognized quite early in the development of high-performance machines (cf. the VAMP study of Senzig and Smith, 1965) that one way to speed up performance for such problems is to include in the instruction set seen by the programmer a set of instructions that perform by themselves both the data-processing kernels and the overhead of loop control. Such instructions can be implemented very efficiently so that little if any of the overhead will interfere with the basic computations. In contrast to conventional instructions that process at most one data element at a time, these new instructions apply some regular sequence of operations (potentially more than one) to all elements from an entire group of data. Such groups of data are typically called *vectors* and the instructions that process them *vector instructions*. They range in complexity all the way from a *vector add,* where corresponding elements of two input vectors are added together to produce an element of an output vector, to a *fast Fourier transform* (*FFT*), where a vector of data undergoes a long and complex sequence of multiplies and adds to produce an output vector, all by the execution of one machine instruction. An example of a primitive vector instruction found in most conventional computer architectures is the MOVE, which moves a vector of bits, bytes, characters, or words from one region in memory to another.

There are a variety of ways such instructions may be added to a computer's repertoire. The simplest is to very carefully hand-code subroutines for each basic instruction type, choosing a sequence of instructions to minimize overhead and maximize performance. This obviously can be done by anyone who knows the detailed timing of a particular machine, but it offers only moderate performance improvement. Another approach, usually attempted only by the computer's manufacturer, is the addition of a vector instruction to a machine's instruction set by microprogramming. Although this usually does not affect the hardware design, it does offer significant performance advantages: now all of the loop control is handled by the very fast microprogram, and the memory system need not be tied up making fetches for the overhead instructions.

The most dramatic performance gain (up to orders of magnitude) can be made by designing the machine with vector instructions in mind from the start. Such machines, called *vector processors,* currently offer the most potential performance of any computer architecture. There are two competing design approaches to machines in this class: the parallel vector processor and the pipelined vector processor. The parallel approach has a multiplicity of arithmetic computational elements; when a vector instruction is being executed each arithmetic element handles a separate element of the input vectors. Machines of this class are the ILLIAC IV (cf. Slotnick, 1967) and the Burroughs Scientific Processor (Stokes, 1977).

The other class of vector processors has one or relatively few arithmetic elements, each of which is pipelined. Machines of this class include the CDC STAR-100 (Hintz and Tate, 1972), the Texas Instrument Advanced Scientific Computer (Watson, 1972a,b), the IBM 3838 Array Processor (IBM, 1976), and the Cray Research CRAY-1 (Cray, 1976). This class is perhaps more common than the parallel approach because the vector instructions themselves represent, for the most part, repeated initiations of the same functions, which in turn are very amenable to the pipelined design techniques of the previous chapters.

In the terminology of this text such designs follow precisely the definition of a statically configured pipeline. In addition, the addressing modes used most often in vector architectures are ones that are relatively easy to generate in a pipelined machine but either inefficient or very costly to implement in a parallel design. This is so because a parallel processor needs to align data with the appropriate processor at the right time, requiring time-consuming and expensive interconnection hardware.

This chapter investigates in detail the properties of pipelined vector processors. Attention is given to both the hardware architecture and how those hardware facilities are visible to the programmer at the machine instruction level. Examples from a variety of real systems show the range of possibilities. How these capabilities are used in actual programming will be discussed in Chap. 5.

4.1 TYPICAL HARDWARE ARCHITECTURE

Regardless of their origin or design goals most current pipelined vector-processing systems have an overall structure similar to Fig. 4-1. In this structure there are six major components:

1 Main memory
2 Scalar processor
3 Vector controller
4 Vector memory address generator and memory controller
5 Local memory
6 Arithmetic pipeline

The *main memory* is similar in function to the main memories of more conventional computers. It is a single memory containing both instructions and data in both vector and nonvector form. However, because the *demand ratio* (memory accesses per clock; see Sec. 2.2.1) is so much higher when vector instructions are being accessed, its organization is much more complex and key to overall system performance. Such memories are typically heavily interleaved and designed to minimize access time for vector operands. Section 2.2.1 describes the range of design alternatives in more detail.

Within all programs, including those that use vectors heavily, there is still a significant requirement for code that cannot be put in vector form. This includes data-dependent tests, I/O, overall program control, memory management, operating system functions, and vector definition and setup. This requirement is best served by a conventional SISD instruction set; therefore, most pipelined vector processing systems include a *scalar processor* separate from the main vector-processing hardware. The scalar processor offloads from the vector hardware all those operations for which it is not a good candidate. Often one of the CPUs from the manufacturer's standard product line is used as a scalar processor.

Once a vector instruction has been fetched and recognized, usually by the scalar

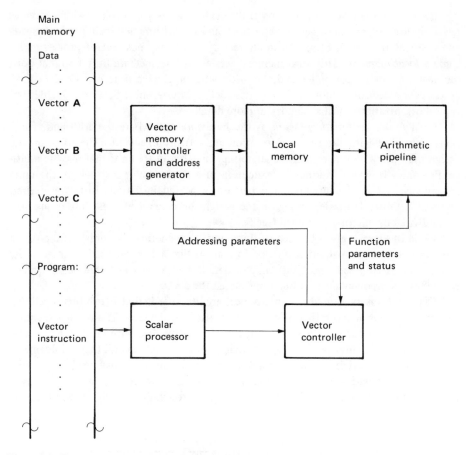

Figure 4-1 Typical pipelined vector processor architecture.

processor, a separate *vector controller* takes over. The functions of this unit include decoding the vector instruction, computing operand-addressing parameters, allocating and setting up the vector memory address generator and the arithmetic pipeline itself, and monitoring the execution of the vector instruction. When the instruction is complete, the vector controller also performs any cleanup or status-gathering that must be done.

Perhaps the most complex, most critical to performance, but least studied set of units in a vector processor is the *vectory memory address generator and controller.* This unit is responsible for taking the addressing parameters generated by the vector controller from the vector instruction and translating them into a series of main memory access requests that will utilize main memory bandwidth efficiently and also will make sure that the arithmetic pipeline has the data it needs when it needs it. The kinds of addressing modes visible to the programmer and the rate at which this unit performs them have a telling effect on the utility of a vector processor for performing a wide range of problems. A later section of this chapter details the major alternatives possible, and Chap. 5 includes discussion of their applications.

Because of the diverse operations of the vector memory controller, which accesses relatively long segments of vectors at a time, and the arithmetic pipeline, which needs one operand from each of several input vectors at a time, most vector processors include a *local memory*. This local memory acts as an intermediate buffer so that both the vector memory controller and the arithmetic pipeline can access the data they need as they need it without mutually destructive interference. Section 2.2.2 defines typical organizations of this memory in more detail.

Finally, the *arithmetic pipeline* is the hardware unit where the arithmetic functions associated with the vector instruction are actually executed. Depending on the design there may be one or more separate pipelined hardware units that may be multiconfigurable. However, during the execution of a single vector instruction, the units are usually statically configured and perform repeated initiations from the desired reservation table. Again depending on the design the control of these initiations may be hardwired or microprogrammed (see Sec. 3.4).

While the names given to each of these units are generic only, with many possible variations of sizes, capabilities, and performance, Fig. 4-1 is remarkably broad in its application. A later section of this chapter details several very different designs, all of which have components whose functions match the above.

One final observation about this typical architecture is that it exhibits pipelining and overlap itself at more than just the arithmetic pipeline level. The whole execution of vector instructions is, at a gross level, a multistage pipeline with local memory serving as some of the intermediate staging latches. At one level beyond that, while one or more vector instructions are in execution, the vector controller may be setting up the next vector instruction, while the scalar processor may be executing instructions leading to the next vector instruction. Figure 4-2 gives a rough idea of what the reservation

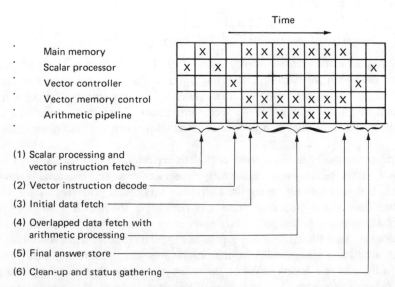

Figure 4-2 Possible vector instruction reservation table.

table for such a system would look like. Note that the vector memory address generator and controller must be active longer than the arithmetic pipeline. This is because at least some data must be read from memory before processing can start, and some final answers must be written back once the computation is complete.

4.2 USER INTERFACE—THE MACHINE-LEVEL INSTRUCTION ARCHITECTURE

The previous section gave an overview of the hardware of a pipelined vector processor. However, as in any computer, a programmer solves a particular problem by dealing not with the hardware but with a program made up of chains of machine-level instructions that in turn control the hardware. Furthermore, the machine-level instruction architecture for a pipelined vector processor is dramatically different from a more classical SISD machine. This section gives an overview of attributes unique to machine-level vector instructions. Throughout the section we will use as an example a *vector element-by-element add* instruction where for all i in some range, the ith element of some vector Y, namely the element $Y(i)$, is replaced by the sum of the ith elements of two other vectors X and U, namely $X(i)$ and $U(i)$. This contrasts with a more classical *scalar add* where the content of some single memory location or CPU register is added to some other memory location or CPU register.

Any instruction, either scalar or vector, must specify at least four generic kinds of information:

1 The function to be performed
2 The operands to use
3 What status to record
4 What instruction to perform next

As in most nonvector instructions the latter two are often implied in vector instructions to be some standard.

4.2.1 The Opcode

In terms of the notation of the previous chapter, the specification of function to be performed in a vector architecture, often called the *opcode,* is equivalent to the selection of which reservation table the arithmetic pipeline should use once data is available. Usually this specification is simply a binary-coded index whose value is used by the vector controller to select both a prestored reservation table and the matching initiation sequence. These reservation tables and initiation sequences are usually built into either hardware or microprograms, and they are not directly modifiable by the machine-level instruction.

Although the total number of operation types for a vector processor may be relatively small, there are still perhaps two to three times as many vector opcodes as there are equivalent scalar opcodes. The reason is that while in a scalar processor there is only one way to do an add, namely, add the two inputs, there are several equally valid variations of a vector add. The first is simply the element-by-element operation described in the previous section where the output is a vector equal in length to the inputs. The second kind of add is typical of the class of *vector reduction* instructions that accept vector inputs and produce a single scalar output. A *vector add reduction* would take all elements of a vector, add them together, and produce a single result. Finally, scalar instructions usually specify only a single operation at a time, while many vector instructions specify a more complex process. Perhaps the most common such vector instruction is the *vector inner product,* which takes two input vectors and produces a single output equal to the sum reduction of the element-by-element product of the inputs. If the input vectors are **X** and **U**, this operation mathematically is:

$$Y = \sum_{i=1}^{N} X(i) \; U(i)$$

Variations of the inner product form the basis for many scientific problems; they can be found in many other instructions to perform convolutions, matrix multiplications, digital filters, and matrix decomposition. In fact many vector processors are designed at the outset with inner products in mind.

In addition, the typical vector instruction set includes opcodes with no counterparts in equivalent scalar sets. Such opcodes are describes as their needs are developed in the following sections.

4.2.2 Operand Specification

The major difference between vector and nonvector instructions at the machine level lies in the specification of operands. In a nonvector instruction an operand (single element) either is implied, such as an accumulator, or is one of a relatively few programmer-visible registers, or is a memory word whose address is directly computed from a base, index, or displacement. A typical instruction format is a two-address mode where two single-element operands are specified for input to the function and one of them is redundantly used to specify where the result goes. At most one of these operand specifications is a memory address. The other is typically a CPU register. The average add instruction found on most scalar machines fits this description.

In a vector machine an operand may consist of many elements, and its length is not usually predictable in advance. Consequently, nearly all vector processors keep their operands in memory. This means that most vector instructions such as a vector add are three-address (two inputs, one result) in format, each address field specifying a separate region of memory. Implied addressing of an operand, where the hardware keeps track of the location of an operand, is very rare.

There are several memory address fields in a typical vector instruction, and each address field must specify much more information than found in nonvector instructions. This information includes:

1 The origin in memory of the vector
2 The number of dimensions in the vector (e.g., one-dimensional array or two-dimensional matrix)
3 The number of elements in each dimension (size)
4 The data type of each element (integer, floating-point, halfword, or byte)
5 The arrangement of elements in memory

The *origin address,* the address of the first element, is roughly equivalent to an address specification in a nonvector instruction. The number of dimensions and size of each dimension specify the mathematical structure the vector is to represent. The data type indicates the format of each element in the vector; it is used not only to size the total number of memory words to be processed but also to determine if any format conversion must be done by the hardware (e.g., fixed- to floating-point).

For a variety of reasons the elements of vectors do not always fall in contiguous memory words. One common example is the accessing of a column of a matrix when the elements of each now are stored contiguously. When this happens, the final piece of information, namely the arrangement of data within memory, becomes important. A later section discusses this subject in more detail.

4.2.3 Status and Sequencing

In addition to performing the specified function, a typical scalar instruction such as an add also detects and records status information as a normal part of its execution. There are at least two kinds of such information. The first deals with properties of the result just computed such as what is its sign or is its value equal to zero. The second indicates data-dependent errors detected during execution of the specified function such as overflow, underflow, or divide by zero. (Note that this does *not* include hardware errors, but only errors due to improper data.)

There are several ways of handling each of these kinds of status. For the first kind, properties of the resulting value, many scalar architecture, particularly accumulator-based ones, do not record such information. Instead the instruction set includes a set of conditional branch instructions that explicitly test the sign and value of the register holding the result of the previous operations. A different approach taken by many general register-based architectures (e.g., that of the IBM System 370) saves such conditions either in a special hardware register termed a *condition code* register or in a special memory location. The branch instructions then simply test these bits without regard to where the actual result is. Finally, many instruction sets include instructions that combine both an arithmetic operation and a sequence control. A common example is a tally and jump-not-zero which decrements some register or memory location, tests the result, and either jumps or continues.

Similar methods are used for data-dependent error conditions. The detection of such conditions can result in the setting of condition code bits and/or the forcing of a branch or interrupt out of the currently executing program to some special subroutine that handles that specific error condition. These special subroutines can set the result to specific values and continue, terminate the program, or branch to a cleanup program. Often the programmer can precondition whether or not a forced branch is taken by setting up beforehand special bits in his *program status word* or *program status area*. Upon detection of such a condition, the hardware will check these bits and decide whether and where a branch is made.

Vector instructions must deal with the same kind of status conditions, but because they are dealing with not just one but many element results, their methods are dramatically different. For example, at least four ways have been proposed for the handling of value-dependent status such as a result equaling zero. The first is to extend the information in the equivalent of a condition code register to include an indication that none, some, or all of the results are zero. The second is to record simply the number of zeros and where the first occurs. The third is to develop a *condition code vector* where each output element has associated with it not only its value but its own condition code. This requires that the vector instruction include addressing not only for the result but also for the condition code vector.

Finally, a common approach is to do no status-saving whatsoever. Instead the instruction set is augmented with vector instructions of the form: "compare vectors for equality" or "test for negative." Each of these accepts as input vector operands and produces as output another vector of the same length as the input, but in which each element is a single bit that records the result of the test. Such vectors are termed *bit vectors*. An example of a vector compare for equality is shown in Fig. 4-3. Note that these are pure vector instructions that may themselves generate status such as none, some, or all of the output bits are 1, or that there are M 1s with the first in position i.

Once bit vectors are included in an architecture, a whole set of additional instructions becomes potentially useful. These include a complete set of logical vector operations that do element-by-element logical operations such as in Fig. 4-4. Such instructions allow tests to be cascaded, for example, "find all elements in **X** whose values are either 0, or negative but not greater than the equivalent element in **Y**." Figure 4-5 lists the vector steps in such a program. We note that none of these instructions does any conditional branches. If conditional branches are needed, other mixed vector/scalar instructions, such as "find next 1 in bit vector," can first determine if there are any 1s in a bit vector and store the result in a scalar condition code, and then store the single scalar index to the first such element. A scalar program can then use this instruction in a loop to find and process all points having the desired condition.

Other uses for bit vectors are given in later sections.

The handling of exceptional conditions is also different in vector instructions as compared to their scalar counterparts, again because a vector instruction performs more than one operation. If an arithmetic exception such as an overflow occurs during a vector instruction, the processor must make an immediate decision whether to continue the execution and record that an error occurred or to terminate it. Programmer-specified control information can be used as in the scalar case to guide the hardware in making the choice. However, in a pipelined machine, by the time one error has been detected, several (potentially many) other initiations of the reservation table may be under way, and it may be impossible to bring the process to a graceful halt from which

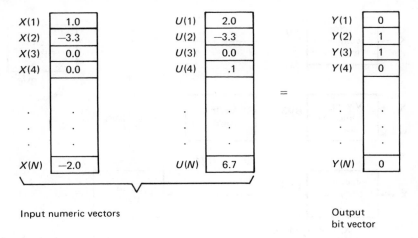

Input numeric vectors   Output
                                                             bit vector

Figure 4-3 Vector compare equal.

it can be restarted after a fix-up subroutine has been called. Consequently, the programmer-specified control information may be extended to include bits that tell the
hardware to record the event but keep the instruction going and "patch up" the output data in some standard way. Typical patch-ups may include replacing a result by
0 if an underflow occurred or forcing the largest representable number in case of an
overflow. Depending on the application this may or may not be an acceptable solution.

Even simply recording the occurrence of an exception causes architectural problems in a vector processor. An extended scalar condition code can indicate whether
there were some or no errors and perhaps where the first one occurred, but it will
not indicate how many or where other errors occurred. A condition code vector can
indicate where multiple errors occurred for many vector instructions, but it is relatively useless when each output depends on several operations and several or all inputs. This is particularly true in reduction operations such as an inner product or
matrix multiplication where it is difficult to identify back to the user which operation encountered an exception; and even if such specification is made, it may be
extremely difficult for the user to translate that back into the input data. Con-

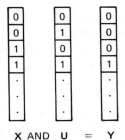

X AND U = Y   **Figure 4-4** Vector AND. **X, U,** and **Y** are all bit vectors.

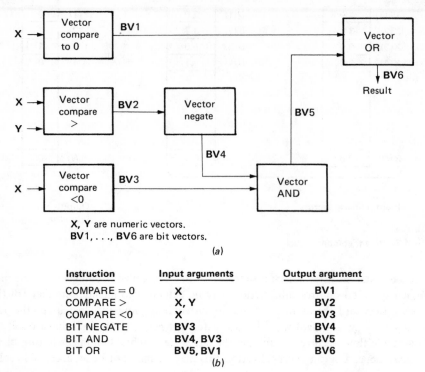

X, Y are numeric vectors.
BV1, . . ., BV6 are bit vectors.

(a)

Instruction	Input arguments	Output argument
COMPARE $= 0$	X	BV1
COMPARE $>$	X, Y	BV2
COMPARE <0	X	BV3
BIT NEGATE	BV3	BV4
BIT AND	BV4, BV3	BV5
BIT OR	BV5, BV1	BV6

(b)

Figure 4-5 Typical use of logical vector operations. (*a*) Program flow. (*b*) Program listing.

sequently, most vector architectures either terminate an instruction or perform some automatic fix-up and continuation, with at most an extended condition code as a record back to the user.

4.2.4 Other Architectural Considerations

Besides the previous topics, there are several other concepts that are unique to vector architectures and that if included in an instruction can have a significant impact on the machine design. Two of these concepts are *padding* and a special *vector floating-point* data format.

Padding refers to the automatic lengthening of a vector to make its length the same as some other vector that is input to the same instruction. The most common example of this is when the inputs to a vector instruction such as an add consist of two vectors one of which has only one element. In this case the one element is replicated as many times as necessary to match the length of the other vector, and the vector operation proceeds as usual. This facility is useful in modifying each element of a vector by a common offset or scale factor. The actual replication is done usually either by the vector memory controller or by use of a special reservation table in the arithmetic pipeline. In either case the single element vector is read from memory only once with a consequent savings of memory bandwidth.

A less common definition of padding occurs when the architecture allows different lengths for each of the input vectors for an instruction. For example, a particular vector add instruction $(X(i) + U(i) = Y(i))$ may specify **X** as having four elements, **U** as having five elements, and **Y** as six elements in length. It is clear how elements $Y(1)$ to $Y(4)$ are computed, but not so for $Y(5)$ and $Y(6)$. If the processor has been designed to pad vectors, both **X** and **U** will be lengthened to six elements. These new elements may be generated in one of two ways. First, the last element may be generated in one of two ways. First, the last element of the vector may be replicated as needed. This is an obvious extension of the scalar approach and in the above example would result in $Y(5) = Y(6) = X(4) + U(5)$. Second and more common, the vector may be extended by simply padding 0s on the end. In the above example this would result in $Y(5) = U(5)$, and $Y(6) = 0$. Figure 4-6 diagrams both approaches.

A second concept that has been discussed from time to time for vector architectures is the inclusion of special *vector floating-point* or *block floating-point* data format (cf. Higbie, 1976). The standard floating-point representation of a number has three components: a sign S, an exponent E, and a fractional value F. Its numeric value is

$$S \times F \times B^{E}$$

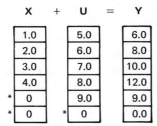

Figure 4-6 Approaches to padding. (*a*) Sample vector add. (*b*) Pad by extension. (*c*) Pad by zero fill.

where B is the base of the number system used by the hardware, commonly 2, 8, or 16. If all elements of some vector $\mathbf{X}$ are in this standard format, then each number $X(i)$ has its own $S(i), F(i),$ and $E(i)$.

However, if all the data in a vector is known to have roughly the same magnitude, then significant memory savings could be made if there were only a single exponent E that is used by all elements of the vector. Typically this common exponent must be the largest exponent required by any of the elements, and elements needing smaller exponents must have their fractions scaled to match the common exponent.

An alternative is to use the memory saved by removing the individual exponents for extending the fraction. This improves the relative accuracy of the numbers considerably.

While superficially attractive, this proposal has a far-reaching effect on the design of a pipelined processor. For example, in the addition of two vectors, one of which is in block floating-point, the final exponent for a block floating-point result is not known until all elements have been added. Consequently, it may be necessary to do the vector add and then read the entire result vector back into the pipeline, scale it accordingly, and write it back. This can have a big impact on performance. In addition, the question of the precision of such a format is a subtle one; it is discussed more fully in Higbie (1976) and Wilkinson (1963).

4.3 VECTOR ADDRESSING MODES

Perhaps the most unusual characteristic of the architecture of pipelined vector processors is the variety of ways that vector operands may be accessed. As the examples of Chap. 5 will show, the performance of vector instructions in real programs very often is determined totally by the rate at which operands may be accessed from main memory and only secondarily influenced by the peak performance of the arithmetic pipeline. Similarly, the performance of entire programs written for vector processors is critically dependent on how easy it is to access the required data patterns as they are needed. This section examines both questions as they relate to processor architecture, namely, the kinds of addressing patterns typically implemented and their relative performance. In terms of the typical processor of Fig. 4-1, the components most affected by the choice of addressing modes are the main memory design and the vector memory controller and address generator.

There are two general classes of vector addressing modes: dense/regular and sparse. The first corresponds to cases where the pattern of data in memory is more or less known in advance. The second corresponds to cases where the desired pattern of data must be computed dynamically. Each is discussed separately below.

4.3.1 Dense/Regular Addressing Patterns

Not unexpectedly, the most common method of storing vectors in the main memories of vector processors is to have neighboring elements stored in locations where addresses are relatively close and structured in an orderly manner. Such patterns are called *dense* or *regular*.

There are three common varieties of such patterns:

1 Sequential
2 Nonsequential but regular
3 Submatrix

Any of a variety of other addressing patterns can be constructed from simple variations of these. Figure 4-7 diagrams each in detail.

In the purely *sequential* mode, neighboring elements of a vector are stored in neighboring words of memory. Thus if element $V(i)$ is stored in location K, then $V(i + 1)$ is in location $K + 1$, $V(i + 2)$ in location $K + 2$, etc. This may be extended to two-dimensional arrays in one of two complementary fashions. In *row order* each row of an $R \times N$ array **M** occupies N consecutive locations with the R rows stored sequentially. Thus $M(i,j)$ is found $(i - 1)N + j - 1$ words from that allocated to $M(1,1)$. *Column order* is identical except that the matrix is stored by columns with each column using R consecutive locations.

The next most common method of vector access typically occurs when a column is desired from a row-ordered matrix, or conversely a row from a column-ordered matrix. Here neighboring elements of a vector are not in consecutive locations but in a *regular* pattern of one element every Nth word (cf. Fig. 4-7*b*). To access such a pattern the vector address generator of Fig. 4-1 must generate a series of addresses whose values differ not by 1 but by N. Further, since only the user knows the actual size of his problem, and since this size may vary from step to step, the value N must be somehow included in the original vector instruction that initiated the transfer.

The third method of accessing data in a regular pattern is an outgrowth of the first two. Its operation is most easily understood by assuming that there is an $R \times N$ array stored in row order in memory, and that a particular vector instruction requires row-ordered access to a rectangular submatrix (Fig. 4-7*c*) of size $m \times n$. To access such data requires m sets of n consecutive addresses, where the start of each set is N higher than the previous start. This corresponds to reading n consecutive words, skipping $N - n$ words, and then starting over.

Inclusion of such a mode in a vector address generator requires at least two extra parameters to be supplied by the vector instruction, namely n and $N - n$, or some variation. In addition, there may be one or two counts supplied to indicate the total number of words transferred, and perhaps there also may be an offset from the base of the original matrix to indicate the start of the submatrix.

This submatrix mode may also be used to access nonsequential but regular vectors when each vector element consists of more than one memory word. For example, if all elements of a two-dimensional $R \times N$ array are double-precision, that is two words per number, then accessing of a double-precision column can be accomplished by a submatrix read that reads two words, skips $2N - 2$ words, and so forth. Another similar example would be a two-dimensional array where each element is a two-word complex number having both a real and imaginary component.

The time to access a vector in any one of these modes depends heavily on the design of the main memory. As described in Sec. 2.2.1, there are two major design

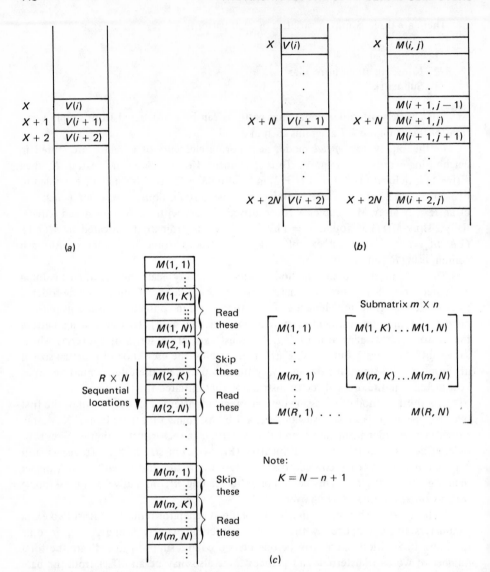

Figure 4-7 Common dense/regular addressing patterns. (a) Sequential vector. (b) Nonsequential but regular vector, or column access. (c) Submatrix accessing.

techniques for high-speed memories, simple interleaving and complex interleaving, with many real systems employing both. In an S-way simple interleaved system, a single access returns S consecutive words. In a C-way complex interleaved system up to C different single-word accesses can be in progress at the same time. In an SC-mixed interleaved design up to C different accesses to blocks of S consecutive words can be in progress at the same time.

In any case the accessing of a purely sequential vector typically can run at the full interleaved rate of the memory. However, as was shown in Sec. 2.2.1, this is not always true for the other two modes. Here the skip values interact with the interleave factor in relatively complex ways to result in sometimes significant slowdowns. For example, Table 4-1 lists, for five different memory organizations, all using the same basic memory module, the average access time for an element of a vector that is scattered at regular intervals. Even within the same design, the performance can fluctuate up to 16 to 1 for different skip values.

The performance of an interleaved memory system is even more complex to describe accurately when a submatrix access is desired mainly because of the varying memory designs and the two parameters involved, access length and spacing value. However, it is possible to derive an upper bound on average word access time that is relatively independent of memory design and spacing value. The following lemma describes this bound.

Lemma 4-1 For a memory design where the time to access a module is T seconds and the interleave factor is IF (S for simple interleave, C for complex, SC for mixed), then the average time to access a word in a submatrix when n consecutive words are read and m words skipped is no greater than:

$$\frac{T(1 + IF/n)}{IF} \quad \text{or} \quad \frac{T}{IF} + \frac{T}{n}$$

Table 4-1 Average Access Time* for Regularly Spaced Vectors

Skip value	Memory Design				
	4-way simple	4-way complex	16-way simple	16-way complex	4 X 4-way mixed
1	4	4	1	1	1
2	8	8	2	2	2
3	12	4	3	1	3
4	16	16	4	4	4
5	16	4	5	1	4.25
6	16	8	6	2	4.25
7	16	4	7	1	4.5
8	16	16	8	8	8
9	16	4	9	1	4.5
10	16	8	10	2	4.25
11	16	4	11	1	4.25
12	16	16	12	4	4
13	16	4	13	1	4.75
14	16	8	14	2	8.5
15	16	4	15	1	12.25
16	16	16	16	16	16
17	16	4	16	1	12.25
18	16	8	16	2	8.5
19	16	4	16	1	4.75
20	16	16	16	4	4

*Assume access time per module is 16 time units.

Proof The average time to read n consecutive words is nT/IF. After the nth word it may take up to T seconds to access the start of the first word of the next block. Thus the total time for n word blocks is $nT/IF + T$. Dividing by n gives the average time per word. Q.E.D.

Table 4-2 lists this bound as a function of n for interleave factors of 4 and 16. Also, assuming a T of 16 allows comparison with Table 4-1. As n gets larger and larger, the bound gets better and the performance approaches that of a purely consecutive access pattern.

4.3.2 Sparse Addressing Patterns

Although the addressing patterns of the last section are by far the most common, there are many applications for which they are either unsuited or very inefficient. Some of these applications include:

1 Data-dependent operations
2 Sparse vector processing
3 Indirect table look-up

Table 4.2   Bound on Access Time for Submatrix Reads*

	Upper bound on average access time per word	
N	$IF = 4$	$IF = 16$
1	20	2
2	12	9
3	9.33	6.33
4	8	5
5	7.2	4.2
6	6.7	3.67
7	6.3	3.29
8	6	3
9	5.8	2.78
10	5.6	2.6
11	5.45	2.46
12	5.33	2.33
13	5.23	2.33
14	5.15	2.15
15	5.07	2.07
16	5	2
17	4.94	1.95
18	4.89	1.89
19	4.84	1.84
20	4.8	1.8

*n, number of consecutive words read before skipping. IF, interleave factor. T is assumed to equal 16 time units.

In a data-dependent operation whether or not a particular element of a vector participates in a particular operation depends on its value. A classic example of this is a "limit" operation of the form

For $i = 1$ to length of vector $\mathbf{A}$ if $A(i) >$ LIMIT   then $A(i) =$ LIMIT

Sparse vector processing is typified by vectors in which the vast majority of elements are zero and the nonzero elements are scattered somewhat randomly. Densities of 5% or less are not uncommon (fewer than 1 out of every 20 elements is nonzero). Circuit analysis, power grid management, and oil reservoir modeling are examples of such problems. For these problems, storing the entire vector costs tremendous amounts of memory space and degrades potential performance considerably since most operations are trivial ones involving only zeros.

Finally, it is often convenient to process vectors that are not data but addresses. Common examples include various forms of table interpolation where each element of a vector is to be used as an index into a table of values. Some kinds of sparse vector processing also fall into this category.

All these applications require methods of accessing vectors termed *sparse addressing* that are not directly compatible with the regular modes of the last section. The two most common vehicles for providing such capabilities are bit vectors and index vectors. This section discusses each separately.

The concept of a bit vector was introduced in Sec. 4.2.3. A bit vector is a vector where each element is a single bit holding only the values 0 or 1. For compactness the elements of a bit vector are packed as tightly as possible into words and the words are stored in consecutive locations. For memories with 32–64 bits per word, the accessing of bit vectors is orders of magnitude faster than that for other kinds of vectors. As described in Sec. 4.2.3, bit vectors may be generated from conditional operations, exception settings, or strings of bit vector instructions such as AND or OR.

Their primary usefulness in sparse vector processing lies in recording and managing in a very natural form those elements of some other vector that are to participate in an operation. There are at least three common ways in which this management is incorporated into vector instructions:

1 Selective store
2 Compression
3 Expansion

In *selective store,* a vector instruction includes in its specification of an output or result vector not only the address of a numeric vector to receive the data but also a bit vector of the same length. During execution of the instruction the ith computed result is stored only if bit i of the bit vector is 1. A 0 suppresses the store and leaves the original value in memory unchanged. Figure 4-8 diagrams an example of this.

This selective store is particularly useful in implementing data-dependent operations. For example, if some operation develops as a condition code a bit vector where a 1 implies that an overflow occurred during the computation of the ith element, then

Original contents of memory	Computed results	Bit vector	Final contents of memory
1	1.1	0	1
2	2.2	1	2.2
3	3.3	0	3
4	4.4	0	4
5	5.5	0	5
6	6.6	1	6.6
7	7.7	1	7.7
8	8.8	0	8

Figure 4-8 Example of selective store.

a selective store into that data array using the bit vector could replace all such elements with some standard pattern such as the largest representable floating-point number. Another example is to add 10 to all elements of a vector that are less than 0. A vector compare with 0 as described in Sec. 4.2.3 could generate the bit vector, and the specification of a selective store using this bit vector on a vector add could implement the rest. Finally, a vector operation to return in $C(i)$ the larger of $A(i)$ and $B(i)$ (where A, B, C are vectors) could be implemented as shown in Fig. 4-9.

The other two operations with bit vectors, *compress* and *expand,* are inverses of each other; they may be used in specifying either the input or the output vectors for a vector instruction. They are equivalent to the compress/expand operation of the programming language APL (cf. Iverson, 1962, or Pakin, 1968) and were first proposed for use in addressing vectors by Senzig (1967). In a compress, the bit vector has the same length as the data vector it is controlling. The data vector actually accessed consists only of those elements of the original data vector for which the equivalent bit of the bit vector is 1. When used as an input vector access specification, a compress greatly reduces the amount of data given to the arithmetic pipeline. When used as an

Initial A	Initial B	BV	Final C
1	2	0	2
2	2	1	2
3	2	1	3
4	10	0	10
−5	−4	0	−4
0	−3	1	0
6	5	1	6
−7	−8	1	−7

Steps

(1) Compare **A** and **B** (generate bit vector **BV**).
(2) Selective store **A** into **C** using **BV**.
(3) Complement **BV**.
(4) Selective store **B** into **C** using **BV**.

Figure 4-9 Use of selective store.

output vector access specification it is similar to a selective store except that the length of the output vector now depends on the number of 1s in the bit vector, not on the length of the calculation. Figure 4-10 diagrams an example.

Bit vector expansion is a partial inverse of compression similar to selective store. Here the length of the original data vector equals the number of 1s in the bit vector, and the length of the final vector equals the overall bit vector length. The ith element of the original data vector goes into the location corresponding to the ith 1 in the bit vector. The elements of the final vector corresponding to 0s in the bit vector may optionally either be zeroed if used in an input vector specification, or left alone if used as an output specification. Figure 4-11 diagrams an example of this.

Compress and expand are clearly useful in handling both data-dependent and sparse vector operations. In addition, by appropriate spacing of 1s and 0s any of the dense/regular access patterns can also be handled. However, implementation of bit vectors in a vector processor has far-reaching effects. First, the design of the vector memory address generation is much more complex since it now must access and accept bit vectors for its own use, then scan the bit vectors for 1s and generate memory addresses accordingly. Then the design of the arithmetic pipeline, or some equivalent resource, must be expanded both to generate bit vectors as the result of comparisons and to do operations on bit vectors such as AND and OR. The whole vector architecture must be adapted to allow specification of bit vectors and the extended instructions needed to control them. Finally, the use of bit vectors makes it very difficult to estimate the actual access time for data vectors, particularly when the 1s are scattered very randomly throughout. About all that can be said without detailed information on the design of a particular system is that there is some performance penalty involved because of the accessing and scanning of the bit vectors themselves; however, versatility is very great.

The second major method of sparse accessing is the use of *sparse index vectors*, which are simply vectors of numbers that are used either as direct memory addresses or as offsets from some memory pointer. With either implementation the accessing of a vector under sparse index control involves reading an element of the sparse index vector and using it to form another memory address containing the actual data. As in the bit vector operations there are several major variations possible, including *sparse pairing* and *selective read/write*. In sparse pairing the index vector is never used to address a vector directly. Instead it merely indicates which elements of a very large vector, which is never in main memory in its entirety, are potentially nonzero. The actual values for these locations are stored in a separate data vector of the same length as the index vector. Figure 4-12 diagrams an example. Instructions to perform more basic vector operations on such vectors must first compare index sets to match up data elements; only then can they do the desired operations. Figure 4-13 diagrams an add of two such entities. Note that the lengths of all three vectors are different.

Selective read/write is similar to bit vector control compress and expand. Each element of the index set points to the next element of the desired vector. Figure 4-14 diagrams an example. As in expand, elements of a vector not directly modified by a selective write may be either zeroed or left alone.

Data vector	Bit vector	After compression
1.1	1	1.1
2.2	0	4.4
3.3	0	5.5
4.4	1	8.8
5.5	1	
6.6	0	
7.7	0	
8.8	1	

Figure 4-10 Bit vector compress.

Data vector	Bit vector	After expansion
1.1	1	1.1
4.4	0	0 *
5.5	0	0 *
8.8	1	4.4
	1	5.5
	0	0 *
	0	0 *
	1	8.8

*Depending on implementation, may be old values.

Figure 4-11 Bit vector expansion.

Index vector	Data vector	Equivalent representation
1	3.1	3.1
3	4.7	0
7	3.1415	4.7
8	2	0
		0
		0
		3.1415
		2
		0
		–
		–
		–

Figure 4-12 Sparse pairing.

Input A		Input B		Output C = A + B	
Index	Data	Index	Data	Index	Data
2	1.1	3	5.5	2	1.1
5	2.2	5	6.6	3	5.5
100	3.3	6	7.7	5	8.8
102	4.4	102	8.8	6	7.7
		103	9.9	100	3.3
				102	13.2
				103	9.9

Figure 4-13 Addition of sparse vectors.

Data vector	Index vector	After compression
1.1	1	1.1
2.2	4	4.4
3.3	5	5.5
4.4	8	8.8
5.5		
6.6		
7.7		
8.8		

Data vector	Index vector	After expansion
1.1	1	1.1
4.4	4	0*
5.5	5	0*
8.8	8	4.4
		5.5
		0*
		0*
		8.8

*Depending on implementation, may be old values.

Figure 4-14 Selective read/write. (Top) Index vector compression. (Bottom) Index vector expansion.

Besides being ideal for implementing sparse vector problems, index vectors are perhaps the only convenient and efficient way of implementing table look-up or interpolation functions on a vector machine. The data vector to be interpolated is first converted into an integer form compatible with address formats. The resulting vector is then used as the index set for one or more selective reads to access the desired table. Other standard vector operations can then complete the process.

Implementation of index vectors in their full generally is even more complex than bit vectors since the vector address generator must now perform two memory accesses per data word delivered to the arithmetic element, one for the index vector and one for the data. In addition, the vector address generator must also add bases, compare index sets, and merge them. If the full generality is included, the vector address generation begins to look like an entire vector processor by itself.

Performance is also difficult to predict because there are two distinct accesses involved. The time required to access the index vector is probably predictable since it is most likely of a dense/regular pattern. On the other hand, the actual access time for the data depends on the statistics of the modules that the addresses of the index vector fall into; therefore the access time depends on the problem.

4.4 SAMPLE SYSTEMS

This section describes the relevant characteristics of several pipelined vector-processing systems. Although the list is by no means complete, the systems described here are either representative of a larger class or have unique features. Further information on these systems is available in the open literature.

For each system the description includes the relevant hardware and instruction set characteristics. The intent is not to fully describe each system; instead the descriptions will demonstrate real implementations of the topics discussed earlier in this chapter. Further, many of the systems employ pipelining in areas other than the vector processor. Such designs are excluded here but will be discussed in later chapters.

4.4.1 IBM 2938 Array Processor

The IBM 2938 Array Processor (IBM, 1968; Ruggiero and Coryell, 1969) is a stored-program computer normally used to augment a conventional computing system, termed the host system, by providing a high-speed vector-processing capability. In terms of Fig. 4-1, it provides the functions of the vector memory controller and address generator, the local memory, the arithmetic pipeline, and much of the vector controller. The rest of the functions reside in the computer to which it is attached.

A partial list of the vector instructions the IBM 2938 may execute includes:

- Element-by-element vector multiply

$$Y(i) = X(i)\, U(i)$$

- Element-by-element vector add

$$Y(i) = X(i) + U(i)$$

- Vector inner product

$$Y = \sum_i X(i)\, U(i)$$

- Sum of vector elements

$$Y = \sum_i X(i)$$

- Sum of squares

$$Y = \sum_i X(i)\, X(i)$$

- Convolving multiply

$$Y(i) = \sum_j U(j)\, X(i + j - 1)$$

- Difference equation
- Partial matrix multiplication
- Vector move
- Vector fixed to floating-point, and floating-point to fixed, conversion

Besides error status the 2938 also keeps status on the largest result computed by the vector instructions. An additional instruction HIGH VALUE READOUT allows the user to access this status value.

Vectors may be in either fixed-point or floating-point format; they may be stored in purely sequential or regularly spaced storage locations. Each vector may have its own length; padding by zero is employed if two vectors in the same instruction have different lengths.

Figure 4-15 diagrams the basic hardware architecture of the IBM 2938. There are two external connections: One is directly to the host's storage system and is used for vector data access; the other connection is with the host's I/O system for a source of vector instructions. The internal architecture of the 2938 includes an *indexing and operand fetch unit* that dynamically generates the addresses of the vector elements as required. Two buffers of 32 words each serve the local memory function. The *X buffer* provides data inputs to the arithmetic pipeline, and the *Y buffer* provides both input and output storage. The arithmetic pipeline is a four-stage linear pipeline that performs a combined floating-point multiply-add at a staging rate of 200 ns. The entire unit is under microprogrammed control.

In addition to containing data the *Y* buffer also has something akin to a bit vector. Each word in this buffer has associated with it an overflow tag bit that is set whenever the arithmetic pipeline generates a result to be stored in that word that is too large for the number system employed. When that result is later transferred to main storage, the value is replaced by one with the largest possible magnitude.

The host computer is responsible for generating programs for the 2938. When such a program is to be executed, the host performs a START I/O command, which

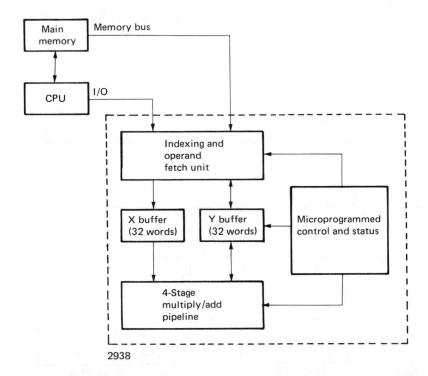

Figure 4-15   IBM 2938 Array Processor.

then delivers to the 2938 the desired sequence of vector instructions in a *channel command word* (*CCW*) chain. Each entry in this chain corresponds to a 2938 instruction, and each entry includes a code giving the desired operation, some flags, and an address of a block of storage that further defines the desired vector operands locations in storage. This list, called an *operand control word* (*OCW*) list, has one entry for each vector operand. The entry defines the format of the data in the vector, the address of the first element, the spacing between elements, and the number of elements in the vector. Once inside the 2938 the OCW list then controls the indexing and operand fetch unit, while the opcode triggers the appropriate microprogram to perform the desired function. Figure 4-16 diagrams this sequence. We note that the host is free to do other work while the 2938 is busy with a program.

Once the 2938 has started a vector instruction, the actual operation depends on the particular operation called for. However, Fig. 4-17 is a simplified reservation table for a typical instruction such as a vector element-by-element multiply or add. First, the next 32 elements of the **X** vector are read from storage into a buffer. Then the next 32 **U** elements are read in while computation is started on each pair. Finally, the 32 results are returned to storage. This pattern is repeated as often as required to process the entire vector.

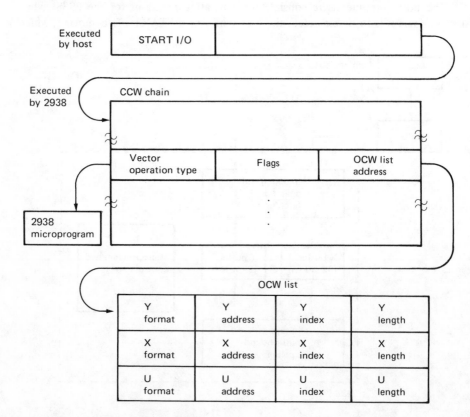

Figure 4-16 IBM 2938 instruction flow.

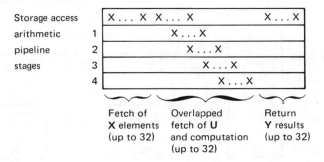

Figure 4-17   Simplified reservation table for typical IBM 2938 vector instruction.

4.4.2   The Texas Instruments Advanced Scientific Computer

The Texas Instruments Advanced Scientific Computer (TI ASC) (Watson, 1972*a,b,* 1974; Stephenson, 1973, 1975; Enslow (Appendix M), 1974) is a heavily pipelined computer with all the elements of Fig. 4-1. Its instruction set contains both scalar and vector instructions, the latter of which includes:

* Vector element-by-element add, subtract, multiply, divide, shift, and logical operations
* Vector inner products, matrix products
* Vector compare, merge, order, search, pick peak, and select

The addressing modes available to the programmer are all dense/regular, but they include several dimensions of addressability, allowing not only vectors but regularly stored matrices of two or more dimensions to be handled. This is an expansion on the submatrix mode of access. No sparse modes are included.

Figure 4-18 diagrams the basic hardware architecture of the ASC. In a typical configuration the main memory is an 8 × 8 -way interleaved design: 8 modules combined into simple blocks, 8 blocks interleaved in complex fashion, with a bandwidth of 4 × 10^8 words/s.

A *memory control unit* (*MCU*) handles not only the interleaved memory, but also simultaneous requests from the I/O, arithmetic pipelines, and instruction units. The *instruction processing unit* (*IPU*) is a heavily pipelined scalar processor that also includes instructions to set up vector operations. Its basic clock is 60 ns.

All vector operations and the actual execution of many scalar instructions are carried out in from one to four *memory buffer unit* (*MBU*)/*arithmetic unit* (*AU*) pairs. Figure 4-19 diagrams this pair in more detail. In terms of Fig. 4-1 the MBU incorporates the functions of the vector address generator and local memory. There are three pairs of eight-word buffers, two pairs for input to the pipeline and one pair for output. They function much as a combination of a swinging buffer and a queue (Sec. 2.2.2), with the MBU loading/unloading the X', Y', Z' buffers while the AU reads X

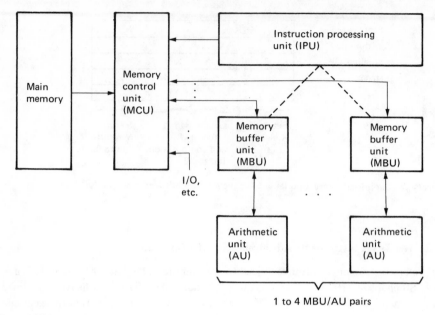

Figure 4-18   TI ASC processor architecture.

and Y, and places its results in Z. Where X or Y are empty, they are loaded from X' or Y' and the cycle repeats.

The AU, which performs the actual arithmetic calculations, is a truly multiconfigurable pipeline with eight stages. It may handle either floating-point or fixed-point operations. Figure 4-20 gives some reservation tables for several typical operations. Notice that the order of usage of stages can vary greatly. A microprogram is responsible for both timing the initiations and controlling the flow through the pipeline. As in the IPU, the basic clock for the AU is 60 ns. Each stage was implemented with 10 or fewer levels of ECL logic.

Vector operations are triggered by the inclusion in a scalar program of one of two special instructions, VECTL and VECT. Both of these instructions make reference to eight special IPU registers called the vector parameter file (VPF). The contents of this file are set up by a conventional SISD program, and when either VECTL or VECT is executed their contents are transferred to an MBU/AU pair for execution of the vector operation. The only difference between the two instructions is that VECT assumes the VPF is loaded, while VECTL provides a memory address of an eight-word block to be loaded into the VPF before processing. The information contained in this VPF includes

- An opcode describing the desired vector operation
- An indication of whether the vectors are one- or two-dimensional
- A base address for each vector operand
- Specification of an IPU register for each vector operand, whose value is to be used as an offset from the base

- Skip value and counts for the first dimension
- Skip values and counts for the second dimension

Because the dimension limits are separate from the vector addresses, all operands are assumed to be of the same size and shape so there is no special padding.

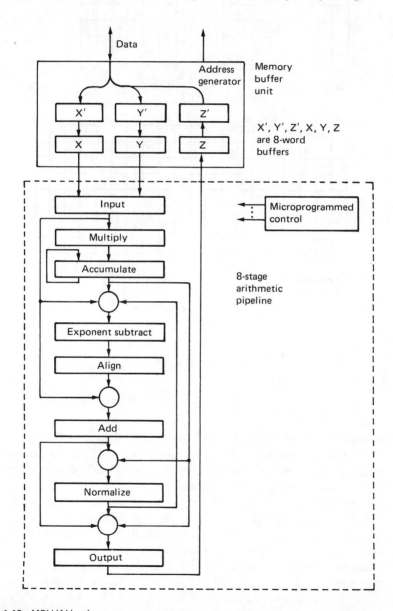

Figure 4-19 MBU/AU pair.

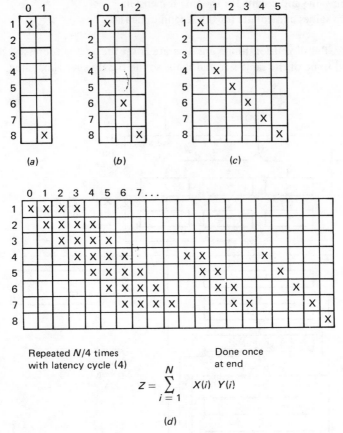

Figure 4-20 Typical operations in the TI ASC AU. (a) Logical. (b) Fixed-point add. (c) Floating-point add. (d) Vector inner product.

4.4.3 Control Data STAR-100

The Control Data STAR-100 (Hintz and Tate, 1972; Jones, 1972; Krider, 1972; Requa, 1972; Control Data Corp., 1975; Ramamoorthy, 1977) is a heavily pipelined computer having all the elements of Fig. 4-1. Like the TI-ASC, its instruction set includes both scalar and vector instructions. However, while the ASC is oriented towards regularly organized matrix type operations, the STAR-100 has a great many sparse vector features built around the use of bit vectors. The primary method for accessing vectors is purely sequential; any other pattern is handled by variation of the selective store, compress, and expand operations described in Sec. 4.3.2.

The hardware architecture of the STAR-100 is shown in Fig. 4-21. The memory is 32-way interleaved, each module holding 2048 512-bit words. Access to the memory is controlled by the storage access controller (SAC), which simultaneously manages four independent memory-request paths with transfers performed in 128-bit packets called quarterwords. Three of these paths provide vector operands and results, and the fourth handles I/O and bit-vector references. The design of these two units permits an aggregate transfer rate of 512 bits every 40 ns.

The stream unit contains both the scalar instruction decode and execution, the vector control functions, and the equivalent of the local memory. This latter consists of 64 quarterwords of buffering. Additional buffering is also included for instructions and control vectors. The stream unit is responsible for generating the memory access requests required to keep these buffers full.

There are two separate pipelined processors connected to the stream unit, each of which may run independently of the other. The first, pipeline 1, contains a four-stage floating-point adder and an eight-stage floating-point multiplier. It is used for many scalar instructions that perform either address calculations or scalar floating-point calculations. Pipeline 2 has not only a floating-point adder but also a general-purpose pipeline unit that can perform floating-point multiply, divide, or square root. It also includes a nonpipelined divider. Its major function is handling vector operations. Both pipelines have a basic clock of 40 ns, and are microprogram-controlled. They are dynamically configurable with several internal paths, and they use the microprograms to perform a static configuration when vector operations are in progress. In addition, the floating-point pipelines are often "splittable"; that is, even though they normally

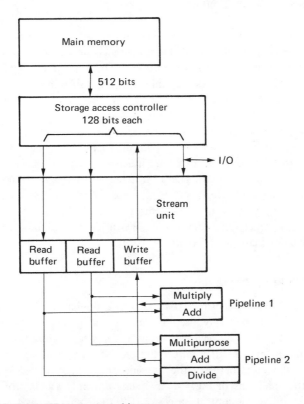

Figure 4-21 CDC STAR-100 hardware architecture.

process 64-bit numbers at one operation per clock, they can be reconfigured to process two 32-bit number operations in the same clock. This provides twice the performance in operations per second when the lesser accuracy is sufficient.

The vector instruction set of the STAR-100 has no equivalent to the TI ASC's vector parameter file. Instead a typical vector instruction is similar in general format to many of the other scalar instructions and specifies various scalar CPU registers as the source of the vector definitions. This allows a program to compute in a conventional fashion the vector-addressing parameters needed by a later vector instruction and to leave them in an arbitrary CPU register until needed. When a typical vector instruction is encountered the opcode indicates the desired vector instruction, and the rest of the instruction specifies seven CPU registers holding the following information:

1   The base address of one vector input operand **A** and its length
2   An offset that is to be added to the above vector base to determine the exact location of the first word of the vector to be accessed
3   The base and length of the second input vector **B**
4   An offset for the second input base
5   The base and length of the result vector **C**
6   The base of a bit vector **CV**
7   An offset for both **C** and **CV**.

In operation the stream unit uses the base and offset for vectors **A** and **B** to determine the first memory word to read; then it directs the storage control unit to read these vectors sequentially into the read buffers. The appropriate pipeline then reads the read buffers, computes the results, and stores the results in the write buffer. Using the control bit vector defined in the instruction, the stream unit then returns the selected results to storage as described in Sec. 4.3.2.

In addition to the typical vector instructions the STAR-100 also includes vector compress and expand instructions, along with instructions to generate and manipulate the bit vectors used for controls. These are much as described in Sec. 4.3.2. Furthermore, the STAR-100 also includes a set of instructions that is a mixture of vector and scalar functions where no vector result is generated. For example, one instruction can compare two vectors **A** and **B** in an element-by-element fashion; it stops as soon as an element of **A** has a larger value than that in **B**. An identification of where this occurs is then saved in a designated CPU register.

4.4.4   IBM 3838 Array Processor

The IBM 3838 Array Processor (IBM, 1976) is similar to the IBM 2938 Array Processor in that it is normally used to augment a more conventional computing system by providing a high-speed vector processing capability. However, there are some substantial differences that reflect the growth in technology and architectural development in the years between the two machines. First, the 3838 has to a large extent all of the functions of Fig. 4-1, including not only a bulk store (BS) to hold vector operands but also a control processor (CP) that functions as a vector controller and provides the user with 15 scalar registers and a set of scalar instructions to assist in vector instruction preparation. Also unlike the 2938, there is only a single connection to the host, a high-speed I/O channel, over which both 3838 programs and data are exchanged. Further, the 3838 can have up to seven independent users simultaneously active within itself, and the processing steps for each user are pipelined at many different levels within the 3838 subsystems.

The 3838 includes in its vector instruction set not only the standard operations found in the 2938 and other vector processors but also a large set of rather complex functions. These include fast Fourier transforms, a variety of different table interpolations, recursive digital filters and optimal filter coefficient derivations, trigonometric and transcendental functions of vector operands, polynomial evaluations, matrix operations and solutions to matrix equations of the form $Ax = b$ for certain classes of matrices, and others. The manufacturer maintains a service that will augment this instruction set with new vector operations to match specific user requirements.

The hardware of the 3838 directly supports the purely sequential, regularly spaced, and submatrix modes of vector accessing as described in Sec. 4.3.1. In addition, a combination of these modes of access and special microcode in other parts of the processor provides some of the capabilities of index sets.

Figure 4-22 diagrams the basic hardware architecture of the 3838. In addition to the bulk store (BS) and control processor (CP) mentioned earlier, there is also an I/O

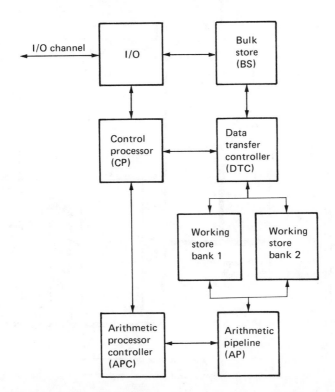

Figure 4-22 IBM 3838 Array Processor architecture.

unit that runs independently of the other subunits during the transfer of programs and data between the host and bulk store. The role of local memory in this processor is assumed by working store, two 8192-byte storage units in a swinging buffer arrangement (Sec. 2.2.2). The transfer of vectors and vector segments between bulk store and working store is the responsibility of the data transfer controller (DTC). This microprogrammed unit takes vector addressing parameters from the CP, generates the appropriate sequence of addresses for both bulk and working store, and performs the desired transfers. The actual transfers are themselves pipelined, and a variety of format conversion options are possible as the data flows through the DTC.

The arithmetic pipeline (AP) is the main computational element in the 3838; it is itself designed around a collection of individually pipelined modules shown in Fig. 4-23. These include floating-point multipliers and adders (four stages each), sine/cosine

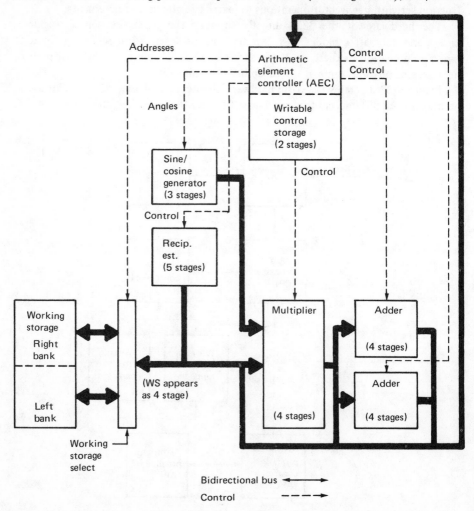

Figure 4-23 Arithmetic processor and working storage.

generator (three stages), and reciprocal estimation (five stages). Even the source of data for the AP, the working store, is treated as a four-stage pipeline. The time for all stages is 100 ns. There are a variety of different modes for each module and different paths between modules all under microprogrammed control. This control is a combination of the time- and data-stationary approaches defined in Sec. 3.4.3. The staging latches coupling most of the modules are register files whose addresses may be varied by the microprogram. This permits the introduction of delays where needed to boost performance (see Sec. 3.2.7). Figure 4-24 diagrams a typical reservation table.

Finally, there is one additional subunit within the 3838, the arithmetic processor controller (APC). This unit has two functions: initialization of the AP to perform the desired sequence of microprograms and synchronization of the AP's usage of working store with the DTC. It too is microprogrammed.

Overall operation of the 3838 is shown in Fig. 4-25. The host computer prepares a 3838 program and the data to be used. It then activates the I/O channel to the 3838 and sends the desired 3838 program in a central information table (CIT). The CIT contains both the vector and scalar operations to be performed by the 3838 and instructions on when to accept data from the host and where in bulk store to place it. Thus when the host end of the I/O channel starts to send the associated data, the 3838 is ready to accept it.

Once the data is in bulk store, the CP begins to execute the other instructions. For each vector instruction it encounters, it prepares for both the APC and the DTC a *link list* describing the microprograms to be executed and the parameters to be used during their execution. For the DTC these parameters consist of base addresses, vector lengths, and spacing parameters. The vector instruction in the CIT either may specify these directly or may indicate that the value may be found in one of the user-accessible scalar registers.

Once prepared, these link lists are passed to the APC and DTC for execution. Synchronization primitives in the 3838 hardware permit the APC and DTC to keep each other in step, so that while the DTC is loading one-half of working store with vector data, the APC is directing the AP to perform the desired vector operation on data in the other half. When both units complete their steps, they reverse the role of the working store banks and continue.

Because the subunits in the 3838 are all independent, effective pipelining can exist at several levels other than within the AP. Up to seven entirely different users may be active simultaneously within a 3838, each with its own CIT, data vectors, and set of scalar registers. While the I/O is transferring data for one user, the CP may be preparing link lists for a second, the APC/DTC/AP may be executing vector instructions for a third, and other user activities may be queued up for service at several spots. The net result is that all elements of the 3838 tend to be fully utilized, maximizing total throughput.

4.4.5 Cray Research CRAY-1

The Cray Research CRAY-1 (Cray, 1976; Johnson, 1978; Ramamoorthy, 1977) is a heavily pipelined computer having all the elements of Fig. 4-1. Its instruction set is a

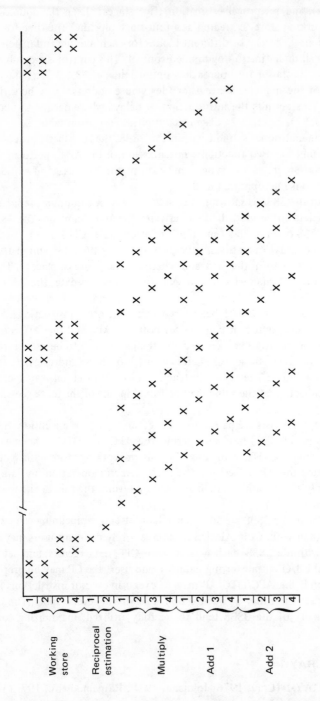

Figure 4-24 A reservation table for the IBM 3838.

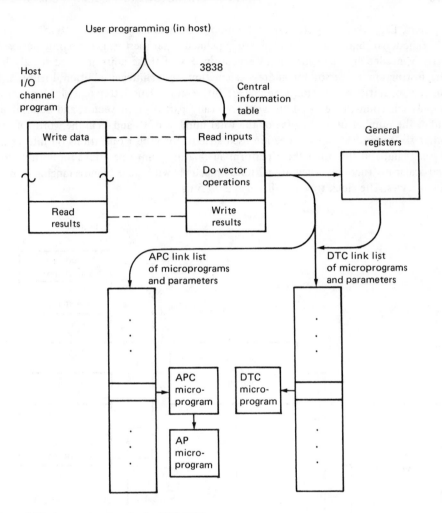

Figure 4-25 Instruction flow in the IBM 3838.

heavily integrated combination of scalar and vector instructions. The elements of vectors may be regularly spaced in memory with some bit-vector capability included to allow selective stores and vector tests. A unique characteristic of this machine is that the local memory is visible to the programmer and can be loaded/unloaded under program control.

The scalar pipeline is described in more detail in Sec. 6.6.3.

The hardware architecture of the CRAY-1 is outlined in Fig. 4-26. The basic clock for the entire system is 12.5 ns. The memory contains both vectors, scalars, and instructions. It is a 16-way interleaved design where each memory module may be read or written every four clocks.

The instruction processor holds all scalar registers and performs all instruction decoding and system control. The local memory function is filled by eight vector registers. Each vector register can contain up to 64 words (vector elements). There are 12 functional units, all of which are pipelined, that perform any computational activity needed by an instruction's execution. Six of these units are used strictly by the instruction processor for address calculation, scalar integer addition, logical, and shifting operations, and for scanning of bit vectors. This latter unit, leading zero/ population count, takes a 64-bit word, typically part of a bit vector, and determines either the number of leading 0s, or the total number of 0s and 1s in the word. Of the other six functional units, three are used strictly for vector operations on integer or logical data, and the other three perform all floating-point operations for both vector and scalar instructions. They are all linear pipelines with stage lengths ranging from 2 to 14 stages. The clock time for all stages is 12.5 ns.

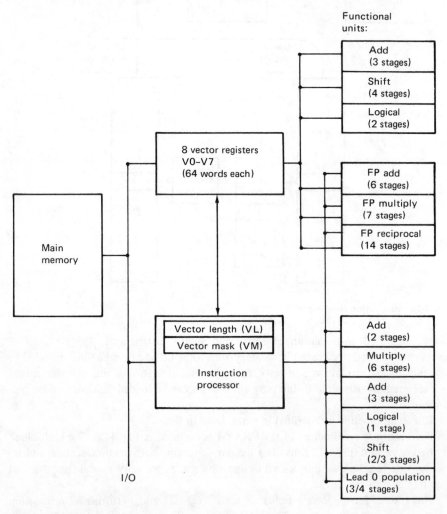

Figure 4-26 CRAY-1 processor architecture. FP = floating point.

Most vector instructions have the same format as their scalar equivalents, that is a 16-bit instruction having a seven-bit opcode and specification of three of the vector registers. The operations that may be specified include add, subtract, multiply, reciprocal estimate, logicals, and shifts. They are all performed on an element-by-element basis. For example, if vector registers Vi, Vj, and Vk are selected, then the mth element of Vj and Vk are run through the appropriate functional unit and back to the mth element of Vi. The *vector length* register in the instruction processor contains the maximum value of m, which can be no greater than 64. Vector registers may be reused, so that an entire vector program can be run strictly on data in these registers without reference to the main memory.

The *vector mask* (*VM*) register contains a 64-bit bit vector for use in a certain selective store-like operation called a merge. The mth bit of the VM register determines which of two vector registers will be used to provide the mth element of the result register. Other uses of the VM register include holding the results of a vector test instruction. Each element of a selected vector register is tested according to some condition, and if it meets the condition, the equivalent bit in VM is set to 1. This may then be used either for a later merge or by scalar instructions that have the capability of accessing selected elements of a vector register.

There are separate instructions for transferring data between the vector registers and main memory. These instructions specify a memory starting address, a space value, and a vector register. Transfers proceed at one element per clock except for certain spacing values that, as described in Sec. 4.3.1, cause memory conflicts and consequent slower transfer rates. At most 64 words may be transferred with a single instruction. Vector operations involving vectors longer than 64 must be explicitly programmed and broken into pieces no longer than 64.

As mentioned in Sec. 4.2.1, reduction operations form an important part of many scientific programs. However, the CRAY-1 includes no specific instructions for such operations. Instead its design permits almost any of its vector instructions to be converted into a reduction operator by simply specifying that one of the input vector registers be the same as the one that receives the result. When this is done, the operation of the vector instruction is changed so that the mth element of the unique vector register is combined with the $m - (d + 2)$ element of the other register, where d is the compute time of the functional unit. Further, this $m - (d + 2)$ element is a value that has just been computed by the pipeline, so that a recursion is formed. The vector operation is thus equivalent to interleaving $d + 2$ different "backed-up" recursions just as described in Sec. 2.4. After completion of the vector operation there remain $d + 2$ partial results which must be combined by scalar operations. For example, a vector add instruction using Vj for one input and Vi for both the other input and the result will take the 64 elements of Vj and sum them into eight partial sums in Vi. (The floating-point add functional unit has six stages.) These eight partial sums can then be added together by a scalar program to compute the final result.

The CRAY-1 also includes other unique features that can enhance performance of vector operations. The first is that vector instructions that do not use any of the same vector registers may execute nearly simultaneously. Thus an add of $V0$ and $V1$ into $V2$ may proceed at the same time as a multiply of $V3$ by $V4$ into $V5$. The other feature is termed *chaining;* it occurs when the result register for one vector instruction is the same as one of the input registers for the next instruction. If the instructions use separate functional units, very often the hardware will start the second vector operation during the clock when the first result from the first operation is just leaving its functional unit. A copy of this result is forwarded directly to the second functional unit and the first execution of the second vector is started. This cycle is then repeated for every clock thereafter; a copy of the result of one functional unit is forwarded to the next. The net result is that the execution of both vector operations takes only roughly d clock units longer than the first vector operation alone, where d is the compute time of the second functional unit. This is equivalent to constructing a new pipeline to compute the aggregate function whose compute time is the sum of the compute times of the individual functional units.

By proper programming, more than two vector instructions can be chained together. This includes not only arithmetic operations but also vector transfers between memory and vector registers. Johnson (1978) includes an example of the chaining of four vector instructions.

PROBLEMS

4-1 For some computer instruction set with which you are familiar, define a set of subroutines that implement basic vector operations. Be sure to include how you specify operand addresses, error flags, and so forth. Do not use bit vectors.

4-2 Repeat the previous problem using bit vectors in the addressing specification.

4-3 What techniques might you use to optimize the performance of a set of hand-coded vector-processing subroutines? Demonstrate with a subroutine to compute the checksum of all elements of a vector.

4-4 Assume that you were going to build a vector-processor attachment to the machine you used in Prob. 4-2. Diagram one possible design and draw a reservation table describing its operation.

4-5 Vector instructions where one operand is a scalar are often implemented as a series of different reservation tables. Why is this? What might be the purpose of the various reservation tables?

4-6 Assume a vector processor where the local memory is implemented as a swinging buffer (cf. Fig. 2-22b) where each buffer is random access to the one unit that currently owns it.

    a Describe via a reservation table how such a system would execute vector instructions, assuming that both buffers are used alternately in the instruction's execution.

    b Describe via a reservation table how this would work if all transfer between the main memory and the arithmetic unit for a single instruction went through just one of the buffers freeing the other buffer for equivalent use on a second vector instruction.

    c Describe the differences between the two approaches.

4-7 Give some estimate of the relative cost/performance of the memory systems used in Table 4-1.

4-8 Assuming each memory module takes 16 clock units per access and that the memory system is a 4 × 4 mixed interleave, how many cycles does it take to read an $N \times 2$, $N \times 3$, $N \times 4$, and $N \times 5$ submatrix out of an $N \times 7$, $N \times 8$, and $N \times 9$ matrix stored in row order?

4-9 Compute the performance of a complex interleaved memory when accessing a vector whose components are from random locations.

4-10 Design a vector memory address controller and generator that implements compress and expand operations within it.

4-11 Design a pipelined vector processor that accesses vectors specified by sparse index sets. Describe how it works for basic vector operations. Use reservation tables where relevant.

4-12 Using the machine of Prob. 4-11 describe in detail how an inner product operation would function.

4-13 Sketch out several ways of summing up all elements of a long vector on the CRAY-1.

4-14 List how much flexibility the sample machines have in dynamically computing vector addressing parameters.

Chapter 5

The Programming
of Pipelined Vector
Processors

The intrinsic nature of a pipelined vector processor makes the task of programming it efficiently rather different than that of more conventional computing machines. The basic data structures and the operations performed by these machines are both more complex and require a different approach to program organization. This chapter explores these differences in detail.

The first section covers the implementation of individual vector instructions, emphasizing how the presence of pipelining affects both the way a vector instruction must be executed and the period of time required for that execution to complete. This is important not because many programmers ever get involved in such areas, but because the way a basic vector instruction is implemented has a dramatic effect on the performance of a machine on a real problem. A good programmer of a pipelined vector-processing system must take these considerations into account when designing a program.

The second section of this chapter emphasizes these performance considerations by using the insights from the first section to construct some models of program behavior when more than one vector instruction is combined into a bigger program. These models are typical of those used in timing analyses of real or proposed vector programs. Their results indicate several specific areas that must be considered in program design.

The final section discusses the "vectorization" of real problems, namely how an algorithm can be constructed expressly to solve problems on a pipelined vector processor and what kinds of tradeoffs are possible to optimize overall performance. Example problems demonstrate these tradeoffs in a hierarchical fashion, each example stressing one particular aspect of vector program design. In addition, there is a short discussion of the differences in program design if the underlying vector processor is parallel rather than pipelined.

5.1 VECTOR INSTRUCTION IMPLEMENTATION

There are several levels of "programming" within any computing system. At the highest level are programs written in a high-order language that specifies operations on data abstractions without concern for the hardware implementing them. Below this is assembly or machine-language coding which specifies operations on memory locations or registers. These are the two levels most familiar to the programmer; however, there are levels below these. Even though a programmer may never be involved at these levels, knowledge of how they function can be of great benefit. This is particularly true of pipelined vector processors. Therefore, the emphasis in this section is on exactly how a vector instruction is developed and how it operates.

In a pipelined vector processor there are at least two levels of programming below the machine-code level. The first describes the implementation of a vector instruction in terms of how vector element addresses are generated, how data is rolled in and out of local memory, and how the arithmetic pipeline is synchronized with these transfers. Below this is the description of how each processing unit such as the arithmetic pipeline performs its specific task. These levels typically are coded only by the manufacturer in either microprogram or sequential logic design. However there are exceptions. For example, some machines (Wittmayer, 1978) allow the programmer access to both levels, down to specifying how each vector element travels through the system. At the other level, machines like the CRAY-1 (Cray, 1976) with its vector registers and chaining features require the machine-level programmer to specify his own vector segmentation and synchronization.

Detailed descriptions of a machine's functioning at these levels is usually found only in the hardware manuals produced by the manufacturer. About the only generally available literature sources are survey articles such as Ramamoorthy (1977), general techniques (Kogge, 1977a,b), and some specific documentation on the TI ASC machine (Stephenson 1973, 1975).

5.1.1 Segmentation

The key problem to be solved by the outer of the two levels of programming is how to handle local memory. Since local memory is never big enough to hold all the data for a vector instruction, it is necessary to *segment* the vector and page these pieces in and out as required. The result is that at this level the processor appears as a two-stage pipeline in its own right, one stage accessing the vector segments to and from main memory and the other processing them in the arithmetic pipeline. Local memory serves as the staging latch between them. Figure 5-1 diagrams typical reservation tables

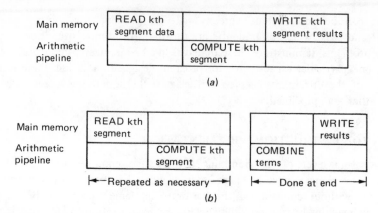

Figure 5-1 Reservation tables for segmentation. (*a*) Vector input/vector result. (*b*) Vector input/ scalar result (reduction operator).

for this segmentation process. Note the difference between the cases where the result itself is a vector and must be segmented and where it is a scalar not known until all data has been processed. Also, there is a deliberate lack of time scale on these tables since many machine-dependent parameters such as addressing modes, vector lengths, and memory designs affect the timing of these processes.

The task of choosing a segmentation strategy is not as easy as it might appear. Given a particular machine design, a time scale can be added to Fig. 5-1 and various segmentation algorithms compared. These strategies will differ in how they answer several basic questions: how will each vector be partitioned, what size are the segments, and in what order are they accessed. These choices are affected in turn by the addressing capabilities of the memory controller, the possible variations in user-supplied addressing parameters, and the structure of the local memory. Furthermore, all this often dramatically affects the arithmetic function actually implemented in the arithmetic pipeline. However, because we are dealing with terms expressible as reservation tables, the theory of Chap. 3 can often provide quick insight into the design process.

The best way to demonstrate the principles involved in the design process is through examples. Following are descriptions of how two different vector instructions might be designed for a typical pipelined vector processor. The first is a simple vector element-by-element add; the second is more complicated and includes a reduction operator.

Example 1 Segmentation of vector element-by-element add One of the most common vector instructions takes two input vectors X and U, assumed to be of equal length, and produces an output vector Y of the same length, where for all i, $Y(i) = X(i) + U(i)$. Here there is only one general approach to segmentation, that is, take Q elements at a time from vectors X and U into local memory, compute Q results, and return to Y. The range of possible Q's depends on the machine

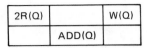

2R(Q)		W(Q)
	ADD(Q)	

Figure 5-2 Reservation table for vector add.

design. The reservation table for one segment looks like Fig. 5-2 with the following definitions:

$$R(Q) = \text{time to read } Q \text{ elements of a vector}$$
$$\text{ADD}(Q) = \text{time to compute } Q \text{ sums in the arithmetic pipeline}$$
$$W(Q) = \text{time to write } Q \text{ results back to main memory}$$

If the machine design does not allow local memory to be used simultaneously by both the arithmetic pipeline and the memory controller, then the MAL bound on the latency between initiations is $L(Q) = 2R(Q) + \text{ADD}(Q) + W(Q)$. If the overlap is allowed, however, then from Chap. 3 the MAL bound is the greatest number of marks per row, or $L(Q) = \text{MAXIMUM } (2R(Q) + W(Q), \text{ADD}(Q))$. Further, the total time is approximately $2R(Q) + (N/Q) L(Q) + W(Q)$, where N is the length of each vector (see Fig. 5-3). We note that the arithmetic pipeline is inactive during the first $2R(Q)$ time units (first data being loaded) and last $W(Q)$ time units (final answers being returned). These are the times required to *start up* and *flush* the two-stage pipe of Fig. 5-1.

For arbitrary values of N, these tend to make the total execution time take on the form

$$a + bQ + \frac{N}{Q} (c + dQ)$$

where a, b, c, d are constants such that $a + bQ$ is $2R(Q) + W(Q)$ and $c + dQ$ is $L(Q)$. The constants a and c are individual start-up/flush times for the pipelined memory controllers and arithmetic units. Figure 5-4 diagrams the generic shape of this total time as a function of Q. As shown, the total time is minimal for certain values of Q in the neighborhood of $Q = \sqrt{Nc/b}$. Whether or not this value of Q

Time

2R(Q*)	2R(Q)	X	W(Q*)	2R(Q)	W(Q)	2R(Q)	W(Q)	X	W(Q)
X	ADD(Q*)		ADD(Q)		ADD(Q)		ADD(Q)		X

| Start-up | | | | Repeat $N/Q - 3$ times | | | | Flush | |

Q	= Standard-sized segment
Q*	= Odd-sized segment
R(Q)	= Time to read Q elements
W(Q)	= Time to return Q results
Add (Q)	= Time to add two vectors in local memory of size Q
X	= Idle time

Figure 5-3 Segmentation of vector add.

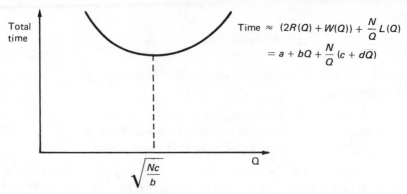

Figure 5-4 Effect of segment size on performance.

can actually be used to implement the algorithm depends to a large extent on the size of the local memory and the expected ranges of N.

Since the values of N are user-dependent, it is usually impossible to guarantee that N will always be an integer multiple of Q. Therefore the processor must be capable of handling small, odd-sized segments of vectors. This can be done by padding the vectors with 0s, at a cost in performance, or by handling one odd-sized initiation. The latter approach is usually taken, even though it means more complex logic in the vector controllers. Further, the odd-sized piece is usually handled first, both because once finished, the controller can handle only Q-sized pieces in a standard fashion, and because it offers a slight performance increase over other possibilities such as odd segment last.

Again from Chap. 3 we recall that more insight can be gained in investigating a pipelined problem by looking at stage utilization. Maximum utilization of the hardware occurs when all rows of the reservation table have the same number of marks. In this example, this occurs when $2R(Q) + W(Q) = \text{ADD}(Q)$. When dealing with purely sequential vectors this is approximately true when the bandwidth of the main memory is three times the basic arithmetic pipeline stage time. However, when dealing with a regularly spaced or sparse access where the skip values clash with the memory's interleaving, this ratio can jump by an order of magnitude and totally dominate the $\text{ADD}(Q)$ component. Therefore the system must be designed with a memory with more bandwidth than needed for normal problems, or there will be a performance penalty because an under-utilized arithmetic pipeline must be accepted for certain problems.

In summary, the typical segmentation philosophy for an element-by-element vector add is to divide it into smaller pieces of size Q (with Q chosen to minimize the overhead), make an initiation of a Q-element vector add every $\text{MAX}\,(2R(Q) + W(Q), \text{ADD}(Q))$ time units, and when N is not a multiple of Q, handle the non-standard-sized piece first.

Example 2 Multiplication of matrix by vector The previous example demonstrated the basic tradeoffs involved for a particular segmentation strategy. This example demonstrates the outcomes when several different segmentation approaches are possible.

The vector instruction to be implemented is one that takes an $N \times M$ matrix **X**, multiplies it by an M-element vector **U**, and stores the N element result in vector **Y**. This may be expressed mathematically at least three different ways, each using an entirely different segmentation approach as shown in Fig. 5-5.

The first approach, *inner product,* is to compute each element of **Y** one at a time using all of **U** and one row of **X**. Segmenting this approach involves breaking **U** and each row of **X** into pieces of size Q and using a reservation table that looks like Fig. 5-1b.

The function performed by the arithmetic pipeline during each initiation is of the form

$$\text{SUM} = \text{SUM} + \sum_{j=1}^{Q} X(j)\,U(j)$$

where the intermediate SUM is kept on the pipeline or in local memory. As in the first example, an optimum Q and initiation sequence can be found.

The second approach, *column scaling,* sums up N-element vectors that are the product of $U(j)$ and the jth column of **X**. The inner loop of this is of the form $Y(i) = Y(i) + U(j) \times X(i,j)$ for $i = 1$ to N. This is the arithmetic function requested of the arithmetic pipeline. The segmentation approach is similar to Example 1, where at each initiation the next Q elements of the jth column of **X** and the next Q element of **Y** are read in, with Q elements going back to **Y** upon completion. Initially a special load of $U(j)$ is performed once and left in local memory during the cycle. The entire process is repeated M times, with the first time all 0s substituted for the **Y** vector input.

The third approach, *submatrix,* assumes that the arithmetic pipeline can be coded to perform $Y = Y + X \cdot U$ for matrices **X** of at most $Q_2 \times Q_1$ size. Segmentation then consists of reading in Q_1-sized pieces of **U**, and then successive blocks of $Q_2 \times Q_1$ submatrices of **X**. Whether or not Q_2 elements of **Y** are paged in and out as partial sums depends on the amount of local memory and the degree of flexibility in the vector controller.

There are several characteristics common to all three approaches. First, they require the vector controller to handle effectively doubly nested loops of computations. Second, some running sums must be initialized to 0 before starting. Finally, some feedback in varying amounts is needed to accumulate partial sums from initiation to initiation.

Despite these common points, the three approaches have some important differences. The first difference, of course, is in arithmetic functions. Second, not all approaches can be implemented on all types of processors. For example, approach 3 requires the vector memory address generator to have a submatrix read capability. If the matrix is stored in row-order (Sec. 4.3.1), approach 2 can be implemented only with a regularly spaced access capability. The same is true of using approach 1 in a

$$
\begin{bmatrix} Y(1) \\ \cdot \\ \cdot \\ Y(N) \end{bmatrix} = \begin{bmatrix} X(1,1) & \ldots & X(1,M) \\ \cdot & & \cdot \\ \cdot & & \cdot \\ X(N,1) & \ldots & X(N,M) \end{bmatrix} \times \begin{bmatrix} U(1) \\ \cdot \\ \cdot \\ U(M) \end{bmatrix}
$$

$$
= \begin{bmatrix} \displaystyle\sum_{j=1}^{M} X(1,j)U(j) \\ \cdot \\ \cdot \\ \displaystyle\sum_{j=1}^{M} X(N,j)U(j) \end{bmatrix} \quad \text{(Inner product)}
$$

$$
= U(1) \begin{bmatrix} X(1,1) \\ \cdot \\ \cdot \\ X(N,1) \end{bmatrix} + \cdots + U(M) \begin{bmatrix} X(1,M) \\ \cdot \\ \cdot \\ X(N,M) \end{bmatrix} \quad \begin{matrix}\text{(Column} \\ \text{scaling)}\end{matrix}
$$

$$
= \begin{bmatrix} Y(iQ_2 + 1) \\ \cdot \\ \cdot \\ Y((i+1)Q_2) \end{bmatrix}
$$

$$
= \begin{bmatrix} X(iQ_2+1,1) & \ldots & X(iQ_2+1,Q_1) \\ \cdot & & \cdot \\ \cdot & & \cdot \\ \cdot & & \cdot \\ X((i+1)Q_2,1) & \ldots & X((i+1)Q_2,Q_1) \end{bmatrix} \begin{bmatrix} U(1) \\ \cdot \\ \cdot \\ U(Q_1) \end{bmatrix} + \cdots +
$$

$$
\text{(Submatrix)}
$$

$$
\begin{bmatrix} X(Q_2+1,N-Q_1+1) & & \ldots & X(iQ_2+1,N) \\ \cdot & & & \cdot \\ \cdot & & & \cdot \\ \cdot & & & \cdot \\ X((i+1)Q_2+1,N-Q_1+1) & \ldots & X((i+1)Q_2+1,N) \end{bmatrix} \begin{bmatrix} U(N-Q_1+1) \\ \cdot \\ \cdot \\ U(N) \end{bmatrix} + \cdots
$$

Figure 5-5 Variations to matrix-vector product.

column-ordered matrix. The final difference is in the ratio of memory bandwidth to arithmetic pipeline cycle time to insure 100% utilization of all hardware. For every NM multiplies required by the arithmetic pipeline, Table 5-1 lists the minimum number of memory accesses required by each approach. Column scaling requires the highest bandwidth; submatrix, the lowest. The actual numbers of course can be much worse depending on the skip value needed and the design of the main memory.

Table 5-1   Minimum Access Per NM Multiplies

Approach	Number of Elements Accessed
(1) Inner product	$2NM + N$
(2) Column scaling	$3NM + M$
(3) Submatrix	Between $(NM + NM/Q_2 + N)$ and $(NM + NM/Q_2 + 2NM/Q_1)$

5.1.2   Implementation of Arithmetic Function—Recursion Removal

The lowest level of coding is the microprograms that implement the arithmetic and transfer functions specified by the segmentation approach. Since these units are usually pipelined, the major problem at this level of programming is the specification of reservation tables and initiation sequences that maximize performance. Chapter 3 described in detail the determination of initiation sequences; therefore, this and the next section will emphasize the determination of an appropriate reservation table. Although only arithmetic functions are considered here, the approaches are fairly general.

The determination of a reservation table for some arithmetic functions such as that for a vector element-by-element add is trivial. Given the function and the hardware, there is only one possible path. However, this is not true for more complex functions such as reduction operators. Here there are ranges of tradeoffs that can affect overall performance. Two of the most important are *recursion removal* and *inner-loop optimization*. The first takes into account dependencies in the calculations, and the latter weighs the amount of problem solved per initiation against the utilization of the various stages in the pipeline. Both use as their guiding criterion Lemma 3-1, the bound on the minimum achievable latency (MAL). The smaller this bound, the greater the chance for high performance when a full state analysis is performed.

The general form of a recurrence problem is the computation of $X(1), \ldots, X(N)$ where

$$X(i) = f(a(i), X(i-1), \ldots, X(i-M))$$

We assume that a reservation table representing one computation of f can be written and has a compute time df. As described in Sec. 2.4, the problem in implementing such problems directly is that the initiation for $X(i)$ cannot be started until that for $X(i-1)$ is nearly complete. This dependency forces the average latency to approach df.

Using additional hardware, the concept of a companion function (Sec. 2.4) can often reduce this average latency to a minimum of 1. Of course when the hardware is fixed, as it is with most vector processors, it is not possible to gain this much performance. However, the same basic concepts can be used to change the function, and thus the reservation table, to yield a reservation table with resulting latency somewhere between 1 and df depending on how many of the $X(i)$'s must actually be computed.

When the actual values of all n $X(i)$'s are desired, not much can be done to eliminate the explicit dependencies in the recurrence. However, the concept of companion functions permits the dependency of $X(i)$ on $X(i-1), \ldots, X(i-m)$ to be weakened to $X(i-K), \ldots X(i-K-m), K > 1$. Then the problem can be expressed as the union of K independent recurrence problems. Although each of these smaller problems has explicit dependencies that prevent any of its initiations from being overlapped, this independence does permit the initiations for different problems to be overlapped, thus reducing overall latency for the original problem.

To be more specific, we assume a recurrence problem of the form

$$X(i) = f(a(i), X(i-1))$$

If f has a companion function g, then the dependency on $X(i-1)$ can be replaced by a dependency on $X(i-2)$ as follows:

$$X(i) = f(g(a(i), a(i-1)), X(i-2))$$

In turn this permits the solution of the original problem to be cast as the union of the two smaller problems:

$$X(2i) = f(g(a(2i), a(2i-1)), X(2(i-2))) \quad \text{(all even index points)}$$
$$X(2i+1) = f(g(a(2i+1), a(2i)), X(2(i-2)+1)) \quad \text{(all odd index points)}$$

for $0 \leqslant i \leqslant n/2$. Clearly this could be carried further to three problems of size $n/3$, four problems of size $n/4$, etc. In practice an optimum point is reached beyond which further backup is counterproductive. The reason is that even though the amount of overlap is increasing, the recurrence for which the reservation table must be formed becomes more complex with each backup, extending the compute time.

As a concrete example, we consider the solution of the recurrence

$$X(i) = a(i) X(i-1) + b(i)$$

on an arithmetic pipeline with the following characteristics:

1 a five-stage multiplier pipeline
2 a five-stage adder pipeline
3 accessing of local memory takes an entire cycle
4 the $a(i)$'s and $b(i)$'s are transferred to local memory as needed
5 there are sufficient paths in the pipeline to connect the multiplier, adder, and local memory in any arbitrary way

With these characteristics, a reservation table for the recurrence looks like Fig. 5-6. Lemma 3-1 indicates that an average latency of 3 may be possible, but the dependencies force actual latency to approach the compute time of 12. Note also that with this latency none of the hardware stages are efficiently used.

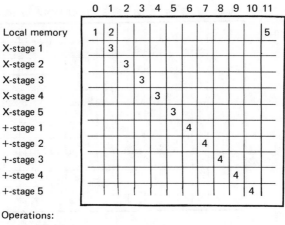

Operations:

1—READ a(i)
2—READ b(i)
3—COMPUTE a(i) X(i − 1)
4—COMPUTE (a(i) X(i − 1)) + b(i)
5—WRITE X(i)

COMPUTE TIME = 12

MAL BOUND = 3

Figure 5-6 Direct solution to $X(i) = a(i) X(i − 1) + b(i)$.

For this problem the use of a companion function

$$g = (a(i) a(i − 1), a(i) b(i − 1) + b(i))$$

changes the recurrence to

$$X(i) = (a(i) a(i − 1)) X(i − 2) + (a(i) b(i − 1) + b(i))$$

The reservation table for this is shown in Fig. 5-7. Here the MAL bound is still 3, but the compute time has stretched to 17. However, because of the relaxed dependencies it is permissible to have two of these initiations overlapped. If this is possible (it may be necessary to insert delays as described in Chap. 3), then an average latency of $17/2 = 8.5$ is possible. This is an improvement over the original solution.

We also note that the utilization of the hardware is much more in balance than in Fig. 5-6. Here for every three local memory accesses, we do three multiplies and two adds, in comparison to one and one.

This process could be continued a step further so that $X(i)$ depends on $X(i − 4)$. In this case the reservation table will have three marks in the local memory access, assuming $a(i − 1) \ldots a(i − 3)$ are kept on the pipeline, five marks in any row for the multiplier, and three marks in any row for the adder. Because of the increased computation, the MAL bound is now up to 5, which means that even with four-way interleaving of recurrences the average latency cannot drop below 5. The actual achievable latency is left as an exercise to the reader.

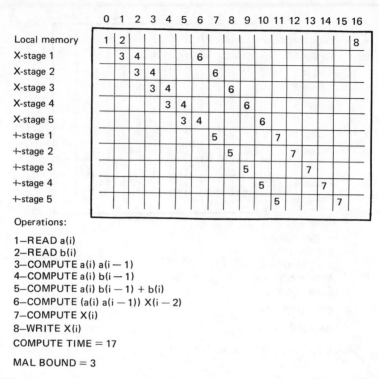

Operations:

1—READ a(i)
2—READ b(i)
3—COMPUTE a(i) a(i − 1)
4—COMPUTE a(i) b(i − 1)
5—COMPUTE a(i) b(i − 1) + b(i)
6—COMPUTE (a(i) a(i − 1)) X(i − 2)
7—COMPUTE X(i)
8—WRITE X(i)
COMPUTE TIME = 17

MAL BOUND = 3

Figure 5-7 Relaxed dependency.

Further relaxation of the dependencies will further increase the amount of overlap possible, but at the expense of reservation tables with even higher MALs. The complexity of the new equations overwhelms the weakened dependencies. Therefore, for this machine and this problem, the best possible latency lies in the range of 5 to 8.5, below what is possible with more hardware (Sec. 2.4) but better than the simple solution of Fig. 5-6. Similar results hold for other recurrences and other machine timings.

More dramatic results are possible when only the final term $X(n)$ is desired, which is the case for most reduction operators. For example, the inner product $\Sigma a(i) b(i)$ is equivalent to the computation of $X(n)$ where $X(i) = a(i) b(i) + X(i − 1)$. Obviously, the previous approach could be used to compute all $X(i)$'s in sequence, but to store only the final point. However, a better solution is possible when the reduction operator (usually addition) is commutative.[1] Then the original problem can be rearranged and split into several independent subproblems. The complexity of these subproblems is the same as the original; therefore, there is no growth in the MAL bound. Because these subproblems are independent, their initiations can be interleaved as before. However, unlike the previous case, after all subproblems have run to completion, a special reservation table must be run once to combine the individual results.

[1] A function f is commutative if for all a and b, $f(a,b) = f(b,a)$.

To further illustrate, we consider implementing the inner product on the same hypothetical machine as the first example. Figure 5-8 diagrams one initiation of the recurrence. The compute time is 12 while the bound on the MAL is 2. A direct solution for $X(n)$ thus involves an average latency of 12 (actually, in this case an average latency of 5 is possible if only feedback around the adder is considered). This direct solution corresponds to a sequence of calculations of the form

$$X(n) = (a(n) b(n) + (a(n-1) b(n-1) + (\ldots(a(2) b(2) + a(1) b(1)\ldots)$$

Using the commutativity of addition permits this to be rewritten as

$$X(n) = (a(n) b(n) + (a(n-6)+(n-6) + \cdots)\cdots)$$
$$+$$
$$(a(n-1) b(n-1) + (a(n-7) b(n-7) + \cdots)\cdots)$$
$$+$$
$$.$$
$$.$$
$$.$$
$$+$$
$$(a(n-5) b(n-5) + (a(n-11) b(n-11) + \cdots)$$

This is equivalent to solving six separate problems of the form

$$X(6i + j) = a(6i + j) b(6i + j) + X(6(i-1) + j) \qquad 0 \leqslant j \leqslant 5$$

This is the same functional form as Fig. 5-8.

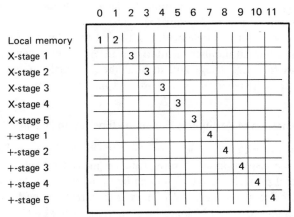

Operations:

1—READ a(i)
2—READ b(i)
3—COMPUTE a(i) b(i)
4—COMPUTE X(i − 1) + a(i) b(i)

Figure 5-8 Basic reservation table for inner product.

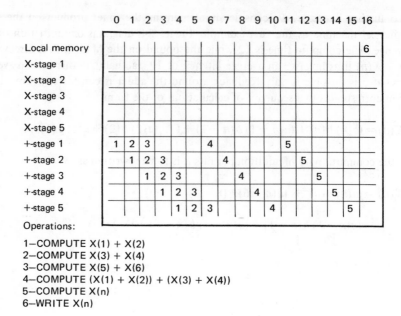

Operations:

1—COMPUTE X(1) + X(2)
2—COMPUTE X(3) + X(4)
3—COMPUTE X(5) + X(6)
4—COMPUTE (X(1) + X(2)) + (X(3) + X(4))
5—COMPUTE X(n)
6—WRITE X(n)

Where X(i) is result of ith subproblem

Figure 5-9 Termination of inner product.

In every 12 clock periods, one initiation from each of these problems can be started, giving an average latency of 2. After $n/6$ such groups of 12 clock periods all six subproblems are complete, and a single initiation of Fig. 5-9 is needed to combine the results by adding them into a single sum. For large n this time is negligible, and the overall solution time is close to $2n$, the MAL limit.

The major constraint to implementing either of these approaches to recursion removal usually is a limited number of internal registers in the pipeline. These registers are needed both to insert delays and to hold the increased number of intermediate terms that appear as the recurrences are separated and backed up.

5.1.3   Implementation of Arithmetic Function—Inner Loop Design

Functions involving recurrences are not the only kind whose implementations can benefit from close inspection and reformatting. In many cases specifying exactly how much of the total problem goes into one initiation of the basic reservation table can significantly affect performance. As it does in recurrences, performance often increases as the complexity of this inner loop increases. The key to when and by how much performance may be increased comes as before from the MAL bound of Lemma 3-1 and the relative utilization of stages by a reservation table. Problems for which such optimization is possible are those where the function is relatively complex and the basic reservation table either has no stage that is 100% utilized or has several stages badly underutilized in relation to others. Changing the function to be performed can bring these relative utilizations into closer alignment. Unlike recursion removal, however, there is no standard approach to finding these new formulations. Different problems will have different solutions. Following are several examples.

Example 1 Matrix-vector product Section 5.1.1 defined a matrix-vector product problem and three ways to implement it. In the submatrix approach the function to be implemented in the arithmetic pipeline is of the form $Y = Y + X U$ where Y and U are vectors of length Q_2 and Q_1, X is a $Q_2 \times Q_1$ array, and all are in local memory. As in the discussion of segmentation, this function can be implemented in three different ways. Which ways are possible depends on the structure of the local memory and how the arithmetic pipeline can access it. For this example we assume the same pipeline as before, a five-stage multiplier and equivalent adder, and a local memory organization that allows any word to be accessed as needed. We also assume sufficient register files within the pipeline itself to hold small submatrixes (e.g., 2×2) without accessing local memory. Thus any of the three variations may be considered for actual implementation on the arithmetic pipeline.

The first approach, repeated inner products, was discussed in detail in Sec. 5.1.2. The MAL bound was 2 and utilization of the multiplier/adder was about 50%. For each row of a $Q_2 \times Q_1$ matrix the execution time is about $2Q_1 + 26$ cycles: $2Q_1$ for the Q_1 initiation, and 26 for start-up/shutdown of the pipeline. The total problem thus takes at least $2\,Q_1\,Q_2 + 26\,Q_2$ cycles (Q_2 rows).

In the column scaling approach each column of X is processed by its own initiation. The first initiation simply reads in a single element of U and holds it as one input to the multiplier. The next Q_2 initiations are of reservation tables that read in one element each of X and Y, multiply the X element by the stored U element and add it to Y, and return the element to storage. This process repeats Q_1 times. Without drawing the reservation table we know immediately that the MAL bound is 3 (three local memory accesses per initiation) and that utilization of the multiplier and adder is at best 33.3% (one mark in any row for these modules divided by the MAL bound). Total time is approximately $3Q_2Q_1 + 14Q_1$ cycles.

The final approach, submatrix combination, segments the already segmented problem in local memory in exactly the same way. Each initiation computes $Y' = Y' + X'\,U'$ where Y' is of length S_2, U' of length S_1, and X' of size $S_2 \times S_1$. Again we can use Lemma 3.1 to bound MAL for any such reservation table as follows:

1 There must be $(S_1 + 2S_2 + S_1\,S_2)$ local memory accesses (S_1 to read U', $2S_2$ to read/write Y', and $S_1\,S_2$ to read X'). We assume sufficient register files in the pipeline to hold all these.

2 There are $S_1\,S_2$ marks per row for the multiplier.

3 There are $S_1\,S_2$ marks per row for the adder.

Again access to local memory is the bottleneck; thus the MAL bound is $S_1 +$

$2S_2 + S_1 S_2$. Total execution time not counting start-up/completion cycles is thus approximately

$$\frac{Q_1 Q_2}{S_1 S_2}\left(S_1 + 2S_2 + S_1 S_2\right) = Q_1 Q_2 + Q_1 \frac{Q_2}{S_2} + 2Q_1 \frac{Q_2}{S_1}$$

As S_1 and S_2 get larger, this approaches twice the performance that the inner product approach provides. Note also that the utilization of the multiplier/adder also grows as these values increase. For $S_1 = S_2 = 2$ the utilization is about 40%, but for $S_1 = S_2 = 8$ it is 72%. Thus performance of this approach is very sensitive to the number of registers inside the pipeline. This is typical of many complex problems.

Example 2. Interwoven calculations The key result of the last example was that alternate representation of the same function can often yield reservation tables that promise higher utilization of all components and generally result in lower MAL bounds and thus higher performance. This example indicates that often the same effect can be achieved by increasing the complexity of the inner loop. We assume that the same hypothetical pipeline as before is to implement the following loop where all variables are in local memory (Fig. 5-10a):

$$\text{For } I = 1 \text{ until N} \quad \text{Do} \quad B(I) = A(I) + H*A(N + 1 - I)$$

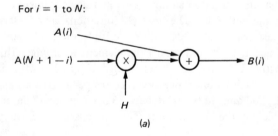

(a)

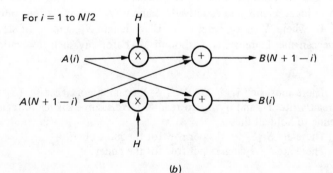

(b)

Figure 5-10 Performance enhancement by expanding inner loop.

Assuming that H is some constant that is kept near the multiplier, a reservation table that implements one iteration of this inner loop has three marks in the local memory row and one each in any multiplier or adder stage. The MAL bound is thus 3 with multiplier/adder utilization of 33%. Total execution time for N iterations is thus approximately $3N$ cycles.

This time can be improved considerably by observing that certain pairs of this inner loop use the same input data and combining those calculations into a single reservation table can result in higher multiplier/adder utilization. The pairing of equations occurs when $I = i$ and $I = N + 1 - i$, for any i. When this occurs the two equations need only $A(i)$ and $A(N + 1 - i)$ to compute $B(i)$ and $B(N + 1 - i)$. This is equivalent to rewriting the original problem as:

For I = 1 Until N/2   Do
Begin
B(I) = A(I) + H* A (N + 1 − I)
B (N + 1 − I) = A (N + 1 − I) + H * A (I)
End

A reservation table to perform this inner calculation (Fig. 5-10b) thus has four marks in the local memory row and two marks in any multiplier/adder stage. This results in a MAL bound of 4, but with 50% increased utilization of the multiplier and adder. Further, since only $N/2$ iteration need be done, the total execution time is about $(N/2)\, 4 = 2N$. Even with the increased MAL, this total time is less than that of the direct approach of $3N$ cycles.

One other potentially valuable attribute of this second approach is that it may be done "in place"—i.e., the output B locations may be the same as the input A's. This is not true of the original formulation—consider the trivial case where $N = 2$. If $A(1)$ is over-written with the value for $B(1)$, the resulting calculation of $A(2)$ will use the wrong value for $A(1)$.

Example 3 Fast Fourier transform Perhaps the most common and interesting application of the technique of inner loop expansion is in the implementation of a fast Fourier transform (FFT) algorithm on a pipeline. This is a problem that has been studied extensively (cf. Groginsky and Works, 1970; Kratz et al., 1974), and one that can be adjusted to match almost any pipeline's capabilities.

Although the theory is somewhat complex, the basic FFT computes a vector $\mathbf{Y}$ from a vector $\mathbf{X}$ via a fast implementation of the equation

$$\mathbf{Y}(j) = \sum_{k=0}^{N-1} \mathbf{X}(K)\, W^{jk}$$

where the elements of $\mathbf{Y}$ and $\mathbf{X}$ are complex, and W is the complex angle $e^{i2\pi/N}$. This fast implementation uses repeated cascades of a "two-point butterfly" calculation (Fig. 5-11) that has two inputs and two outputs. Note the resemblance to

A, B, C, D, W are complex

Real (C) = Real (A) + Real (B) × Real (W) — Imag (B) × Imag (W)
Imag (C) = Imag (A) + Real (B) × Imag (W) + Imag (B) × Real (W)
Real (D) = Real (A) — Real (B) × Real (W) + Imag (B) × Imag (W)
Imag (D) = Imag (A) — Real (B) × Imag (W) — Imag (B) × Real (W)

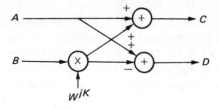

Figure 5-11   Two-point butterfly.

Fig. 5-10b. For an N-point transform (N elements in **X** or **Y**), this cascading consists of $\log_2 N$ columns of $N/2$ of these basic butterflies as in Fig. 5-12. For more detail see Rabiner and Rader (1972).

There are a variety of methods of implementing the inner loop of this FFT on a pipelined processor. To demonstrate, we assume the same hypothetical machine as before, except that the adder is capable of summing up three separate inputs. We also assume that some other unit provides the complex angles as needed. One of the simplest uses of such a configuration is development of a reservation table that computes the two-point butterfly of Fig. 5-11. This reservation table can be initiated $(N/2) \log_2 N$ times, with the addressing of local memory set up so that the appropriate data is available as needed. Recalling that all data is complex, the reservation table will have eight marks in the local memory row (two marks for each input and output), four marks in any stage of the multiplier, and four marks in any stage of the adder (each mark corresponds to an add of three numbers). From Lemma 3.1 this gives a bound on MAL of 8 clocks for a total of $4N \log_2 N$ clock units plus pipeline start/stop. During this time the multiplier and adder are at best 50% utilized.

In this case, one way of expanding the inner loop to increase utilization is to execute with one reservation table all those butterflies in two or more columns that share common inputs. The dotted lines in Fig. 5-12 diagram four- and eight-point butterflies. For the four-point case, the calculation consists of those four two-point butterflies that share common inputs at each column. When looked at in this fashion, there are $(\log_2 N)/2$ columns of $N/4$ four-point butterflies per column. The resulting reservation table has 16 marks for local memory (there are four complex inputs and four complex outputs), 16 marks in any multiplier stage (four from each of the four internal butterflies), and 16 marks for the adder. The MAL bound is now 16, but the total time is $16 * (N/4) \times (\log_2 N)/2 = 2N \log_2 N$. This is twice as fast as the two-point implementation. In addition, with a latency of 16 there are marks in every slot of every row—all elements of the hardware are 100% utilized.

Once all relevant hardware is fully utilized it is usually not worthwhile to continue to expand the inner loop. For example, if for the FFT and our hypothetical machine we coded an eight-point butterfly as the inner loop, the resulting reservation table would have 32 marks for local memory and 48 marks in any row for the multiplier or adder. The MAL bound is now 48, and for $(\log_2 N)/3$ columns of $N/8$ butterflies per column the result is $2N \log_2 N$—the same as the previous attempt. Note, however, that now the multiplier and adder are 100% utilized, but local memory drops to 66% utilization. Larger butterflies only exaggerate this reversal.

It should be clear that any of these loop expansion techniques can be implemented only if there are sufficient internal arithmetic pipeline registers to hold all the intermediate terms. Furthermore, changing the ratio of multipliers and adders or changing

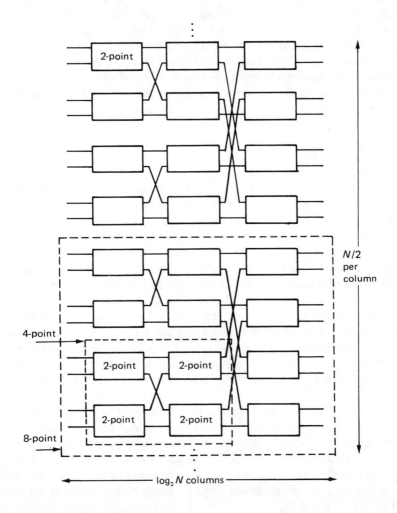

Figure 5-12 Computational structure of FFT.

the local memory access rate totally changes the analysis. Note, however, the power of Lemma 3-1—we have only to know that the modules are pipelined, with the results relatively independent of the actual number of stages.

5.2 EFFECTIVE PERFORMANCE OF VECTOR INSTRUCTIONS

In the previous sections the implementation of pipelined vector instructions was discussed. The performance considerations were limited primarily to minimizing the average latency between two initiations within the execution of the instruction. In overall system behavior, however, this is not the only consideration: two others play almost equally important roles in determining the performance of a program including vector construction. These are the effect of pipeline start-up/flush and the effect of the presence of nonvector instructions in a heavily vectorized program. Although not recognized in many early studies, the significance of these factors has been realized in recent years; now most studies of real algorithms for vector processors go into great detail in analyzing these effects (cf. Rudsinski and Worlton, 1977; Voight, 1977; Ward, 1976; Calahan et al., 1976). Early leaders in this area were the studies of Chen (1971, 1975) on the efficiencies of pipelines as functions of utilizations.

The following subsections develop simple models for each of these factors and indicate the implications in the programming of vector processors.

5.2.1 Effects of Start-Up Times

In all the implementation studies of Sec. 5.1, the overall times for a vector instruction take the form $s + a n$ where n is the number of elements (initiations), a the average latency per initiation, and s the start-up and stop times. As the name implies, this latter time is the sum of the time required to start up the pipeline, from the start of the vector instruction to the first initiation, and the time to shut the pipeline down i.e., from the last initiation to the end of the instruction. When several levels of pipelining are involved, such as managing the local memory on top of the arithmetic pipeline, these start-up/flush times tend to be additive from level to level, with the overall time the sum of that for each level. For example, a close examination of the vector element-by-element add instruction reveals that the start-up time is the sum of the time to set up the vector memory controller, the time for an overlapped memory to access the first element, and the time to load the first segment of both operands into local memory. Likewise, the flush time consists of the time to do the last add and transfer it to local memory and the time to write the last segment back to main memory.

In real systems, this overhead can go anywhere from a few to several hundred equivalent pipeline clock cycles. Its effect on a program can be understood by recasting the equation for vector instruction time $(s + an)$ into an equivalent form $p(n)an$, where $p(n)$ is a *performance degradation factor*. This value will always exceed 1, but the closer it is to 1, the closer the overall performance of the system approaches the average latency a of the calculation loop. By simple algebra this term $p(n)$ can be derived as

$$s + an = \left(\frac{s}{an} + 1\right) an$$

$$= \left(\frac{s/a}{n} + 1\right) an$$

$$= p(n) \, an$$

Thus $p(n)$ depends on n and on the ratio of start-up to average latency. Again in real systems this ratio can vary greatly, and even in the same machine it can be different for different instructions.

Figure 5-13 diagrams $p(n)$ for various values of s/a and n. As can be seen, $p(n)$ does not approach 1 closely until n is on the order of 10 times the s/a ratio. The number of iterations n is directly related to the length of the input vectors, which means that the relative processing time per vector element is significantly larger for short vectors than it is for long ones. This is known as the *short-vector problem*. Its effect in the programming of vector processors is to favor algorithms that call for a few long vector operations over those with many short vectors even if the total number of elements processed in both cases is the same.

5.2.2 Effects of Scalar Instruction Performance

Very few programs for pipelined vector processors involve only vector instructions. To the contrary, a great percentage of the code involves operations of the following kinds:

- computing parameters (addresses or lengths used to describe vectors)
- setting up and starting vector instructions
- testing for exception conditions
- performing I/O

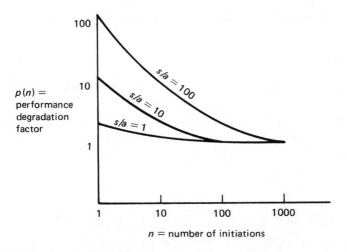

Figure 5-13 Effects of start up/flush time.

- doing scalar data analysis (e.g., has the process converged?)
- doing nonvectorizable data calculations
- governing overall loop and program control

These operations involve inherently single elements randomly addressed; they are characterized by nonrepetitive, data-value-dependent execution sequences. They are typically coded in a classical nonvector language; in terms of the general architecture of Fig. 4-1, they are executed in the scalar processor part of the system.

The significance of these operations to overall program execution speed is that usually not all of their execution can be overlapped with (i.e., executed at the same time as) the vector instructions. This is particularly true of the vector set-up, the scalar data analysis, and nonvectorizable calculations that determine what vector instructions are executed on what data. As a result the time required to execute that code must be counted in the overall time to execute the total program. This slows down the effective ratio at which operands are processed by the system.

There are several ways that this situation can be modeled. The first is simply to compute the time for the scalar code and lump it in as extra start-up times on the vector instructions. Although reasonable, this approach is problem-dependent and gives little insight into the general dynamics of the situation. A better model was proposed by Chen (1971a,b); it is much more general but somewhat removed from the problem posed here.

A third model, patterned after one proposed by Rudsinski and Worlton (1977), gives more intermediate but more useful results. For this model we first define the average time for any vector instruction as $s + an$, where as before s is the average start-up/flush time, a the average latency between initiations, and n the number of initiations of the underlying reservation table. Further, we define q as the average number of significant operations per initiation. For simple element-by-element operations like an add this is 1; for more complex instructions it is higher. An inner-product, for example, might have a q of 2, a multiply and an add. The value used for q here is an average.

With these definitions, the *average time per operation* in vector mode is

$$\frac{s + an}{nq} = \frac{s}{nq} + \frac{a}{q}$$

We also assume that the scalar processor can do an average operation in t (a/q) seconds for some value t. The value of t for real systems can vary anywhere from 1 to 100. Now if m is the total number of nonoverlapped operations in a program (sum of all operations performed by vector instructions plus nonoverlapped scalar operations), and f is the percentage done in vector mode, then the total program time is

$$fm\left(\frac{s}{nq} + \frac{a}{q}\right) + (1 - f)\, mt\, \frac{a}{q}$$

Dividing this by m yields the average time per operation over the whole program:

$$f\,\frac{s}{nq} + \frac{a}{q}\,[t + f(1 - t)]$$

This could be graphed for various values of the parameters; but for our purposes it is more revealing to assume a perfect vector processor where the start-up overhead is negligible (i.e., $s/nq = 0$). This gives an upper bound for performance that becomes reasonable for large vector size. In this case the average time per operation is

$$\frac{a}{q}\,[t + f(1 - t)]$$

As before, the term a/q represents the minimum time possible if all operations are done in vector instructions and $t + f(1 - t)$ is a *performance degradation factor* due to scalar operation.

Figure 5-14 diagrams this degradation factor as a function of t and f. As indicated, for nontrivial values of t a factor near 1 requires extremely high values of f—often in excess of 95%. The value is even higher when start-up costs are included.

To the programmer this again implies that programs with long vectors are preferable to those with shorter ones. However, it also means that in any case it is imperative to keep the scalar overhead as low as possible. In programming style it may mean doing things like always setting up to do another sequence of vector instructions while the current one is in progress and before it is known whether another sequence is needed.

5.2.3 Construction of Vectorized Programs

As might be expected from the previous sections, the construction of efficient programs for computers having vector capabilities can be very nontrivial. Many of the complexities that appear in the implementation of the individual vector instructions have strong analogs when the same instructions are combined into large programs. The processes involved are sufficiently different from that for more sequential pro-

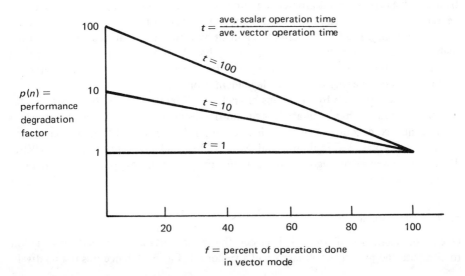

Figure 5-14 Effects of scalar operation.

gramming so that they are often called by their own special term *vectorization* techniques. In fact the introduction of a new vector-processing computer system is often accompanied by concerted attempts to help potential users understand the concepts and recast their problems in orientations that can take advantage of vector capabilities (cf. Krider, 1972; Kishi and Rudy, 1975; Johnson, 1978).

As in the implementation of vector instructions, there is little solid theory to guide the process of vectorizing a program, so the best description of problems and approaches may be through examples, which is the purpose of this section. Five sample problems are given, each chosen to demonstrate different aspects of the vectorization process. No particular vector machine or architecture is assumed. Instead we will describe the solution in terms of the common vector operations found on most vector processors, such as vector element-by-element operations, vector inner-products, and bit vector or conditional vector select operations. Likewise, no particular performance numbers are assumed, although general formulas of the form $s + an$ will be used when necessary where s is related to start-up time, a to average latency, and n the length of the vectors participating in the operation. A symbolic subscript of + will be used for formulas related to element-by-element additions, X for multiplicatins, and IP for inner products. Where necessary, reference is made to earlier sections that discussed in detail the particular tradeoffs involved.

The five examples are arranged hierarchically to show different aspects of the programming with emphasis on where knowledge of the pipelined implementation can be significant. The first example, matrix-vector product, is similar to the earlier instruction implementation discussions; it points out how interleaved memory and instruction speed affect choice of a program design. The second example discusses a matrix-matrix multiplication problem where the matrices are sparse in certain well-defined patterns. This demonstrates the advantages possible by defining a data structure that both matches the problem and provides long vectors. The third example is the classical tridiagonal matrix solution problem and how a seemingly nonvectorizable problem can be vectorized. It also demonstrates the problem of "vector temporaries" and necessary scalar processing. The fourth example, element-by-element rounding, shows how seemingly data-value-dependent processing can be handled on a vector processor without conditional branching or scalar testing. The final example, sorting, demonstrates the vectorization of a heavily data-value-dependent problem.

These examples are by no means all-inclusive. There are many other problems for which vectorization has been attempted and the results published. Some recent results include matrix decomposition (Calahan et al., 1976), partial differential equations (Ortega and Voigt, 1977; Fulton and Noir, 1975), and eigenvalue problems (Ward, 1976). Other vectorized algorithms and vector program analyses appear almost daily in the open literature.

5.2.4 Matrix-Vector Product

One of the examples of Sec. 5.1 discussed the implementation of a vector instruction to compute the product of a matrix and a vector (cf. Fig. 5-5). Since this is a relatively common process in scientific and engineering computing, and since not all vector processors include such an instruction in their repertoire, a vector program to implement it is an excellent first example of vectorization.

When only the simple vector instructions described earlier are available, there are at least two approaches to writing such a program, the inner product technique and the column scaling technique, both described in Fig. 5-5. The inner product technique takes a vector, i.e., a row, of the matrix X and a vector representing U and performs an inner-product instruction. The resulting single value is an element of Y. This process is embedded in a loop that executes N times with each iteration selecting a different row of X. An equation for the overall execution time is of the form

$$N(s_{IP} + a_{IP} M + \text{LOOP}) = a_{IP} NM + (s_{IP} + \text{LOOP}) N$$

where LOOP = the scalar overhead in the outer loop

The second approach, column scaling, selects columns of X, multiplies each by a scalar from U, and adds the vectors together one at a time. When coded the resulting program is a loop containing a vector element-by-element multiply between a column of X and single element of U repeated N times, and an element-by-element addition to sum this with the previous operations. All vectors are of length N and the loop is repeated M times. The resulting equation is of the form

$$M(s_X + a_X N + s_+ + a_+ N + \text{LOOP}) = (a_X + a_+) NM + (s_X + s_+ + \text{LOOP}) M$$

Although both approaches are of the same form, roughly proportional to NM, the difference in actual performance can be dramatic. If the matrix X is laid out in main memory in a column-ordered fashion, then the coefficient a_{IP} for the inner-product approach may have to include a large degradation due to memory interleaving. Likewise, for a row-ordered matrix the column-scaling approach may see a large value for a for certain values of M.

Even if the terms a_{IP} and $a_X + a_+$ are approximately equal, the resulting performances may still be dramatically different due to the second-order terms. For many processors the start-up time for an inner product s_{IP} is much larger than that for a simple vector operation such as multiply or add. On the other hand, the equation for column scaling consists of the sum of two startups, s_X and s_+. Further, each of these terms is multiplied by a different coefficient: N for the inner-loop approach, and M for column scaling. This indicates that the inner-product approach is better for short, fat matrices, where the vectors are long and the loop executed a relatively few number of times. In contrast, the column-scaling approach favors tall, thin matrices, again because the operations involve long vectors.

As mentioned earlier, either technique may suffer if the matrix is not properly oriented in main memory and if the skip value needed to read the row or column is one that is bad for the particular interleaving used in the main memory design. This is a very common problem for which a variety of programming techniques have been proposed as at least partial solutions. One of the earliest and most direct solutions is *matrix skewing* (cf. Budnik and Kuck, 1971; Kraska, 1969). Although several variations are possible, the basic idea can be shown by a simple example. We assume a 4 × 4 matrix stored in row order in a four-way interleaved memory assuming complex interleaving. Accessing a column out of such a matrix takes four times longer than a row. However, one way to overcome this is to add a fifth dummy column to the matrix making it a 4 × 5. The start of each row has been skewed by one word relative to the previous row. Now when a column is to be read, every fifth word is read from the memory rather than every fourth. Referring back to Chaps. 2 and 4, however, we see that a skip value of 5 in such a memory permits data accessing at the same speed as that for a sequential row. Thus either a row or column can be accessed in the same amount of time at the cost of some extra storage. Variations of this technique are available to allow fast access to diagonals and submatrices.

In summary we see that even for this simple problem of matrix-vector multiplication, the production of an optimum program for a pipelined vector processor is decidedly nontrivial. One can easily conceive of a program which includes vector code for both approaches along with an initial driver in scalar code to select dynamically on the basis of N, M, the memory interleave factor, and matrix orientation, which computational approach and data structure should be used.

5.2.5 Diagonal Matrix-Matrix Products

The previous example assumed that the matrices were dense; that is, any of the N by M elements can have a nonzero value. There are, however, many problems where the matrices are very sparse; that is, most of the elements are known to be always 0. In such cases an efficient vector program must take this sparseness into account in both data structures and processing sequences. This example considers the case of the multiplication of two sparse matrices **X** and **U** of size $N \times N$ where the sparseness is of a special kind: only certain *diagonals* of the matrices are potentially nonzero, and all other elements are always 0. Figure 5-15 diagrams a simple problem with diagonal sparse matrices of size 5 × 5 with three to four diagonals. We note the use of a numbering system to label the diagonals where the main diagonal is denoted as the 0th, where a diagonal whose first element starts in the ith element of the first row is the $(i - 1)$st diagonal, and where a diagonal starting in the ith element of the first column is the $-(i - 1)$st diagonal.

Real problems are typically much more sparse than this sample. Matrices of sizes up to 10,000 × 10,000 with only five to seven nonzero diagonals (only 1 out of 2000 points is nonzero) are common. Direct attempts to solve problems, such as obvious extensions of the previous example, are doomed because they use incredible amounts of storage and huge amounts of time multiplying and adding zeros. They have both the wrong *data structure* and the wrong *computationed approach*. Efficient vectorization of this problem requires more novel thinking. The approach described here is similar to that of Madsen et al. (1976).

When confronted by·such a problem, a natural response is to attempt to define a data structure that holds only the nonzero elements, and then to use some variation of the classical row-column algorithm to efficiently generate the result. This presents two problems. First, the sequence of calculations turns out to be heavily dependent on which point of **Y** is being calculated. For example, the expression for $Y(2,2)$ in the sample problem of Fig. 5-15 is

$$Y(2,2) = X(2,2)\,U(2,2) + X(2,3)\,U(3,2)$$

while the calculation for $Y(2,3)$ (on the same row as $Y(2,2)$) is

$$Y(2,3) = X(2,3)\,U(3,3)$$

The second problem is that even if some clever indexing method is found to perform these operations, the vector lengths are still rather small, leading to inefficient programs.

The more efficient approach is to use the natural vectors of the problem—namely the diagonal. Rather than trying to express an $N \times N$ matrix with **d** diagonals in some kind of reduced row-column form, a more natural representation is as a set of **d** vectors, each vector representing a diagonal. Note that these vectors may be of different lengths since the ith diagonal has only $N - i$ elements.

The next step is to look at what happens when we multiply two matrices where each has only one diagonal. Figure 5-16 shows the case where both matrices are diagonals with negative indices; other cases are similar. Not surprisingly the result of

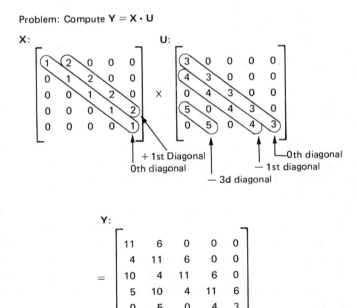

Figure 5-15   Sample multiplication of two sparse diagonal matrices.

Matrix representation

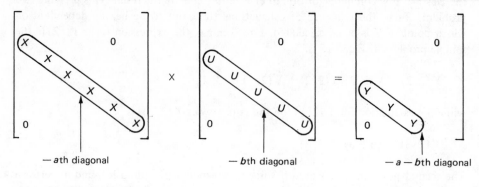

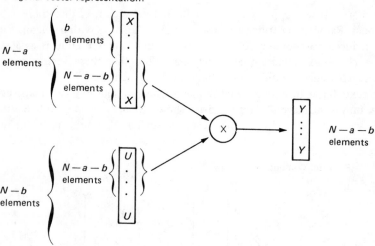

Figure 5-16 Product of matrices with one diagonal.

this product is a matrix with only one diagonal whose index is simply the sum of the indices to the two input diagonals. Further, the computation involved is a simple vector element-by-element multiply of sequential parts of each input. This is both easy to implement and efficient.

Generalization of this idea to matrices with more than one diagonal is straightforward. For each possible pair of diagonals, one from **X** and one from **U**, we compute what diagonal the product will produce and perform the vector element-by-element multiply. Further, if some other diagonal product has already generated a diagonal with this index, this new vector is added to the previous one. Thus the product of diagonals with indices +2 and +3 would be added to the product of diagonals with indices +9 and −4.

The actual code depends on the particular machine being used, but in general it has the following characteristics. First, it uses simple vector operations on data that is in sequential elements of vectors in main memory. Second, the vectors tend to be relatively long, on the order of N. Finally, a significant amount of scalar code is needed to cycle through the diagonals, compute for which diagonal a product is destined, and determine offsets and lengths needed to control the individual vector operations. If the programs are written for matrices where the diagonal structures never change, then the code can be replaced largely by table look-ups; otherwise, it must be run dynamically with the vector instructions. The net result, however, is still a program whose aggregate performance on a pipelined processor is superior to those of other approaches.

5.2.6 Tridiagonal Systems of Equations

In the previous two examples there was nothing intrinsic in the mathematics to force the calculations to be performed in any particular order. Vectorization thus is reduced to finding the most efficient ordering. This is not true of all problems; a great many include dependencies in their description that must be explicitly dealt with. This example is one such problem. We wish to compute an N-element vector $\mathbf{X}$ from the equation $\mathbf{AX} = \mathbf{K}$ where $\mathbf{A}$ is an N-by-N matrix with three diagonals at indices -1, 0, and 1 (using the definitions of the previous examples), and $\mathbf{K}$ is an N-element vector of known quantities. The vectorization of this problem has received a great deal of attention, both in algorithm development (cf. Stone, 1973) and in actual performance analysis on real machines (cf. Madsen and Rodrique, 1976). The approach described here is not as optimal as some of the others, but it exhibits several properties of educational interest.

The classical method for solving such problems is Gauss Elimination. Figure 5-17 diagrams both the original problem and the steps involved in its solution. Basically, the N-by-N matrix $\mathbf{A}$ is split into two matrices $\mathbf{L}$ and $\mathbf{U}$ such that both have only two diagonals and their product $\mathbf{LU}$ equals $\mathbf{A}$. Once these matrices are known two recurrences (see Secs. 2.4 and 5.1) can successively compute a vector $\mathbf{Z}$ from $\mathbf{LZ} = \mathbf{K}$ and $\mathbf{X}$ from $\mathbf{UX} = \mathbf{Z}$.

At first glance, only a small part of this procedure can be vectorized, namely the computation of the vector $\mathbf{f}$ from $\mathbf{c}$ and $\mathbf{b}$ and the vector $\mathbf{e}$ from $\mathbf{c}$ and $\mathbf{d}$, once the latter has been computed. These are simple vector element-by-element operations of length $N-1$. The rest of the problem, however, is not so obvious.

One solution relies on the existence of companion functions (see Sec. 2.4) for each of the three recurrences; that is, computations of the main diagonal of $\mathbf{U}$ and vectors $\mathbf{Z}$ and $\mathbf{X}$. From this, the techniques of Sec. 2.4 can be generalized to allow the introduction of vectorization (cf. Kogge, 1973a, 1974). As one example, the computation of $\mathbf{Z}$ can be rewritten as:

(1) $E(i) = -e_i \quad 1 \leqslant i \leqslant N$
(2) For $m = 1$ to $\log_2 (N-1)$ do
     (a) $T(i) = E(i) K(i - 2^{m-1}) \quad 2^{m-1} + 1 \leqslant i \leqslant N$
     (b) $K(i) = K(i) + T(i) \quad 2^{m-1} + 1 \leqslant i \leqslant N$
     (c) $E(i) = E(i) E(i - 2^{m-1}) \quad 2^{m-1} + 1 \leqslant i \leqslant N$
(3) $T(i) = E(i) K(1) \quad 2 \leqslant i \leqslant N$

(4) $X(1) = K(1)$
(5) $X(i) \ = K(i) + T(i) \quad 2 \leqslant i \leqslant N$

This particular representation is easily vectorizable since steps 2*a*, 2*c*, and 3 are vector element-by-element multiplies, and steps 2*b* and 5 are vector element-by-element addition. The only unique constraints are that for each iteration of steps 2*a*, 2*b*, and 2*c*, the length of the vector operation changes as a function of *m*, and for some operations the elements that participate come from the middle of the storage allocated to the main vector. Both these lengths and offsets must be computed by a scalar program before each sequence of vector operations.

Another characteristic of this and many other vectorized programs is the appearance of *vector temporaries.* Such vectors are similar to a temporary variable in conventional programming in that they hold intermediate results; but because they are vectors, much more storage space in memory must be allocated to them. Thus while

Compute vector **X** from

$$\overset{\mathbf{A}}{\begin{bmatrix} a_1 & b_1 & & & 0 \\ c_2 & a_2 & b_2 & & \\ & \cdot & \cdot & \cdot & \\ & & \cdot & \cdot & \cdot \\ & & & \cdot & b_{N-1} \\ 0 & & & c_N & a_N \end{bmatrix}} \overset{\mathbf{X}}{\begin{bmatrix} X_1 \\ \cdot \\ \cdot \\ \cdot \\ X_N \end{bmatrix}} \overset{=}{=} \overset{\mathbf{K}}{\begin{bmatrix} K_1 \\ \cdot \\ \cdot \\ \cdot \\ K_N \end{bmatrix}}$$

Step 1: Decompose into **L** and **U**

$$\overset{\mathbf{L}}{\begin{bmatrix} 1 & & & 0 \\ e_2 & 1 & & \\ & \cdot & 1 & \\ & & \cdot & 1 \\ 0 & & e_2 & 1 \end{bmatrix}} \overset{\mathbf{U}}{\begin{bmatrix} d_1^{-1} & b_1 & & 0 \\ & \cdot & \cdot & \\ & & \cdot & \cdot \\ 0 & & \cdot & b_{N-1} \\ & & & d_N^{-1} \end{bmatrix}}$$

for $i = 2, \ldots, N$:

$f_i = c_i b_{i-1}$
$d_1 = 1/a_1$
$d_i = 1/(a_i - f_i d_{i-1})$
$e_i = c_i d_{i-1}$

Step 2: Solve for **Z** from **LZ** = **K** (forward elimination)

$Z_1 = K_1$
$Z_i = K_i - e_i Z_{i-1}$

Step 3: Solve for **X** from **UX** = **Z** (back substitution)

$X_N = Z_N d_N$
$X_i = (Z_i - X_{i+1} b_i) d_i$

Figure 5-17 Solution of tridiagonal equations.

only about $5N$ words of storage are needed to solve Fig. 5-17 on a conventional non-vector machine, the introduction of intermediate vector variables such as f, t, and z can balloon this to $8N$ words or more. Unless care is taken by the programmer in using storage, very large problems may badly overrun the amount of memory available. To avoid this overrun the programmer of a vector machine must spend significant time mapping out the available memory and determining which is the best sequence of use and reuse. This often means, for example, using the same temporary vector in several different places for several different intermediate results that are not needed at the same time.

The actual timing for such an algorithm on a pipelined vector processor is also unique. The major part of the computation takes place at step 2, where for the mth step the time for $2a$, $2b$, and $2c$ is roughly

$$2s_X + s_+ + (2a_X + a_+)(N - 2^{m-1} - 1)$$

Summing over all values of m yields:

$$(2a_X + a_+)(N - 1)(\log_2 (N - 1) - 1) + (\log_2 (N - 1))(2s_X + s_+)$$

This time grows roughly as $N \log_2 N$. In comparison, a conventional approach on a scalar machine requires time proportional to N. This is an odd result indeed; the vectorized program is computationally more complex than the straightforward sequential one. This happens relatively frequently with vector code. It does not mean, however, that the vectorized version is slower than the scalar version. In fact if the average time per operation (see Sec. 5.2) is better than $\log_2 N$ times faster in vector mode than in scalar mode, then even with the $N \log_2 N$ multiplier the time may still be less. Of course, for large enough N a simple scalar version will be faster.

Similarly for small N the start-up costs may become excessive in the vector version, and again the scalar equivalent may be faster. The net result is that there may be a limited region of N for which vectorization in this fashion makes sense. Outside this region other approaches must be considered.

5.2.7 Rounding

So far none of the examples have dealt with problems where the value of each data element in a vector affects the computations performed on it. This example investigates a problem with these characteristics. Although relatively simple, it still demonstrates the steps in reasoning involved in vectorizing other more difficult problems.

The problem to be solved is that of rounding each element of a vector of floating-point numbers to its nearest integral value. Thus if an input vector includes the values 4.49, 4.51, −4.49, −4.51 the resulting vector should include 4.0, 5.0, −4.0, −5.0. We note that this is more complex than simply adding .5 to each element and taking the integer part, since for negative numbers the answer is wrong (e.g., $−4.49 + .5 = −3.99$ $= −3.0 \neq −4.0$). The algorithm to compute this must somehow test both the sign of each vector element and the value of its fraction.

There are a variety of ways to solve this using only vector operations. The one described here assumes a processor with bit vector and selective-store capability. It is not necessarily optimal but it does demonstrate the principles involved. In addition, we also assume that in the number system used to express floating-point numbers in a particular machine there exist certain "unnormalized zeros." These zeros have the property that when added to a nonzero floating point number, the value returned is the original number with the fractional part truncated. Thus numbers like 4.1 and −4.9 when added to this zero will yield 4.0 and −4.0 respectively. Most current machines include such zeros in their number representation (e.g., 0×16^7 in IBM System/370 representation).

Figure 5-18 diagrams the complete process. The first step is to compare the vector of data and produce a bit vector whose elements are 1 if the corresponding data values are nonnegative, and 0 otherwise. Then the data vector is added to a vector of values 0.5 using a selective store and the bit vector of step 1. This adds 0.5 to each positive number. Step 3 complements the bit vector, and step 4 adds −0.5 with a selective store using the complemented bit vector. This adds −0.5 to just the negative elements. Finally, the resulting vector is added to one containing only the special unnormalized zero. The result is the desired answer.

5.2.8 Sorting

The previous example demonstrated the vectorization of problems where the computation depends on the value of the element involved, but where the value of one vector

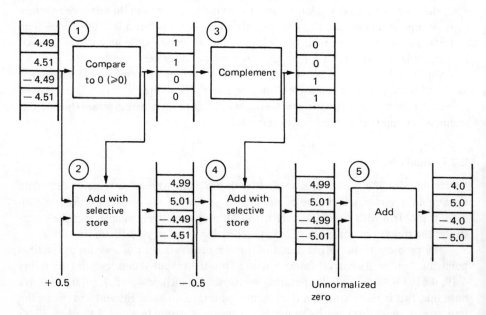

Figure 5-18 Rounding using selective store.

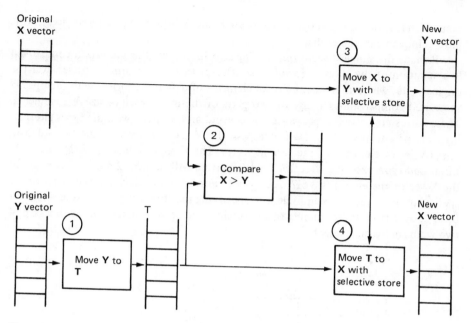

Figure 5-19 Vectorized comparison exchange.

element has absolutely no effect on the computation for other elements. Problems that do have such dependencies are considerably more complex and require perhaps the most original thought in order to vectorize them efficiently. The most classic problem of this kind is that of sorting a vector of numbers into ascending or descending order. As before, the approach described here is chosen for explanatory purposes and is guaranteed to be nonoptimal. For more efficient algorithms, the reader is challenged to try vectorizing the algorithms in Knuth (1973), particularly variations of Batcher's (1968) sorting networks.

Most sorting algorithms amenable to vectorization are based on the concept of a *comparison-exchange* operation. This operation has two inputs X and Y and two outputs X' and Y'. If $X \leqslant Y$, then X' is set to X and Y' set to Y. If $X > Y$, then the outputs are exchanged, i.e., X' set to Y and Y' to X. A vectorized comparison-exchange operation is similar. It accepts two input vectors X and Y and produces two output vectors X' and Y' where $X'(i)$ and $Y'(i)$ are the result of a comparison exchange between $X(i)$ and $Y(i)$. Normally such a process is done *in place;* that is, the output vectors X' and Y' take up exactly the same main memory locations as do X and Y respectively.

This vectorized comparison-exchange procedure is relatively easy to implement on a vector processor having bit vector and selective store capabilities. Figure 5-19 diagrams the steps involved. The first step is to make a copy of vector Y in the vector temporary T. This is necessary to prevent losing the Y elements involved in exchanges before their values are needed. The second step is to do a vector compare that generates a bit vector. A 1 in this vector indicates that an exchange is to be made.

Steps 3 and 4 then do selective stores from **X** and **T** into **Y** and **X** respectively. This process implements the exchange.

Perhaps the simplest vectorized sorting algorithm using this vectorized comparison is a variation of the classical *bubble sort*. This procedure performs N passes over the original data, where N is the number of elements of data to be sorted, with each pass a vectorized comparison-exchange of two parts of the input, each of size $N/2$ elements. These passes are of two types—an even pass and an odd pass—with the types alternating from pass to pass. In an *even-type* pass, the **Y** vector consists of the 1st, 3rd, 5th, ..., $(N-1)$st elements of the current vector. The **X** vector holds points $2,4,6,\ldots,N$. In an *odd-type* pass, the **Y** vector holds elements with indices $2,4,6,\ldots,N-2$ and the **X** vector the elements $3,5,7,\ldots,N-1$. For a typical pipelined vector processor specifying these vectors is equivalent to specifying that the first point is at an offset of 0, 1, 2, or 3 from the beginning of the original vector in main memory with a skip of two words between elements.

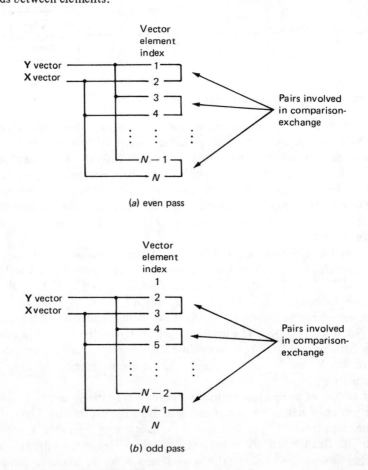

Figure 5-20   Vectors for sorting algorithm.

	After ith pass							
Original	Even	Odd	Even	Odd	Even	Odd	Even	Odd
vector	$i = 0$	$i = 1$	$i = 2$	$i = 3$	$i = 4$	$i = 5$	$i = 6$	$i = 7$
8	7	7	5	5	3	3	1	1
7	8	5	7	3	5	1	3	2
6	5	8	3	7	1	5	2	3
5	6	3	8	1	7	2	5	4
4	3	6	1	8	2	7	4	5
3	4	1	6	2	8	4	7	6
2	1	4	2	6	4	8	6	7
1	2	2	4	4	6	6	8	8

Figure 5-21 Sample vectorized sort for $N = 8$.

Figure 5-20 demonstrates which elements of the original vector are involved in a comparison-exchange for each pass and which elements make up the vectors **X** and **Y** for the vectorized operation. Figure 5-21 diagrams a simple example. As can be seen, there is a great resemblance to a bubble sort. At each pass the larger numbers tend to move one position down, while the smaller numbers tend to move up. Unlike a pure bubble sort, however, no part of the vector is guaranteed to be in proper order before the last pass has been executed.

5.3 COMPARISON WITH PARALLEL VECTOR PROCESSORS

A pipelined vector processor is not the only way of implementing SIMD architectures. At least one major alternative is a parallel organization where there are many arithmetic units, each with its own memory but all executing the same instruction simultaneously. Figure 5-22 is representative of such designs (cf. the ILLIAC IV—Barnes et al., 1968; or the Burroughs Scientific Processor—Stokes, 1977). In contrast to a pipelined machine where vector elements in a vector operation are handled one at a time, on a parallel machine a vector operation proceeds by having each arithmetic unit handle one element of the vector simultaneously with every other unit. If there are more elements than there are arithmetic units, the process is repeated an integral number of times. Although conceptually the design of good algorithms is the same for both types of machine designs, there are some important differences. This section highlights these differences.

The first major difference lies in the ease of accessing different data structures. For example, we consider accessing a column out of a row-oriented matrix. The pipelined machine simply requires a skip value specified during the vector accessing. This may cause a performance penalty if the skip value clashes with the interleaving of main memory. For a parallel machine, a row-oriented matrix means that each memory unit has a column of the matrix. Thus in one access time up to N elements of a row may be read simultaneously. However, if each memory unit is connected to one and only one arithmetic unit, accessing a column is extremely costly because each element of the

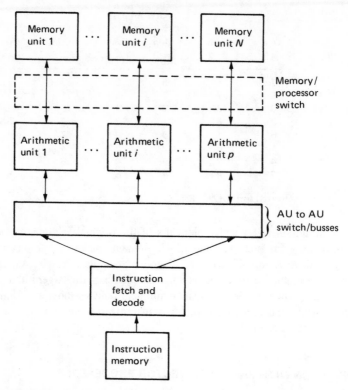

Figure 5-22 General parallel SIMD architecture.

column must be read out the same arithmetic unit one at a time and shifted somehow to the other units. To avoid this problem, switches are often imposed between memory units and the arithmetic units, and variations of the skewed matrix concept are used to speed up the access time. This switch is very often one of the more costly parts of a parallel SIMD design.

Note, however, that the degradation also works in the other direction. For example, accessing a diagonal in a parallel machine is often as fast as a row, while on a pipelined machine it requires a skip value that may cause slow-downs. Thus, a good data structure to use in programming one kind of vector processor may be less than ideal for the other.

Another difference between the two is that the equations for the execution time of a vector instruction are totally different. For the parallel case, if the length of the vector is less than P (the number of arithmetic units), then the total time is independent of N since all elements can be done simultaneously. For N greater than P the process is repeated Ceiling (N/P) times, with P elements at a crack. This makes the *time per operation* of a totally different form than for pipelining. If a is the time to process P elements in one cycle, then the total time for a vector instruction on a parallel machine is of the form

$$\left(P \times \frac{\text{Ceiling}\ (N/P)}{N}\right) \frac{a}{P}\ N$$

As in the pipelined case (Sec. 5.2.1), the first term represents a degradation factor, but it has an entirely different shape than for the pipelined case (Fig. 5-13). Figure 5-23 diagrams the two shapes. As shown, there is still a short-vector problem, but it goes away faster than for pipelined designs, only to recur to some extent whenever the vector length is just over a multiple of P.

On the other hand, the existence of scalar code affects a program written for a parallel machine in much the same way that it does for a vector machine except that the effects can be much more significant, particularly when P is large. This is because the time for a scalar operation will probably approximate the time for one arithmetic unit to do that operation. However, in this time period the entire array of processors can be doing P operations on different elements. Since values of P of 64 or more are not unusual, large values of t in Fig. 5-14 are entirely possible, resulting in significant loss of system throughput.

A final difference lies in expressions for the *computational complexity* of vector algorithms. Since a pipelined machine still processes each element of a vector sequentially, while a parallel design processes P of them at a time, the expression for the total time for an algorithm will often include an extra factor of N for the pipelined case which does not always appear in the parallel case, particularly when N is less than P. For example, the time required to process the first-order recurrence by the algorithm of the previous section grows as $N \log_2 N$ for all N on a pipelined machine, while for N less than P the time on a parallel machine grows only as $\log_2 N$. Of course, for N greater than P, the growth rate resembles Ceiling $(N/P) \log_2 N$—similar to the pipelined version.

In summary, although there are a great many similarities between a pipelined vector machine and one based on a parallel design, a vector algorithm written for one

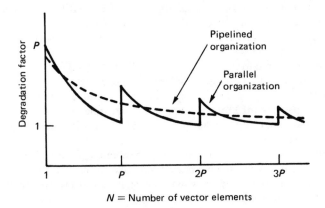

Figure 5-23 Vector instruction time degradation.

is not necessarily a good vector algorithm for the other. It is important for the programmer to know not only that the underlying machine handles vectors, but also the way in which that processing is performed.

PROBLEMS

5-1 Assuming that the loading and unloading of local memory never interferes with operation of the arithmetic pipeline, exactly how much time is spent by the pipeline computing n initiations of a reservation table with compute time d and latency cycle (m)? Redo for cycle (m_1, m_2).

5-2 For the sample segmentation of a vector add instruction, derive an exact equation for the execution time as a function of Q when:

  a one input vector is spaced every 17 words in memory,

  b the other is spaced every three words,

  c the output is spaced every five words;

and the machine characteristics are:

  a the arithmetic pipeline is a five-stage adder,

  b in one cycle the arithmetic pipeline can read two arbitrary values and write a third into local memory,

  c in one cycle the memory controller can write two words and read one into local memory,

  d it takes the memory controller one cycle to compute the first address,

  e each memory module has an access time of 16 cycles.

Define the equation for the cases where the memory is 16-way complex interleaved, 16-way simple interleaved, and 4×4 mixed interleave. Graph for $N = 1000$. Pick an optimal Q.

5-3 The number of elements N in a vector is not always an exact multiple of the segment size Q. Why is it usually more efficient to handle the one nonstandard piece of input vector first rather than last? Redo Prob. 5-2 assuming that the nonstandard piece is handled last. What is the difference?

5-4 Verify Table 5-1. Assuming $N = M$ and $Q_2 = Q_1$, what is the optimal value of Q_1?

5-5 For the sample recurrence of Sec. 5.1.2, $X(i) = a(i) X(i-1) + b(i)$, develop a reservation table that permits four-way interleaving of initiations; i.e., express $X(i)$ in terms of $X(i-4)$. What is the actual achievable latency?

5-6 For the equations for Prob. 5-2, graph the performance degradation factor for $Q = 8$ as a function of n. At what point would you say the machine begins to work most efficiently?

5-7 Assuming a four-way complex interleaved memory, diagram how a 4×4 matrix A would map into the memory, assuming row order and $A(1,1)$ goes into location 0. Diagram the mapping when skewing is used. Draw timing diagrams showing how skewing speeds up column access.

5-8 What is the minimum number of dummy columns needed to add to an $M \times M$ matrix to allow fast access to a column out of an N-way complex interleaved memory?

5-9 What does skewing do to the accessing of matrix diagonals?

5-10 Try implementing Example 2 of Sec. 5.1.3 on the TI ASC (Sec. 4.4.2). List assumptions you think necessary.

5-11 Define and sketch out the implementation of a vector instruction to compute $Y(i) = A(i) Y(i-1) + B(i) Y(i-2)$ on a vector processor like the IBM 3838 (Sec. 4.4.4). List whatever assumptions you think necessary.

5-12 Write out a general vectorized algorithm to compute the product of two matrices **X** and **U** where **X** has diagonals at 0 and +1, and **U** has diagonals at 0, −1, and −3. Verify that given the data of Fig. 5-15, it yields the proper results. Develop a rough equation for total time. When does the algorithm become most efficient?

5-13 Find an alternative vector algorithm for rounding (Sec. 5.2.7) that does not require vector tests or bit vectors.

5-14 Write an expression for the time required to perform the sort algorithms of Sec. 5.2.8. Develop a better algorithm.

5-15 Describe some techniques that might be used to take a nonvector program in any form you wish: machine code, assembly, or high-level source, and vectorize it to use vectors. Would there be any difference if the target machine were parallel rather than pipelined?

Chapter 6

Pipelining in SISD
Machine Designs

Perhaps the oldest and most enduring use of pipelining is in the design of conventional SISD (single instruction stream/single data stream) computers. Nearly all computers on the market today have SISD architectures, many of them employing various degrees of internal pipelining. The primary reason for the use of pipelining is as always increased performance over a nonpipelined design; the general design principles are those described earlier in this text. However, unlike the SIMD (single instruction stream/multiple data stream) machines of Chaps. 4 and 5, the pipelining in these machines is normally not visible to the programmer because it is the implementation of the instruction set architecture and not its specification that is pipelined. Furthermore, the process being pipelined namely machine-level instruction execution, is much more dynamic with greater dependencies than those in vector machines. The combination results in pipelines that are both complex and highly self-organizing. In the terminology of Secs. 1.2 and 3.1 they are asynchronous and multifunction with dynamic scheduling of initiations.

There are two reasons to shield the programmer from the pipelined aspects of an SISD machine design. First, it is a common practice to define a single instruction set architecture for an entire family of computers, each of which will properly execute the same programs but whose underlying implementations may be different. In such cases any visible side-effects of the pipelining, good or bad, must be detected and suppressed by the hardware. The second reason for shielding the programmer from the pipelining is the conceptual complexity of keeping track of the location of each of several instructions currently in the pipeline and exactly what values they receive when they request operands. There is simply too much bookkeeping involved.

The effects of pipelining that might be visible to the programmer if not properly considered divide into two classes. The first deals with dependencies between adjacent instructions in a program and how overlapping their execution in a pipeline can affect the operands they use and the results they compute. Although this can show up in many subtle ways, typically it occurs when, for example, one of instructions i or $i + 1$ needs to read some datum and the other needs to change it. When overlapping the execution of instructions in different stages of a pipeline, care must be taken to guarantee that the read and modification occur in the order the programmer expects, not in whatever order is easiest for the hardware. Such dependencies are termed *hazards;* if they are to be made invisible to the machine-level programmer, they must be detected and handled by *interlocks* in the hardware.

The second class of pipelining effects comes about from the handling of events asynchronous to the normal operation of a program that do in fact change what the CPU is executing. Such events are classified as *interrupts* because they force an unexpected branch in the program. The problem with handling interrupts on a pipeline is that often it is difficult to determine, first, where the forced branch should be inserted, and second, exactly how to restart the interrupted program once the cause of the event has been handled. This is particularly true of interrupts caused by *program exceptions*—that is, where the expected execution of the program causes some constraint to be violated. Examples include overflows and underflows in arithmetic operations and addresses out of bounds in memory operations.

None of these effects dictates that no one other than the actual hardware designer should consider pipelining. On the contrary, there are computers in which the instruction set itself was designed to minimize the possibility of hazards and unmanageable interrupts, thus mapping very easily onto a pipelined structure. An example of this is the scalar part of the CRAY-1 (Cray, 1976). Alternatively, for certain applications it may be useful to force the programmer to deal with at least some of the hazards directly, to minimize the hardware costs, maximize the possible performance, or both. A common example occurs at the microinstruction level of many machines where only a small amount of code will be written and where performance and cost make the extra effort in programming a worthwhile endeavor.

This chapter discusses the pipelining of SISD computers in detail. To keep the discussions general we assume throughout that the implementation must explicitly handle all hazards and other complications that might affect the user's view of the machine. In a sense we are solving the hardest problem and by implication simplifying cases where the programmer sees the pipelining.

We start with definitions of a model SISD instruction set that has many of the characteristics of real machines. Coupled with a simple performance measure, this model will be used to demonstrate the various design principles and their effectiveness. Following these definitions is a formal definition of interinstruction dependencies, the hazards they cause, and generic ways of implementing interlocks to handle them. A third section combines these descriptions into a series of hypothetical designs of increasing complexity. These designs make it clear that the most critical subsystem of SISD machines, particularly high-performance models, is the *prefetch buffer* or *cache*. A separate section covers on this subject in more detail.

The fifth section analyzes the effects of pipelining on the handling of interrupts and program exceptions. Finally, the last section demonstrates the current state of the art through a series of detailed examples of real machines. These machines cover the gamut from one-chip microprocessors such as the 8086 to the scalar portions of high-speed machines such as the CRAY-1. They include machines for which the instruction set was, and machines where it was not, designed with pipelining in mind.

6.1   A MODEL SISD ARCHITECTURE

A prerequisite for any attempt to design a pipelined structure is a thorough understanding of the process to be pipelined. Never is this more evident than when the process consists of the execution of machine-level instructions for conventional SISD architected machines. Although a great number of such architectures exist, they all share common characteristics relevant to pipelining. This section summarizes these characteristics and constructs a model that covers them without going into excessive detail. The level of abstraction should be high enough to allow most programmers to relate it to the architecture they are most familiar with. In addition, an arbitrary but plausible performance measure is included to allow at least first-order calculations of the effectiveness of the various pipelining techniques described later in this chapter.

Before continuing, we must emphasize the difference between the architecture of a computer as seen by a programmer and its implementation. The architecture is primarily a *description* of:

1   Objects visible to the programmer that hold data (register, memory, I/O ports, etc.)
2   Operators available to change the contents of objects (instruction set)
3   How these operators may be chained together to create new functions (instruction formats and sequencing).

The implementation of the computer architecture is the actual hardware that functions according to these rules. Often a family of machines may have the same architecture (program-compatible) but radically different implementations. Pipelining is one method that can be used in varying degrees to implement the same architecture.

Most programmers are familiar with one or more SISD architectures. Although there are many variations, the classic architecture of this type has several common characteristics. First, the objects that may hold data and are visible to the programmer include a relatively small number of registers and a much larger number of memory locations. Each of these objects holds only one basic data element (number or character) at a time.

Next, the basic operators compute only one data-element result at a time, usually from only one or two other single-element data operands. The architecture does not explicitly deal with more complex structures such as vectors or arrays, although there may be assists available to ease access to particular elements within such structures. Thus, while an add of the contents of two 16-bit registers may be present, there are no multielement vector adds defined in the basic instruction set.

An instruction is one set of bits specifying a single operator and zero to three sets of bits defining the single-element operands required by the operator. These operand descriptions may specify either a register, a memory location, or a short procedure to use for computing a memory location. They may make reference to registers or other memory locations before determining the final address.

Finally, as seen by the programmer, these instructions are executed one at a time in the order in which they appear in memory. Each instruction runs to completion before the next one is started. A special register, termed the *program counter* or *instruction counter,* keeps track of which instruction is to be executed next. The only deviation from strictly sequential execution, not counting interrupts, occurs when a particular instruction explicitly changes the program counter. This change may be either unconditional, e.g., jump, skip, or subroutine call, or conditional on some value computed by previous instructions.

The model architecture assumed for this chapter has all the above characteristics. In particular we assume the following:

    1 a special CPU register termed the instruction counter (IC) to keep track of the instruction location

    2 several other programmer-visible CPU registers that hold data (e.g., one or more accumulators, index registers, general purpose registers)

    3 a two-address format where two operands are specified, with the result, if there is one, always returning to one of the input operand locations

    4 a complete set of unconditional branch instructions

    5 a complete set of conditional branch instructions

    6 two sizes (number of bits) in the instruction formats, a short size for register to register (RR) instructions and one twice that length for most others.

Note that much of the detail is left undefined. This includes number of registers, methods of computing memory addresses, and more detailed instruction formats. Although critically important to a real design, these details have little effect at the level of discussion in this chapter. Some detail, such as exactly how the conditional branches make their data-dependent tests, is of some importance and discussed where relevant.

From the above description it is possible to determine the degree of partitioning possible in the process of executing instructions. Figure 6-1 diagrams the normal flow of activity in a partitioned fashion for a typical instruction like an ADD. The instruction is fetched, decoded, operands fetched, result computed, and the instruction completed. Perhaps the only segment whose functions are not perfectly clear is that labeled ENDOP. This phase includes setting error flags (overflow, etc.), setting condition codes (e.g., "This result was zero"), incrementing the IC, and testing for pending interrupts. These are all housekeeping functions needed to maintain an orderly flow to the instruction execution process.

Figure 6-1 shows a natural partitioning to the instruction-processing sequence, but

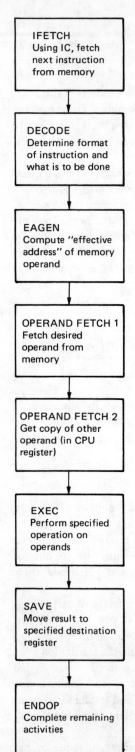

IFETCH
Using IC, fetch
next instruction
from memory

DECODE
Determine format
of instruction and
what is to be done

EAGEN
Compute "effective
address" of memory
operand

OPERAND FETCH 1
Fetch desired
operand from
memory

OPERAND FETCH 2
Get copy of other
operand (in CPU
register)

EXEC
Perform specified
operation on
operands

SAVE
Move result to
specified destination
register

ENDOP
Complete remaining
activities

Figure 6-1 Partitioning of typical instruction execution.

it is by no means the only example. Some of the stages, such as the two operand fetches, are independent of each other and may be reordered arbitrarily. Other phases, such as ENDOP, have components that could be moved elsewhere. This is true of the IC updating which can be done almost any time after instruction fetch. Clearly either more or less partitioning is possible. Stages may be condensed (e.g., combine EXEC and SAVE) or expanded (e.g., break EAGEN into smaller stages). Figure 1-5 diagrammed one such partitioning for a real machine.

Perhaps more important than these relatively static partitioning differences are other variations that occur dynamically from instruction to instruction. For example, the process of effective address generation may vary from almost nothing (simply use some bits of the instruction as the address) to a relatively complex procedure that might benefit from several internal levels of partitioning (such as indirect addressing from a base, plus index register, plus displacement address). Similarly, the execution phase may vary tremendously from a simple load to a double-precision floating-point division.

Even larger variations occur when the instruction is not like an ADD. Figure 6-2 diagrams three such alternatives: a store, an unconditional branch, and a conditional branch.

A STORE instruction moves a copy of some CPU registers into a designated memory location. This requires neither an operand fetch from memory nor an execution phase to compute a result. Similarly, the activities of ENDOP are greatly reduced since no error flags or test results need be recorded.

An unconditional JUMP has an even simpler partitioning because now the instruction ends as soon as the "effective address" has been jammed into the IC. Again the ENDOP activities are pared down even further since the IC is not to be updated.

The most radical variations in partitioning occur in the conditional BRANCH class of instruction. Here there are two entirely distinct partitionings depending on the result of the test specified by the instruction; the test itself represents a major phase of the instruction execution. If the test fails, completion of the instruction is simply an ENDOP activity similar to that for the store class. If the test succeeds, the partitioning is similar to the unconditional JUMP class.

Note that throughout this chapter a capitalized BRANCH, ADD, or STORE refers to an instruction in the model architecture, while branch, add, or store refers to that operation.

Along with this description of a model SISD architecture, a somewhat arbitrary but not unrealistic performance model is needed. This model simply specifies in general units the time required to do each of the major partitions of Figs. 6-1 and 6-2. These roughly approximate the time spent doing these functions on a processor of conventional design with absolutely no pipelining or overlap. Later sections will modify these times as appropriate.

Table 6-1 lists each partition type and the time spent in that position by each of the four classes of instructions discussed earlier.

The IFETCH, OPFETCH 1, and STORE entries all assume a memory access that typically takes longer than a CPU activity. The effective address generation EAGEN assumes that on the average the required computation reduces to something like the

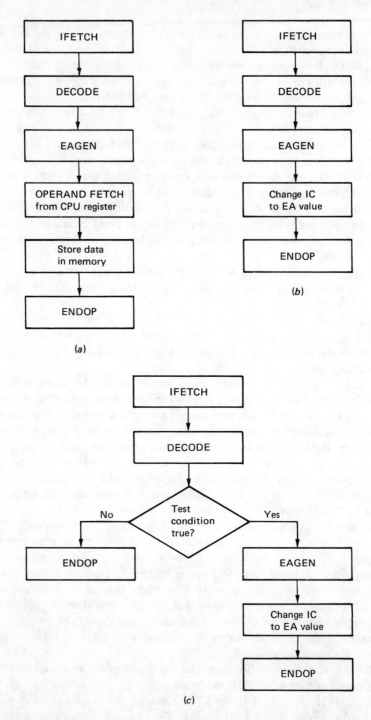

Figure 6-2 Partitioning of other instruction classes. (*a*) Store. (*b*) Unconditional jump. (*c*) Conditional branch.

Table 6-1   Time Allocation to Model Partitions

Partition name	ADD class	STORE class	JUMP class	Conditional BRANCH yes/no
IFETCH	5	5	5	5/5
DECODE	2	2	2	2/2
TEST				1/1
EAGEN	2	2	2	2/0
OP FETCH 1	5			
OP FETCH 2	1	1		
EXECUTE	3			
SAVE	1			
CHANGE IC			1	1/0
STORE		5		
ENDOP	1	1	1	1/1
TOTAL	20	16	11	12/9

addition of a displacement found in an instruction to a copy of some CPU register. Similarly, the execution phase for ADD-like instructions is an average between relatively quick operations such as an add, load, or logical operations, and longer operations such as multiply, divide, or shift. The totals at the bottom of Table 6-1 give the average time for instructions in each class and are the sum of the individual partition times.

One assumption made in Table 6-1 is that each instruction, whether short or long format, always goes to memory for the same period of time. This means that the memory system can deliver with one access a single long-format instruction but is no faster at accessing a short-format instruction. Such an access would probably deliver two short-format instructions, one of which is discarded. Later sections will examine how modification of this procedure can increase performance.

The time per instruction is not a sufficient model to accurately judge a computer design's potential performance. Any real program the computer must execute consists of combinations or *mixes* of instructions of each class. Although the mixes depend on each program's structure, some overall statistics to use as guides have been determined (cf. Gibson, 1970; Connors et al., 1970; and Table 11-2 in Fuller, 1975). Table 6-2 lists one such mix corresponding to the classes of instructions defined earlier.

Table 6-2   An Approximate Mix of Instruction

Class of instruction	Percent of execution
ADD-like (load, add, multiply, etc.)	60%
STORE-like	15%
Unconditional JUMP	5%
Conditional BRANCH—taken	12%
Conditional BRANCH—not taken	8%
	100%

As shown, the majority of instructions are of the class of Fig. 6-1, with branches of various kinds coming next in number. From this table and Table 6-1 a reference number is derived of about 17.11 time units per instruction executed for a nonpipelined computer implementation of the model SISD architecture.

One other statistic that will prove relevant is the percent of instructions that are of a short format. For this model we assume 30% of the total fall in this category.

6.2 INTERINSTRUCTION DEPENDENCIES AND HAZARDS

In a nonpipelined computer design all the operations involved in executing a single instruction (cf. Figs. 6-1 and 6-2) are completed before the next instruction is started. Thus the actual order of execution matches the logical order assumed by the programmer when the program was written. This is not true in pipelining. Instruction executions are overlapped so that some of the operations required for instructions $i + 1$, $i + 2, \ldots$, may be started and completed before instruction i is completed. This difference can cause problems if not sufficiently considered during the design phase because the operations started by $i + 1$, $i + 2, \ldots$, may depend on results from instructions i that have not yet been completed. The existence of these dependencies causes hazards (Ramamoorthy, 1977) that must be detected by the computer implementation, and resolved so that the actual results produced by the program match what the programmer expected. The hardware technique that implements detection and resolution of a hazard is termed an *interlock*.

A hazard occurs whenever some data object within the computer (e.g., register, memory location, flag) is accessed or modified by two separate instructions that are close enough so that the pipelining overlaps their execution. There are three classes of such hazards formally called *read-after-write* (RAW) hazard, *write-after-read* (WAR) hazard, and *write-after-write* (WAW) hazard. To demonstrate the differences among these, consider the following piece of code:

```
        .
        .
        .
STORE   X
        .
        .
        .
ADD     X
STORE   X
        .
        .
STORE   X
        .
        .
        .
```

A read-after-write hazard between two instructions i and j (j assumed to logically follow i) occurs when j attempts to read some object that is modified by instruction i. If the operation in i that modifies the object is not complete before j starts to access it, then j will read the wrong value of that object. In the above code a RAW hazard exists between the first STORE to X and the ADD. If the ADD reads memory before the first STORE has a chance to update it, the wrong value will be added into the CPU register. Instruction j will have gotten a value that is "too old."

A write-after-read hazard exists when instruction j (logically following i) wishes to modify some object that is read by i. If j modifies the object before i has accessed it, i will again get the wrong value, although now the value is too new rather than too old. In the above sample code a WAR hazard potentially exists between the ADD and the second STORE. If the second STORE is overlapped with the ADD, it might be possible for the second update of X to occur before the ADD accesses X.

A write-after-write hazard exists when both instructions i and j attempt to update the same object, but i's store can occur after j's. The result is that after both instructions are complete, the object may be left with an intermediate value (from i) and not the final value (from j). On the sample code this might occur between the last two STOREs. If the second STORE is completed after the third, the value in X will not be what the programmer expects.

By symmetry there is a fourth possibility, read-after-read. However, such a condition alone is not a hazard.

A more formal and rigorous definition of these hazards can be found in Keller, (1975). The basis for this formulation lies in two definitions:

Definition 6-1

The *domain* of an instruction i, denoted $D(i)$, is the set of all objects (registers, memory locations, and flags) whose contents in any way affect the execution of instruction i.

Definition 6-2

The *range* of an instruction i, denoted $R(i)$, is the set of all objects (register, memory locations, and flats) whose contents may be modified by the execution of instruction i.

$D(i)$ is thus the set of all objects read by instruction i, and $R(i)$ the set of all objects modified by i. With this in mind, a hazard condition between an instruction i and a logically later instruction j now occurs whenever any one of three conditions[1] is satisfied:

Condition 1.   (RAW) $R(i) \cap D(j) \neq \Omega$
Condition 2.   (WAR) $D(i) \cap R(j) \neq \Omega$
Condition 3.   (WAW) $R(i) \cap R(j) \neq \Omega$

---

[1] $X \cap Y$ is set intersection, i.e., the set of all elements common to both sets X and Y. Ω is the null set, i.e., the set with no members.

These conditions are pictured in Fig. 6-3. Note the one-to-one relationship between the conditions and the hazards defined earlier.

To make these conditions more concrete, Table 6-3 summarizes the domains and ranges of each class of instruction in the model architecture.

Although this may not be totally representative of real architectures (e.g., those with some form of address generation through indirect pointers), it is very representative. Table 6-4 then uses these domains and ranges to list the kinds of hazards that might be present between two instructions. For example, a STORE instruction that uses an index register computed by a previous ADD would represent a possible RAW hazard. Likewise, two JUMPs in a row represent a WAW hazard since both change the IC. Finally, a conditional BRANCH depends on the condition code or register value set by a previous add-like instruction. It should not depend on the condition code of a following instruction; this represents a WAR hazard.

One hazard not explicitly shown in Table 6-4 can occur any time there is "self-modifying code" where one instruction (typically a STORE) writes into memory a word that shortly thereafter is executed as an instruction. This code can pose a RAW-like hazard between the STORE instruction and the IFETCH phase of the instruction initiation that executes out of that location.

The above discussion describes when hazards might occur. As mentioned earlier it is up to the hardware designer building a pipeline machine to detect the actual occurrences and resolve them so the machine performs as expected. There are a wide variety of techniques used to do these functions, but for the most part they fall into standard classes. For the detection problems there are two opposing approaches. The first is to centralize all the hazard detection in one stage, usually associated with IFETCH, and compare the domain and range with all those instructions already in the pipeline. The second approach to detection is to allow an instruction initiation to travel through the pipeline until it reaches any point where an element out of either the domain or range is needed. It then makes a test to see if there is a potential hazard with any other instruction in the pipeline. The latter case is more flexible than the former, but the hardware needed to do the comparisons can grow as rapidly as the square of the number of stages.

There are similarly two approaches to resolving a hazard once it is detected. The first is simply to "stop the pipe" if a hazard is found. Thus if instruction j is discovered to have a hazard condition with a previously initiated instruction i, then all initiations in progress for instructions $j, j + 1, j + 2, \ldots,$ are stopped in their tracks until i has passed the point of conflict. The second approach is more complex; it simply stops j but allows $j + 1, j + 2, \ldots,$ to continue through the pipeline. This permits $j + 1, j + 2, \ldots,$ to race ahead of j in the pipeline. Of course the hazard checks for $j + 1, j + 2, \ldots,$ must include comparisons with the delayed instruction j, and if a hazard is found they must also be put aside until the original hazard for j has been resolved and j is permitted to resume.

A final comment deals with speeding up the resolution of RAW hazards. As might be deduced from the sample code sequence, one of the most common RAW hazards occurs when an ADD-like instruction makes reference to a memory location modified by a previous STORE. In such cases the direct solution would be to hold up the ADD

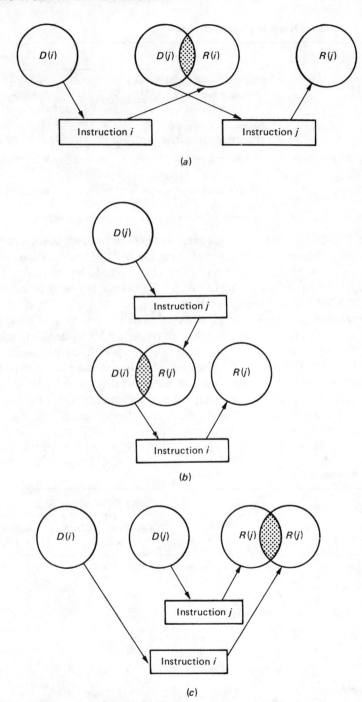

Figure 6-3 Represention of hazards. (a) Read-after-write (RAW) hazard. (b) Write-after-read (WAR) hazard. (c) Write-after-write (WAW) hazard.

Table 6-3   Domain and Range in Model Architecture

Instruction	Domain	Range
ADD-like	Memory locations (operands) Registers (operands) Registers (EAGEN)	Registers (results) Condition codes Flags
STORE	Registers (operands) Registers (EAGEN)	Memory locations
UNCONDITIONAL JUMP	Registers (EAGEN)	Instruction counter
CONDITIONAL BRANCH	Condition (codes/flags) registers (EAGEN)	Instruction counter

until the STORE has completed the memory modification, at which point a fetch from the same memory location would allow the ADD to restart. However, a faster solution, called *short-circuiting,* gives a copy of the data to be stored directly to the waiting ADD, saving it from having to wait for the STORE to complete and then to do another READ. Figure 6-4 diagrams this.

A generalization of this process, termed *forwarding,* can be used throughout the machine to help speed up the resolution of all types of RAW hazards. At each point in the pipeline where data is to be accessed as input to some function, there are multiple staging latches to catch the data. If the data for an instruction passing through a stage is in a RAW hazard with an earlier instruction, one of the staging latches is loaded not with the data, which isn't available yet, but with an index or *tag* to the stage that will produce it. The instruction waiting for the data is then frozen at that stage until the data is available. Note that multiple staging latches at the input to a stage allow other instructions to move through the stage while the RAW-dependent one is frozen. This is

Table 6-4   Possible Hazards in Model Architecture

Instruction i	Instruction j			
	ADD-like	STORE	UNCONDITIONAL JUMP	CONDITIONAL BRANCH
ADD-like	RAW WAR WAW	RAW WAR	RAW	RAW
STORE	RAW WAR		WAW	
UNCONDITIONAL BRANCH	WAR		WAW	WAW
CONDITIONAL BRANCH	WAR		WAW	WAW

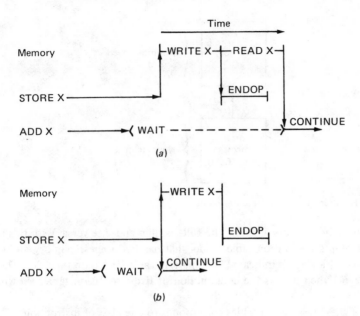

Figure 6-4 RAW hazard resolution speed-up. (*a*) Without short-circuiting. (*b*) With short-circuiting.

similar to the data-stationary control technique of Chap. 3. Finally, whenever a stage completes a computation it checks all other relevant staging latches to see if any has a tag equal to its own ID; and if so, the stage receives copies of the data. This completion reactivates the frozen instructions, permitting them to continue through the pipeline.

The concept of short-circuiting goes back at least as far as the STRETCH machine (Block, 1959). The general concept of forwarding, as defined above, seems to have been developed by Tomasulo (1967), with references as early as 1965 (Flynn and Amdahl, 1965). A detailed discussion on the question of hazard resolution can be found in Keller (1975).

6.3 DEVELOPMENT OF PIPELINED DESIGNS

This section explores the ramifications of pipelining on SISD computer design by using the model architecture of Sec. 6.1 and describing a succession of implementations for it, each of which uses incrementally more pipelining than the previous one. A crude performance model for each design is developed to permit a contrast with the nonpipelined design. The basis for these models is the assumed partitionings and timings of Sec. 6.1.

Before discussing these designs, however, it is worthwhile developing reservation tables that model a totally nonpipelined implementation. This design consists of a noninterleaved memory connected to a nonpipelined central processing unit (CPU), Fig. 6-5.

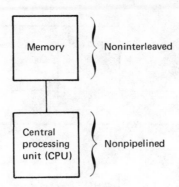

Figure 6-5 Nonpipelined SISD computer model.

Whenever the memory is busy, the CPU is idle, and vice versa. With this in mind, one can develop a reservation table model that has two stages, memory and CPU. As before, usage of a stage is indicated by a mark in the appropriate time slot. The timing from Table 6-1 then directs the construction of five reservation tables shown in Fig. 6-6.

Each of these reservation tables corresponds to one class of instructions. The ADD class, for example, consists of five units of instruction fetch, followed by four units of CPU activity for decode and effective address generation, followed by five units of data fetch, and finally six units of CPU activity. The others are similar in the terms of Chap. 3.

The initiation control strategy for the nonpipelined design is to execute each instruction (initiation of a reservation table) to completion. No new initiation is started before the previous completes. Using this strategy gives an average latency (average time to execute an instruction) of 17.11 time units.

6.3.1 Simple Prefetch

Any pipelining of the instruction execution process must begin with an attempt to overlap one instruction execution with the next. An examination of Fig. 6-6, particularly the most common ADD class, indicates that there are several times when a second initiation could be started without causing collision with the first. The simplest of these cases merely starts the instruction fetch for the next instruction while the current instruction is doing its last bit of processing in the CPU. Figure 6-7 times out a sequence of ADDs using just this amount of overlap. On a repetitive basis the average time for each ADD-like instruction drops from 20 units to 15—a substantial performance increase.

The technique of fetching the next instruction during the termination of the current one, called *instruction prefetching,* is usually easy to add to a computer design. Despite its simplicity, there is a subtle but important difference between a design with prefetching and a more conventional design. In the conventional design instruction, execution always starts with the fetching of the instruction from memory. When prefetching is employed, execution starts with the assumption that the instruction is already in the CPU and it is the responsibility of the execution process to fetch the next instruction before it can complete.

This distinction not only complicates the execution of each instruction by forcing it to handle part of its successor, but it also introduces potential hazards that must be avoided. The clearest occasion of hazard occurs in any JUMP or conditional BRANCH classes. Here the branch address of the next instruction to be executed is not known until nearly the end of the branch, and consequently any prefetching of the next in-

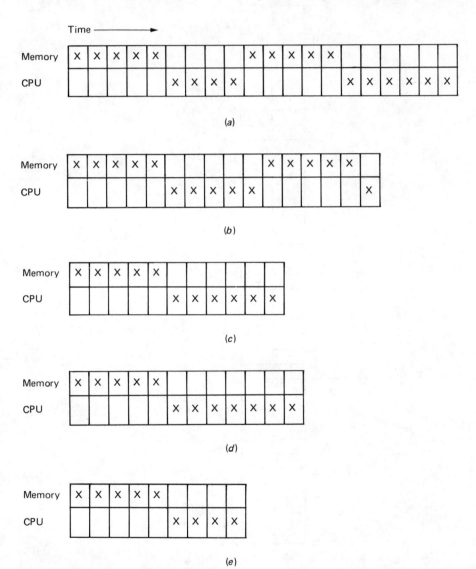

Figure 6-6 Reservation tables for nonpipelined design. (a) ADD class. (b) STORE class. (c) JUMP class. (d) Conditional class—branch taken. (e) Conditional class—branch not taken.

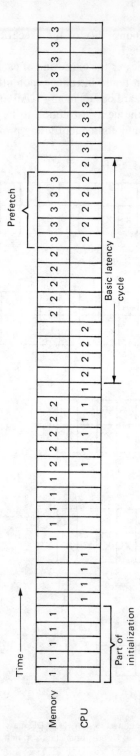

Figure 6-7 Simple overlap of multiple ADD-like instructions.

struction may be wasted. This corresponds to a RAW hazard around the updating of the IC register.

Another possible RAW hazard occurs within the execution of a STORE instruction. When prefetching occurs after the STORE operation in memory is complete, no hazard is possible. However when the prefetch is started before the STORE operation (e.g., during times 5-9 in Fig. 6-6b), the wrong instruction will be fetched if the STORE is part of a sequence of self-modifying code that changes the next instruction word in memory. The prefetched word in this case must be suppressed.

Figure 6-8 diagrams some reservation tables for a design using prefetch where all of the above hazards are avoided. There is no overlap during any of the BRANCH instructions, and the prefetch for the store occurs only after the STORE has modified

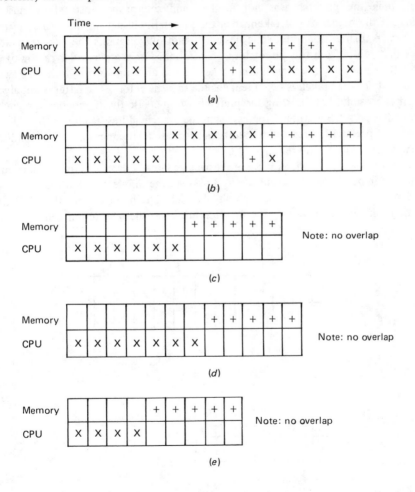

+ = Prefetching of next instruction

Figure 6-8 Reservation tables for simple prefetch design (hazard-free). (a) ADD class. (b) STORE class. (c) JUMP class. (d) Conditional class—branch taken. (e) Conditional class—branch not taken.

memory. A + is used instead of an "X" to mark the periods where activity related to prefetch is in progress. Note that for the ADD and STORE classes extra CPU activity is needed to support the prefetch, namely the updating of the IC and its passage to the memory system. This activity used to be part but not all of the ENDOP functions.

Using the mix of Table 6-1, the average latency of such a design drops from 17.11 to 13.96, a performance increase of about 18%.

It is possible to expend more hardware to move the prefetch up in the reservation table and then do the required hazard detection and resolution. For example, a conditional BRANCH instruction could always initiate a prefetch of word IC + 1 just after being decoded, but before the effective address of the branch has been computed and the decision as to whether or not the branch should be taken is made. If the branch is taken, then the prefetch was not needed, and the proper instruction must be fetched. If the branch is not taken, then the prefetch will deliver the desired instruction earlier than a nonprefetching design. Figure 6-9 diagrams the two reservation tables that result from this prefetch mechanization. For the particular timing of our model, the case where the branch is not taken speeds up from 13 time units to 7, while the case where the branch is taken remains the same as before. The latter is not always true; it is possible that inserting the prefetch will increase the time when a branch is taken if the prefetch is still in progress when the branch address is known. In addition, this unused prefetch represents an additional request to the memory system and thus increases the demand ratio required of it.

With the timing shown in Fig. 6-9 the average latency decreases by .48 time units, an increase in performance of only about 3.4% over the simple prefetch design.

Some additional performance can also be picked up by modifying the STORE instruction. This involves starting the prefetch just after the instruction is decoded but

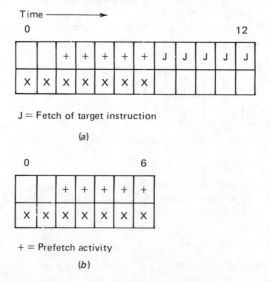

Figure 6-9 Variations in conditional BRANCH with prefetch. (a) Branch taken. (b) Branch not taken.

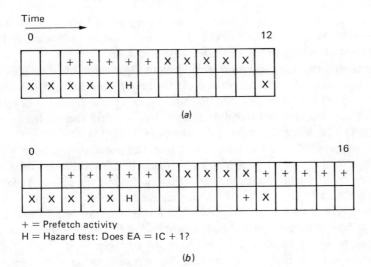

+ = Prefetch activity
H = Hazard test: Does EA = IC + 1?

(b)

Figure 6-10 Variations in store reservation table due to hazard resolution. (a) No hazard, EA ≠ IC + 1, or hazard and short circuit. (b) Hazard, EA = IC + 1, no short circuit.

also adding a test between the updated IC and EA of the STORE. If they don't match, there is no hazard and the prefetched instruction word is the proper one. If they do match, the prefetched word is worthless. In this case either the modified location must be read again or a copy of the data that was just stored must be forwarded as the next instruction. This latter approach is an example of the short-circuiting technique defined in Sec. 6.2.

Figure 6-10 diagrams the timing of a STORE for the model architecture. Note the extra cycle of CPU activity added to do the hazard check. If short-circuiting is employed, the time per STORE drops from 16 in the nonpipelined design to 13, a decrease in the average latency of another .45 time units. If short-circuiting is not employed, when the hazard is detected the time actually exceeds the nonpipelined case.

Using all these prefetching techniques would reduce the average latency per instruction execution in the model architecture from 17.11 to 13.03 time units. This corresponds to a design with 24% more performance than a nonpipelined design. Numbers for real architectures are typically in the same range. Furthermore, in most real designs the associated hardware cost is small, making the cost-performance ratio of the prefetching technique very attractive. Consequently, prefetching can be found in most modern designs.

6.3.2 Instruction Overlap

As effective as prefetching is, it still does not provide all the performance possible from the computer's hardware. For example, Fig. 6-8 shows that for a series of ADD-like instructions the CPU is used in only 11 out of 15 cycles, while the memory is used even less, 10 out of 15. Neither is utilized 100%. However, Lemma 3-1 and Theorem

3-4 applied to Fig. 6-6a indicate that an average latency of 10 for a series of ADDs should be possible. At this rate both CPU and memory would be used fully, and the average time per ADD would be half of the nonpipelined design.

Simply applying the delay insertion techniques to Fig. 6-6a in isolation does give a reservation table that, at least for a series of ADDs, achieves the bound of 10. Figure 6-11 shows this modified table. Basically, the start of the decode activity is delayed 1 time unit, and the final unit of ENDOP is delayed 5 time units. The result is a table with compute time 26, but which accepts the latency cycle (5, 15).

The obvious question to ask at this point is: Could all reservation tables of Fig. 6-6-6 be modified by delay insertion so that they approach 100% utilization of at least one of the two units? Theoretically, the answer is yes. Assume the mix of Table 6-2 gives an average of 8.75 time units of memory activity and 7.6 time units of CPU activity per instruction; by Lemma 3-1, an average instruction time of 8.75 time units is thus possible with sufficient delays. This is almost half of the nonpipelined time.

The next question is whether designing logic for a nonpipelined CPU to follow these reservation tables is feasible or practical. The answer is no for several reasons:

1 The insertion of a delay anywhere in a reservation table is equivalent to inserting new stages which may themselves require CPU time.

2 When reservation tables are overlapped the CPU must keep track of not one instruction, or even one instruction plus the prefetch of the next, but of bits and pieces of several different instructions. (An exercise to the reader to verify this is to apply the cycle (5,15) to Fig. 6-11. Such control becomes extremely complicated to implement with conventional state logic or microprogrammed control techniques.)

3 Increased overlap makes possible many of the hazards of Table 6-2. This not only further complicates the control logic, but also may require new CPU activity for hazard detection and dynamically introduced delays for their resolution.

All the above factors cause the average latency actually observed to increase dramatically over the bound of 8.75 time units.

6.3.3 Separate I/E Units

The solution to the dilemma of the previous section is to pipeline the CPU. Since the instruction fetch appears relatively easy to overlap with other activities, it is a good candidate for one stage of the pipeline. Similarly, the actual computation requested by the instruction, such as an add or multiply, is also a good candidate for another stage. This partitioning is so natural and so often used that the stages performing these functions have come to be known by standard names. The stages performing the instruction fetch, some of the decode, and much of the ENDOP functions are the *instruction unit* or *I-unit*. The stages performing the execution functions plus the rest of the ENDOP are the *execution unit* or *E-unit*. Figure 6-12 demonstrates the resulting design. There is some ambiguity in Fig. 6-12 as to where many of the intermediate functions such as effective address generation are placed. This ambiguity is deliberate because it is possible to find almost any partitioning of these functions actually used in real machine designs.

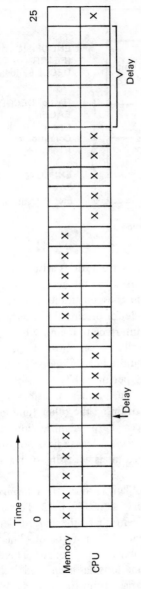

Figure 6-11 "Optimal" ADD instruction reservation table.

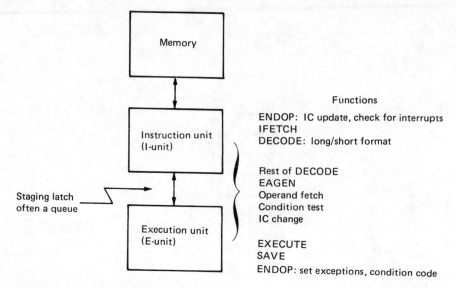

Figure 6-12 Classical SISD CPU partitioning.

Besides this ambiguity several other questions arise from a study of Fig. 6-12. The first issue is the memory interface used for the accessing of operands. The I-unit has clear responsibility for instruction fetches, but there is no equivalent responsibility for data accesses. Arguments can be made for placing this interface almost anywhere. Placing it in the I-unit creates a single interface to memory but somewhat limits the range of possible partitioning. It practically forces most of decode, EA generation, and operand access to be done in the I-unit. For the model architecture all but the ADD class of instructions would be totally performed by the I-unit.

Another alternative is to make the E-unit responsible for operand accessing. This gives much more flexibility in partitioning the other functions but it also requires a memory system with two interfaces. Perhaps more important, it complicates the hazard detection and resolution process because now both the I-unit and the E-unit must know precisely what the other unit is accessing or has accessed recently to prevent hazards.

A common solution to this problem is to create a *storage control unit* (SCU) between the I-unit, E-unit, and memory, as in Fig. 6-13. This unit not only handles the separate access requests, but also centralizes the hazard detection that must occur around use of memory locations. This SCU may be pipelined and may show up as a separate stage in the instruction execution process. There are examples of real machines where each of these combinations has been tried.

Another serious question that arises from Fig. 6-12 is: Which unit owns the programmer-visible registers? For example, it is clear that the I-unit owns the IC in that it is primarily responsible for updating, modifying, and using it for instruction fetching. Therefore, the IC should be packaged in the I-unit. Likewise, registers that are primarily accumulators are owned by the E-unit. There are others, however, that either unit may modify. This is particularly true of architectures where registers may be used either as accumulators, indexes, or bases, and the EA generation process permits modification of the registers (e.g., autoincrementing of index registers). Such registers must be handled very carefully because they introduce a great many additional hazards that must be detected and resolved.

Figure 6-14 diagrams a typical solution to the register ownership problem. Those registers that are owned by a unit are packaged with it, and those that are common to both are packaged separately. Each register in the common set has special *tag* logic to aid in hazard detection and resolution. Typically, the I-unit decodes a new instruction to the point of determining which of these registers are read or modified by that instruction. For each register that is to be modified, its tag is set to indicate to future instructions that the contents of the register are undergoing change. Similarly, the tag is read for each register that is to be read by the new instruction. If the tag indicates that the register is undergoing modification by a previous instruction, the new instruction must be held up. This is like detecting and resolving a RAW hazard; similar uses of the tags prevent WAW and WAR hazards.

When an instruction has finished computing the modification of one of these registers, the modified value is sent to the appropriate register, and its tag is reset. Resetting the tag permits any instructions suspended on it to resume.

There are several choices of when to suspend an instruction and what to do with instructions following it. An instruction can be suspended as soon as it enters the I-unit and released only when all hazards are resolved (needed registers available); or it can be allowed to proceed until it actually needs the contents of a register. At this point, if the register contents are still unavailable, the instruction is frozen. Similarly, if the execution of instruction i is frozen, it is a design option whether to suspend in-

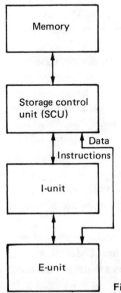

Figure 6-13 Use of storage control unit in SISD pipeline.

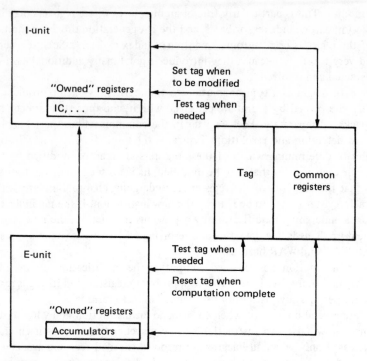

Figure 6-14 Ownership of registers.

structions $i + 1$, $i + 2$, ... Suspending these instructions simplifies the tag process but at a cost in performance. Allowing the instruction to continue permits instructions to be executed out of sequence as soon as their operands are available. This option increases hardware utilization at the cost of complicated hazard circuitry. Examples of each design are given later.

This centralization of common registers often can be a bottleneck because both the I-unit and E-unit and separate stages within each unit may demand simultaneous access to the registers. Even though the demand may be for different registers, the normal construction of the register as a small semiconductor memory usually precludes more than one or two accesses at a time. To prevent this limitation from significantly degrading potential performance, many systems replicate the entire register logic several times and give one copy to each stage that needs it. This permits simultaneous reads of many different registers without conflict. However, when a register or its tag is to be modified, the modification must be performed on all copies simultaneously so that all stages have up-to-date information. This may require stealing a cycle from each unit.

In addition to registers and memory, the following other machine resources may introduce hazards to be handled between the two units: condition codes, flags, test results, and other processor status information. These resources are usually handled in the same way as the registers.

6.3.4 Range of I-Unit Partitions—Branch Processing

As mentioned in the discussion of Fig. 6-12 there is a whole range of partitionings possible for the instruction execution process when there are at least two stages in the CPU. This section examines the more obvious choices, particularly how they affect the I-unit.

The I-unit is primarily concerned with instruction fetching. Therefore one natural line of partitioning is to place in the I-unit most or all activities that affect this process. In terms of the model architecture, this activity includes not only ENDOP activities from ADD- and STORE-like instructions, but also all the activity associated with BRANCH and JUMP instructions. Figures 6-16, 6-17, and 6-18 diagram the functioning of the I-unit for a range of such partitions.

Before describing each of these functions in detail, it is worthwhile to comment on the nature of the connection between the I-unit and the E-unit. Because they are two stages of a pipeline, a staging latch between them is expected. The simplest structure is a single register that holds the next instruction to be processed by the E-unit. If this register is full because the E-unit is busy executing it, then activity in the I-unit must eventually come to a stop. In this case the two units are *rigidly connected* and reservation tables that describe the activity of both can be produced and analyzed.

A more widely used interconnection replaces this latch by a first-in-first-out (FIFO) queue that can contain multiple entries (see Fig. 6-15). This effectively decouples the two units and allows each to work at its own pace. It also levels out extremes in processing times (e.g., E-unit time to do a load versus a divide or I-unit delay due to conditional BRANCH) so that both units continually have work to do. In turn this eliminates most of the difficulties with instruction overlap as mentioned in Sec. 6.3.2, allowing total performance to approach a bound like Lemma 3-1. However, it does make the compute time of individual instructions difficult to predict when they enter the I-unit. This reduces the applicability of the theories of Chap. 3 to modeling the overall system.

All the samples of I-unit partitioning described in this section assume a staging latch that is a FIFO. It is termed the *I-queue*. Since the maximum depth of this queue is not specified, it may have any value including 1. This latter case corresponds to defaulting the FIFO to a single latch and rigidly connecting the two units.

Figure 6-16 is the simplest partitioning; it basically assumes that the I-unit handles only the IFETCH and ENDOP functions. In general it corresponds to the prefetching procedures of Sec. 6.3.1. As long as there is space in the I-queue, the I-unit will increment the IC and fetch the next instruction. These are placed in the I-queue for eventual execution by the E-unit. The only exception is when the E-unit encounters a branch to be taken; it must signal the I-unit, which in turn must flush the I-queue of its contents and reload the IC with the value provided by the E-unit. The E-unit stops until this instruction has been fetched, at which point it resumes execution.

For this partitioning, hazard detection and resolution are relatively simple. The only areas of contention between the I-unit and the E-unit are around the value of the IC and memory. For the IC the only hazards are around branches, and these are

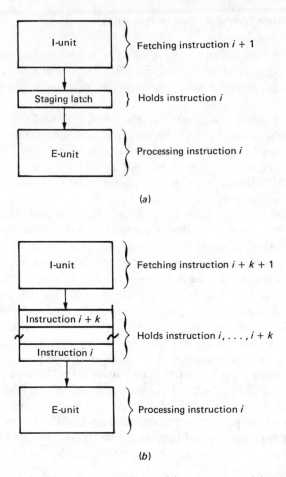

Figure 6-15 Staging latch between I-unit and E-unit. (a) Single register. (b) FIFO.

handled explicitly. Hazards around memory occur only during execution of self-modifying code where one store instruction affects a memory location already prefetched by the I-unit. Detection of this hazard requires the I-unit to compare the memory address during all stores with the addresses of all instructions already read into the I-queue. Occurrence of a match requires flushing all or part of the I-queue.

The timing for this partitioning greatly resembles that for the prefetch strategy of Sec. 6.3.1. Except when branches are taken, the E-unit is never idle waiting for instructions. Only when a branch is taken will the instruction fetch show up. In fact, it is expected that the time for such branches is actually longer than for the nonpipelined design because of the overhead of signaling and I-queue flushing. For our model architecture, Table 6-5, column c, lists some times that might be reasonable. The average instruction latency shows about an 18% improvement over a nonpipelined design.

The next level of partitioning might be to include in the I-unit enough of the decode to detect just BRANCH instructions, plus all of the associated EA generation

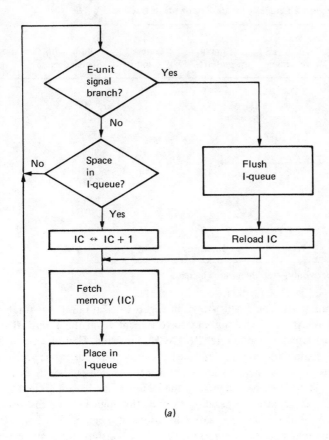

(a)

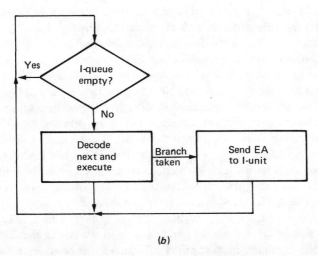

(b)

Figure 6-16 I-Unit as prefetcher (hazard-free). (a) I-unit. (b) E-unit.

Table 6-5   Approximate Latencies for Variety of I-Unit Designs

	(a) No pipelining	(b) Simple prefetch	(c) Simple I-unit	(d)* I-unit with branch decode	(e)* I-unit with target fetch
ADD-Like	20	15	15	15	15
STORE	16	15	15	15	15
JUMP	11	11	13	0	0
Conditional BRANCH (taken)	12	12	14	7	2
Conditional BRANCH (not taken)	9	9	5	7	2
Averages	17.11	13.96	13.98	12.65*	11.65*

*Lower bounds only—real-life hazards increase this.

and ENDOP functions. The result shown in Fig. 6-17 is an I-unit that totally executes unconditional BRANCHes without any involvement from the E-unit. The only interaction occurs when a conditional BRANCH is reached. Here the I-unit halts until the test result is known from the E-unit, usually after the I-queue has been emptied by the E-unit. The potential hazards in this design are more complex than the previous case. Although there is no hazard around the IC usage, the hazard around the stores in self-modifying code requires more complex detection logic because the instructions in the I-queue may be from nonconsecutive locations in memory. Furthermore, the EA generation phase may require access to index or base registers that may be dynamically changed by the E-unit. This represents a RAW hazard that must be detected and resolved. A tag or forwarding mechanism is often used for this.

The existence of these additional hazards makes timing of average instruction latency more difficult than for previous cases. Table 6-5, column d, gives an estimate of a lower bound if none of the hazards occur. The effective times for ADD-like and STORE classes are roughly the same as before because they are E-unit bound. As long as there is no long chain of unconditional JUMPs, the effective time for such branches is zero, since the I-unit totally overlaps their execution with the E-unit. For conditional BRANCHes, the I-unit stops until the E-unit is complete, at which point the next instruction is fetched. Again if there are no long chains of BRANCHes, the only time directly associated with such instructions is the time to test the E-unit's result, fetch the instruction, and place it in the I-queue. The overall result is an average latency that approaches 26% less than the nonpipelined case.

Although Fig. 6-17 has minimized the effects of JUMPs, there is still a significant component of average latency due to I-unit suspension at a conditional BRANCH. An obvious approach to minimizing this effect is to prefetch in one or even both possible directions when a conditional BRANCH is encountered. Then when the E-unit has

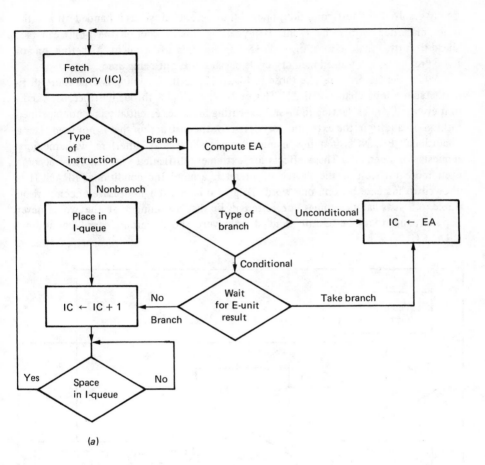

(a)

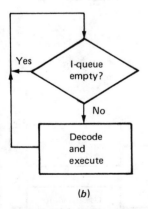

(b)

Figure 6-17 I-Unit including branch decode. (a) I-unit. (b) E-unit.

finally resolved the test condition, one of the prefetched words is handed off and the other discarded. While the E-unit is processing this instruction the I-unit can race ahead to further instructions. Figure 6-18 diagrams this arrangement. As before, one of these prefetches is a wasted memory cycle because it is not being used.

While the hazards are like those in Fig. 6-17, accurate timing is even more difficult. Again a long chain of BRANCHes or JUMPs cripples throughput because the E-unit eventually idles, leaving the I-unit executing branches essentially in a nonpipelined fashion. In addition, the extra memory fetch for the instruction that is not used after a conditional BRANCH requires memory time which may interfere with memory requests for operands. These effects are extremely difficult to model. They become even more difficult if the degree of prefetch around the conditional BRANCH is allowed to increase beyond one word. To give at least a rough measure of comparison Table 6-5 lists latency times for different I-units, assuming that the worst never happens and that the E-unit is idled only very shortly around each conditional BRANCH.

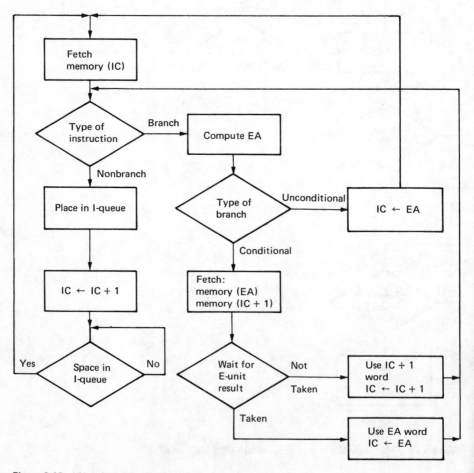

Figure 6-18   I-Unit including branch target prefetch.

A technique that is applicable to any of these designs has the I-unit "guess" which way the conditional BRANCH may go. This guess may be based on gross statistics (over 50% of all conditional BRANCHes are taken), on opcodes (e.g., a BRANCH ON COUNT nearly always taken), or some elaborate scheme for predicting the test result. Clearly, performance increases with increasing the probability of correct guesses.

6.3.5 Further Pipelining—One Instruction Per Cycle

So far the CPU has had essentially two stages. Of these stages, the E-unit is the major bind; the I-unit becomes idle either when the I-queue is full or a conditional BRANCH is encountered. This situation is similar to the inner loop designs for vector instructions (cf. Sec. 5.1.3). Then overall performance can be increased if the functions are repartitioned to more equally distribute the workload. In this case a natural repartitioning would move at least the EA generation (and some of the decode functions needed to drive it) from the E-unit to the I-unit. If the I-unit is already assumed to have the functions shown in Figs. 6-17 or 6-18, then this may not cost much in direct hardware. The logic used for EA generation for JUMPs and BRANCHes can be expanded to do EA generation for all instructions.

Further, if the registers used to do EA generations are from the same set as those used as operands in ADD-like instructions, it is equally reasonable to also move the operand 2 fetch activity into the I-unit.

The net result is to equally balance usage of the I- and E-units for the most common ADD class of instructions. For the other classes of instructions, the I-unit handles almost the entire load. In fact, the average utilization of the I-unit per instruction is about six time units for the model architecture.

The primary penalty is the increased possibility of hazards around the CPU registers that are now accessed by both the I-unit and the E-unit. Interlocks, usually in tag form, must be added to each register; and hardware logic in the I- and E-units must be added to detect and resolve improper accessing. Variations in these solutions will be described later in this chapter when a series of real machine designs are discussed.

This partitioning does not conclude CPU performance enhancement. Instead it virtually begs for more pipelining. The I-unit can now go through a fairly rigid pattern of ENDOP, IFETCH, partial decode, and EA generation. This maps well into a linear pipeline. Likewise the E-unit now receives predecoded instructions and either the operands themselves or at worst their memory/register address. Its functioning includes completing the fetch of the operands, doing the designated operations, and storing the result and any condition code or status. This in turn maps into a multiconfigurable arithmetic pipeline where the different types of reservation tables are well-controlled. Such a pipeline might have a strong resemblance to the arithmetic pipelines of Chap. 4.

The two I-unit and E-unit pipelines can now run independently with the I-queue or its equivalent buffering them. Figure 6-19 diagrams this arrangement. Execution of an instruction now corresponds to not one but two different reservation tables on two separate pipelines.

Good design of these pipelines results in a CPU where every stage takes the same amount of time and where at least theoretically a latency of one instruction per stage

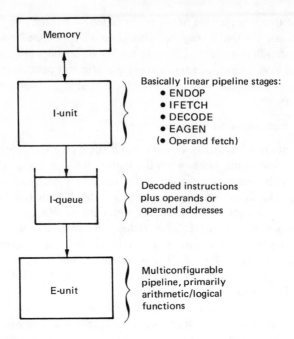

Figure 6-19 Typical fully pipelined CPU.

cycle is possible. There are two primary obstacles to achieving these conditions, memory bandwidth and slow-downs caused by hazard resolution. In our model architecture the average instruction requires 1.75 memory accesses; and if the memory system of the nonpipelined assumptions is used (5 time units per access), the average memory time of 8.75 time units would destroy a pipeline whose stage time is one time unit. The demand ratio gets even higher and performance is further degraded when techniques like prefetching are employed that result in potentially unneeded accesses. Better memory organizations are clearly needed. Fortunately, just as for vector processors, there is a strong technology for designing memory systems that match well with CPU pipelines as in Fig. 6-19. These techniques are described in a later section.

Speeding up the memory system to match the CPU pipeline leaves only interinstruction hazards as potential performance degradation factors. The effects of such hazards are heavily architecture-dependent and even more heavily individual-program-dependent. As such, they almost totally have resisted attempts to model them mathematically. Instead most investigation has focused on cycle-by-cycle simulation of individual CPUs or proposed extensions of CPU designs (cf. Peuto and Shustek, 1977; Foster and Riseman, 1972; Riseman and Foster, 1972). Reams of statistics have been derived from these simulations, but few detailed insights have been revealed. The overall conclusion from these studies is that the average instruction latency for a fully pipelined CPU with a good memory system lies between 1.6 and 3 stage-time units, and the exact number depends on the program.

6.3.6 Effects of Instruction Size

One attribute of the model architecture that has been ignored up to now is the existence of two instruction formats: long and short. All previous designs assumed each instruction fetch required exactly one memory access whether it or a previous instruction was long or short. This kept the I-unit design discussions conceptually simple but ignored a complication that must be handled by real designs. This section investigates this complication.

The existence of different length instructions can have both good and bad effects on a system's performance, primarily because of its effect on the memory bandwidth needed to support IFETCH. If, for example, a memory system can deliver with one access a word capable of holding two short or one long instruction, then if the I-unit is able, a series of n short instructions should require only $n/2$ accesses. As shown in the previous section, a fully pipelined CPU can easily be bound up waiting for a much slower memory. Any reduction in the memory bandwidth the CPU needs can translate directly into increased performance. The converse of this is also true: if a memory access can delivery only one short instruction, and two accesses are needed for long formats, then the previous designs were overly optimistic.

The model architecture gives an example. If each instruction is the same length, then on the average each instruction requires 1.75^2 memory accesses for a demand ratio (Sec. 2.2.1) of 1.75 if the CPU is fully pipelined and no hazards are encountered. If each memory access returns two short instructions, and short instructions occur 30% of the time, then the demand ratio drops to 1.6. On the other hand, if two memory accesses are needed for each long instruction, the demand ratio expands to 2.5.

This situation is even more complex for many modern architectures that have more than two different sized formats. The formats can range from very short ones that pack four instructions to a memory word, to very long ones that require three or more accesses. Accurate sizing of the demand ratio needed of the memory system requires knowing both the formats of the instruction set and their probability of occurrence.

The typical method of handling this variation in size is to replace the stages performing the ENDOP (IC update) and IFETCH functions by an I-unit operation that resembles Fig. 6-16 but has enough decoding to determine the format size of the next instruction and some local memory to remember the lengths of the previous instructions. Often the output staging latch of this logic is called an *instruction register* (IR); it is always long enough to hold a single instruction of maximum length. It is here that all the pieces of an instruction are assembled. The local memory, often called a *prefetch buffer* (PB), is at least the width that can be accessed by one memory operation and holds whatever parts of one access are not needed by the instruction required by that access. Some flags associated with the PB indicate at all times how full it is. Finally, the IC is part of this stage. Figure 6.20 diagrams this structure.

---

[2] The ADD class and STORE class each require one extra memory access and occur 75% of the time, assuming each data access corresponds to exactly one memory word.

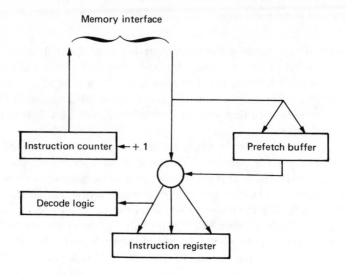

Figure 6-20 IFETCH stage.

In general the logic associated with the IFETCH stage must be capable of handling any sequence of instructions in any format. To demonstrate the kind of function performed by this logic, we look at the two cases for the model architecture: one where a memory word (result of one access) holds one short instruction or half a long one and the other where it holds two shorts or one long. In the latter case a long instruction can straddle a word boundary with half in each of two consecutive words. A design for a real architecture must handle all combinations of the above for all format sizes.

Figures 6-21 and 6-22 diagram the general operation of the IFETCH stage for each case. In both cases the time required to fetch the next instruction is not constant. Therefore later stages in the pipeline must be told when an instruction has been totally assembled. The function marked "Signal next stage" does this. To avoid frequent delays and holdups while an assembly is in progress, many real designs replace the IR by an IR-queue which, like the I-queue, has room for several assembled instructions and allows the IFETCH and later stages to proceed at their own rate. Other designs perform an equivalent function by expanding the prefetch buffer to hold several memory words.

6.4 CACHES

The previous section indicated that instruction latencies as low as one per cycle with a very small cycle time are possible. Many of the machines described later in this chapter are in fact designed with minimum latency as a goal. Regardless of the practicality of the CPU design, however, there is one major system component that has not yet been discussed: the memory system. As in the pipelined vector processors, a simple memory design quickly becomes the limiting factor in achievable performance. For example, for our model architecture it may be possible to design a pipelined CPU where one stage-time equals one of the time units used in Table 6.1. However, the memory to drive this pipeline takes on the average 6 to 10 time units per instruction, totally overwhelming the high-speed pipeline. The required *demand ratio* is much higher than the available memory bandwidth.

Rectifying this imbalance usually involves combining a variety of techniques. Perhaps the simplest is to physically partition memory into two halves each of which can be accessed simultaneously. Placing all instructions in one half and all data in the other increases the average bandwidth of the memory as seen by the CPU by almost a factor of two. Although dividing the memory requires attention from the programmer during program load, it is an effective technique that can often satisfy the demands of a less than fully pipelined CPU. Machine designs using this technique date back at least as far as the STRETCH (Block, 1959).

The next technique is memory interleaving (see Sec. 2.2). Although it does not decrease the access time seen by one instruction, it does increase the number of accesses in operation at one time, thus increasing effective memory bandwidth.

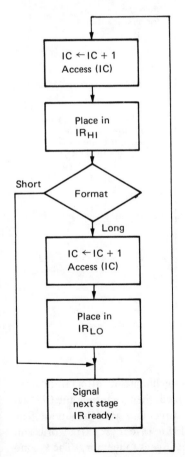

Figure 6-21 IFETCH logic: long = two words; short = one word.

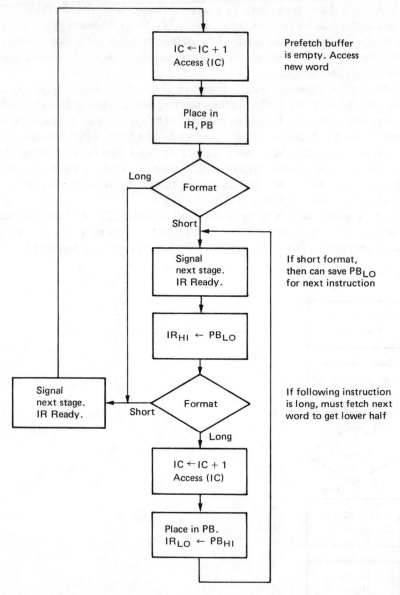

Figure 6-22 IFETCH logic: long = one word, short = $\frac{1}{2}$ word.

Although memory interleaving can be an effective technique, it suffers from some potential problems. First, if simple interleaving is assumed, then each time the CPU requests an item it gets not only that item but copies of memory words around it. The only effective way to use this bandwidth is for the CPU to save these extra words and to check if any of them are what it needs the next time it goes to memory. The second problem occurs in either simple or complex interleaved designs because, as mentioned before, interleaving per se does not speed up the access time for a particular word. This means that the IFETCH mechanism in the CPU must make its requests far in advance of when the instruction is to be executed by the rest of the pipeline. In some cases, like branches, this is not always possible.

As with the pipelined vector processors, the typical solution to both problems is to insert between main memory and the CPU pipeline a high-speed local memory that matches the requirements of each unit more closely (see Fig. 6-23). In recent years this local memory has become known by the term *cache.* The following subsections discuss the design of such caches in more detail.

Historically, the cache is one part of the overall concept of *storage hierarchies* where faster but less dense memories are placed closer to the CPU, and slower but more dense or bigger memories back them up. This takes advantage of the *locality of reference* observed in most programs where most references over a short period of time come from certain neighborhoods, called *working sets,* of storage locations; these neighborhoods drift slowly as the program progresses. The fast, less dense memories in a hierarchy track these neighborhoods, while the slower memories hold bigger parts of the program which are rolled into the faster levels as needed. Using this concept, the overall speed of the memory system approaches that of the fastest level, and the overall storage limits are that of the slowest, and usually cheapest.

The concept of storage hierarchies dates back to the late 1950s (e.g., the LARC: Eckert et al., 1959). However, the first documented use of a cache as an explicit part of a computer's design was in the IBM System/360 Model 85 (Liptay, 1968). This was followed by development of simple models of cache performance (Lee, 1969; Kaplan

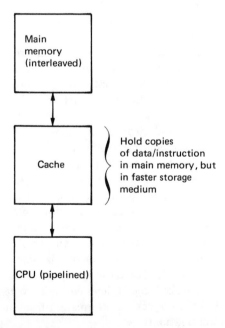

Figure 6-23 Typical cache placement.

and Winder, 1973) and formal definitions of classes of cache organizations (Bell et al., 1974). During that time cache design techniques were based on simulations and "benchmark" programs where long series of instructions were run through machine simulators in which the characteristics of the cache could be varied from run to run. Examples of such studies can be found in Meade (1972), Bell et al. (1974), Strecker (1976), and Peuto and Shustek (1977). Recent work has been in developing more theoretical models that do a better job of predicting cache behavior in advance (cf. Rau and Rossmann, 1977; Smith, 1978; Rao, 1978). Additional work has concentrated on system costs (Welch, 1978) and the effect of processor "cold start" on cache performance (Easton, 1978).

6.4.1 General Operation and Characteristics

At any one time a cache contains in high-speed storage (3–10 times faster than main memory in access time) copies of memory words containing bits and pieces of programs and data. When the CPU needs to make a request of memory, it generates the address of the desired word and searches the cache for the desired quantity. If the quantity is available a *hit* occurs, and a copy of the object is passed back to the CPU without making a request of memory and in much less time. If the desired object is not in the cache, then a *miss* or *cache fault* occurs. The address must then be passed to the memory for access. In addition, room must be found in the cache to save a copy of the desired word and any extra word delivered as a matter of design by the interleave in the memory. When the data returns, copies are stored in the cache and the desired object is relayed to the CPU.

In the vast majority of designs the cache is not visible to the programmer except in terms of program execution time. Nothing special is needed to manage the cache. The process of searching the cache and requesting memory vs. cache access is handled entirely by hardware. Of course, knowing the nature of the cache allows a programmer to write a program that runs at very high hit ratios, but the same program would still run on a noncache machine, just as a nonoptimized program would run on a cache-based machine at perhaps less than optimal performance.

This cache operation is considerably different from that for a local memory found in a pipelined vector processor and discussed in Chaps. 4 and 5. First, a cache is more passive than its vector processor equivalent. Activity is usually triggered only by CPU requests will no real equivalent to the vector memory address generator and controller function. Second, the addressing patterns are more random than in the vector case. Operand accesses need not fall in any particular order, and the existence of branches can change the locality of references radically at unpredictable moments. Even the existence of different sized instructions and data from reference to reference introduces unique complications. On the other hand, there is a greater chance of reuse of data in a cache than in a local memory for a vector machine. Instructions often form loops that are executed repeatedly. Subroutines may be called from several places in a program. Data may be referenced several times during a program. For each of these a well-designed cache will fetch the desired information from memory only once, and each subsequent access will find a hit.

A simple model quickly gives insight into the performance enhancement possible by use of a cache. The relevant terms are:

h = hit ratio = percentage of accesses that a memory request is found in cache
c = time to search cache and extract desired object if hit occurs
m = time to search cache, request object from memory, and save in cache, if miss occurs
a = m/c = ratio between memory access time and cache time as seen by CPU

Of these, h, the *hit ratio*, is the criterion of most concern to cache designers practically since the introduction of the cache concept. The maximum value of 1 is not achievable because of the randomness of reference and the typical size difference between cache and memory, often two or more orders of magnitude. Likewise, h will not be 0 because of the buffering of multiple data words from interleaved memory and because of all the data reuse mentioned earlier. In real systems, hit ratios of around 80% seem relatively easy to achieve; careful design can up this to the 95% range. With these definitions the average access time seen by the CPU is a weighted average of cache and memory access times:

$$hc + (1 - h)\, m$$

Dividing by c gives the average access time in units of cache access time:

$$h + (1 - h)\, a$$

For any nonunity hit ratio this indicates how much slower the combined memory system is over a memory consisting of a single huge cache. Figure 6-24 diagrams this factor for a variety of a values. As can be seen, achieving access rates anywhere near the pure cache rate requires very high hit ratios.

Another way to look at the cache is in terms of how much it "amplifies" the memory system's bandwidth. If the memory bandwidth is $1/m$ and that for memory plus cache is $1/[hc + (l - h)m]$, then the ratio is

$$\frac{m}{hc + (l - h)m} = \frac{a}{h + (l - h)a}$$

Figure 6-25 diagrams this for a variety of a's. As before, hit ratios of above 80% are needed to attain a desirable level of amplification. In fact for large hit ratios the curves become quite steep; a slight change in hit ratio causes a significant change in the speedup factor. Furthermore, the hit ratio is never a simple constant—it can change dynamically with different programs running on the same machine (e.g., a loopless program vs. one with tight loops) and with the design of the cache. Consequently it is the designer's task to understand the range of problems for which performance optimization is desired, and to pick a cache design that is satisfactory over that range.

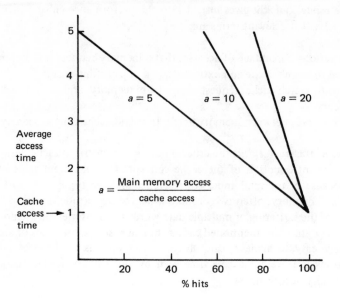

Figure 6-24 Hit ratio.

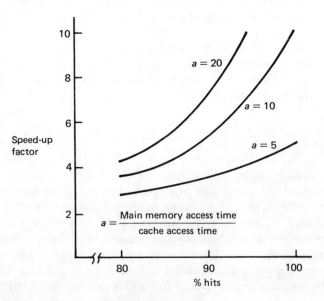

Figure 6-25 Effect of cache on bandwidth seen by CPU.

6.4.2 Basic Cache Organizations

Over the first few years a formal set of terms has developed to define variations in cache designs. The first is definition of the term *line* as the basic unit of information that moves between memory and cache. In an interleaved memory design the line is often a multiple of the number of words accessed in one request from one module times the interleave factor. Memory thus consists of a large set of lines with consecutive addresses. Likewise the storage within the cache holds multiple lines but not necessarily in any particular order. At any one time the lines in the cache represent copies of a set of lines from the memory. When the CPU wishes to access an item, it searches the cache to see if the line containing that data is present. This search is often associative in nature, each line or set of lines in the cache having an associated *address tag* indicating which lines in memory these lines represent. These tags are usually compared simultaneously with the CPU-provided line address. A match indicates a hit.

When a miss or cache fault occurs a line must be chosen to receive the new line from memory. Usually special hardware containing line replacement information guides this selection. The hardware can be status tags associated with each line, queues of cache line usage traces, or counters.

Figure 6-26 diagrams the basic organization of any cache in the terms defined above. A CPU address enters the cache and goes through an address map to strip out the line address and determine which line or set of lines from the cache storage should be searched. The address tags from these lines are then compared to the CPU line address. If a match occurs the desired line is read out of the cache, and the rest of the CPU address is used to select the desired byte or word, for relay back to the CPU. If a miss occurs the line address is passed to the memory system; while the access is in progress the line replacement information is interrogated and updated. This operation selects one of the cache lines to receive the incoming line. As before, the desired information is then stripped out and passed to the CPU.

The major as yet undefined characteristic of such a cache is the mapping between memory lines and cache lines. Since the size of the memory is so much bigger than that of the cache, each cache line may have to hold over a period of time many different memory lines. It also may be desirable to hold any combination of memory lines in the cache at one time. Thus over time each memory line may be found in one of several different cache lines. In the extreme this is a many-to-many mapping, and is one place where a designer can make tradeoffs between cache complexity and cache performance. Following is a formal definition of the kinds of mappings possible. In this section we assume that 2^N is the number of lines in the memory and 2^n is the number of lines in the cache. For each kind of mapping a simple diagram will be included where $N = 4$, $n = 2$, and the CPU desires information from memory line 6.

The most general but most costly method of mapping is termed *fully associative.* Any line of the memory can be found in any of the cache lines, in any combination. In the case diagrammed in Fig. 6-27 each line has its own address tag and its own comparator. When the CPU wants a line it must search against all 2^n lines for resolution. This can get quite expensive if 2^n is in the hundreds or thousands. Further, when a cache fault occurs any of the lines can be loaded with the new information.

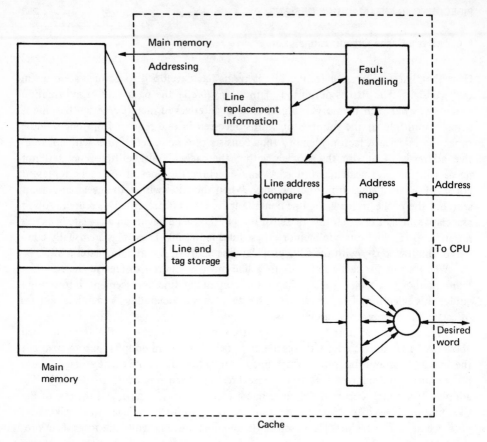

Figure 6-26 Typical cache organization.

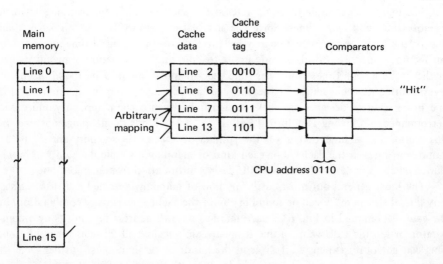

Figure 6-27 Fully associative cache.

The other extreme of cache design is the *direct mapped* approach. Each cache line may contain only one of a certain subset of memory lines, and the subsets for different cache lines do not usually overlap. The search in this case consists of determining in which subset the CPU line address falls, going to the single corresponding line in cache, and doing a single compare to see if it is the desired line.

Because implementation is simple the typical direct mapping uses a *bit map* to select memory subsets. For example, if there are N bits in a memory line address the lower n of them selects to which cache line it may be copied. All memory lines with the same lower n bits in their address thus fall into the same subset and may appear in only one line in the cache. Thus in Fig. 6-28 cache line 0 can contain only copies of memory lines 0, 4, 8, and 12. Likewise cache line 1 can contain only copies of lines 1, 5, 9, and 13.

The major advantage of this approach is its simplicity and low cost. Only one comparator is needed and, perhaps more important, the storage in the cache can be in the form of a standard memory. Very fast, dense semiconductor memory components are ideal; fewer levels of logic are needed between an address and the memory chips than for other approaches. This translates into fast access times. In addition, the address tags need be only $N - n$ bits. The major disadvantage to this approach is the

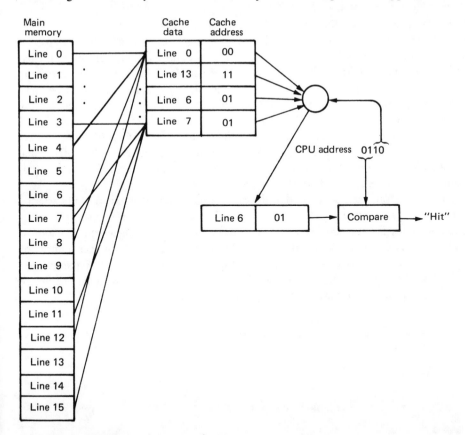

Figure 6-28 Direct mapping (bit-mapped) cache.

restricted number of combinations of lines that may be present in the cache. For example, if a program alternately references lines 6 and 10 in Fig. 6-28, each reference would cause a cache fault since lines 6 and 10 cannot be in the cache at the same time. In contrast the fully associative cache would quickly organize itself so that this "thrashing" did not occur.

The number of valid combinations can be computed mathematically. For the direct bit-mapped approach each of the 2^n lines in cache can come from one of the 2^{N-n} lines in its subset in main memory. There is thus a grand total of

$$(2^{N-n})\,2^n \qquad \text{combinations possible. In contrast, there are}$$

$$2^N \cdot (2^N - 1) \cdot \ldots \cdot (2^N - 2^n + 1) = \frac{2^N!}{(2^N - 2^n)!}$$

valid combinations in the fully associative approach. In cases where $N \gg n$ this is roughly

$$(2^N)\,2^n \qquad \text{combinations.}$$

The difference from the direct approach can be enormous.

A more general technique that includes both direct and fully associative as special cases is termed *set-associative*. Here the cache is divided into disjoint sets of lines. Each line in the memory may go to any line in a particular set in the cache. When the cache is to be searched a direct map uses the CPU line address to select a set of cache lines. Then a fully associative search over just the selected set determines if the line is in the cache. As before, a bit-mapping usually implements the direct map. If there are 2^n lines in the cache divided into 2^s sets, then the bottom s bits of the CPU line address selects which set in the cache should be searched. The upper $N - s$ bits of the line address are then compared against each line address tag in the set. Figure 6-29 diagrams the case where $s = 1$, that is, there are two sets.

If there is only one set ($s = 0$) in the cache, this technique is exactly fully associative. If there is only one line per set ($n = s$) it is exactly direct-mapped. For intermediate values it is an amalgam of both, thus allowing the designer the freedom to trade off between the low complexity of direct mapping and the higher number of combinations, and thus potentially higher hit ratio, of fully associative. In comparison with the other approaches, each set of 2^{N-s} lines can hold any combinations of the 2^{N-s} memory lines that may reside in that set. There are a total of

$$\frac{2^{N-s}!}{(2^{N-s} - 2^{n-s})!} \qquad \text{combinations per set}$$

or approximately

$$(2^{N-s})\,2^n \qquad \text{total combinations over } 2^s \text{ sets}$$

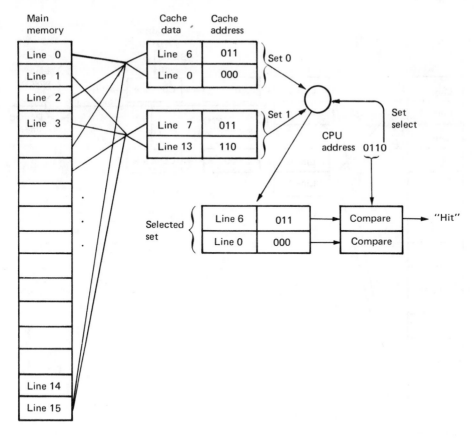

Figure 6-29   Set-associative cache.

It is possible to generalize the direct and fully associative techniques in a manner opposite to the set-associative approach. This is called a *sector mapping*; as before, it is assumed that the cache lines are divided into disjoint sets. However, each set, termed a *sector,* has associated with it a single address tag, not one per line. The lines within a sector then correspond to consecutive memory lines starting at the line address in the sector address tag. Searching such a cache is the reverse of the set-associative approach and starts with an associative match between the CPU line address and all the sector address tags. When a match is found, the line within the sector is accessed via a direct map. This mapping is usually a bit-mapping which, if there are 2^s sectors, takes the bottom $n - s$ bits of the CPU line address and directly accesses the sector with the matching address tag. When $s = n$, this mapping becomes fully associative; for $s = 0$, it becomes a trivial direct map. Figure 6-30 diagrams a design where $s = 1$—i.e., there are two sectors.

The advantage of this approach, as in the set-associative method, is simplicity. Each sector can consist of a small, high-speed semiconductor memory with even fewer

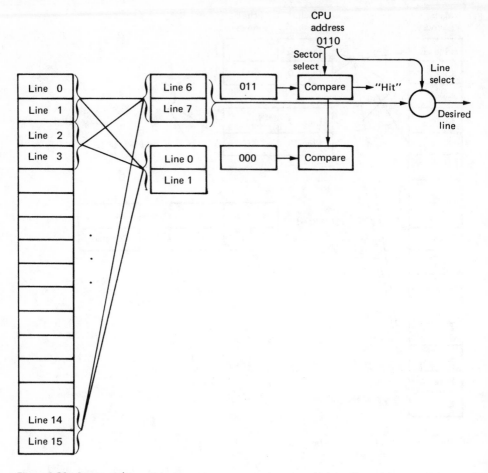

Figure 6-30 Sector cache.

address tags and comparators than the set-associative approach. The disadvantage is that the number of line combinations containable within the cache can be quite small in comparison to set-associative. Once an address tag has been set up in a sector, there is only one way that memory lines can map into lines within the sector. The only variability is in the combination of sectors, and there are exactly

$$2^{N-n+s} \cdot (2^{N-n+s} - 1) \ldots (2^{N-n+s} - 2^s + 1) \quad \text{unique combinations}$$

This is approximately

$$(2^{N-n+s})^{2^s} \quad \text{unique combinations}$$

For s in the typical range of 4 to 16, this is much less than a set-associative or direct map.

With all these options it is difficult to see how a designer can make the optimal choice of organization, size, etc. As mentioned earlier, mathematical models of cache behavior are becoming available (cf. Rao, 1978), but they still require detailed knowledge of statistics of line usage, which in turn depends heavily on the instruction set of the CPU, the program being run, and perhaps even how the program was loaded into memory. Therefore rather than attempt to develop any detailed theory here, we simply present some graphs drawn from a composite of published design tradeoffs, particularly from Lee (1969) and Strecker (1976). Since they are composites, they may not be an accurate match for any particular computer design, but should at least give ideas of the shape of actual curves.

The first curve, Fig. 6-31, lists the number of valid line combinations that may be found in caches of various organizations as a function of cache size. The ordinate of this graph is really log-log in nature, so that even a slight difference in two curves spells a tremendous difference in actual values. As can be seen, the typical sector cache allows nowhere near the number of combinations that any set-associative design does. This suggests that a set-associative cache is more likely to contain any arbitrary working set that a program might use, and therefore it probably achieves a higher hit ratio than a sector cache of the same size. This may be one reason why in practice sector caches do not tend to be used as often as set-associative caches.

As mentioned previously the actual hit ratio achieved by a cache depends on many factors. Figure 6-32 lists ranges of hit ratios achieved by different set-associative designs for a variety of programs as a function of cache size. Although the actual values may not reflect reality precisely, the "bent-arm" shape of the curve seems universally characteristic. Up to a point, increasing the cache size has a great effect on hit ratio, after which a point of diminishing returns is reached. However, this second region of hit ratio is also the area where even a small increment results in a significant increase in the effective speed-up of the memory system (see Fig. 6-25). Therefore it

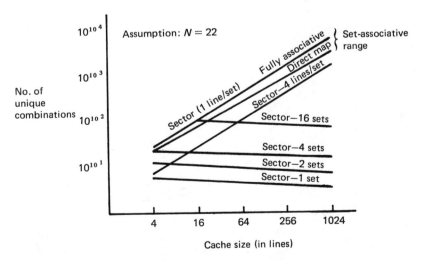

Figure 6-31 Combinations vs. cache size.

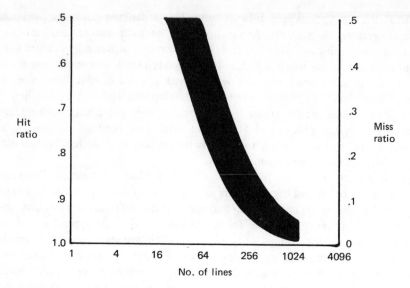

Figure 6-32   Typical hit ratio vs. cache size.

may be advantageous to design a cache further into the relatively flat region of Fig.
6-32 than one would normally go.

The final graph, Fig. 6-33, indicates the effect of set size on the performance of a
set-associative cache. As before, the curves have the bent-arm shape. The topmost
curve corresponds to one line per set. However, this is the definition of a direct-
mapped cache. No associative search is needed within the set. The next line represents
two lines per set. As can be seen, even a very slight increase in associativity results in a
few percentage points' improvement in hit ratio. Increasing the associativity to four

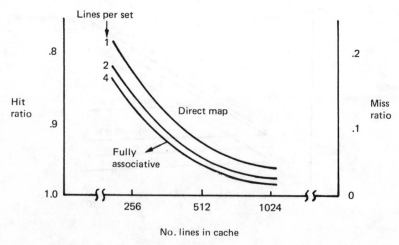

Figure 6-33   Effects of set size.

lines per set again improves the hit ratio, but not as much as before. Increasing the set size above four tends to make the cache more fully associative but with declining paybacks.

6.4.3 Status Bits, Handling Stores, and Line Replacement Strategies

Selecting a basic cache organization does not complete the cache designer's task. In addition, there are a variety of design decisions that can have a large effect on overall cache complexity and performance.

The first decision has to do with how the cache determines that a particular cache line contains a valid copy of data. In some circumstances, such as just after power-on or in a sector cache after a cache fault, there may be cache lines with invalid "junk" in them. None of the search techniques mentioned thus far have taken this possibility into account.

The nearly universal technique used to detect this possibility extends each line in the cache by one bit, called a *validity bit.* Upon power-on or when a line is erased from the cache, these bits are turned off. Whenever a line is copied from the memory system into a cache line, that cache line's validity bit is set "on." Then whenever the cache is searched and a line found with the right address, a final check of the line's validity bit determines whether or not a hit can be declared.

The next design decision deals with a store operation that needs to modify a memory word. The question in this case is whether or not the cache is modified, and when the memory is actually updated. At least three different approaches have been used to resolve this in real designs. The first, *store through* or *write through,* updates both the cache and the memory at the same time if the cache contains a copy of the line to be modified. This technique requires that Fig. 6-24 and 6-25 be modified, since a memory operation occurs on all stores even though a hit may have occurred in the cache. On the other hand, it has the advantage of guaranteeing that the memory always has the most current copy of all variables. This is a distinct advantage in multiprocessing systems or systems with independent I/O channels where there are multiple uses of the same memory system.

The second approach to handling stores might be called *store and invalidate.* As above, it always changes the memory; however, if a word is in the cache it is not changed. Instead, the validity bit for the line that it is in is turned off. This approach has the same advantages as the store-through approach, with the added advantage of simpler cache hardware—no data path is needed from the CPU into cache. However, it does tend to lower the hit ratio because lines are invalidated as soon as a single bit is changed anywhere in them.

The third approach, *store in,* is to change only the cache if the cache has a match with the CPU line address. This has the advantage of speed and potentially higher hit ratios. Figures 6-24 and 6-25 need not be modified. However, the approach presents problems in a multiprocessor environment, because now external processors may need access to the cache to guarantee that they are receiving the latest copy of all information.

Another problem with the latter approach is guaranteeing that updated information that exists only in the cache is not lost when a cache fault occurs and a new line is to be brought in. One solution is to simply copy a cache line's contents back to the memory before loading in a new one. This can significantly affect overall performance because many lines, particularly those containing instructions, are never modified, making the write-back simply wasted time. A better solution is to add yet another bit, termed a *modification bit,* to each line in the cache. This bit is reset when the line is initially loaded; it is set only when a store operation changes something in it. Then when a line is to be replaced, the modification bit is tested. Only if it is set does the line need to be copied back to the memory.

Some sources (cf. Bell et al., 1974) indicate that a variation to either the store-through or store-in approach can have a beneficial effect on hit ratios. In this variation, whenever a store is to be done, if the cache does not contain the desired line and memory must be updated, the modified copy of the line is brought into the cache just as if a miss on a real operation had occurred.

The final design decision that has to be made to complete a cache is the choice of a *replacement strategy* to determine which line in the cache is to be bumped when a new line is to be brought in after a cache fault. For a purely direct-mapped cache there is no choice. Each line in the memory may reside in one and only one line position in the cache. However, for any cache with an associative map there are several cache line positions that can receive a particular main memory line. The task of the replacement strategy is to pick which one.

There are three major strategies discussed in the literature: random, first-in-first-out, and least-recently-used. Under *random selection,* the choice of which line from a set is to be replaced is done "randomly." This randomness may be generated by a digital pseudorandom number generator, by "hashing" the address or data bits in some fashion, or by reading low-order bits on a time-of-day counter. Although it has the advantage of simplicity and relative ease of modeling, the approach has the drawback of nonrepeatability. The same program can be run twice on the same machine and take different amounts of time.

Another easily implemented technique is *first-in-first-out* (FIFO). This is a form of "round robin" scheduling in which a list of the order in which lines were changed is kept with each set of lines. At the bottom of the list is an index to those lines changed most recently; at the top are those that were changed farthest back in time. When a new line is to be brought in, it replaces the line at the top of the list, and the entire list is rotated up one position so that the line that was at the top is now at the bottom. The most direct implementation of this is a counter associated with each set which at each miss in that set is incremented by 1. The value of this counter indicates which line is to be replaced.

Theoretically the most powerful replacement strategy is the *least-recently-used* (LRU). This is a modification of FIFO where at every hit, rather than miss, the list is modified. The index to whichever line is accessed is moved from where it is in the list to the bottom-most position, and the rest moved up to fill the gap. On a miss, the line to be replaced is the one at the top of the list. This is equivalent to "time tagging" each cache line as to when it was last used. The line chosen to replace the old line is the one which has not been referenced in any way in the longest time. Although LRU is more complex to implement than the other strategies, studies have indicated that it can provide measurably better hit ratios.

6.4.4 Relationship to Virtual Memories

Many modern computers include variations of the concept of *virtual memory,* where the amount of storage addressable by the programmer exceeds the amount of real memory directly connected to the computer. Typically, all this virtual storage resides in a disk unit or other fast-access mass-storage device and is brought into the real memory only as needed.

Generally this concept sounds much like a higher order cache, and in fact there are similarities. The virtual memory equivalent of a line is a page; the real memory now fills the role of the cache storage. Whenever an address is generated, a check must be run to see whether that particular page is in the real memory or in the mass storage device. The latter case corresponds to a *page fault,* or a miss in cache terminology. In the case of a hit, the hardware must determine which real page corresponds to the desired one.

However, there are some important differences between a cache and virtual memory. Although both speed up the effective access rate of their respective backing stores, the primary purpose of a cache is to speed up the computer's instruction rate, and the purpose of virtual memory is to increase the amount of storage that a programmer can deal with directly. Thus control of the former is normally done in total by hardware; the latter has significant operating system help. Likewise the mapping between addresses and eventual storage locations is different. A cache uses associative searches to quickly determine where a line resides. A virtual memory system typically employs a series of tables to translate between a virtual address and a real one. By manipulating these tables, the relationship between virtual and real addresses can be changed arbitrarily.

One case where a designer must consider both storage techniques is in the design of a cache for a system with virtual memory. Here the addresses generated by the CPU are virtual, but real addresses are needed on a cache miss. There are several approaches to handling this dichotomy; the most typical one employs an associative table that is compared against part of the virtual address. If a match occurs, the other part of the matching entry indicates how to form the real address. This table is often integrated with the address tags on the cache, permitting both the cache search and address translation to be done at once.

6.5 INTERRUPTS AND PIPELINED CPUs

One characteristic of modern computer architecture that can present unique problems to the pipelined CPU design is the interrupt system. An *interrupt* is a signal that indicates the occurrence of an event. It is different from a *discrete* signal in that its occurrence forces the CPU through hardware to suspend the currently running program and start execution at some predetermined point. There are two classes of interrupts: program and external. A *program interrupt* usually results from something that occurs in relation to the currently running program. Examples include indication of program exceptions (overflows, underflows, invalid instructions, and addressing errors), hardware malfunctions, or requests for system supervisory services. An *external interrupt* usually comes from a device external to the CPU; it signals such things as I/O operation complete and request for service.

Interrupts cause problems for the designer of a pipelined CPU in two areas: logical timing and performance. The first problem, that of *logical timing*, is determining when in relationship to the current program the interrupt occurred. In a conventional non-pipelined CPU design there is usually a well-defined time period, often part of ENDOP, when interrupts are sampled. If an interrupt is present, the current program can logically be suspended immediately and restarted at the next instruction when desired. The routine to which control is given when the interrupt occurs can identify when the interrupt occurred to within one instruction time.

This preciseness does not always exist in a pipelined CPU. First, there is no clearly absolute time reference because many different instructions execute concurrently. Second is the problem of stopping the pipeline in a controlled fashion so that a restart is possible. This is particularly true of program interrupts indicating program exception; these are typically due to program-related errors that are not detected until the offending instructions have traveled significantly down the pipeline. At this point other instructions in back of the offending instruction may have already reached the point of no return where they have partially executed and changed the machine state so that a reverse in the computation is not possible. This usually happens only when a pipeline design permits instructions to be executed "out of order." Furthermore, the instruction counter, which is usually owned by a very early stage in the pipeline, may have already been updated several times by branches so that its contents cannot be counted on to identify where in the program the offending instruction occurred. In such circumstances, the best the hardware can do is to indicate to the interrupt-handling software that an event of a certain class occurred near some IC value. This lack of precise information and inability to restart at the cause of the problem effectively prevents the system software from "fixing up" a program and allowing it to continue.

In some machines such interrupts are identified as *imprecise* or *fuzzy* interrupts. The only general way to design around this imprecision is to use extensive amounts of internal *checkpointing*. This basically involves saving much of the state of the machine (IC, registers and flags) in a local memory each time a new instruction is started through the pipeline. If an interrupt ever requires "backing up" to that instruction, all the information is available. Needless to say, this can be an expensive proposition depending upon the amount of information that must be stored. Again, it is typically worst when the pipeline permits out-of-order execution. Simpler pipelines can get away with less checkpointing.

The second major problem interrupts cause is in performance, particularly in operation of the CPU and, if one is present, in the cache. First, to permit an orderly suspension of the current task, it may be necessary to permit all instructions currently in the CPU pipeline to complete before saving program status and starting the interrupt routine. The same effect may occur on return from the interrupt processing. This translates into unusable CPU cycles and loss in CPU performance.

The second and potentially more significant performance constraint occurs when there is a cache in the system. An interrupt, once accepted, represents a total change in the effective working set of the program running on the CPU. This in turn means that for a period of time after an interrupt routine has been started there will be an extremely high miss ratio. Aggravating this situation is the characteristic of many interrupt-handling programs of being relatively linear, loop-free programs with a large percentage of conditional branches. Additionally, the working set again radically changes when control is returned to the suspended programs, since the cache now contains interrupt programs and data. Under conditions of frequent interrupts, this effect can significantly degrade a CPU's effective performance rate.

In the literature this problem and several related ones have come to be known as the *cold start* problem; the problem has been studied by several researchers including Easton (1978) and Kaplan and Winder (1973). The results usually tend to be cast in terms of the extra number of cache faults that occur over what would be measured if no task switch had happened. One simulation by Kaplan and Winder (1973) places this extra number of misses at a number about equal to 80% of the cache size in lines. Estimates like this can then be brought back into the average access time and performance measured for any particular machine. Examples are left as problems to the reader.

There are some techniques, both hardware and architectural, that can help alleviate this problem. The first is simply to include in the instruction set commands to "turn the cache off." When an interrupt is accepted, such an instruction can save the cache's contents from being lost. The interrupt routine then runs directly out of main memory as if it had encountered a 100% miss ratio. This is probably not much worse than with the cache on, but it prevents a significant number of misses when the suspended program is restarted and the cache "turned on" again. The second approach is to *partition* or *compartmentalize* the cache so that separate pieces of the cache are devoted to programs like interrupt routines or operating system services and do not require destroying the interrupted task's working set. This has the advantage of reducing misses on all types of programs, but it does increase hardware costs. Clearly detailed tradeoffs are needed.

Because of all these problems, there is a growing trend in computer designs to include special processors, possibly a microprocessor, dedicated to handle only interrupts. These processors field the interrupts and handle all the "ordinary" events. The interrupts are passed to the pipelined machines only if absolutely necessary.

6.6 SAMPLE SYSTEMS

This section describes the relevant characteristics of several real pipelined SISD machines. Although by no means a complete list, the systems described here either represent a larger class or exhibit unique characteristics. Further information on these systems is easily available in the open literature.

At attempt has been made to keep the terminology consistent with the rest of this chapter. Consequently there may be some discrepancy in naming conventions between these descriptions and those in the source material. However, this discrepancy is in name only and does not reflect any change or proposed change to the system's functioning.

The systems chosen are the INTEL 8086, the IBM System/360 Model 91, the scalar processor from the CRAY-1, and the IBM 3033 processor complex. The INTEL 8086 demonstrates how pipelining can be used even at the level of microprocessor designs. The IBM System/360 Model 91 merits description because of its extensive documentation in the literature and extensive use of pipelining and hazard detection and resolution techniques. The scalar processor from the CRAY-1 demonstrates what can be done when an instruction set is deliberately designed with pipelining in mind. Finally, the IBM 3033 illustrates the current state-of-the-art in pipelined CPU design.

6.6.1 INTEL 8086 Microprocessor

The INTEL 8086 (McKevitt and Bayless, 1979; INTEL, 1978) is a good example of how the techniques of pipelining have influenced even the neweset of computer designs, namely an LSI one-chip microprocessor CPU. This processor was designed as an upward extension of the 8080 family, and includes many 8- and 16-bit operations in its instruction set. Physically it uses a single set of 20 pins for both memory address and data (16 bits per access). Internally the CPU uses prefetching and a separate E-unit for speed. Microprogramming is used to control the E-unit.

The limitation on pins to a large extent dictates memory system design. The most that one memory access can provide is 16 bits. Consequently none of the memory design techniques described earlier can do much to increase aggregate memory bandwidth. This very definitely bounds the maximum performance that is possible.

The major goal in the logic design of the CPU was thus to come as close as possible in performance to the memory bandwidth bound. This goal, however, had to be tempered with the real-life constraint between amount of logic on a chip and *yield*, that is, percent of manufactured chips that are free from defects. Adding more logic decreases yield, and consequently increases the cost of the part. This presents the designer with a classic tradeoff between performance and cost.

To explore this range of possibilities, the designers of the 8086 developed four trial designs with varying degrees of pipelining. Each design was sized for amount of logic, and a gross simulation performed on each to determine approximate performance. The candidate that appeared best from these four then underwent more extensive simulation to tie down the various design parameters.

The four candidates included (*a*) a nonpipelined design (a "classical" benchmark); (*b*) a design with a simple prefetch mechanism similar to that described earlier in this chapter; (*c*) a three-stage pipeline with IFETCH, DECODE and EAGEN, and execute stages; and (*d*) a two-stage pipeline prefetch/E-unit design with an I-queue between the prefetcher and the E-unit. This E-unit also overlapped ENDOP of one instruction with the decoding phase of the next. Figure 6-34 diagrams each candidate.

The results of the logic and performance sizing are given in Fig. 6-35. Here the amount of logic is expressed in terms of the area it uses up in the LSI chip. In addition, to simplify comparison all quantities are normalized to that used by the classical nonpipelined baseline. The results indicate that as predicted for the model architecture described earlier in this chapter, a design with just simple prefetch can be quite effective. In this case it increased performance by 35% at a cost of only about 15% in logic

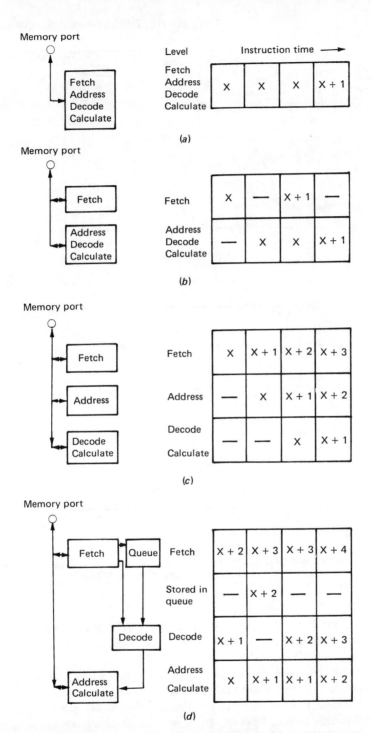

Figure 6-34 8086 Trial designs. (a) Nonpipelined. (b) Single prefetch. (c) Three-stage pipeline. (d) Two-stage with I-queue. Copyright © 1979 by The Institute of Electrical and Electronics Engineers, Inc. Adapted, by permission, from IEEE Spectrum, vol. 16, no. 3, March 1979, pp. 28–34.

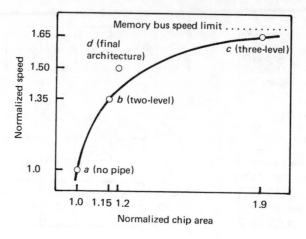

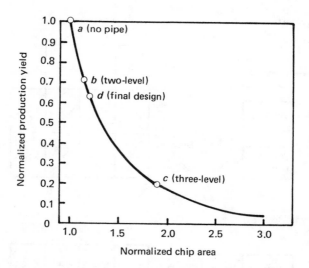

Figure 6-35 Performance and yield vs. chip size. Copyright © 1979 by The Institute of Electrical and Electronics Engineers, Inc. Adapted, by permission, from IEEE Spectrum, vol. 16, no. 3, March 1979, pp. 28–34.

area. Further up the curve, a full three-stage pipeline very nearly achieves full utilization of the memory system, but at a cost of 90% more logic area and only about 20% the yield of the baseline.

Design d, the two-stage pipeline with an I-queue, appears to have significantly better performance than the simple rigid two-stage, but at much better yields than the full three-stage design. For this reason it was chosen as the baseline 8086 design.

Even within this design, however, there were some pipelining tradeoffs to be made, primarily in the size of the I-queue. Too long an I-queue would hurt performance by wasting memory operations just before a branch. Too short an I-queue would not provide the E-unit with sufficient work to keep busy 100% of the time. To determine the best size, the designers of the 8086 performed a series of instruction-level simulations. Various programs were written and run through a CPU simulator where the depth of the I-queue could be varied. The results, shown in Fig. 6-36, indicated that in all cases after a depth of six bytes very little additional performance was achieved. This led to a choice of 6 bytes (a little over two average instructions).

6.6.2 IBM System/360 Model 91

Of all the machines of any particular generation, only a few are of more than historical interest 10 to 15 years after their design. In the field of pipelined computers the IBM System/360 Model 91 is one such machine.[3] Although certainly not the first machine to employ pipelining, it was one of the first to use pipelining in a consistent and pervasive fashion. Practically every design technique described in this chapter, except the cache, was used on the Model 91. There are, for example, at least four different techniques used for hazard detection. Further, the pipelining was used to support an instruction-set architecture that was developed not just for this machine but was already supported by many other nonpipelined designs. For these reasons an understanding of the Model 91 is of great value in studying pipelining.

The overall objective for the design of the Model 91 was to produce a machine where an instruction latency of one instruction per cycle was possible. The cycle time

---

[3]The January 1967 issue of the *IBM Journal of Research and Development* was devoted to this machine.

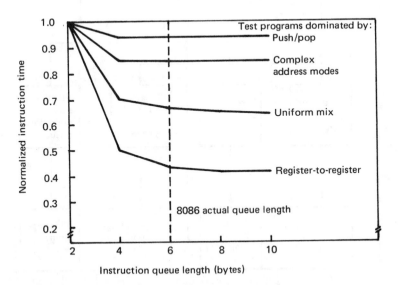

Figure 6-36 Performance vs. I-queue depth. Copyright © 1979 by The Institute of Electrical and Electronics Engineers, Inc. Adapted, by permission, from IEEE Spectrum, vol. 16, no. 3, March 1979, pp. 28–34.

was 60 ns. In overall performance this goal was 10 to 100 times faster than the older IBM 7090. Technology alone was insufficient to meet this goal; in fact estimates at the time indicated that the latest circuit and hardware advances would give only a factor of 4. The rest had to come from sophisticated organizational techniques.

Figure 6-37 diagrams the basic structure of the CPU for the Model 91. There is a pipelined I-unit and not one but two separate E-units. One of these handles all fixed-point calculations while the other handles all floating-point work. The fixed-point E-unit is of conventional design and performs most of its required operations in single cycles. The floating-point E-unit is heavily pipelined and includes some sophisticated

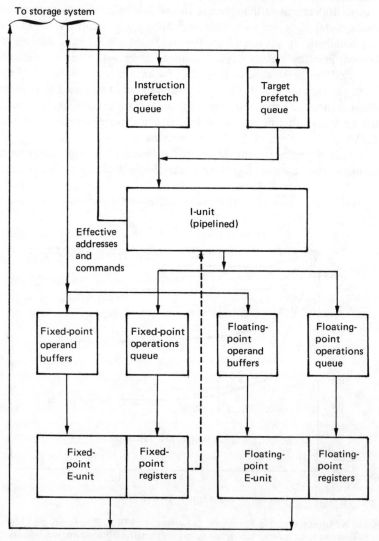

Figure 6-37 IBM System/360 Model 91 CPU architecture.

forwarding techniques to handle hazards. Between the I-unit and each of the E-units is the equivalent of an I-queue to buffer up instructions processed by the I-unit. In turn the I-unit has two prefetch buffers, one for normal sequential instruction fetches and a smaller one for prefetching ahead on branches.

To the programmer the System 360 architecture includes two sets of registers: four floating-point registers (FPRs) and 16 fixed-point general purpose registers (GPRs). Because the FPRs involve only floating-point calculations, they are exclusively owned by the floating point E-unit. In contrast the GPRs are owned by the fixed-point E-unit, but the I-unit has fast access to them to allow it to do address calculations.

Besides handling the ENDOP, IFETCH, and much of the decode functions, the I-unit also performs all effective address calculations and initiation of requests for all storage operations involving operands. However, it does not handle the returning data on reads from memory or gather the data for writes. Instead when it makes a memory request it indicates the register in the CPU (usually not visible to the programmer through the instruction set) to which memory is to communicate. For example, on reads from memory the I-unit provides the memory system with the identity of a register at the input to either of the E-units. There are several of these registers, termed *operand buffers,* for each E-unit. When the data is accessed, a copy is transmitted by the storage system to the designated register. To match this, when the I-unit prepares the instruction for one of the E-units, it encodes into the instruction not the required memory address but this same operand buffer register designation. Subsequent interlocks in the E-units prohibit them from processing such instructions until the memory system has provided the data.

Writes to memory are handled similarly. The I-unit sends the memory system the address and the identity of a *store-data register* that will contain a copy of the data to be stored. The instruction that is passed on to the E-unit directs it to deliver the desired data to this register. Only when the register is loaded will the store take place.

Figure 6-38 diagrams the memory subsystem of the Model 91 in more detail. As mentioned earlier in this chapter, a great many hazards are possible around the memory. In the Model 91 there is a significant amount of hardware to explicitly detect and resolve such hazards efficiently. This hardware consists of three stacks of registers and comparators between their contents and the address provided by the I-unit. These stacks consist of the *store-address register,* the *request stack,* and the *accept stack.* The store-address register maintains the memory addresses of all store (write) operations for which an E-unit has not yet provided data. The request stack contains all memory operations that have not yet been performed because of busy memory modules. The accept stack is a list of all memory operations currently in some phase of execution. There can be up to 16 different modules arranged to provide complex interleaving (see Sec. 2.2.4). The accept stack contains a unique entry for each such module.

In operation, when the I-unit makes a read request the address it provides is compared with all registers in these stacks. A match with an entry in the store-address stack corresponds to a RAW hazard. When such a match occurs, the address is sent to the request stack until the previously designated write data becomes available. When this happens, a *multiaccess operation* occurs that in addition to storing the data in

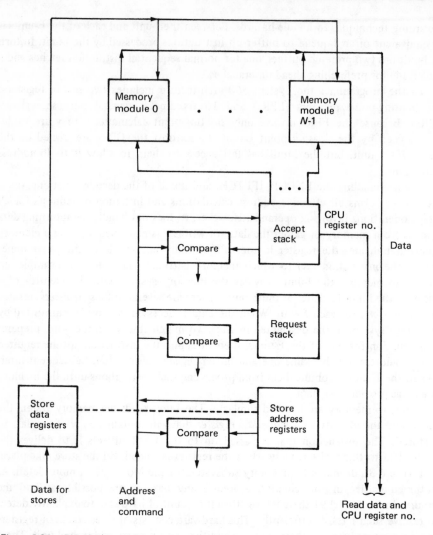

Figure 6-38 IBM 360/Model 91 storage system.

memory, "short circuits" the memory and sends a copy of the data to the designated operand or prefetch buffer. This both resolves the hazard and saves making an extra memory operation.

If there is no match with the store-address stack, but there is with an entry in the request stack or accept stack, then as above the request is sent to the request stack and a multiaccess operation set up. This again saves memory operations when there are two or more outstanding requests for the same word.

A request may also be placed in the request stack if no comparisons occur but the desired memory module is busy with a different request. When the module becomes free, the request will be started.

If no match occurs and the memory module is not busy, then the address is gated into the accept stack and the module started. Completion of the operation causes the data to be forwarded to the designated CPU register and all others to be chained to that address via the multiaccess feature.

As mentioned before, the I-unit itself is heavily pipelined. Figure 1-5 in Chap. 1 lists the stages and a sample reservation table. In light of the discussions in this chapter, the purpose of each stage should be obvious.

One aspect of the I-unit design that is not obvious is the design of the hazard interlocks. There are two separate mechanisms, one for handling the access to GPRs and one for conditional branches. To handle the first, namely hazards associated with the GPRs, each GPR has associated with it a *status counter*. Whenever an instruction that intends to modify a GPR reaches the decode stage, that stage's logic increments the status counter associated with that GPR. Several instructions in a row that alter the same GPR will thus increment this counter several times.

When these instructions reach the fixed-point E-unit, in the same order they passed the decode stage, the E-unit does the appropriate modifications and then decrements the status counter for that GPR.

Consequently, whenever the decode stage encounters an instruction that wishes to use a GPR in address calculations in the I-unit, it first checks the status counter for that GPR. If the status is nonzero, then some instructions that have been previously decoded but not executed are waiting to modify this GPR. The current instruction at the decode stage must then wait for the counter to reach zero before advancing. During this wait no other instructions are decoded. This guarantees that the sequence of instructions passing through the decode stage is exactly what the programmer expects. Maximum performance is thus one per cycle with delays occurring only if a hazard around a GPR develops.

The other major interlock in the I-unit handles conditional branching. The System 360 architecture defines a *condition code register* as one which is set by many instructions to indicate what happened during the last calculation. There are, for example, codes to indicate that the last ADD generated a zero, negative, nonnegative result with or without overflows or underflows. This condition code is set by each instruction as it completes. A conditional BRANCH instruction compares the last value of this code with a programmer-specified pattern. If a match occurs, the branch is taken.

In the Model 91 many different instructions may be in execution at a stage at the same time. They may even be executed by the E-units out of order. To guarantee that this has no effect on the logical condition code values, a simple interlock mechanism associates a one-bit flag with each stage in the CPU. At any one time only one of these flags can be set; all others are reset. As in the GPR interlock, the decode stage has a major responsibility for managing these flags. Each time it encounters an instruction that will change the condition code, it resets all flags throughout the CPU except the one for the very next stage, which it sets. Then as the instruction travels through the pipeline the value of this flag follows it. When the instruction is complete, the hardware associated with the last stage resets the flag.

When the decode stage encounters a conditional branch, it tests all these flags in the CPU. If all are zero, then no currently executing instruction will change the condition code register, and its current value is correct. The branch is then either taken or not taken. If some flag is set, then the condition code is not valid. However, rather than simply wait as was done for the GPRs, in this case the decode unit "guesses" that the branch will not be taken and allows other instructions to pass through the decode and later I-unit stages, but not to E-units. However, these instructions are all marked "conditional." Only when the final condition code flag is reset does the CPU know whether or not it guessed right. If it did, then the conditional marking is removed and operation proceeds. However, if it guessed wrong, all stages holding instructions marked conditional are reset, and the new target instruction must be decoded.

To reduce the lost time if a guess fails, the decode stage upon detection of a conditional branch requests several instructions to be fetched from the branch target address. These are placed in the target prefetch queue and discarded if not needed.

The other unit of interest in the Model 91 is the floating-point E-unit. Figure 6-39 diagrams its basic structure. The major components are a decoding stage, the floating-point register, a floating-point adder, and a floating-point multiplier/divider. The adder is itself a two-stage pipeline. The multiplier/divider is internally pipelined at 20 ns stage-times, but the pipelining feeds back on itself. Therefore, to the rest of the unit this logic is nonpipelined with three 60-ns cycles taken for multiplies and 12 cycles for divides.

At the input to the adder and multiplier/divider unit are staging latches of a unique design called *reservation stations*. There are three at the input to the adder and two at the input to the multiplier/divider. Each reservation station contains room for two input numbers and two 4-bit *tags*. The tags are part of the forwarding system, to be described shortly.

The FLRs are similar in design, each register containing a 4-bit tag and a *busy bit*.

In addition, the *store-data* registers for the E-unit that reside in the memory subsystem also have 4-bit tags.

Connecting all these units is the *common data bus* (CDB). All registers that may be changed by calculations in the E-unit, namely all those with tags, receive their data from the CDB. All units that may generate results contend for permission to place their data on the CDB. Each unique source of changes has its own 4-bit *ID*. For example, each of the operand buffers has an ID in the range 1 to 6. Furthermore, each reservation station represents a potentially new calculation. Thus the reservation stations at the adder have IDs 10 to 12, and those at the multiplier/divider have IDs 8 and 9. Whenever a result is placed on the CDB, the ID of the originator accompanies it. Placing an ID on the CDB causes all registers with tags to compare the contents of their tags with the ID. If a match occurs, a copy of the data on the CDB is shunted into that register and the tag is reset to 0000. This permits one data source to satisfy many demands.

The operation of this E-unit proceeds as follows. Instructions are stacked up by the I-unit at the input operation stack in the order that the programmer would expect. These pass through the decoder stage in the E-unit at a maximum rate of one per cycle. For each instruction the decoder looks at the opcode and selects a free reservation station of the appropriate type. Then the decoder checks the status of each speci-

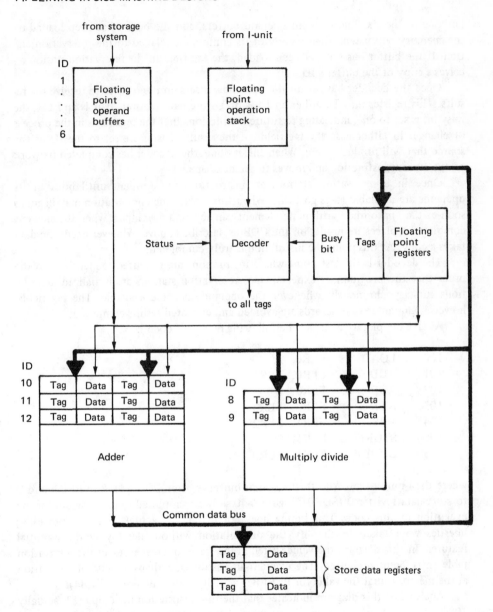

Figure 6-39 IBM 360/Model 91 floating-point E-unit.

fied operand register. If an operand is an FLR and its busy bit is 0 then the current data in the FLR is valid, and a copy of its contents is copied into the chosen reservation station. A busy-bit value of 1 indicates that some instruction currently in execution will change that register. In this case the tag field in the reservation station receives a copy of the tag field in the FLR register. If the operand is from memory, i.e., one of the six floating-point operand buffers, and the buffer has been loaded by the memory subsystem, then a copy of its contents is relayed to the reservation station. If the buffer has not yet been loaded, the tag field in the reservation station receives a copy of the buffer's ID.

Once the decoder has set up the operands, it sets up the register to receive the results. This register may be either an FLR or a store-data register. If it is an FLR, the busy bit is set to one, indicating to future instructions that the register is in the process of change. In either case the tag fields of the result register are set to the ID of the source that will produce them. When this is done, the decoder has completed its work on the current instruction and moves to the next one.

Once in a reservation station, an instruction lies dormant until both of its operands are available (tags go to 0). When this occurs the computation may begin as soon as the appropriate arithmetic element can accept a new input. When the element completes it places its results on the CDB as described above. Whoever needs the data takes a copy. At this point the instruction is truly completed.

The decoder is the last point where instructions are executed sequentially in the order that the programmer expects. Once reservation stations are initialized, instructions run asynchronously whenever the operands become available. The tag fields, however, guarantee that hazards are avoided and expected results computed.

As an example, we consider the following piece of "code":

100	LOAD	FLR0, A
101	ADD	FLR0, FLR1
102	ADD	FLR0, B
103	ADD	FLR2, FLR3
104	MPY	FLR1, FLR2
105	STORE	FLR1, C
106	DIVIDE	FLR1, FLR0

where the I-unit assigns A to floating-point buffer register 4 (FLB4), B to FLB3, and C to store-data register 0 (SDR0). Figure 6-40 shows a simplified timing diagram for the execution of this code. This timing does not match the actual Model 91 precisely; liberties were taken to simplify the presentation without destroying the essential features. In this diagram the values listed in the stage squares represent the reservation table entry being processed. The diagram also assumes, perhaps because of contention at the memory, that the value for B (FLB3) actually arrives before A (FLB4).

Analysis of this diagram indicates that the first instruction to complete is actually 103, since both of its operands were available. Because instruction 100 changed FLR0's tag, instruction 101 cannot begin execution in the adder until time 7. Instruction 102 cannot begin until 101 completes. Instruction 104 starts as soon as 103 completes, but it uses the multiplier for three cycles. Once 104 completes, however, both instructions 105 and 106 start, with 105 taking no time whatsoever from the E-unit. Finally, it is worth noting that during this entire period the physical register FLR0 is changed only once after 102 completes, even though the program specified three changes. The same is true for FLR1. Clearly, starting at time unit 8, more instructions

Time	1	2	3	4	5	6	7	8	9	10	11	12	13	//	19	20	21
Decoder	Load	Add	Add	Add	Mpy	St	Div										
Multiplier													9		9		
Adder 1					12		10			11	11						
Adder 2						12		10	10		8	11					
CDB tag					3	4	12		10		8	11				9	
FLR 0	0,–	1,4	1,10	1,11	1,11	1,11	1,11	1,11	1,11	1,11	1,11	1,11	0				
FLR 1	0,–					1,8	1,8	1,9	1,9	1,9	1,9	1,9	1,9	1,9	1,9	1,9	0
FLR 2	0,–				1,12	1,12	1,12	0,–									
FLR 3	0,–																
SDR 0	–						8	8	8	8	8	0					
RS8L ×	–					0	0	0	0	0	–						
RS8R	–					12	12	0	0	0	–						
RS9L ×	–							8	8	8	8	0	–				
RS9R	–							11	11	11	11	11					
RS10L +		4	4	4	4	4	0										
RS10R +		0	0	0	0	0	0										
RS11L +	–			10	10	10	10	10	10	0	–						
RS11R +	–			3	3			0	0	0	–						
RS12L +	–				0	0											
RS12R +	–				0	0											

Note: Tags are tag values at *beginning* of clock.
For FLRs, values are busy bit, tag.
RSX = Reservation station X (Left or Right)
× = multiplier
+ = adder.

Figure 6-40 Timing for sample code.

277

could be decoded and set up in the E-unit. In fact if the entire program segment were duplicated over and over, the physical floating-point register would hardly ever be changed, but the results as seen in memory would still be correct. Further, the decoder would be delayed only occasionally in issuing instructions because of a lack of available reservation stations.

The whole concept of the common data bus and reservation stations is a perfect example of dynamic configuration of a multifunction pipeline.

6.6.3 Scalar Processing in the CRAY-1

The Cray Research CRAY-1 (Cray, 1976; Johnson, 1978) is a heavily pipelined and overlapped computing system that includes both vector and scalar processing. Section 4.4.5 described the overall hardware characteristics and vector hardware in particular; this section describes briefly the operation of the scalar portion.

The scalar instruction set of the CRAY-1 is a good example of one designed explicitly for implementation in pipelined/overlapped hardware. It is an evolution of the architecture of previous machines such as the Control Data Corp. 6600 (Thornton, 1970); as such it has three unique characteristics. First, the registers visible to the programmer are strictly partitioned by function. There is a separate set of registers for computing addresses and a separate set of registers for computation. This tends to reduce hazards around registers. Second, the instruction set explicitly acknowledges the speed penalty paid when operands must be fetched from memory by giving the programmer a relatively large set of high-speed registers positioned between memory and the registers associated with computation. One set of instructions allows fast "random access" to these intermediate registers for computation; another set permits block transfer to and from the heavily interleaved memory. The resulting structure has many of the characteristics of a programmer-managed cache for data operands.

Finally, the instruction set directly exploits the concept of *functional units* that, when given operands, perform well-defined functions and return results to prespecified destinations. Thus nearly all computational instructions include an opcode to select a specific functional unit and specification of three registers, two to provide inputs to the functional unit and one to receive the result. This simplicity and regularity of function has two immediate effects. First, individual instructions do not partition into as many subfunctions as, for example, our model architecture. This reduces the length and complexity of any instruction decoding pipeline. Second, the universal use of a register-to-register format minimizes hazards around memory accesses and permits relatively clean forwarding-like techniques to handle the conflicts that still occur around the registers.

The hardware design of the CRAY-1 explicitly mirrors all three of these characteristics. Four sets of programmer-visible registers are pictured in Fig. 6-41. The two *primary* sets are termed S and A and hold eight registers each. The S-registers, 64 bits wide, are the principal registers for scalar computation. The A-registers, 24 bits wide, hold all address computations. These registers have fast and direct access to the functional units of which there are nine:

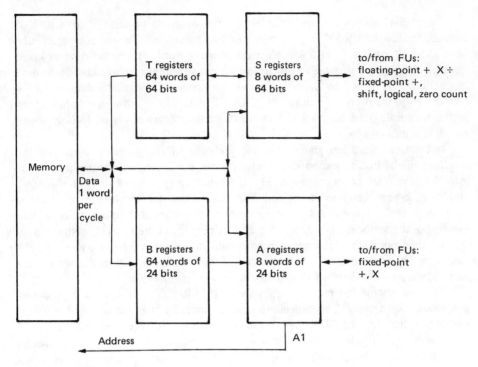

Figure 6-41 Memory/register hierarchy in CRAY-1.

- 24-bit fixed-point adder
- 24-bit fixed-point multiplier
- 64-bit floating-point adder
- 64-bit floating-point multiplier
- 64-bit floating-point reciprocal estimator
- 64-bit fixed-point adder
- 64-bit shifter
- 64-bit logical unit
- 64-bit leading-zero count

All these functional units are pipelined and during any cycle may receive operands from primary registers to start a new calculation and deliver a result to a primary register to complete a previously issued instruction.

Backing up these primary registers are two sets of *intermediate registers* named T and B. Each has 64 words of the same width as the primary registers they back up. A word may be transferred between a primary register and an intermediate register in one cycle. In contrast the path between a primary register and main memory can take 11 cycles, mainly because of the much slower access time of memory. Block transfers between main memory and these intermediate registers pay this latency penalty only once and then use the interleaved capabilities of the memory for high-rate transfers.

Figure 6-42 shows the instruction fetch and decoding pipeline of the CRAY-1. Instructions for the CRAY-1 come in one or two *parcel* units, where one parcel is 16 bits, and four parcels fit into a single main memory word. The *parcel counter* keeps track of the location of which word and which parcel within that word holds the next instruction. It is owned by the first stage of the pipeline. To minimize demand on the memory from instruction fetching, the CRAY-1 includes an *instruction buffer* which in the terminology of Sec. 6.4 is a sector cache with four sectors of 16 lines where each line equals 64 bits.

Instruction execution starts with the updating of the parcel counter and the searching of the instruction buffer. If a hit occurs, the appropriate parcel is read out into the *next instruction register* (*NIR*). If a miss occurs, termed an "out-of-buffer" condition, a new sector must be loaded. A two-bit counter which is incremented at each out-of-buffer condition selects the sector to be loaded in a round-robin fashion. Loading of the sector starts with the word containing the desired parcel, so the instruction pipeline can restart, and wraps around until the sector is full. Transfers between main memory and the cache occur at a rate of four words per cycle and make exactly one reference to each bank of the 16-way interleaved memory.

Once an instruction parcel reaches the NIR, initial decoding proceeds to detect and resolve all hazards. This procedure includes checking that the desired functional unit is free, that none of the primary registers needed by the instruction are "reserved" by a previous instruction, and that this instruction will not collide with a previous instruction when it comes time to store results. A reservation on a register means that

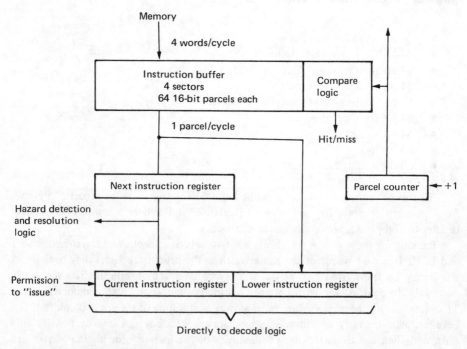

Figure 6-42 CRAY-1 instruction fetching.

there is a previous instruction still in execution that will modify that register. If any of these conditions occurs, updating of the parcel counter and fetching the next instruction halts. When all hazards have cleared, a reservation is placed on the primary register receiving the result of the computation (if any), and the instruction is allowed to continue to the next stage. The latch for this stage is termed the *current instruction register* (CIR). Once an instruction reaches the CIR there is no more hazard detection, and the instruction "issues." The *lower instruction register* (LIR) is usually a copy of the NIR and holds the lower parcel of two-parcel instructions.

Issuance of an instruction consists of gating copies of any operand registers to the appropriate functional unit and initializing the functional unit. It is then up to the functional unit to complete this instruction, freeing the CIR to issue the next instruction. The only exceptions are branches which are completed locally and update the parcel counter for the next fetch.

When a functional unit completes, it stores the result in the designated register and removes any reservation on it.

In summary, instruction execution follows a rigid pipeline from the instruction buffer through the NIR and CIR, with all hazard detection and resolution done at the NIR stage. However, once past the CIR the rigidity disappears; instructions complete whenever they leave their particular functional unit pipelines. Since these pipelines vary anywhere from 1 to 14 cycles in length, the order of completion can become quite scrambled.

6.6.4   IBM 3033 Processor Complex

The IBM 3033 Processor Complex (IBM, 1978; Connors et al., 1979) is a good example of the most recent generation of high-performance SISD pipelined computers, having virtually all the features discussed earlier in this chapter. Its general structure (Fig. 6-43) includes an interleaved memory, an SCU-like unit called the *processor storage control function* (PSCF), a cache, an I-unit called the *instruction preprocessing function* (IPPF), and an E-unit called the *execution function*. The following description will start with the cache and work down through the I- and E-units; it will follow with the storage system. The basic cycle time assumed throughout is 57 ns.

The cache is a set-associative design with 64 sets of 16 lines each. A line consists of eight double-words (64 bytes). A typical request is for a single double-word. In timing, the cache is itself a two-stage pipeline, the first stage corresponding roughly to the fetch of the appropriate set of 16 address tags and the comparison with the desired line address. The second stage is active only on a hit; it corresponds to the selection of the actual line of data. This design is similar to, but has twice the capacity of, the cache on the IBM 3168 CPU, which had reported hit ratios of at least 92% (Connors, et al., 1979).

All store operations change both the cache, if a hit occurs, and the primary memory system. This corresponds to the *store-through* philosophy discussed earlier. When the object to be stored is less than a double-word and a cache hit has occurred, the object is merged into its proper place in the cache's double-word and a copy of the modified double-word is sent to storage.

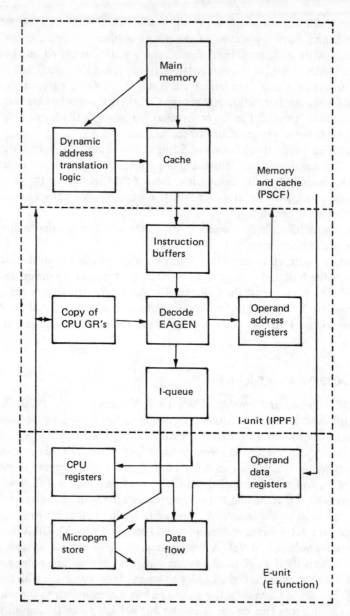

Figure 6-43 IBM 3033 organization.

The replacement strategy used in the cache design is a modified *least recently used* (LRU). To drive this algorithm the cache includes a *replace array* that holds an 18-bit record for each of the 64 sets. This record includes the following information:

1 division of the 16 lines into four groups of four lines each and the order in which these groups have been accessed;

2 division of each group into two pairs of lines, and indication of which of these pairs was accessed last;

3 division of each pair into two lines with indications of which of these lines was accessed last.

On each access, the appropriate replace record is read out and modified. When a hit occurs, this modification consists of changing the group ordering information to indicate that the group in which the current line resides is now the "most recently used." In addition, the pair and line within pair information for the group is changed if necessary. When a miss occurs, the line selected for replacement is the least recently used line of the least recently used pair of the least recently used group. No replace modification occurs on a store operation.

Figure 6-44 diagrams the I-unit (IPPF) of the IBM 3033. It employs nearly all the

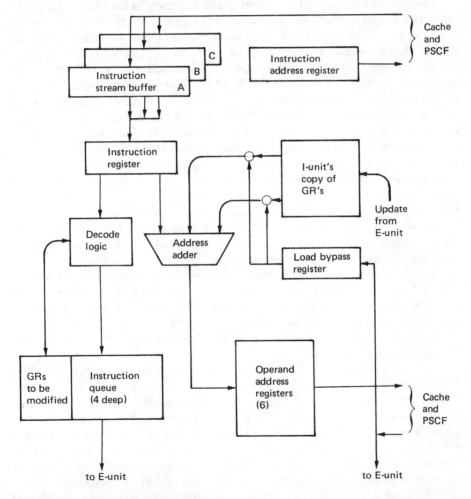

Figure 6-44 I-Unit (IPPF) for IBM 3033.

techniques described earlier for I-unit design. The logic at the top of the diagram fulfills a prefetch-like function, with the instruction address register serving as the IC by providing instruction addresses to the cache and storage units. When a line returns, it goes into one of three instruction stream buffers which serve as prefetch buffers. One of these buffers holds prefetched instructions assuming no branches are taken. The other two hold prefetched instructions for the targets of up to two branch instructions that have been decoded by later logic.

At any particular time, one of these buffers is feeding appropriate parts of its contents into the instruction register, which in turn is the input staging latch for the decode and effective address generation stage. This stage can run at a rate of one new instruction per cycle, but will slow down if certain RAW hazards appear or needed resources are not available. The major output is to a four-entry instruction queue that delivers decoded instruction to the E-unit.

Effective address generation consists of the addition of a displacement from the instruction to two instruction-designated general registers, one as a base and the other as an index. To implement this the 3033 I-unit includes a three-way adder and its own copy of the GRs, (which is updated as required by the E-unit). Since instructions are decoded and executed sequentially by the I- and E-units, there are no WAR or WAW hazards surrounding the GRs needed by the I-Unit. There are, however, two sources of RAW hazards. The first is modification of a GR needed by one instruction in the I-unit by an instruction not yet completed in the E-unit. This hazard is detected by adding to each entry in the I-queue tags with indication of which GRs, if any, will be changed by that instruction. Part of the decode logic then compares all GRs needed by the I-unit with these tags. The occurrence of a match causes the I-unit to freeze until the E-unit completes that instruction. The other GR hazard handled explicitly by the I-unit occurs when certain previously initiated load instructions need to load from memory GRs needed by the current I-unit instruction. In this case a special path, called *load bypass*, allows the I-unit to capture a copy of such data just as it comes from storage without having to wait for the E-unit to complete. This is an example of the "short-circuiting" technique described in Sec. 6.2.

The output of the address adder goes to one of six *operand address registers* (*OAR*). Each of these has a matching *operand data register* (*ODR*) in the E-unit to receive the desired quantity from the cache/memory system. This system is similar to that described earlier for the IBM System/360 Model 91.

Lack of space in either the I-queue or the OARs also causes the I-unit to freeze until space is available.

Another major source of hazards handled by the I-unit is in the instruction prefetching and the occurrence of STORE instructions that affect the prefetch region. There are two separate tests. The first occurs each time a prefetch request is made: if the desired address matches the store address associated with any store instruction currently in the I-queue, then that request is delayed until the store completes. The second test occurs each time a STORE instruction is decoded; the test compares the store address with any of the data in any of the instruction stream buffers. A match causes those buffers to be reset and restarted only after the STORE completes.

The final characteristic of interest in the IBM 3033 IPPF is its handling of branches. The general approach is similar to that of Fig. 6-18. The E-unit is ultimately responsible for deciding whether a branch (particularly a conditional one) is to be taken, but the I-unit does not sit idle waiting for the decision. Instead, when it encounters a branch instruction in its instruction register, the I-unit requests that one of the other two instruction stream buffers be loaded from the cache line specified by the branch. Further, the I-unit then makes an independent guess as to whether or not the branch will be taken. This guess is a "wired-in" function based on the kind of branch, various machine status bits, and designer experience. On the basis of this guess the I-unit continues to decode further instructions from the appropriate instruction stream buffer. These instructions are fed to the I-queue as normal. If the E-unit decides the guess is correct, these decoded instructions are immediately available for execution. If the guess was wrong, these instructions are purged, and the E-unit must wait until the I-unit can go to the alternate instruction stream buffer and restart the decode process.

It is possible for the I-unit to encounter a second branch in the instruction stream guessed at by the first before the E-unit has verified the guess. In such cases the I-unit prefetches yet another possible line of program into the third instruction stream buffer. No attempt is made to handle a third such branch.

Figure 6-45 is a general outline of the E-unit (execution function). It is microprogrammed with the decoded information in each entry in the I-queue indicating which microprogram to execute next. There is a one-to-one correspondence between microprograms and instructions decoded by the I-unit. Further, these microprograms are executed in the sequence expected by the programmer. There is no attempt as in the

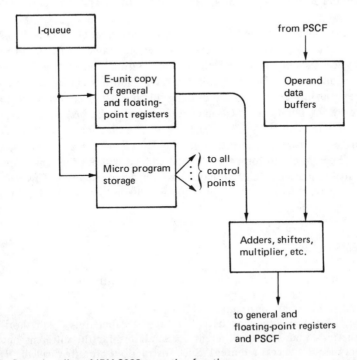

Figure 6-45 General outline of IBM 3033 execution function.

IBM 360/Model 91 to have the hardware dynamically change the order of execution. In operation, the E-unit is itself a small pipeline. The first "stage" is directed by the bottom entry in the I-queue; it involves fetching the first microinstruction of the desired microprogram and accessing any general or floating-point register needed as a data operand. The second through $(N-1)$st cycles correspond to execution of the desired function in the single E-unit data flow stage. This may involve waiting for data to arrive in response to a previous I-unit request. The final stage involves updating the results into required registers in either the E- or I-units. Since most instructions involve only a single cycle (such as LOAD or ADD), this overlap is generally useful in keeping several instructions in some phase of execution at once, thus maximizing throughput.

The final major unit of the IBM 3033 is the *processor storage control function* (PSCF), which includes the cache (discussed earlier), the main processor system storage, and several functions to handle virtual memory addressing. The main memory is an eight-way complex interleaving of double-word memory modules. When a cache miss occurs, the PSCF automatically transfers a double-word from each of these modules into the cache line that the replacement algorithm has chosen. The actual double-word that caused the cache miss is read out first. A bypass path exists around the cache to deliver this double-word as soon as possible to the ultimate I-unit or operand data registers.

Store operations are also largely handled by the PSCF. When the E-unit executes an instruction that requires a store operation, it delivers the data to be stored to the PSCF. The I-unit normally has previously provided the address. The PSCF then checks the cache and if a hit occurs, updates both the cache and the appropriate memory module.

The final function of the PSCF is to handle the *virtual memory* addressing option. When this mode is active, all memory addresses generated by the I-unit refer not to exact physical memory locations but to some "virtual" memory map. A full virtual-to-physical address translation requires several additions and table look-ups. These tables are in main memory. To avoid doing this translation on every memory address generated by the I-unit, the PSCF includes a *directory lookaside table* (DLAT) which functions like the address tags in a cache. Part of each memory address generated by the I-unit is compared with entries in the DLAT. If a match occurs, the DLAT indicates directly how to form the physical address without the table look-ups. Only on a mismatch must the full translation procedure be employed. This match process executes in parallel with the first stage of the cache so that no additional time is spent unless absolutely necessary.

PROBLEMS

6-1　For the sample architecture of Sec. 6.1 what is the theoretical minimum time per instruction in a pipelined implementation, how did you compute it, and what is the major constraint?

6-2　Many SISD architectures have "multiple accumulators," and short-length instructions that specify different accumulators for the different operands (no data memory access required). Such instructions are often called "RR" format instructions. Assume that of the 60% ADD-like instructions in the mix of Table 6-2, 15% are RR and the other 45% require a memory access (RS format). How does this affect hazards in the architecture? Draw a new set of reservation tables for a nonpipelined design and determine expected performance. Derive a theoretical bound if pipelining was used.

6-3 How would the inclusion of "autoincrementing" of base or index registers affect Table 6-4 for the model architecture?

6-4 Verify that the reservation table of Fig. 6-11 and the latency sequence (5,15) are compatible. In a long series of ADDs, how many different instructions can be simultaneously active?

6-5 Take some architecture that you are familiar with and develop a hazard table like Table 6-4. List where each hazard came from.

6-6 Write a program to compute factorials in the architecture chosen for Prob. 6-5. Show where each hazard occurs.

6-7 Consider the possibility of pipelining a cache into two stages, one to search for a match and one to access the data if a hit occurs. Redo Figs. 6-24 and 6-25 assuming the time for each stage is $C/2$. Is this as effective as doubling the speed of a single-cycle cache?

6-8 The equation for Figs. 6-24 and 6-25 assume a *store-in* cache. Redo them for a *store-through* cache. To get an estimate of the number of store operations, use the statistics of Sec. 6.1. Graph the results and compare with Figs. 6-24 and 6-25.

6-9 If h is the hit ratio for a store-through or store-in cache, will the hit ratio for a store-and-invalidate cache be the same size, larger, or smaller? Develop a simple model to demonstrate the general effects.

6-10 Consider an SISD CPU with a cache running a timesharing system where all users are totally independent of each other, and every t ms the CPU rapidly (in 0 time) switches from one user to another. Assume also that when running one user, the CPU can execute 10^6 instructions per second at 90% hit ratio, that the cache access time is 0.1 μs, that the memory is 1 μs, that each instruction requires 1.75 accesses, and that the number of extra misses due to the task switch is 80% of the size of the cache in lines. Derive the effective hit ratio and average instruction execution rate for various values of t and cache size. What seem to be good combinations?

6-11 Outline an instruction set for an SISD CPU where the cache is directly visible to the programmer. Indicate how overall performance might be affected.

6-12 Redo the timing for the sample piece of code for the IBM System/360 Model 91 assuming that there is no tagging and an instruction freezes the E-unit decoder if any register it needs has a busy-bit set. How much performance is lost?

Chapter 7

Future Trends

The first six chapters of this book addressed the state of the art in pipelining and overlap techniques as they existed in the late 1970s. However, as in any computer-related field of study, novel designs, untried concepts, and different insights abound, with new ones appearing almost daily. This final chapter will try to capture the essence of some of these new concepts and predict how they may affect future computer system designs. The material runs the gamut from experimental systems currently in the design stage to comments that might be called philosophical at best. As with any prediction, these comments reflect, both intentionally and unintentionally, the biases of the author and thus should not be taken as a definitive statement of the future of pipelining. They have served their purpose if they trigger new discussion and research that will in fact lead to future machines and design techniques.

The general topics cover five major areas. First is a discussion of how pipelining may influence the components produced by future technologies. Next are descriptions of several radically different processor organizations that try to beat the slow-down and performance losses from hazards and interlocks in pipelined SISD computers. The third section shows that pipelining techniques need not be limited to CPU designs and may in fact be used throughout whole systems. The fourth section then attempts to predict how the art of programming may evolve to recognize and exploit pipelining. Finally, it has occurred to the author that the whole concept of programming may itself be simply another, but unique, form of pipeline design. The fifth section discusses this idea.

7.1 FUTURE TECHNOLOGIES

Over the last 30 years the techniques of pipelining have grown hand-in-hand with the component technologies that implemented them, from relays and vacuum tubes to integrated circuits. This section predicts how the two will interact both in the near future in terms of LSI and farther ahead in radically new technologies.

7.1.1 Impacts of Pipelining on LSI

The primary technology for computer components over the last 15 years has been solid-state semiconductor. The most recent emphasis in this area has been in large-scale integration (LSI) and very large-scale integration (VLSI). More and more gates have been packed into smaller and smaller areas of silicon. The actual growth rates in density have been phenomenal—several orders of magnitude per decade. Further, it appears that the technology has not come anywhere near the ultimate limitation.

To date very little application of pipelining has been made in the design of individual solid-state components. The obvious question is whether this will continue into the LSI and VLSI world.

In the author's opinion pipelining will become one of the dominant techniques of LSI circuit and chip design. Two observations form the basis for this opinion. First, the inherent speed of individual gates is increasing only slightly in comparison with gate density. This can be seen in the basic cycle times of computers over the last 15 years. With only one or two exceptions, high-performance machines have consistently had cycle times between 50 and 80 ns, with more moderate performance machines having equivalent times in the 100 to 400 ns range. This has been true of everything from the largest multiprocessors to the simplest microprocessors. Only architectural techniques such as parallelism or pipelining have greatly increased the aggregate performance of the computing systems. LSI of itself will not alter this situation; its major contribution is reduced size, not circuit speed.

The second major observation behind the prediction of pipelining in LSI is that the packaging of mass-produced integrated circuits, particularly in terms of available signal pin-outs, has changed even less than basic gate speeds. A 40-pin package is roughly the state of the art, and even it dwarfs the actual size of the LSI chip.

The trick to designing high-speed LSI components thus is to find some architectural technique that can utilize extra logic gates without increasing the number of signal pins needed. Pipelining is an obvious and ideal solution. Just as the flow rate of a pipeline is largely independent of its length, so is the total number of pins. One set is needed for inputs, another for outputs. This is no different from a nonpipelined part. However, with proper design the intermediate stages of a pipelined LSI chip need not contribute extra pins. They do contribute to overall throughput by reducing the stage time. In fact, with greater circuit densities it is quite realistic to expect designs using variations of the Earle latch, with stage times approaching modifications of Hallin and Flynn's (1972) bounds (see Sec. 2.1.1).

As one example, a conventional medium scale integration (MSI) arithmetic logic unit (ALU) chip currently can perform a four-bit add operation in 30 to 60 ns. With internal staging of four gates per level and 1- to 2-ns gates, pipelining may increase performance by factors of 3 to 10. The only cost might be a pin or two for clocks.

Another more relevant example is the typical 40-pin microprocessor chip. Pin limitations and memory chip technology place an upper limit on available memory bandwidth between a standard microprocessor and its memory subsystem. As was shown in the previous chapter (the INTEL 8086 example), relatively simple CPU pipelining can very quickly utilize all this bandwidth. With LSI and VLSI one might consider packaging more memory on the CPU chip to avoid the pin limitations. This probably will be done for reasons of total system size. However, perhaps a better way to augment the total throughput of a microprocessor system is to include in the CPU chip not memory per se but a "memory amplifier," namely a cache. This cache, when combined with much more extensive pipelining to use the extra bandwidth available from the cache, might promise as much as an order of magnitude in performance.

This section would be incomplete without a brief discussion of one possible drawback of pipelining in LSI parts—namely, design time—and of how the use of pipelining might compare with the use of various forms of parallelism. In today's technology the time required to design a part is a major factor in its economic viability. A part that is complex and requires extensive design effort and time may not be used as much as a slower but less complex part that was available earlier. The uses of pipelining may both hinder and help this design time. For smaller LSI parts like specialized I/O chips, the design is straightforward enough that the introduction of pipelining, while it may increase the speed of the chip, will probably increase the design complexity and time.

The situation tends to reverse when the LSI chip is large enough to hold an entire function like a microprocessor. Here the design is complex to begin with; and the very discipline imposed by identifying individual stages and working with each in relative isolation may actually improve the design time, not to mention improving the performance.

As LSI densities grow larger, the use of pipelining may become more important just for the design vigor it imposes. However, a point will be reached, probably when the equivalent of several complete microprocessor systems can be embedded on a single chip, where the complexity is too great even for pipelining. It is here that parallelism, or the replication of identical functions, really comes into play. Perhaps the only economical way to use such very large gate densities is to replicate functions designed for less dense LSIs many times on the same chip and interconnect them to run in parallel to solve the problem. We note, however, that these less dense functions may themselves be pipelined. At these densities the two techniques complement each other nicely.

7.1.2 Emerging Technologies

On the near horizon are technologies radically different from those of today. Examples include surface acoustic waves (SAWs), charge-coupled devices (CCDs), magnetic bubbles, and Josephson devices. Many of these technologies appear more than simply amenable to pipelining; it is almost as if some were developed with pipelining explicitly in mind.

As examples, both CCDs and bubbles seem ideal candidates. Unlike conventional transistor-based technologies where transient current or voltage levels represent data, both these technologies use physically persistent phenomena such as packets of electrical charge or small magnetic domains to represent data, with manipulation of the data done by physically moving these packets. Besides their obvious and well-publicized applications to memory systems, they may also be used for logic (cf. Miller and Zimmerman, 1975; Minnick, 1975). Their advantages for pipelined logic are also obvious: The technology is basically self-latching, the packets physically moving from stage to stage. For CCDs a stage is defined by a set of electrodes placed at some voltage potentials that would maintain a charge beneath them if one was initially placed there. In Fig. 7-1 three electrodes are used for each stage, and by use of a three-phase clock the charge can be moved from one set of three electrodes to the next. Magnetic bubbles are similar, but here rotating magnetic fields are used to move the charge by attraction/repulsion. Figures 7-2 and 7-3 diagram a typical bubble device and the timing of a move.

Complex logic elements can be constructed arbitrarily out of either technology, but with one unique feature: The elements themselves are pipelined. For example, Fig. 7-4 (Lapidus, 1972) diagrams a two-input bubble logic gate with two outputs, one for the AND of the two inputs, and one for the OR. Counting each "T" as a stage this is a three-stage pipeline. More complex circuits such as adders could be built out of combinations of such devices; instead of representing the logic for one stage as they do in

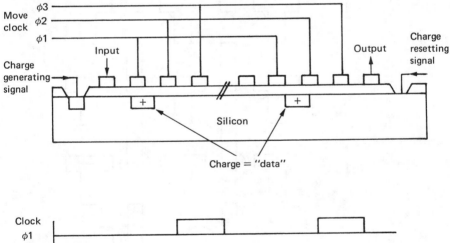

Figure 7-1 Typical CCD device.

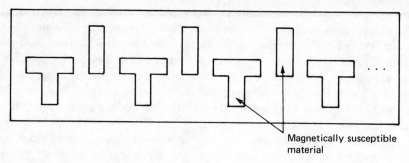

Magnetically susceptible
material

Figure 7-2   Top view of magnetic bubble track.

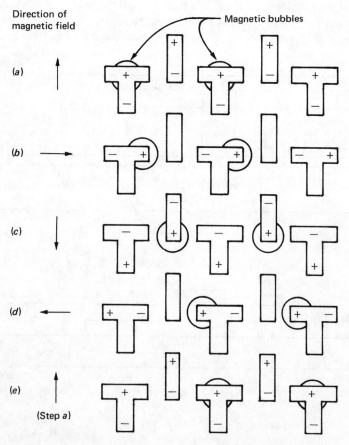

Figure 7-3   Movement of bubbles.

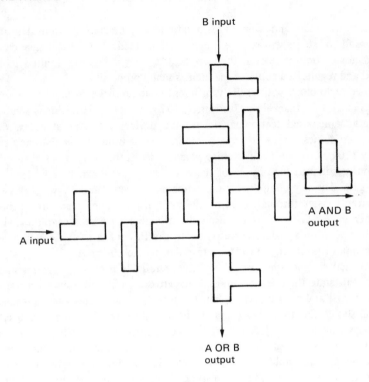

Figure 7-4 Magnetic bubble AND/OR gate pipeline.

current technology, in bubbles or CCDs such devices would be complete multistage pipes.

Such technologies have several advantages over the current generation. First, the self-latching property means that latches and all their complications need not be considered. This in turn eases the clock skew problem. Then, if entire machines are placed on one or a few chips, the clock distribution problem is also simplified, because of both short distances and the nature of the actual clocking mechanism in the device. In addition, the problems with different gate delays and wiring delays virtually disappear because it is the bubble or charge itself that progresses in steps through the circuit, and any circuit-to-circuit wiring is pipelined as a "shift register" whose length can be precisely controlled.

Perhaps the major problems with the use of such technologies in future pipelined systems are speed and control. Since it is a physical entity that is being moved, typical transport velocities are much slower than the speed of light. Current upper limits to staging rates are in the range of 10^7 stages per second. In comparison, current high-speed, semiconductor pipelines already can run about an order of magnitude faster. It will take a few years for speeds to become truly competitive.

The control problems come about from the potentially extremely long pipelines inherent in any complex circuit built with such technologies. Typical modern pipelines employ perhaps a few dozen stages, with circuitry included to keep track of where individual data items are and when new operations may be started. Equivalent designs with thousands of stages will require much more sophisticated scheduling and control than used now. For this reason, their application may always be limited to highly specialized and regularized applications such as signal processing.

Another technology with entirely different characteristics is based on Josephson tunneling (JTL) (cf. Anacker, 1979; Herrel, 1974; Schlig, 1976). This is a superconducting, cryogenic-based technology where the devices are kept at a few degrees absolute. It combines speeds potentially orders of magnitude faster than any current technology (10s of ps) with self-latching characteristics that may be ideal for pipelining. Without going into the physics of the device, Fig. 7-5 diagrams a typical Josephson AND gate. The key component is a switching element that has two states when a supply current passes through it. In parallel with this element is an output line that drives other gates. Each input corresponds to a line that runs near the switching element. In operation a logic 1 corresponds to the flow of current through a control line, either input or output. A logic 0 corresponds to the no-current flow.

The normal state of the switching element reflects itself as a zero resistance to current. In this state there is no voltage drop across the element, thus no current flow through the output line. However, when the total current in the input lines passes a certain threshold, the switching element changes state to one where there is some finite voltage drop across it. This finite drop allows current to flow through the output line. Further, this switch is irreversible in regard to the input lines. Once the input current passes the threshold for a sufficient period of time, the device switches and stays switched regardless of what happens to the inputs. The only way to return the switching element to the 0 state is to remove the supply current.

This self-latching makes pipelining almost a necessity in any large combination of JTL gates. The clock in this case consists of the power supply which must be turned off periodically to reset the logic. To avoid losing the state of the machine when a set of logic is being reset, the output must be saved. This could be in an explicit staging register whose clock is simply the inversion of the one for the logic. However, a more

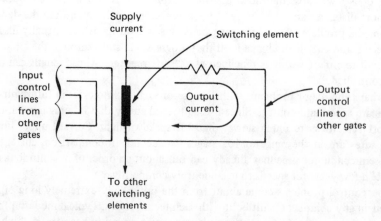

Figure 7-5 A Josephson AND gate.

interesting alternative is to use the logic itself for the staging function. Figure 7-6 portrays one possibility. The function to be performed is designed totally in combinational logic, each level of logic driven by one of three supply clocks. During each time period, one level of logic is being reset, while the level that was just reset is being latched with a new set of values from a third level to which power has not been cut off recently. During the next clock time this third set of logic is reset, while signals from the second set are allowed to propagate forward and latch up the first set. In the next clock it is the second set that is reset, and the third reloaded. This three-phase cycle then repeats itself indefinitely. The entire logic then appears as a pipeline running at a staging rate approaching the time of one JTL gate transition. The only limitations are clock skew, sharpness of clocks, and variation in reset time. Even so, the net bound is much better than that derived by Hallin and Flynn (1972) for semiconductor technologies. Coupled with the inherent speed of the technology, the potential performance of computers built in JTL appears to be enormous by today's standards. The major problems appear to be in the physical packaging and maintenance of such devices, along with organization and control of the relatively long pipelines that result.

7.2 PROCESSOR ARCHITECTURES TO BEAT HAZARDS

Chapter 6 addressed the design of pipelined SISD computers. As should have been apparent, the major conceptual difficulty with such design was not the pipelining itself, but the many and often subtle interinstruction hazards that had to be detected and resolved. Very often this resolution involved all or part of the pipeline, resulting in performance losses of a factor of 3 or more over what might be possible if there were no hazards. These performance losses are equivalent to underutilized hardware and as such lead to the obvious question of what can be done to reclaim the lost cycles. This section describes several processor designs that attempt to do just that. All appear feasible; some are actually under prototype design.

7.2.1 Sharing a Pipeline

The problem in overlapping many instructions from the same program within a pipeline at the same time is that they often place sequencing constraints on each other, forcing some stages of the pipeline to stop temporarily. This stoppage does two things: First, it creates empty cycles that percolate through the pipeline, and second, it makes the time required for executing an instruction practically impossible to predict in advance. A suggestion by Shar and Davidson (1974) may alleviate both problems. The basic idea is to execute not one but several instruction streams on the same pipeline. This in effect superimposes an MIMD multiprocessor architecture on an outgrowth of an SISD-based pipeline design. Proper design of this modification can then virtually eliminate the problems associated with instruction hazards. First, the pipeline can be made quite rigid, with well-defined reservation tables totally determining the path of each instruction type in the instruction set. This fixes the instruction timing variation. Second, for each instruction stream there is one and only one instruction active at any

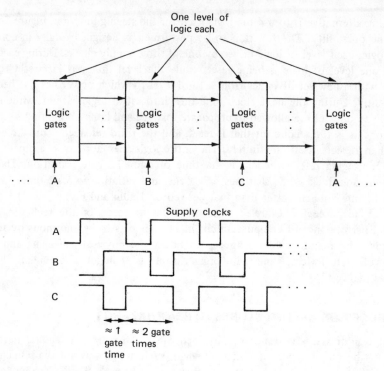

Figure 7-6 A possible JTL pipeline.

time in the pipeline. This avoids the uncertainties due to hazards; it also eliminates the hardware needed to detect and resolve hazards. Finally, a control mechanism is needed to choose from among each instruction stream that does not have a currently executing instruction the one to initiate next. This choice will try to optimize stage usage while avoiding collisions. In turn this eliminates many wasted cycles and increases total throughput of the hardware. Figure 7-7 diagrams this general configuration.

In the terminology of Chap. 3 such a pipeline corresponds almost exactly to a dynamically configured multifunction pipeline. All of the scheduling theory and hardware initiation controller designs discussed there thus are directly applicable.

There are several unique characteristics of such designs worth mentioning. First is the question of processor state, which usually includes those registers, status indicators, and other state information that are visible in some way to the programmer. In a conventional pipelined SISD computer, there may be several physical copies of this information throughout the pipeline, but they all contain copies of the same conceptual information. This is not true on an MIMD pipeline since each instruction stream must have its own unique processor-state information. The common approach to acknowledging these multiple states is to augment the latches for each stage in the pipeline with enough bits to totally contain the processor state for a single instruction stream. This state follows the execution of its next instruction around the pipeline in a ring-like fashion shown in Fig. 7-8a.

An alternative approach is to centralize all the processor states in a single multi-ported memory and to augment each staging latch by only enough bits to identify which instruction stream is currently using that stage. When a particular stage needs access to some state information (such as a register), it uses this identity latch as part of its access to this central memory. Figure 7-8*b* diagrams this variation.

A similar situation occurs in the memory system. Again there are two approaches. First, all instruction streams can see exactly the same memory, perhaps augmented by a single common cache. This is convenient for many MIMD programs. It is also cheaper to implement in a pipelined MIMD structure than in multiple physically independent processors, since no complex multiprocessor switch is needed. The second approach is to dedicate a separate memory subsystem to each instruction stream; when the pipeline issues a memory access request it includes the "identity" of the instruction stream. This increases effective memory bandwidth by "interleaving by instruction stream," and is much cheaper and easier to implement than other forms of interleaving.

As an example of the effectiveness of this technique, Shar and Davidson (1974) studied pipelines that implemented instruction streams based on the Hewlett-Packard 2116 computer instruction set. They partitioned the flow of instruction execution for one instruction into seven distinct phases and looked at several different pipeline organizations that supported this partitioning in different ways. One advantage of the instruction-set architecture they chose was that all instruction types could follow exactly the same reservation table. This permitted them to derive optimal scheduling rules from the static configuration theory, thus simplifying the initiation control. The result of the study was a range of configurations with different costs and performances. In terms of cost/performance ratios, the best configuration could do the processing of seven conventionally designed 2116s at about 3.5 times the amount of hardware.

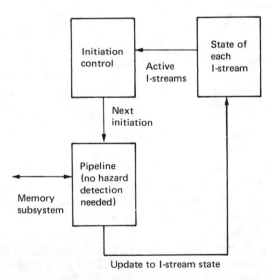

Figure 7-7 MIMD architecture on single pipeline.

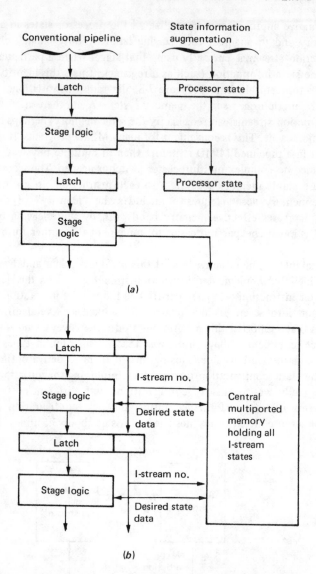

Figure 7-8   Location alternatives for state information. (a) Ring structure. (b) Central structure.

Although Shar and Davidson were the first to formally document the tradeoffs and advantages possible from such techniques, they were not the first to propose or actually use them. The Control Data 6600 computer system (Thornton, 1970) physically implemented 10 independent peripheral processors (as seen by a programmer) in a single piece of hardware where a "barrel switch" successively rotated each stage past each processor's registers. Flynn et al. (1970) proposed generalizations of this where "skeleton" processors consisting primarily of register sets and processor status competed for central pools of logic.

7.2.2 Explicit Hazard Recognition

Another approach to regaining the cycles lost to hazards is to explicitly recognize their existence at the instruction-set level and allow either the programmer or the support software package to handle them. This is the approach taken by Peled (1977) and Tsui (1980) in the design of a low-cost computer for signal processing applications, termed the simple signal processor (SSP). The instruction set of this machine is basically accumulator-oriented, with an index register for addressing and some special features for signal processing. In design it consists of a rigid four-stage pipeline with two separate memory interfaces. The first stage of the pipeline performs the instruction fetch function and is the sole user of one of the memories. The second stage performs decode and EAGEN functions. The third stage is the sole user of the other memory and performs all data accesses. The fourth stage completes the pipeline by performing all execution activities. ENDOP functions are distributed among all four. Figure 7-9 diagrams this organization.

Figure 7-10 shows reservation tables for the major classes of instructions. With the exception of MULTIPLY and DIVIDE, all instructions follow a linear path through the pipeline. This promises an instruction latency of 1. We note that on a branch the IC is changed early enough in the second stage to affect the IFETCH in the first stage for the next instruction. The key difference between this and other pipelined machines is that with one exception there are no interlocks built into the hardware. A new instruction is initiated at each clock regardless of what instructions preceded it into the pipeline. The only exception is with MULTIPLY and DIVIDE which freeze the pipeline once they reach the fourth stage.

This lack of hardware hazard detection and resolution forces the construction of the programs running on this machine to take hazards into account. While this would be difficult or impossible on many typical pipelines, the very rigidity and simplicity of the SSP design make the task very manageable. First, the linearity of the pipeline and the separation of memories guarantee that there are no hazards around memory,

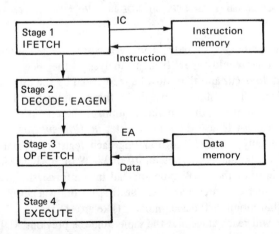

Figure 7-9 SSP pipeline.

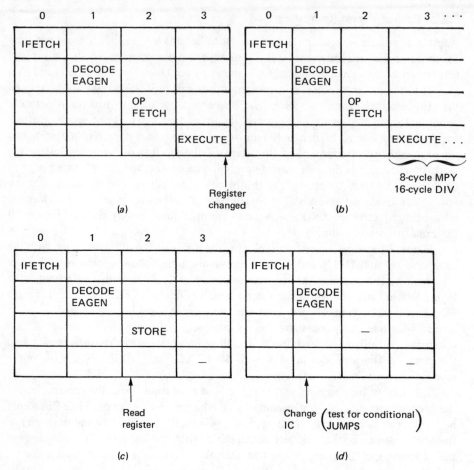

Figure 7-10 Reservation tables for SSP. (*a*) ADD-like, (*b*) MULTIPLY/DIVIDE, (*c*) STORE, (*d*) JUMP.

particularly data memory. All data memory accesses are performed in exactly the order the programmer would expect from an analysis of the code.

Hazards that do occur and that must be recognized by the programmer are around the machine's internal registers, particularly the accumulator. However, as in the memory, the very rigidity of the pipeline minimizes the effects. Only when neighboring instructions attempt to use the same register *in different stages* of their execution does a hazard actually occur. Since updating each register is usually done only in a specific stage, this eliminates the possibility of WAW or WAR hazards. The resulting hazards are primarily of the RAW type and fall into a few easily recognizable classes. Figure 7-11 diagrams two such hazards. The first occurs whenever a STORE follows any instruction that modifies the accumulator (like an ADD).

The STORE will reach stage 3 at the same time the previous ADD reaches stage 4. However, the ADD will not update the accumulator until the end of the time unit, while the STORE needs it at the beginning. The result is that what is stored is the value in the accumulator because of the instruction before the ADD, not the ADD. If the results of the ADD are to be stored, then some additional instruction must be inserted between the two. At worst this is a no-operation instruction (NOP) that merely delays one time unit. Usually, however, an instruction that goes after the store can be moved up before the store, and the NOP avoided.

The other major hazard class in Fig. 7-11 occurs when a conditional BRANCH is to test some value in the accumulator. The test occurs at the beginning of a time unit by stage 2, while the update to the accumulator is at the end of a time unit in stage 4. Thus following an ADD-like instruction by a conditional BRANCH will test not the result of the ADD, but the result left in the accumulator by the instruction initiated

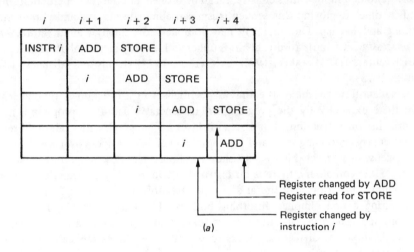

(a)

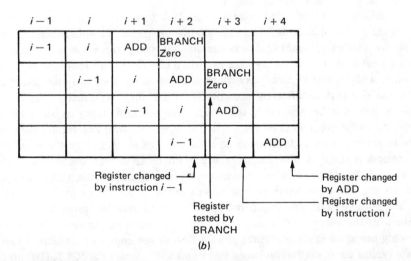

(b)

Figure 7-11 Hazards in SSP. (a) ADD-STORE hazard. (b) Conditional BRANCH.

two time units before the ADD. To make the test on the value of this last ADD requires either adding two NOPs between the ADD and the BRANCH, or moving two instructions from the other side of the BRANCH between the ADD and the BRANCH. The latter may make the program look somewhat odd but allows it to use the full performance capability of the machine.

7.2.3 Data-Flow Architectures

Hazards very often exist in conventional sequential programs for SISD machines simply because of the sequentialism of the representation. One instruction is tied to the next by placement in the program, and the computer's logic must expend considerable effort to determine if this constraint can be broken and the two instructions overlapped in time. Removing this sequentialism can eliminate hazards and permit more pipelining and overlap. One radically new approach to computer architecture, *data-flow processing*, attempts to do this; it is under active study at several universities and research centers (cf. Miranker, 1977; Syre et al., 1977; Dennis and Misunas, 1975; Kosinski, 1973).

In a data-flow machine, the only sequentialism in a program is that which is placed there explicitly by the programmer. In general a data-flow program is not a sequential list of instructions, but instead it is a directed graph with nodes that represent elementary processing steps and links interconnecting the nodes over which values, called tokens, may travel. Figure 7-12 shows a simple data-flow program. Unlike conventional SISD computers, there is no instruction counter (IC) or equivalent. Instead an elementary operation may fire at any time after tokens have arrived on each of its inputs. Firing a node implies absorbing both of the input tokens, performing the operation, and generating an output value token that is placed on an output link. A token on a link that divides and leads to several other nodes replicates itself with copies traveling into each destination.

The definition of the firing rules and the lack of an IC immediately eliminates many of the potential hazards found in sequential programs. Since there is no intrinsic limit to the number of nodes that may fire simultaneously, there is at least the potential for a great deal of concurrency. The execution of different operations may overlap each other without fear of interlocks. However, there are at least two other aspects of data-flow design that permit even more overlap. First, there is no reason why individual nodes may not be pipelined, with each firing corresponding to an initiation. Second, the entire program itself may often be pipelined, with new input tokens permitted to enter as soon as there is no possibility of collisions. In a real sense, a data-flow program is simply a programmable way of interconnecting nodes or stages into a particular pipeline to compute some function, i.e., a reservation table. Proper design of the nodes and firing mechanisms then permit much of the theory of Chap. 3 to be directly applicable to the generation and optimization of data flow programs.

Much of the theory and techniques of pipeline design also show up in the most commonly proposed implementation of data flow driven computers. Figure 7-13 diagrams a typical configuration proposed by Dennis and associates at M.I.T. (Dennis and Misunas, 1974). The data-flow program is stored in a set of instruction cells whose

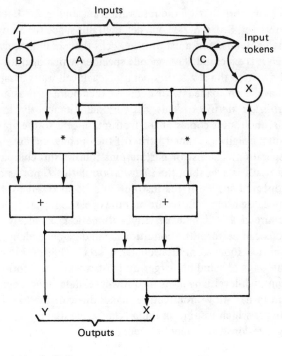

Input A, B, C
$$Y = A * X + B$$
$$X = Y/(C * X + A)$$
Output X, Y

Figure 7-12 Representation of a data-flow program.

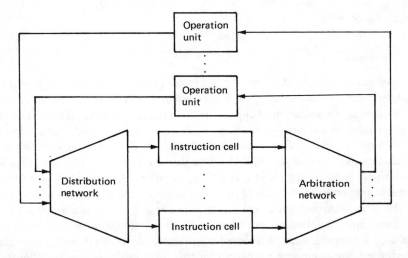

Figure 7-13 Basic data-flow processor.

operation closely mirrors that of the reservation stations in the E-unit of the IBM System/360 Model 91 (cf. Sec. 6.6.2). Each cell contains space for an opcode, several data values for input operands, and a list of other cells that should receive the result of this instruction when it is executed. The opcode specifies which operation unit is to receive the inputs and generate the result. In operation each cell waits passively until all its input operands have been loaded with data. At that point it fires and requests service from the *arbitration network*. This network simultaneously handles many fired instruction cells, and routes copies of the instruction cells to the appropriate *operation units*. These units, usually pipelined, strip off the opcode and data values and perform the specified operation. The list of destinations follows this computation through the unit. When the result is available, the *distribution network* routes copies of the result back into the operand spaces of the instruction cells specified by the destination list. In turn this may cause other cells to fire and the cycle to repeat.

This procedure clearly handles strictly arithmetic tasks nicely. Further, relatively simple extensions can perform the conditional and data-dependent kinds of operations needed to support a fuller computational range. The big problems, however, are in finding efficient ways of handling larger units of work in the form of procedures and in mapping from high-level languages into low-level data-flow programs. The very lack of sequentialism in data-flow architecture makes difficult the translation from current high-level languages which assume an underlying sequential machine. Entirely new languages and language constructs may be needed.

7.3   SYSTEM DESIGNS USING PIPELINING

This book has primarily addressed the design of individual computing systems using pipelining. However, the techniques are not quite so limited in scope. There are several possibilities for applications in much broader contexts. This section describes two of the more interesting ones: certain forms of computer networks and certain types of distributed processing.

7.3.1   Networks

A *network* is a system whereby several geographically separate "users" can interchange information. Very often the users are local computer systems or humans at terminals, and the network is a collection of computers interconnected by digital communication links (cables, telephone lines, or satellite links). There are many such designs, but perhaps the most common fall into the general category of *packet-switched store and forward*. Examples include the ARPANET (Roberts and Wessler, 1970), ETHERNET (Metcalfe and Briggs, 1976), and CYCLADES (Pouzin, 1973). In such networks, all messages are represented as series of *packets*, usually of fixed size. Each packet travels from the source, through links and nodes connecting links, to the destination. The nodes interconnecting the links are often small computers themselves. When a packet enters such a computer node, it is stored in a memory block buffer until the computer has performed any required error checks, further route selection, and link allocations. When the link is free, the message is forwarded to the next node. Figure 7-14 diagrams a typical organization of such a network.

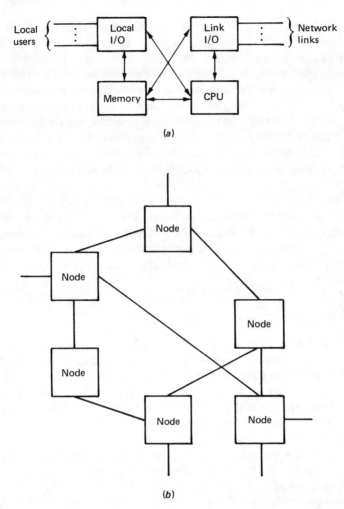

Figure 7-14 Network structures. (*a*) A node. (*b*) A network.

With the proper view, a packet-switched store and forward network becomes an almost exact model of a dynamically configured multifunction pipeline. The stages are equivalent to nodes, with the node memory buffers serving as staging latches. Transmission of a packet from one node to another corresponds to picking a reservation table (the route control) and making an initiation into the pipeline (starting transmission). A multipacket message transmission that uses the same path corresponds to a temporary static configuration (a "vector" operation). A collision can correspond to the simultaneous transmission of two packets in the same link or too many packets attempting to enter the memory buffers of a node at the same time.

For this model much of the theory of Chap. 3 is directly applicable, particularly if there is a central source that governs the routes taken by messages entering the network. For the latter approach the entry of a new message causes the node receiving the message to forward to the route controller an indication of the length of the message and its ultimate destination. The route controller then constructs a route reservation table, inserts delays to avoid collisions, and determines a latency sequence to optimize total network throughput. It then returns this information to the original node for execution. We note that in this case delays correspond to some data packets stagnating in memory buffers while other packets pass through the node more quickly. As such, delays are more meaningful than in conventional pipelines because they correspond to transport delays in getting a message across the network, thus they are directly visible to the end user. Consequently, the algorithms for selection of a reservation table and delay insertion may be modified to look for solutions which minimize user waiting time.

One other research topic of potential value is to modify the pipeline control theory of Chap. 3 for the case where each stage has its own set of reservation tables and can make scheduling decisions on its own with only limited knowledge of what the other nodes are doing. This would eliminate the need for a central route controller and perhaps put some of the currently used route-control algorithms on a more sound theoretical basis.

7.3.2 Distributed Processing

One topic that currently arouses a great deal of interest is *distributed processing*. While there is no single universally agreed-upon definition of distributed processing, many think of it as a network where each intermediate node in some way processes the data passing through it. The major difference from networks is that now it is the path taken, not the source/destination pair, that is of importance. This path in some sense models the computational sequence applied to the data.

This view fits the concept of a pipeline even better than a network did. When data enters a node to be processed by other nodes, the desired path is like a reservation table. As the path taken by the data becomes more and more rigidly definable in advance, the analogy becomes even stronger.

One very good example of a case where representation of a path by a fixed reservation table is extremely valid is in a signal-processing system where the processors are distributed. One processor may do nothing other than digital filtering, while another performs Fourier analysis, and a third does display formatting. Data enters the system at fixed intervals and follows a relatively rapid and unchanging path through the system. In this case, the theory of Chap. 3 may be of direct benefit since it can aid the system designer in scheduling all the various activities so that no processor is asked to do two things simultaneously. The delay insertion techniques then indicate exactly when various buffers in the system hold data, which in turn can be used to predict accurately exactly how much and where temporary storage is needed.

7.4 EFFECTS OF PIPELINING ON PROGRAMMING

To date, the complications introduced by pipelining have been largely hidden from the average programmer by combinations of hardware interlocks and support software translations. While this trend will probably continue, there will be a growing realization of the existence of pipelining in a system and of the techniques that may be used to exploit its capabilities. This section addresses some of the techniques that may become more widespread.

7.4.1 Programming of SISD Pipelines

Most larger conventional SISD computing systems of today employ some kind of pipelining within the CPU. When used to execute conventional sequential oriented programs, much of the pipeline's capability (up to 66%) is lost in handling interlocks caused by hazards between individual instructions. While a programmer need not be concerned with these interlocks to produce correct programs, recognition of the pipeline's existence can pay off in substantial performance increases. This includes such things as tightening data structures so that the most frequent methods of accessing them do not hit the memory interleave, unrolling loops and centralizing data-dependent choices to minimize the effects of branches, and keeping commonly used sequences of code and data close together to enhance cache hit ratios. All these things can be done by a programmer even in a high-level language.

If programming is done at the assembly-code level, other techniques can reduce the effects of hazards even further. Chief among these low-level techniques is avoidance of the use of a single register for most calculations. In addition, using several different registers for different calculations and interleaving two different calculations into one piece of code can go a long way toward minimizing hazards. One well-known example of a set of programs optimized in this fashion is STACKLIB (McMahon et al., 1972) for the CDC 7600 series machines. These programs perform basic vector operations out of essentially scalar instructions. The placement of each instruction within the loops is carefully chosen to minimize hazards and maximize throughput.

To date, most compilers, even "optimizing" ones, have not done much to automate these techniques. However, as pipelining becomes more and more extensive, it will become increasingly difficult for the average programmer to understand, much less optimize around, the potential interlocks in the underlying pipelines. Compilers and other support software will have to evolve to handle them. An example of software that is tending in this direction is the FORTRAN compiler for the ASC machine (cf. Gaulding and Madison, 1975).

Opposite trends may occur at lower levels of programming, such as detailed microprogramming of a CPU or a vector processor arithmetic unit. Here it is critical that the programmer see the pipeline and how data flows through it. However, this visibility must not be lost when several different initiations overlap. The concept of a reservation table seems excellent for resolving such problems because it allows the programmer complete visibility into the pipeline for one set of calculations, and with proper support software it can be automatically modified to meet some desired latency sequence. Other support software can then interleave different initiations as required to produce actual microcode. To date only preliminary attempts have been made to produce such systems.

7.4.2 Programming of Vector Pipelines

As demonstrated in Chaps. 4 and 5, pipelined vector processors are capable of truly enormous processing rates. However, achieving these rates requires even more attention from the programmer than for efficient use of pipelined SISD machines. Consequently, the development of such machines and their parallel processing equivalents has been coupled closely with the development of languages and compilers that deal directly with vectors.

The most well-known vector language is APL (cf. Pakin, 1968). While it has influenced the design of particular vector processors, it has not become a prime language for the programming of such machines. Instead a variety of languages have developed, often targeted for specific vector machines both pipelined and parallel in basic design. These include TRANQUIL (Budnick and Kuck, 1969), LRLTRAN (Zwakenburg et al., 1973), and VECTRAN (Paul and Wilson, 1975), to name just a few. An excellent paper by Gary (1977) summarizes major characteristics.

The major difference between these languages and more conventional ones is the explicit recognition of vectors and vector operations. The programmer can deliberately identify data structures as vectors and arrays and specify computation on all or subsets of the elements in single statements without loops.

Another emphasis has been on production of compilers that *vectorize* code; that is, take a program written without vectors and recast it into an equivalent program that uses vectors. In FORTRAN-like languages this process primarily involves analyzing DO loops and recognizing when they can be recorded as vector operations. One example can be found in Remund and Taggart (1977).

While substantial progress has been made in both language definition and compiler techniques, the major problem in efficiently programming such machines has not changed. As demonstrated in Chap. 5, the entire approach to developing algorithms changes dramatically when vectors are used. The difficulties are so great that it may be quite some time before the library of high-quality vector algorithms and techniques even begins to rival the current libraries for more standard scalar-based code. The problem seems to be not in the machine designs or language constructs as much as it is in the typical way a human thinks.

7.5 IS PROGRAMMING REALLY A FORM OF PIPELINE DESIGN?

In the process of writing this book, it occurred to the author that there are strong analogies between the concepts of pipelining and programming, and that a cross-fertilization of ideas may be of value to both areas. This section attempts to construct this analogy, and, it is hoped, to foster some insights by the reader.

For any conventional computer architecture the construction of a program corresponds to partitioning the problem into small pieces called computer instructions. Executing such a program is equivalent to traveling through some paths of these instructions. In pipeline terminology, each instruction is a small stage with a single execution of the program corresponding to an initiation. The instruction counter (IC) corresponds to the pipeline's clock because every time it changes, the initiation moves to the next stage. The CPU and memory registers function as staging latches since they carry the data from stage to stage. The CPU registers in particular represent a unique staging latch since they are not dedicated to a particular stage but instead "follow" the IC around the program. In addition, because there is only one IC, only one stage at a time is active. In terms of a reservation table analog this means that there is at most one mark in any column.

Each initiation in a program pipeline may take a different path through the pipeline. In this sense a program is equivalent to a multifunction pipeline.

A reentrant program is one that can have more than one execution pending in it at one time. This corresponds to the overlap of several initiations within the pipeline. A collision of two initiations occurs when both are in sequence of code that attempts to change exactly the same resource at the same time (usually memory). In programming terminology such references of code are termed *critical sections* and are protected by a variety of synchronization and interlocking techniques. This corresponds to hazard resolution and detection. In fact, even the classification of hazards in a pipeline (Sec. 6.2) can carry over.

The major difference between a program pipeline and the pipelines studied earlier in this book is that very seldom is the path taken by a computation through a program known when the initiation is made.

How might the concept of a program as a pipeline affect future advances in the state of the art? One way might be in increased understanding of communication between multiple, concurrently executing processes (initiations of a program). This whole area is one of the toughest and most important in the theory of programming for exactly the same reasons that its analog of hazards are to pipeline theory. Development of clean and efficient communication and synchronization primitives may shed light on ways to design instruction sets and processor architectures that are not so hazard prone.

The emergence of data-flow machines may do the same thing in reverse. Perhaps if architectures can be developed to handle multiple, independent, but related instructions, the same principles can be updated to handle multiple communicating processes.

Another area where programming might benefit from pipeline theory is in the selection of length and location of critical sections within an operating system. Unlike most application programs, the modules of an operating system are somewhat rigidly connected, permitting them to be modeled as pipelines with stages corresponding to the critical sections. Extensions of the theory of Chap. 3 might be used to control entry of processes into the operating system in a way that either reduces or eliminates the possibility of collisions in critical sections.

Finally, the whole area of pipelining as a subtopic in the theory of computational complexity is virtually untouched. There are models and theories of computation for parallel structures, but as mentioned at the end of Chap. 5, very little of it carries over to pipelined structures. Much of the scheduling theory for production, lines, and the like maps into linear pipelines, but very little is known about more complex structures.

PROBLEMS

7-1 Take some standard MSI part for which you have good documentation and attempt to design an equivalent part that is pipelined. What might be the performance increase? What, if any, additional pins are needed? By how much has the complexity of the chip been increased?

7-2 Given the pin constraints of a typical microprocessor, sketch out the design of a cache memory that could be placed on the same chip as the CPU. What are the variables affecting the design? How does the cache system interact with the external memory? How many extra pins are needed?

7-3 Describe exactly how the magnetic bubble AND/OR gate of Fig. 7-4 works. Design a magnetic bubble half-adder. What problems did you have to face? How many stages are there in the pipeline? (Consider each 360-degree rotation of the magnetic field as one cycle.)

7-4 Sketch out a simple pipeline that could handle multiple instruction streams of the type of the model architecture of Chap. 6. Compute an estimate of the total throughput. What problems did you encounter?

7-5 Derive bounds on stage timing similar to those of Sec. 2.1 for a technology like that of Josephson.

7-6 Write a data flow program for computing some simple function like $N!$ on a data flow computer. It may be necessary to "invent" operations that produce or use logical tokens that take on only true/false values. Attempt to develop a reservation-table model of the computation.

7-7 Assuming the same computation chosen for Prob. 7-6, write a program for a computer like SSP. Assume a simple single-accumulator instruction set. Identify each hazard you encountered and how you wrote or modified the code to overcome it.

7-8 What do you think of the analogy proposed in Sec. 7.5?

Collision Vector Characteristics

Table A-1 lists, for all collision vectors up to nine bits in length, the minimum achievable latency (MAL), all cycles that achieve this average latency, both greedy and nongreedy, and all other greedy cycles that are valid for the collision vector but are not optimal. For this appendix a greedy cycle is any cycle in the modified state diagram that starts at some state and, selecting only the arcs with lowest latencies, returns to that state without traversing any other state more than once.

All cycles are listed in a canonical order where each cycle has been rotated until its equivalent representation as a number (base the compute time of the collision vector) is minimal.

For the nonoptimal greedy cycles, the average latency is included in square brackets before the cycle.

The listing of cycles here is not exhaustive, and although all optimal and all greedy simple cycles are included, there may be (and usually are) other nonoptimal nongreedy simple cycles. This is certainly true if nonsimple cycles are considered.

The programming that produced these cycles is due to Jordan B. Pollack.

Table A-1

Collision vector	MAL	Optimal nongreedy	Optimal greedy	Nonoptimal greedy
11	2.00		(2)	
101	2.00		(1,3)	
111	3.00		(3)	
1001	2.00		(1,1,4)	
			(2)	
1011	2.50		(1,4)	
1101	2.00		(2)	
1111	4.00		(4)	
10001	2.00		(1,1,1,5)	
			(1,2,3,2)	
10011	2.33		(1,1,5)	
10101	3.00		(1,5)	
			(3)	
10111	3.00		(1,5)	
11001	2.50		(2,3)	
11011	3.50		(2,5)	
11101	3.00		(3)	
11111	5.00		(5)	
100001	2.00		(1,1,1,1,6)	
			(1,2,1,3,3)	
			(1,1,2,4,2)	
			(2)	
100011	2.25		(1,1,1,6)	[3.00] (3)
100101	2.00		(2)	[2.67] (1,1,6)
100111	2.67		(1,1,6)	
101001	2.33		(1,3,3)	
101011	3.00		(3)	[3.50] (1,6)
101101	3.50		(1,6)	[4.00] (4)
101111	3.50		(1,6)	
110001	2.00		(2)	[3.00] (3)
110011	3.00		(3)	[4.00] (2,6)
110101	2.00		(2)	
110111	4.00		(2,6)	
111001	3.00		(3)	
111011	3.00		(3)	
111101	4.00		(4)	
111111	6.00		(6)	
1000001	2.00		(1,1,1,1,1,7)	
			(1,1,1,2,5,2)	
			(1,1,2,1,4,3)	
			(1,1,3,4,1,2)	
			(1,3)	
			(1,2,2,3,2,2)	

Table A-1. (*Continued*)

Collision vector	MAL	Optimal nongreedy	Optimal greedy	Nonoptimal greedy
1000011	2.20		(1,1,1,1,7)	[2.75] (1,3,4,3)
1000101	2.50		(1,1,1,7)	
			(2,3)	
			(1,2,5,2)	
1000111	2.50		(1,1,1,7)	
1001001	3.00		(1,1,7)	
			(2,2,5)	
			(1,4,4)	
1001011	3.00		(1,1,7)	[4.00] (4)
1001101	3.00		(1,1,7)	[3.50] (2,5)
1001111	3.00		(1,1,7)	
1010001	2.00		(1,3)	
1010011	2.75		(1,3,4,3)	
1010101	4.00		(1,7)	
			(3,5)	
1010111	4.00		(1,7)	
1011001	3.00		(1,4,4)	
1011011	4.00		(1,7)	
			(4)	
1011101	4.00		(1,7)	[5.00] (5)
1011111	4.00		(1,7)	
1100001	2.33		(2,2,3)	
1100011	3.50		(3,4)	[3.67] (2,2,7)
1100101	2.50		(2,3)	
1100111	4.50		(2,7)	
1101001	3.00		(2,2,5)	[4.00] (4)
1101011	3.67		(2,2,7)	[4.00] (4)
1101101	3.50		(2,5)	
1101111	4.50		(2,7)	
1110001	3.50		(3,4)	
1110011	3.50		(3,4)	
1110101	4.00		(3,5)	
1110111	5.00		(3,7)	
1111001	4.00		(4)	
1111011	4.00		(4)	
1111101	5.00		(5)	
1111111	7.00		(7)	
10000001	2.00		(1,1,1,1,1,1,8)	
			(1,1,1,1,2,6,2)	
			(1,1,1,2,1,5,3)	
			(1,1,2,1,1,4,4)	
			(1,1,1,3,5,1,2)	
			(1,1,3,1,4,1,3)	
			(1,1,2,2,4,2,2)	
			(1,2,2,1,3,2,3)	
			(1,2,1,2,3,3,2)	
			(2)	

Table A-1. (*Continued*)

Collision vector	MAL	Optimal nongreedy	Optimal greedy	Nonoptimal greedy
10000011	2.17		(1,1,1,1,1,8)	[2.60] (1,3,1,4,4)
				[2.60] (1,1,3,5,3)
10000101	2.00		(2)	[2.40] (1,1,2,6,2)
				[3.00] (3)
				[2.40] (1,1,1,1,8)
10000111	2.40		(1,1,1,1,8)	[4.00] (4)
10001001	2.20		(1,2,3,3,2)	[2.75] (1,1,1,8)
10001011	2.75		(1,1,1,8)	[3.25] (2,3,5,3)
10001101	2.75		(1,1,1,8)	[3.00] (3)
10001111	2.75		(1,1,1,8)	
10010001	2.00		(2)	[2.50] (1,4)
				[2.50] (1,1,4,4)
10010011	3.00		(1,4,4)	[3.33] (1,1,8)
10010101	2.00		(2)	[3.33] (1,1,8)
10010111	3.33		(1,1,8)	[4.00] (4)
10011001	3.33		(1,1,8)	[4.00] (2,6)
				[3.67] (1,5,5)
10011011	3.33		(1,1,8)	[5.00] (5)
10011101	3.33		(1,1,8)	[4.00] (2,6)
10011111	3.33		(1,1,8)	
10100001	2.25		(1,3,1,4)	[3.00] (3)
10100011	2.60		(1,3,1,4,4)	
10100101	3.00		(3)	[3.67] (1,3,6,3,1,8)
				[4.00] (4)
10100111	4.00	(1,8,3)	(1,3,8)	
			(4)	
10101001	3.00		(3)	
10101011	4.00		(3,5)	[4.50] (1,8)
10101101	3.00		(3)	[4.50] (1,8)
10101111	4.50		(1,8)	
10110001	2.50		(1,4)	
10110011	3.00		(1,4,4)	
10110101	4.00		(4)	[4.50] (1,8)
10110111	4.00		(4)	[4.50] (1,8)
10111001	3.67		(1,5,5)	
10111011	4.50		(1,8)	[5.00] (5)
10111101	4.50		(1,8)	[6.00] (6)
10111111	4.50		(1,8)	
11000001	2.00		(2)	[2.67] (2,3,3)
11000011	3.25		(2,3,5,3)	[4.00] (2,2,8)
				[4.00] (4)
11000101	2.00		(2)	[3.00] (3)
11000111	4.00		(2,2,8)	
			(4)	
11001001	2.67		(2,3,3)	
11001011	3.25		(2,3,5,3)	
11001101	3.00		(3)	[4.00] (2,6)

Table A-1. (*Continued*)

Collision vector	MAL	Optimal nongreedy	Optimal greedy	Nonoptimal greedy
11001111	5.00		(2,8)	
11010001	2.00		(2)	
11010011	4.00		(2,2,8)	
			(4)	
11010101	2.00		(2)	
11010111	4.00		(2,2,8)	
			(4)	
11011001	4.00		(2,6)	[5.00] (5)
11011011	5.00		(2,8)	
			(5)	
11011101	4.00		(2,6)	
11011111	5.00		(2,8)	
11100001	3.00		(3)	[4.00] (4)
11100011	4.00		(3,5)	
			(4)	
11100101	3.00		(3)	[4.00] (4)
11100111	4.00		(4)	[5.50] (3,8)
11101001	3.00		(3)	
11101011	4.00		(3,5)	
11101101	3.00		(3)	
11101111	5.50		(3,8)	
11110001	4.00		(4)	
11110011	4.00		(4)	
11110101	4.00		(4)	
11110111	4.00		(4)	
11111001	5.00		(5)	
11111011	5.00		(5)	
11111101	6.00		(6)	
11111111	8.00		(8)	
100000001	2.00		(1,1,1,1,1,1,1,9)	
			(1,1,1,1,1,2,7,2)	
			(1,1,1,1,2,1,6,3)	
			(1,1,1,2,1,1,5,4)	
			(1,1,1,4,5,1,1,2)	
			(1,1,1,1,3,6,1,2)	
			(1,1,1,3,1,5,1,3)	
			(1,1,3,1,1,4,1,4)	
			(1,1,1,2,2,5,2,2)	
			(1,1,2,2,1,4,2,3)	
			(1,1,3,2,4,1,2,2)	
			(1,1,2,1,2,4,3,2)	
			(1,2,1,2,1,3,3,3)	
			(1,1,2,3,4,2,1,2)	
			(1,2,3,1,3,2,1,3)	
			(1,2,2,2,3,2,2,2)	
			(2)	

Table A-1. (*Continued*)

Collision vector	MAL	Optimal nongreedy	Optimal greedy	Nonoptimal greedy
100000011	2.14	*	(1,1,1,1,1,9)	[2.50] (1,1,1,3,6,3)
				[2.50] (1,1,3,1,5,4)
				[2.50] (1,1,4,5,1,3)
				[2.50] (1,4)
				[3.00] (3)
100000101	2.33	*	(1,1,1,1,1,9)	
			(1,1,1,2,7,2)	
			(2,2,3)	
			(1,2,2,5,2,2)	
100000111	2.33		(1,1,1,1,1,9)	[3.50] (1,4,5,4)
100001001	2.17	*	(1,2,1,3,3,3)	[2.60] (1,1,1,1,9)
				[2.60] (1,1,2,7,2)
100001011	2.60		(1,1,1,1,9)	[3.00] (3)
100001101	2.60		(1,1,1,1,9)	[3.50] (3,4)
100001111	2.60		(1,1,1,1,9)	
100010001	3.00	*	(1,1,1,9)	
			(1,2,7,2)	
			(1,6,3,2)	
			(1,1,5,5)	
			(1,2,3,6)	
			(1,5)	
			(2,3,2,5)	
			(3)	
100010011	3.00		(1,1,1,9)	[3.67] (1,5,5)
			(3)	
100010101	3.00		(1,1,1,9)	
			(2,3,2,5)	
			(1,2,7,2)	
100010111	3.00		(1,1,1,9)	[5.00] (5)
100011001	3.00		(3)	
			(1,1,1,9)	
100011011	3.00		(1,1,1,9)	
			(3)	
100011101	3.00		(1,1,1,9)	
100011111	3.00		(1,1,1,9)	
100100001	2.20	*	(1,1,4,1,4)	[2.75] (2,2,2,5)
				[6.00] (6)
100100011	2.50		(1,4)	
100100101	3.00		(2,2,5)	[3.67] (1,1,9)
100100111	3.50		(1,4,5,4)	[3.67] (1,1,9)
100101001	3.25	*	(2,2,2,7)	[3.67] (1,1,9)
				[3.83] (1,6,4,2,4,6)
100101011	3.67		(1,1,9)	[4.00] (2,4,6,4)
100101101	3.67		(1,1,9)	
			(2,2,7)	
100101111	3.67		(1,1,9)	
100110001	3.00		(1,5)	[3.50] (2,5)
			(1,1,5,5)	

*Because of the large size of the state diagrams, a full search for all optimal nongreedy cycles was not performed.

Table A-1. (*Continued*)

Collision vector	MAL	Optimal nongreedy	Optimal greedy	Nonoptimal greedy
100110011	3.67		(1,1,9) (1,5,5)	
100110101	3.50		(2,5)	[3.67] (1,1,9)
100110111	3.67		(1,1,9)	[5.00] (5)
100111001	3.67		(1,1,9)	[4.50] (2,7) [4.33] (1,6,6)
100111011	3.67		(1,1,9)	[6.00] (6)
100111101	3.67		(1,1,9)	[4.50] (2,7)
100111111	3.67		(1,1,9)	
101000001	2.50	*	(1,3,1,5) (1,3,3,3) (1,4)	[7.00] (7)
101000011	2.50		(1,4)	[3.00] (3)
101000101	3.50	*	(1,3,1,9) (1,3,7,3) (1,4,5,4) (3,4)	
101000111	3.50		(1,3,1,9) (1,4,5,4)	
101001001	2.50		(1,3,3,3)	
101001011	3.00		(3)	[3.83] (1,3,6,3,1,9)
101001101	3.50		(1,3,7,3) (3,4)	
101001111	4.33	(1,9,3)	(1,3,9)	
101010001	3.00		(1,5) (3)	
101010011	3.00		(3)	[3.67] (1,5,5)
101010101	5.00		(1,9) (3,7) (5)	
101010111	5.00		(1,9) (5)	
101011001	3.00		(3)	
101011011	3.00		(3)	[5.00] (1,9)
101011101	5.00		(1,9) (3,7)	
101011111	5.00		(1,9)	
101100001	2.50		(1,4)	
101100011	2.50		(1,4)	
101100101	3.50		(1,4,5,4)	
101100111	3.50		(1,4,5,4)	
101101001	4.25		(1,6,4,6)	
101101011	5.00		(1,9) (4,6)	
101101101	5.00		(1,9)	[5.50] (4,7)
101101111	5.00		(1,9)	
101110001	3.00		(1,5)	
101110011	3.67		(1,5,5)	

*Because of the large size of the state diagrams, a full search for all optimal nongreedy cycles was not performed.

Table A-1. (*Continued*)

Collision vector	MAL	Optimal nongreedy	Optimal greedy	Nonoptimal greedy
101110101	5.00		(1,9)	
			(5)	
101110111	5.00		(1,9)	
			(5)	
101111001	4.33		(1,6,6)	
101111011	5.00		(1,9)	[6.00] (6)
101111101	5.00		(1,9)	[7.00] (7)
101111111	5.00		(1,9)	
110000001	2.25		(2,2,2,3)	[3.00] (3)
110000011	3.00		(3)	[3.75] (2,2,2,9)
				[3.63] (2,3,6,3,2,4,5,4)
110000101	2.33		(2,2,3)	
110000111	4.33		(2,2,9)	[4.50] (4,5)
110001001	3.00		(3)	[3.25] (2,2,2,7)
110001011	3.00		(3)	[3.75] (2,2,2,9)
110001101	3.50		(3,4)	[3.67] (2,2,7)
110001111	4.33		(2,2,9)	
110010001	3.00		(3)	
			(2,3,2,5)	
110010011	3.00		(3)	[4.17] (2,3,6,3,2,9)
				[5.00] (5)
110010101	3.00		(2,3,2,5)	
110010111	4.67	(2,9,3)	(2,3,9)	[5.00] (5)
110011001	3.00		(3)	[4.50] (2,7)
110011011	3.00		(3)	[5.50] (2,9)
110011101	4.50		(2,7)	
110011111	5.50		(2,9)	
110100001	2.75		(2,2,2,5)	
110100011	3.75		(2,2,2,9)	
			(2,4,5,4)	
110100101	3.00		(2,2,5)	
110100111	4.33		(2,2,9)	[4.50] (4,5)
110101001	3.25		(2,2,2,7)	[4.00] (2,4,6,4)
110101011	3.75		(2,2,2,9)	[4.00] (2,4,6,4)
110101101	3.67		(2,2,7)	
110101111	4.33		(2,2,9)	
110110001	3.50		(2,5)	
110110011	5.00		(5)	[5.50] (2,9)
110110101	3.50		(2,5)	
110110111	5.00		(5)	[5.50] (2,9)
110111101	4.50		(2,7)	[6.00] (6)
110111011	5.50		(2,9)	[6.00] (6)
110111101	4.50		(2,7)	
110111111	5.50		(2,9)	
111000001	3.00		(3)	
111000011	3.00		(3)	[4.50] (4,5)
111000101	3.50		(3,4)	
111000111	4.50		(4,5)	[6.00] (3,9)
111001001	3.00		(3)	

Table A-1. (*Continued*)

Collision vector	MAL	Optimal nongreedy	Optimal greedy	Nonoptimal greedy
111001011	3.00		(3)	
111001101	3.50		(3,4)	
111001111	6.00		(3,9)	
111010001	3.00		(3)	[5.00] (5)
111010011	3.00		(3)	[5.00] (5)
111010101	5.00		(3,7)	
			(5)	
111010111	5.00		(5)	[6.00] (3,9)
111011001	3.00		(3)	
111011011	3.00		(3)	
111011101	5.00		(3,7)	
111011111	6.00		(3,9)	
111100001	4.50		(4,5)	
111100011	4.50		(4,5)	
111100101	4.50		(4,5)	
111100111	4.50		(4,5)	
111101001	5.00		(4,6)	
111101011	5.00		(4,6)	
111101101	5.50		(4,7)	
111101111	6.50		(4,9)	
111110001	5.00		(5)	
111110011	5.00		(5)	
111110101	5.00		(5)	
111110111	5.00		(5)	
111111001	6.00		(6)	
111111011	6.00		(6)	
111111101	7.00		(7)	
111111111	9.00		(9)	

Bibliography

Anacker, Wilhelm. 1979. "Computing at 4 Degrees Kelvin," *IEEE Spectrum*, May, vol. 16, no. 5, pp. 26–37.

Anderson, S. F., J. G. Earle, R. E. Goldschmidt, and D. M. Powers. 1967a. "The IBM System/360 Model 91: Floating Point Execution Unit," *IBM J. Res. Dev.*, January, pp. 34–53.

Anderson, D. W., F. J. Sparacio, and R. M. Tomasulo. 1967b. "The IBM System/360 Model 91: Machine Philosophy and Instruction Handling," *IBM J. Res. Dev.*, January, pp. 8–24.

Barnes, G. H., R. M. Brown, M. Kato, D. J. Kuck, D. L. Slotnik, and R. A. Stokes. 1968. "The ILLIAC IV Computer," *IEEE Trans. Comp.*, vol. C-17, no. 8, pp. 746–757.

Batcher, K. E. 1968. "Sorting Networks and Their Application," *AFIPS Proc. SJCC*, pp. 307–314.

Bell, James, David Casasent, and C. Gordon Bell. 1974. "An Investigation of Alternative Cache Organizations," *IEEE Trans. Comp.*, vol. C-23, no. 4, pp. 346–351.

Block, E. 1959. "The Engineering Design of the STRETCH Computer," *Proc. EJCC*, pp. 48–59. See also *Computer Structures: Readings and Examples*. 1971. McGraw-Hill, New York, pp. 421–439.

Boland, L. J., G. D. Granito, A. U. Marcotte, B. U. Messina, and J. W. Smith. 1967. "The IBM System/360 Model 91: Storage System," *IBM J. Res. Dev.*, January, pp. 54–67.

Briggs, F. A., and E. S. Davidson. 1977. "Organization of Semiconductor Memories for Parallel-Pipelined Processors," *IEEE Trans. Comp.*, vol. C-26, no. 2, February, pp. 162-169.

Bucholz, W. 1962. *Planning a Computer System: Project STRETCH*, McGraw-Hill, New York.

Budnik, P., and D. J. Kuck. 1969. *A TRANQUIL Programming Manual*, Computer Science Dept., Univ. of Ill., file no. 316, December.

Budnik, P., and D. J. Kuck. 1971. "The Organization and Use of Parallel Memories," *IEEE Trans. Comp.*, vol. C-20, no. 12, December, pp. 1566-1569.

Calahan, D. A., W. N. Joy, and D. A. Orbits. 1976. "Preliminary Report on Results of Matrix Benchmarks on Vector Processors," SEL Report 94, Univ. of Michigan, Ann Arbor, May 24.

Chen, T. C. 1971a. "Parallelism, Pipelining, and Computer Efficiency," *Computer Design*, January, pp. 69-74.

Chen, T. C. 1971b. "Unconventional Superspeed Computer Systems," *AFIPS Proc. SJCC*, pp. 365-371.

Chen, T. C. 1975. *Introduction to Computer Architecture*, chap. 9, SRA, Chicago.

Connors, W. D., V. S. Mercer, and T. A. Sorlini. 1970. "S/360 Instruction Usage Distribution," TR 00.2025, Systems Development Division, IBM Corp., Poughkeepsie, N.Y., May 8.

Connors, William D., John H. Florkowski, and Samuel K. Patton. 1979. "The IBM 3033: An Inside Look," *Datamation*, May, pp. 198-218.

Control Data Corp. 1975. *Control Data STAR-100 Computer Hardware Reference Manual*, Publication No. 60256000, Control Data Corp., Minneapolis.

Cotten, L. W. 1965. "Circuit Implementation of High-Speed Pipeline Systems," *AFIPS Proc. FJCC*, pp. 489-504.

Cotten, L. W. 1969. "Maximum-rate Pipeline Systems," *AFIPS Proc. SJCC*, pp. 581-586.

Cray Research Inc. 1976. *CRAY -1 Computer System*, No. 2240004, Cray Research Inc., Bloomington, Minn.

Davidson, E. S. 1971. "The Design and Control of Pipelined Function Generators," *Proc. 1971 Int. IEEE Conf. on Systems, Networks, and Computers*, Oaxtepec, Mexico, January, pp. 19-21.

Davidson, E. S. 1974. "Scheduling for Pipelined Processors," *Proc. 7th Hawaii Conf. on System Sciences*, pp. 58-60.

Davidson, E. S., A. T. Thomas, L. E. Shar, and J. H. Patel. 1975. "Effective Control for Pipelined Computers," *Proc. Spring COMPCON*, IEEE no. 75CH 0920-9C, pp. 181-184.

Dennis, Jack B., and David P. Misunas. 1975. "A Preliminary Architecture for a Basic Data Flow Processor," *Proc. Second Annual Symposium on Computer Architecture*, IEEE no. 75CH 0916-7C, January, pp. 126-132.

Deverell, J. 1975. "Pipeline Iterative Arithmetic Arrays," *IEEE Trans. Comp.*, vol. C-23, no. 3, March, pp. 317-322.

Earle, J. 1965. "Latched Carry-Save Adder," *IBM Tech. Disclosure Bulletin*, vol. 7, no. 10, March, pp. 909-910.

Easton, Malcolm C. 1978. "Computation of Cold-Start Miss Ratios," *IEEE Trans. Comp.*, vol. C-27, no. 5, May, pp. 404-408.

Eckert, J. P., J. C. Chu, A. B. Tonik, and W. F. Schmitt. 1959. "Design of UNIVAC-LARC System: I," *Proc. EJCC*, pp. 59-65.

Emer, J. S., and E. S. Davidson. 1978. *Control Store Organization for Multiple Stream Pipelined Processors*, Coordinated Science Laboratory, University of Illinois, Champaign-Urbana.

Enslow, P. (ed.). 1974. *Multiprocessors and Parallel Processing*, John Wiley, New York.

Flynn, M. J. 1966. "Very High-Speed Computing Systems," *Proc. IEEE*, vol. 54, no. 12, December, pp. 1901–1909.

Flynn, M. J., and G. M. Amdahl. 1965. "Engineering Aspects of Large High Speed Computer Design," *Proc. Symp. Microelectronics and Large Systems*, Spartan Press, Washington, D.C., pp. 77–95.

Flynn, M. J., and P. R. Low. 1967. "The IBM System/360 Model 91: Some Remarks on System Development," *IBM J. Res. Dev.*, January, pp. 2–7.

Flynn, M. J., A. Podrin, and K. Shimizer, 1970. "A Multiple Instruction Stream with Shared Resources," L. C. Hobbs (ed.), *Parallel Processor System Technologies and Applications*, Spartan Books, Washington, D.C., pp. 251–286.

Foster, Caxton C., and E. Riseman. 1972. "Percolation of Code to Enhance Parallel Dispatching and Execution," *IEEE Trans. Comp.*, December, pp. 1411–1415.

Fuller, Samuel H. 1975. *Introduction to Computer Architecture*, chap. 11, SRA, Chicago.

Fulton, R. E., and A. K. Noir. 1975. "Impact of CDC STAR-100 Computer on Finite Element Systems," *ASCE J. Structures*, April, pp. 731–750.

Gary, John M. 1977. "Analysis of Application Programs and Software Requirements for High Speed Computers," *High Speed Computer and Algorithm Organization*, D. J. Kuck, D. H. Lawrie, and A. H. Samueh (eds.), Academic Press, N. Y., pp. 329–354.

Gaulding, S. N., and D. P. Madison. 1975. "Optimization of Scalar Instructions for the Advanced Scientific Computer," *Proc. Spring COMPCON*, IEEE No. 75CH 0920-9C, pp. 189–193.

Gibson, Jack C. 1970. *The Gibson Mix*, TR 00.2043, Systems Development Division, IBM Corp., Poughkeepsie, N.Y., June 18.

Groginsky, H. L., and G. A. Works. 1970. "A Pipeline Fast Fourier Transform," *IEEE Trans. Comp.*, vol. C–19, no. 11, November, pp. 1015–1019.

Hallin, T. G. 1970. *Pipelining of Arithmetic Units*, M.S. thesis, Dept. Elec. Engr., Northwestern University, Evanston, Ill.

Hallin, T. G., and M. J. Flynn. 1972. "Pipelining of Arithmetic Functions," *IEEE Trans. Comp.*, vol C–21, no. 8, August, pp. 880–886.

Herrell, D. J. 1974. "Femtojoule Josephson Tunneling Logic Gates," *IEEE J. Solid State Circuits*, vol. SC–9, no. 5, pp. 277–281.

Higbie, L. C. 1976. "Vector Floating-Point Data Format," *IEEE Trans. Comp.*, vol. C–25, no. 1, January, pp. 25–32.

Hintz, R. G., and D. P. Tate. 1972. "Control Data STAR-100 Processor Design," *Proc. COMPCON*, IEEE No. 72CH 0659-3C, pp. 1–4.

Husson, S. S. 1970. *Microprogramming Principles and Practice*, Prentice-Hall, Englewood Cliffs, N.J.

IBM Corp. 1968. *IBM System/360 Custom Equipment Description: 2938 Array Processor*, no. 6A 24-3519-1, IBM Corp., Endicott, N.Y.

IBM Corp. 1976. *IBM 3838 Array Processor Functional Characteristics*, no. 6A24-3639-0, file no. S370-08, IBM Corp., Endicott, N.Y., October.

IBM Corp. 1978. *3033 Processor Complex Theory of Operation/Diagrams Manual*, vols. 1–5, SY22-7001 through SY22-7005, IBM Corp., January.

INTEL Corp. 1978. *MCS-86 Preliminary User's Manual*, INTEL Corp., June.

Iverson, K. E. 1962. *A Programming Language*, John Wiley, New York.

Johnson, P. M. 1978. "An Introduction to Vector Processing," *Computer Design*, February, pp. 89–97.

Jones, P. D. 1972. "Implicit Storage Management in the Control Data STAR-100," *Proc. COMPCON*, IEEE no. 72CH 0659–3C, pp. 5–7.

Kamal, A. K., H. Singh, and D. P. Agrawal. 1974. "A Generalized Pipeline Array," *IEEE Trans. Comp.*, May, pp. 533–536.

Kaminsky, W. J., and E. S. Davidson. 1977. "Organization of Multiple Stream Pipelined LSI Processors," Coordinated Sciences Laboratory, Univ. of Illinois, Champaign-Urbana.

Kaplan, K. R., and R. V. Winder. 1973. "Cache-Based Computer Systems," *Computer*, March, pp. 30–36.

Karp, R. M. 1972. "Reducibility Among Combinatorial Problems," Tech. Report 3, Dept. of Computer Science, University of California, Berkeley.

Keller, Robert M. 1975. "Look Ahead Processors," *Computing Surveys*, vol. 7, no. 4, December, pp. 177–195.

Kishi, T., and T. Rudy, 1975. "STAR TREK," *Proc. Spring COMPCON*, IEEE no. 75CH 0920–9C, pp. 185–188.

Kogge, P. M. 1973a. "A Parallel Algorithm for the Efficient Solution of a General Class of Recurrence Equations," *IEEE Trans. Comp.*, vol. C-22, no. 8, August, pp. 786–793.

Kogge, P. M. 1973b. "Algorithm Development for Pipelined Processors," *Proc. 1977 Proc. 1st Ann. Conf. on Computer Arch.*, December, pp. 71–80.

Kogge, P. M. 1974. "Parallel Solution of Recurrence Problems," *IBM J. Res. Dev.*, vol. 18, no. 2, March, pp. 138–148.

Kogge, P. M. 1977a. "The Microprogramming of Pipelined Processors," *Proc. 4th Ann. Conf. Computer Arch.*, IEEE No. 77CH 1182–5C, March, pp. 63–69.

Kogge, P. M. 1977b. "Algorithm Development for Pipelined Processors," *Proc. 1977 Internat. Conf. Parallel Processing*, IEEE No. 77 CH1253–4C, August, p. 217.

Knuth, D. E. 1969. *The Art of Computer Programming*, vol. 1, Addison-Wesley, Reading, Mass.

Knuth, D. E. 1973. *The Art of Computer Programming*, vol. 3, Addison-Wesley, Reading, Mass.

Kosinski, P. R. 1973. "A Data Flow Programming Language," Report RC4264, IBM, T. J. Watson Research Center, Yorktown Heights, N.Y., March.

Kraska, P. W. 1969. "Array Storage Allocation," M. S. thesis, Dept. Computer Sci., University of Illinois, Champaign-Urbana, Rep. 344.

Kratz, G. L., W. W. Sproul, and E. T. Walendziewicz. 1974. "A Microprogrammed Approach to Signal Processing," *IEEE Trans. Comp.*, vol. C-23, no. 8, August, pp. 808–817.

Krider, L. D. 1972. "STAR-A De-education Problem," *Proc. COMPCON*, IEEE No. 72CH 0659–3C, pp. 9–12.

Kuck, D. J. 1968. "ILLIAC IV Software and Application Programming, *IEEE Trans. Comp.*, vol. C-17, no. 8, August, pp. 758–770.

Lambritte, J. I., and R. G. Voigt. 1975. "The Solution of Tridiagonal Linear Systems on the CDC STAR-100 Computer," *ACM Trans. Math Software*.

Lapidus, G. 1972. "The Domain of Magnetic Bubbles," *IEEE Spectrum*, September, pp. 58–62.

Larson, A. G. 1973. "Cost-Effective Processor Design with an Application to Fast Fourier Transform Computers," Digital Systems Lab Report SU–SEL–73–037, Stanford University, Stanford, Calif., August.

Larson, A. G., and E. S. Davidson. 1973. "Cost Effective Design of Special Purpose Processors: A Fast Fourier Transform Case Study," *Proc. 11th Ann. Allerton Conf. Circuits and System Theory*, University of Illinois, Champaign-Urbana, pp. 547–557.

Lee, Francis F. 1969. "Study of 'Look Aside' Memory," *IEEE Trans. Comp.*, vol. C–18, no. 11, pp. 1062–1064.

Liptay, J. S. 1968. "Structural Aspects of the System/360 Model 85 II The Cache," *IBM Sys. J.*, vol. 7, no. 1, pp. 15–21.

Loomis, H. H. 1966. "The Maximum Rate Accumulator," *IEEE Trans. Comp.*, vol. EC–15, no. 4, August, pp. 628–639.

Madsen, N. K., and G. H. Rodrique. 1976a. "A Comparison of Direct Methods for Tridiagonal Systems on the CDC-STAR 100," UCRL–76993, Lawrence Livermore Lab., May 28.

Madsen, N. K., G. H. Rodrique, and J. I. Karush. 1976b. "Matrix Multiplication by Diagonals on a Vector/Parallel Processor," *Info. Processing Letter*, vol. 5, no. 2, June.

McKevitt, James, and John Bayliss. 1979. "New Options from Big Chips," *IEEE Spectrum*, March, pp. 28–34.

McMahon, F. H., L. J. Sloan, and G. A. Long. 1972. "STACKLIB–A Vector Function Library of Optimum Stack-loops for the CDC 7600," Lawrence Livermore Laboratory Report LTSS–510, November.

Meade, Robert M. 1972. "How a Cache Memory Enhances a Computer's Performance," *Electronics*, January 17, pp. 58–63.

Metcalfe, Robert M., and David K. Briggs, 1976. "ETHERNET Distributed Packet Switching for Local Computer Networks," *CACM*, vol. 19, no. 7, July, pp. 345–404.

Miller, C., and T. Zimmerman. 1975. "Applying the Concept of a Digital Charge Coupled Device Arithmetic Unit," *1975 Internat. Conf. Application of Charge-Coupled Devices*, pp. 199–207.

Minnick, R. C. 1975. "A System of Magnetic Bubble Logic," *IEEE Trans. Comp.*, vol. C–24, no. 2, February, pp. 217–218.

Minnick, R. C., P. T. Bailey, R. N. Sandfort, and W. L. Semon. 1975. "Cascade Realizations of Magnetic Bubble Logic Using a Small Set of Primitives," *IEEE Trans. Comp.*, vol. C–24, no. 2, February, pp. 215–217.

Miranker, G. S. 1977. "Implementation of Procedures on a Class of Data Flow Processors," *Proc. Internat. Conf. Parallel Processing*, IEEE No. 77CH 1253–4C, pp. 77–86.

Ortega, J. M., and R. G. Voigt. 1977. "Solution of Partial Differential Equations on Vector Computers," ICASE Report 77-7, NASA Langley, Hampton, Va., March 30.

Pakin, S. 1968. *APL\360 Reference Manual*, Science Research Associates, Palo Alto, Calif.

Patel, Janek H. 1976. "Improving the Throughput of Pipelines with Delays and Buffers." Coordinated Science Lab. Report R-747, University of Illinois, Champaign-Urbana, October.

Patel, Janek H. 1979. "Pipelines with Internal Buffers," *Proc. 6th Ann. Symp. Computer Arch.* IEEE 79CH 394–6C, pp. 249–254.

Patel, J. H., and E. S. Davidson. 1976. "Improving the Throughput of a Pipeline by Insertion of Delays," *IEEE/ACM 3rd Ann. Symp. Computer Arch.*, IEEE No. 76CH 0143-5C, pp. 159-163.

Paul, George, and M. Wayne Wilson. 1975. *"The VECTRAN Language: An Experimental Language for Vector/Matrix Array Processing,"* IBM Palo Alto Scientific Center Report 6320-3334, August.

Peled, A. 1977. "On the Architectural Implications of Recent Reduced Computational Complexity Signal Processing Algorithms," *Tech. Report 055*, IBM Israel Scientific Center, Haifa, Israel, August.

Peuto, Bernard L., and Leonard J. Shustek. 1977. "An Instruction Timing Model of CPU Performance," *Proc. 4th Ann. Symp. Computer Arch.*, IEEE 77CH 1182-5C, pp. 165-178.

Pouzin, L. 1973. "Presentation and Major Design Aspects of the CYCLADES Computer Network," *Proc. 3rd ACM/IEEE Data Communications Symp.*, November, p. 80.

Pullman, R. E. 1977. "Control Data 480 Series Microprogrammable Computer Family," *Computer*, October, pp. 45-53.

Rabiner, L. R., and C. M. Rader. 1972. *Digital Signal Processing*, IEEE Press, New York.

Ramamoorthy, C. V. 1977. "Pipeline Architecture," *Computing Surveys*, vol. 9, no. 1, March, pp. 61-102.

Ramamoorthy, C. V., and K. H. Kim. 1974. "Pipelining—The Generalized Concept and Sequencing Strategies," *Proc. NCC*, pp. 289-297.

Ramamoorthy, C. V., and H. F. Li. 1974. "Efficiency in Generalized Pipeline Networks," *AFIPS Proc. NCC*, pp. 625-635.

Ramamoorthy, C. V., and H. F. Li. 1975. "Some Problems in Parallel and Pipeline Processing," *Proc. COMPCON*, IEEE No. 75CH 0920-9C, pp. 177-180.

Rao, Gururaj S. 1978. "Performance Analysis of Cache Memories," *J. ACM*, vol. 25, no. 3, pp. 378-395.

Rau, B. Ramakrishna, and George E. Rossman. 1977. "The Effect of Instruction Fetch Strategies upon the Performance of Pipelined Instruction Units," *Proc. 4th Ann. Symp. Computer Arch.*, IEEE 77CH 1182-5C, pp. 80-89.

Remund, R. N., and K. A. Taggart. 1977. " 'To Vectorize' or to 'Vectorize' ": 'That is the Question,' " *High Speed Computer and Algorithm Organization*, D. J. Kuck, D. H. Lawrie, and A. H. Sameh (eds.), Academic Press, New York, pp. 399-410.

Regua, J. E. 1972. "STAR—A System Programmer's View," *Proc. COMPCON*, IEEE No. 72CH 0659-3C, pp. 13-16.

Riseman, E. M., and C. C. Foster. 1972. "The Inhibition of Potential Parallelism by Conditional Jumps," *IEEE Trans. Comp.*, December, pp. 1405-1411.

Roberts, L., and B. Wessler. 1970. "Computer Network Development to Achieve Resource Sharing," AFIPS. *Proc. SJCC*, vol. 36, pp. 543-549.

Rudsinski, L., and J. Worlton. 1977. "The Impact of Scalar Performance on Vector and Parallel Processors," *High Speed Computer and Algorithm Organization*, D. J. Kuck, D. H. Lawrie, and A. H. Sameh (eds.), Academic Press, New York, pp. 451-452.

Ruggiero, J. F., and D. A. Coryell. 1969. "An Auxiliary Processing System for Array Calculations," *IBM Sys. J.*, no. 2, pp. 118-135.

Schlig, E. S., 1976. "A Proposed Distributed Josephson Logic Circuit," *IEEE J. Solid State Circuits*, June, pp. 424-426.

Senzig, D. N., and R. V. Smith. 1965. "Computer Organization for Array Processing," *AFIPS. Proc. FJCC*, pp. 117–128.

Senzig, D. N. 1967. "Observations on High-Performance Machines," *Proc. FJCC*, pp. 791–799.

Shapiro, H. D. 1977. "A Comparison of Various Methods for Detecting and Utilizing Parallelism in a Single Instruction Stream," *Proc. 1977 Internat. Conf. Parallel Processing*, IEEE No. 77CH 1253-4C, pp. 67–76.

Shar, L. E. 1972. "Design and Scheduling of Statically Configured Pipelines," Digital Systems, Lab Report SU-SEL-72-042, Stanford University, Stanford, California, September.

Shar, L. E., and E. S. Davidson. 1974. "A MultiminiProcessor System Implemented Through Pipelining," *Computer*, February, pp. 42–51.

Siegal, H. J. 1977. "Analysis Techniques for SIMD Machine Interconnection Networks and the Effects of Processor Address Masks," *IEEE Trans. Comp.*, vol. C–26, no. 2, February, pp. 153–161.

Slotnick, D. L. 1967. "Unconventional Systems," *Computer Design*, December, pp. 49–52.

Smith, Alan J. 1978. "Comparative Study of Set Associative Memory Mapping Algorithms and Their Use for Cache and Main Memory," *IEEE Trans. Software Engr.*, vol. SE-4, no. 2, March, pp. 121–130.

Stephenson, C. M. 1973. "Control of a Variable Configuration Pipelined Arithmetic Unit," *Proc. 11th Allerton Conf. Circuits and System Theory*, University of Illinois, Champaign-Urbana, pp. 558–567.

Stephenson, C. M. 1975. "Case Study of the Pipelined Arithmetic Unit for the TI Advanced Scientific Computer," *Proc. 3rd Ann. Symp. Computer Arith.*, pp. 168–173.

Stokes, R. A. 1977. "Burroughs Scientific Processor," *High Speed Computer and Algorithm Organization*, D. J. Kuck, D. H. Lawrie, and A. H. Sameh (eds.), Academic Press, New York, pp. 85–90.

Stone, H. S. 1973. "An Efficient Parallel Algorithm for the Solution of Tridiagonal Linear Systems of Equations," *J. ACM*, vol. 20, pp. 27–38.

Strecker, William D. 1976. "Cache Memories for PDP-11 Family Computers," *Proc. 3rd Ann. Symp. Computer Arch.*, January, pp. 155–158.

Swan, R. J., S. H. Fuller, and D. P. Sieviorek. 1977. "CM*–A Modular, Multi-Processor," *AFIPS Conf. Proc.*, vol. 46, NCC, pp. 637–644.

Syre, J. C., D. Comte, and N. Hifdi. 1977. "Pipelining, Parallelism, and Asynchronism in the LAU System." *Proc. Internat. Conf. Parallel Processing*, IEEE 77CH 1253-4C, pp. 87–92.

Sze, D. T., and J. T. Tou. 1972. "Efficient Operation Sequencing for Pipeline Machines," *Proc. COMPCON*, IEEE No. 72CH 0659-3C, pp. 265–268.

Thomas, A. T., and E. S. Davidson. 1974. "Scheduling of Multiconfigurable Pipelines." *Proc. 12th Ann. Allerton Conf. Circuits and System Theory*, University of Illinois, Champaign-Urbana, pp. 658–669.

Thompson, C. D. 1978. "Generalized Connection Networks for Parallel Processor Intercommunication," *IEEE Trans. Comp.*, vol. C-27, no. 12, December, pp. 1119-1126.

Thornton, J. E. 1964. "Parallel Operation in the Control Data 6600," *Proc. SJCC*, pp. 33–39.

Thornton, J. E. 1970. *Design of a Computer–The Control Data 6600*, Scott, Foresman and Co., Glenview, Ill.

Thornton, J. E. 1977. "Networks and Interconnection Schemes," *High Speed Computer and Algorithm Organization*, D. J. Kuck, D. H. Lawrie, and A. H. Sameh (eds.), Academic Press, New York, pp. 91–100.

Tomasulo, R. M. 1967. "An Efficient Algorithm for Exploiting Multiple Arithmetic Units," *IBM J. Res. Dev.*, January, pp. 25–33.

Tsui, Frank. 1980. "JSP—A Research Signal Processor in Josephson Technology," *IBM J. Res. and Dev.*, March, pp. 243–252.

Voigt, R. G. 1977. "The Influence of Vector Computer Architecture on Numerical Algorithms," ICASE Report 77–8, NASA Langley, Hampton, Va., March 31.

Wallace, C. S. 1964. "A Suggestion for a Fast Multiplier," *IEEE Trans. Elec. Comp.*, vol. EC-13, February, pp. 14–17.

Ward, R. C. 1976. "The QR Algorithm and Hyman's Method on Vector Computers," *Math. of Comp.*, vol. 30, no. 133, January, pp. 132–142.

Watson, W. J. 1972a. "The TI ASC—A Highly Modular and Flexible Super Computer Architecture," *AFIPS Proc. FJCC*, pp. 221–228.

Watson, W. J. 1972b. "The Texas Instruments Advanced Scientific Computer," *Proc. COMPCON*, IEEE No. 72CH 0659-3C, pp. 291–293.

Watson, W. J., and H. M. Carr. 1974. "Operational Experiences with the TI Advanced Scientific Computer," *Proc. 1974 NCC*, pp. 389–397.

Welch, Terry A. 1978. "Memory Hierarchy Configuration Analysis," *IEEE Trans. Comp.*, vol. C-27, no. 5, May, pp. 408–413.

Wilkinson, J. H. 1963. *Rounding Errors in Algebraic Processes*, Prentice-Hall, Englewood Cliffs, N.J.

Wittmayer, Woodrow R. 1978. "Array Processor Provides High Throughput Rates," *Computer Design*, March, pp. 93–100.

Wulf, W. A., and C. G. Bell. 1972. "C.mmp—A Multi-mini-processor," *AFIPS Proc. FJCC*, pp. 765–777.

Zwakenburg, Z., J. Engle, D. Gotthoffer, and M. River. 1973. "Vector Extensions to LRLTRAN," *Proc. ACM SIGPLAN Conf. Programming Languages and Compilers for Parallel and Vector Machines*, March, pp. 77–87.

Index